ILLUSTRATED COMPUTER DICTIONARY FOR DUMMIES®

2ND EDITION

by Dan Gookin
and Wally Wang

IDG Books Worldwide, Inc.
An International Data Group Company
Foster City, CA ♦ Chicago, IL ♦ Indianapolis, IN ♦ Braintree, MA ♦ Dallas, TX

Illustrated Computer Dictionary For Dummies®, 2nd Edition

Published by
IDG Books Worldwide, Inc.
An International Data Group Company
919 E. Hillsdale Blvd.
Suite 400
Foster City, CA 94404

Library of Congress Catalog Card No.: 95-77668

ISBN: 1-56884-218-X

Printed in the United States of America

10 9 8 7 6 5 4 3 2 1

2A/QW/QX/ZV

Distributed in the United States by IDG Books Worldwide, Inc.

Distributed by Macmillan Canada for Canada; by Computer and Technical Books for the Caribbean Basin; by Contemporantea de Ediciones for Venezuela; by Distribuidora Cuspide for Argentina; by CITFC for Brazil; by Ediciones ZETA S.C.R. Ltda. for Peru; by Editorial Limusa SA for Mexico; by Transworld Publishers Limited in the United Kingdom and Europe; by Al-Maiman Publishers & Distributors for Saudi Arabia; by Simron Pty. Ltd. for South Africa; by IDG Communications (HK) Ltd. for Hong Kong; by Toppan Company Ltd. for Japan; by Addison Wesley Publishing Company for Korea; by Longman Singapore Publisher Ltd. for Singapore, Malaysia, Thailand, and Indonesia; by Unalis Corporation for Taiwan; by WS Computer Publishing Company, Inc. for the Philippines; by WoodsLane Enterprises Ltd. for New Zealand.

For general information on IDG Books Worldwide's books in the U.S., please call our Consumer Customer Service department at 800-762-2974. For reseller information, including discounts and premium sales, please call our Reseller Customer Service department at 800-434-3422.

For information on where to purchase IDG Books Worldwide's books outside the U.S., contact IDG Books Worldwide at 415-655-3021 or fax 415-655-3295.

For information on translations, contact Marc Jeffrey Mikulich, Director, Foreign & Subsidiary Rights, at IDG Books Worldwide, 415-655-3018 or fax 415-655-3295.

For sales inquiries and special prices for bulk quantities, write to the address above or call IDG Books Worldwide at 415-655-3200.

For information on using IDG Books Worldwide's books in the classroom, or for ordering examination copies, contact Jim Kelly at 800-434-2086.

About the Authors

Dan Gookin, the author of *Buy That Computer!, DOS For Dummies,* and *Word For Windows 6 For Dummies,* is a writer and computer "guru" whose job is to remind everyone that computers are not to be taken too seriously. Presently, Mr. Gookin works for himself as a freelance writer. Gookin holds a degree in Communications from the University of California, San Diego. Dan lives in rustic Idaho with his wife and many sons.

Wallace Wang, a stand-up comic by night, also writes a software review column for a comedy newsletter, teaches computer classes for local companies, and has written other computer books. Both Dan and Wallace once had a computer radio show on KVSD in San Diego.

ABOUT IDG BOOKS WORLDWIDE

WINNER
Eighth Annual Computer Press Awards 1992

WINNER
Ninth Annual Computer Press Awards 1993

Welcome to the world of IDG Books Worldwide.

IDG Books Worldwide, Inc., is a subsidiary of International Data Group, the world's largest publisher of computer-related information and the leading global provider of information services on information technology. IDG was founded more than 25 years ago and now employs more than 7,500 people worldwide. IDG publishes more than 235 computer publications in 67 countries (see listing below). More than 60 million people read one or more IDG publications each month.

Launched in 1990, IDG Books Worldwide is today the #1 publisher of best-selling computer books in the United States. We are proud to have received 8 awards from the Computer Press Association in recognition of editorial excellence, and our best-selling *...For Dummies™* series has more than 17 million copies in print with translations in 25 languages. IDG Books Worldwide, through a recent joint venture with IDG's Hi-Tech Beijing, became the first U.S. publisher to publish a computer book in the People's Republic of China. In record time, IDG Books Worldwide has become the first choice for millions of readers around the world who want to learn how to better manage their businesses.

Our mission is simple: Every one of our books is designed to bring extra value and skill-building instructions to the reader. Our books are written by experts who understand and care about our readers. The knowledge base of our editorial staff comes from years of experience in publishing, education, and journalism — experience which we use to produce books for the '90s. In short, we care about books, so we attract the best people. We devote special attention to details such as audience, interior design, use of icons, and illustrations. And because we use an efficient process of authoring, editing, and desktop publishing our books electronically, we can spend more time ensuring superior content and spend less time on the technicalities of making books.

You can count on our commitment to deliver high-quality books at competitive prices on topics consumers want to read about. At IDG Books Worldwide, we value quality, and we have been delivering quality for more than 25 years. You'll find no better book on a subject than an IDG book.

John J. Kilcullen

John Kilcullen
President and CEO
IDG Books Worldwide, Inc.

IDG Books Worldwide, Inc., is a subsidiary of International Data Group, the world's largest publisher of computer-related information and the leading global provider of information services on information technology. International Data Group publishes over 235 computer publications in 67 countries. More than sixty million people read one or more International Data Group publications each month. The officers are Patrick J. McGovern, Founder and Board Chairman; Kelly Conlin, President; Jim Casella, Chief Operating Officer. International Data Group's publications include: **ARGENTINA'S** Computerworld Argentina, Infoworld Argentina; **AUSTRALIA'S** Computerworld Australia, Computer Living, Australian PC World, Australian Macworld, Network World, Mobile Business Australia, Publish!, Reseller, IDG Sources; **AUSTRIA'S** Computerwelt Oesterreich, PC Test; **BELGIUM'S** Data News (CW); **BOLIVIA'S** Computerworld; **BRAZIL'S** Computerworld, Connections, Game Power, Mundo Unix, PC World, Publish, Super Game; **BULGARIA'S** Computerworld Bulgaria, PC & Mac World Bulgaria, Network World Bulgaria; **CANADA'S** CIO Canada, Computerworld Canada, InfoCanada, Network World Canada, Reseller; **CHILE'S** Computerworld Chile, Informatica; **COLOMBIA'S** Computerworld Colombia, PC World; **COSTA RICA'S** PC World; **CZECH REPUBLIC'S** Computerworld, Elektronika, PC World; **DENMARK'S** Communications World, Computerworld Danmark, Computerworld Focus, Macintosh Produktkatalog, Macworld Danmark, PC World Danmark, PC Produktguide, Tech World, Windows World; **ECUADOR'S** PC World Ecuador; **EGYPT'S** Computerworld (CW) Middle East, PC World Middle East; **FINLAND'S** MikroPC, Tietoviikko, Tietoverkko; **FRANCE'S** Distributique, GOLDEN MAC, InfoPC, Le Guide du Monde Informatique, Le Monde Informatique, Telecoms & Reseaux; **GERMANY'S** Computerwoche, Computerwoche Focus, Computerwoche Extra, Electronic Entertainment, Gamepro, Information Management, Macwelt, Netzwelt, PC Welt, Publish, Publish; **GREECE'S** Publish & Macworld; **HONG KONG'S** Computerworld Hong Kong, PC World Hong Kong; **HUNGARY'S** Computerworld SZT, PC World; **INDIA'S** Computers & Communications; **INDONESIA'S** Info Komputer; **IRELAND'S** ComputerScope; **ISRAEL'S** Beyond Windows, Computerworld Israel, Multimedia, PC World Israel; **ITALY'S** Computerworld Italia, Lotus Magazine, Macworld Italia, Networking Italia, PC Shopping Italy, PC World Italia; **JAPAN'S** Computerworld Today, Information Systems World, Macworld Japan, Nikkei Personal Computing, SunWorld Japan, Windows World; **KENYA'S** East African Computer News; **KOREA'S** Computerworld Korea, Macworld Korea, PC World Korea; **LATIN AMERICA'S** GamePro; **MALAYSIA'S** Computerworld Malaysia, PC World Malaysia; **MEXICO'S** Compu Edicion, Compu Manufactura, Computacion/Punto de Venta, Computerworld Mexico, MacWorld, Mundo Unix, PC World, Windows; **THE NETHERLANDS'** Computer! Totaal, Computable (CW), LAN Magazine, Lotus Magazine, MacWorld; **NEW ZEALAND'S** Computer Buyer, Computerworld New Zealand, Network World, New Zealand PC World; **NIGERIA'S** PC World Africa; **NORWAY'S** Computerworld Norge, Lotusworld Norge, Macworld Norge, Maxi Data, Networld, PC World Ekspress, PC World Nettverk, PC World Norge, PC World's Produktguide, Publish& Multimedia World, Student Data, Unix World, Windowsworld; **PAKISTAN'S** PC World Pakistan; **PANAMA'S** PC World Panama; **PERU'S** Computerworld Peru, PC World; **PEOPLE'S REPUBLIC OF CHINA'S** China Computerworld, China Infoworld, China PC Info Magazine, Computer Fan, PC World China, Electronics International, Electronics Today/Multimedia World, Electronic Product World, China Network World, Software World Magazine, Telecom Product World; **PHILIPPINES'** Computerworld Philippines, PC Digest (PCW); **POLAND'S** Computerworld Poland, Computerworld Special Report, Networld, PC World/Komputer, Sunworld; **PORTUGAL'S** Cerebro/PC World, Correio Informatico/Computerworld, MacIn; **ROMANIA'S** Computerworld, PC World, Telecom Romania; **RUSSIA'S** Computerworld-Moscow, Mir - PK (PCW), Sety (Networks); **SINGAPORE'S** Computerworld Southeast Asia, PC World Singapore; **SLOVENIA'S** Monitor Magazine; **SOUTH AFRICA'S** Computer Mail (CIO),Computing S.A.,Network World S.A., Software World; **SPAIN'S** Advanced Systems, Amiga World, Computerworld Espana, Communicaciones World, Macworld Espana, NeXTWORLD, Super Juegos Magazine (GamePro), PC World Espana, Publish; **SWEDEN'S** Attack, ComputerSweden, Corporate Computing, Macworld, Mikrodatorn, Natverk & Kommunikation, PC World, CAP & Design, Datalngenjoren, Maxi Data,Windows World; **SWITZERLAND'S** Computerworld Schweiz, Macworld Schweiz, PC Tip; **TAIWAN'S** Computerworld Taiwan, PC World Taiwan; **THAILAND'S** Thai Computerworld; **TURKEY'S** Computerworld Monitor, Macworld Turkiye, PC World Turkiye; **UKRAINE'S** Computerworld, Computers+Software Magazine; **UNITED KINGDOM'S** Computing /Computerworld, Connexion/Network World, Lotus Magazine, Macworld, Open Computing/Sunworld; **UNITED STATES'** Advanced Systems, AmigaWorld, Cable in the Classroom, CD Review, CIO, Computerworld, Computerworld Client/Server Journal, Digital Video, DOS World, Electronic Entertainment Magazine (E2), Federal Computer Week, Game Hits, GamePro, IDG Books Worldwide, Infoworld, Laser Event, Macworld, Maximize, Multimedia World, Network World, PC Letter, PC World, Publish, SWATPro, Video Event; **URUGUAY'S** PC World Uruguay; **VENEZUELA'S** Computerworld Venezuela, PC World; **VIETNAM'S** PC World Vietnam. 05/17/95

Acknowledgments

I would like to extend special thanks the following folks who helped make this dictionary happen. First, kudos goes to my co-author, the ineffable Wally Wang. I'd also like to acknowledge the contributions from the first edition made by the earnest Chris Van Buren. Thanks also go to this book's original editor, Laurie Smith. And I'd also like to point out Drew Moore among the IDG staff for doing such a blasted fine job with the illustrations. Gratis to Kevin Spencer for looking up some of the words no one could find anywhere. No one named "Webster" was involved with this project.

Dan Gookin

(The publisher would like to give special thanks to Patrick J. McGovern, without whom this book would not have been possible.)

Credits

Senior Vice President and Publisher
Milissa L. Koloski

Editorial Director
Diane Graves Steele

Acquisitions Editor
Megg Bonar

Brand Manager
Judith A. Taylor

Editorial Manager
Kristin A. Cocks

Editorial Executive Assistant
Richard Graves

Editorial Assistants
Stacey Holden Prince
Kevin Spencer

Acquisitions Assistant
Suki Gear

Production Director
Beth Jenkins

Supervisor of Project Coordination
Cindy L. Phipps

Pre-Press Coordinator
Steve Peake

Associate Pre-Press Coordinator
Tony Augsburger

Media/Archive Coordinator
Paul Belcastro

Project Editor
A. Timothy Gallan

Editors
Jeffrey W. Waggoner
Pat Seiler
Laurie Smith
Diane L. Giangrossi
Diana R. Conover

Technical Reviewer
Christine Whetstone

Associate Project Coordinator
Sherry Gomoll

Production Staff
Gina Scott
Carla C. Radzikinas
Patricia R. Reynolds
Melissa D. Buddendeck
Dwight Ramsey
Robert Springer
Theresa Sánchez-Baker
Kathie S. Schnorr
Dominique DeFelice
Angie Hunckler
Drew R. Moore
Laura Puranen

Proofreader
Kathleen Prata

Cover Design
Kavish + Kavish

Introduction

Here it is, the *Illustrated Computer Dictionary For Dummies, 2nd Edition,* your shield in the constant word battle that takes place between the nerds, geeks, and technoweenies and people like us who have to put up with the jargon. We've scoured the magazines, manuals, and books for these terms. Hunted them down in dark programmers' dungeons, listened to taped conversations of bigwigs talking in acronym-speak, and we've even made up a few words ourselves. The end result is this lighthearted approach to understanding computer terms and — if you dare — learning how to incorporate such terms into your everyday conversation.

The Logical Approach

After long periods of careful thought, we decided to lay this book out in alphabetic format and, further, to alphabetize all the words for your referencing needs. Symbols (@#$%^&*!) and numbers (0-9) are listed first in their own chapters. But after that, it's A to Z — with all the letters in between in proper order. (And we're assuming you know the alphabet here, sung to the tune of "Twinkle Twinkle"; in case you forgot, ask any 4-year-old.)

The words are presented in the following format. First, we give you the word itself, then a pronunciation guide, followed by the word's meaning or a definition, and then comes sample usage:

dictionary

Pronunciation: *dik-shun-aery*

Meaning: A book that contains a list of words, their pronunciations, and their meanings. When you don't know what a word means, you look it up in a dictionary. When you want to be sure you're using a word properly, you look it up in the dictionary. When you're losing an argument and need some random, though professional-sounding source to quote, you use the dictionary.

Sentence: "My kid keeps asking me what words mean, so I tell him to 'look it up in the *dictionary,*' since I'm too embarrassed to admit I don't know what the words mean myself."

Philosophical Stuff

Our purpose behind this dictionary is to both enlighten and inform. Oh, and we've tossed in some entertainment value as well. Computers are always thought of as these big, frowning, cold, and serious devices of torment — like nuns in Catholic schools. The truth is, they aren't. They aren't nuns, that is. (And the nuns aren't big and frowning either!) Instead, computers have a vast potential for humor and enjoyment (just like the nuns). This book presents technical information with that attitude in the hopes that you will understand it better. And if not that, then at least you'll be able to tolerate the terminology with a modicum of levity.

\

Symbol name: *backslash*

Uses: The symbol used in MS-DOS to separate directories and filenames such as C:\WINDOWS\SYSTEM or A:\PASCAL. Don't get the backslash key mixed up with the forward slash (/) that's found on the same key as the question mark (?). Otherwise, MS-DOS won't have the slightest idea what you're trying to do.

.

Symbol name: *star-dot-star*

Uses: The *.* designation uses the * wildcard, which can take on any value. In MS-DOS, *.* refers to all files. To delete every file in a directory, you type **DEL *.*** and press the Enter key. (Don't try this at home unless you know what you're doing.)

&

Symbol name: *ampersand*

In computer programming, & sometimes represents a "logical and." For example:

```
IF(NUMBER=1 & LETTER=A) THEN "We're at the
beginning."
```

In the C programming language, two ampersands are used — &&.

The character is correctly called an ampersand. *Ampers* comes from the ancient Vulcan for "this squiggly symbol means" and *and* means "and."

+

Symbol name: *plus*

Uses: This symbol is used in addition because (thankfully) it's on the keyboard and makes a poor impostor for the letter T.

```
2 + 2 = 5
```

(This used to happen a lot with older spreadsheets.)

The plus sign may also be used to connect two items. For example:

```
COPY A.DOC+B.DOC AB.DOC
```

In DOS, this command glues the file B.DOC to the end of the file A.DOC, creating a new file AB.DOC. This is known as *concatenation,* which is literally translated as "sticking two cats together," though the more common "sticking two things together" is generally accepted.

#

Symbol name: *pound, number, or tic-tac-toe*

Uses: The pound symbol, located above the 3 on American keyboards. This symbol is used in written language to represent numbers or items: "All right, Becky, you chose #3, 'Medical Instruments I've Found on the Beach.'"

In some versions of UNIX, the # is the system prompt.

The # symbol also has appeal as a nice solid character. Some people use it decoratively or to produce crude graphics:

```
 #######
#       #
#  # #  #
#       #
# ##### #
#  ###  #
#       #
 #######
```

On British keyboards, the # symbol is replaced by £, which really means "pound." (# is the "hash" character.)

>>

Symbol name: *ap-end (as in append)*

Uses: There is really no way to pronounce any of these symbols, though "ugh-ugh" is often used. Some say "Double greater-than." Others may just say "append," which is what these characters do in DOS.

```
TYPE SIGNATUR.TXT >> LETTER.DOC
```

The preceding DOS command takes the information in the file SIGNATUR.TXT and sticks it to the end of the file LETTER.DOC. Note that this trick works only with text files, not documents created with a word processor or formatted documents.

>=

Symbol name: *greater-than-or-equal-to*

Uses: These symbols are used to compare two values in a test (as in a database query, for example). The test passes if the first value is greater than or equal to the second value. For example:

10 >= 9 is true
10 >= 10 is true
10 >= 11 is false
good >= evil — we hope is true

<=

Symbol name: *less-than-or-equal-to*

Uses: These symbols are used to compare two values in a test. The test passes if the first value is less than or equal to the second value. For example:

9 <= 10 is true
10 <= 10 is true
10 <= 9 is false
Hollywood <= "real life" is always true

!

Symbol name: *exclamation point; bang*

Uses: The exclamation point is used at the end of a sentence to denote excitement: "Your wife is here!" Or maybe surprise, "My heart!" In Spanish, a preceding exclamation point alerts the reader to the excitement level of the sentence: "¡Su esposa esta aqui!" Y "¡Mi corazon!"

In the C programming language, the ! is used to mean "not." For example:

```
!TRUE = FALSE
```

This statement means "not true is the same thing as false," almost a universal truth anywhere but in Washington, D.C.

!=

This symbol means "not equal to." "Watching baseball on TV is just != being at the ballpark."

In the USENET electronic mail system, ! is called a *bang,* and it's used in someone's electronic address — like a highly effective ZIP code. For example:

```
crash!dang
```

This is the electronic address of *dang* on the *crash* system. The address is "crash, bang, dang." (It's Dan's old address, by the way, so don't try to reach him there.)

Did you ever notice that all the sentences in *Mad Magazine* end in either an exclamation point or a question mark?

"

Symbol name: *double quotes*

Uses: This symbol is often used to *hug* what's called a *string* of text. For example:

"The pastry was bad, and the coffee tasted like it had been strained through a dirty gym sock."

The text between the quotes is the "string," but the quotes themselves are not.

$

Symbol name: *dollar sign; string; hex*

Uses: The dollar sign is used in a number of ways, most of which really have to do with money. Obviously, when followed by a number, as in $1,000,000, the dollar sign means "dollars, big bucks, moola."

In the BASIC programming language, a dollar sign is used to identify a *string* or text variable. FIRST$ would be a variable named "FIRST" that holds a string value. It's pronounced *first string,* by the way; not *first SS* or *first dollar sign.*

Some programming languages use the dollar sign to denote a *hexadecimal* (base 16) number. For example, $14 is the hexadecimal value 14 (20 decimal). $A1 would be the hexadecimal value A1 (161 decimal). In this usage, the $ is pronounced *hex.* $A1 is *hex A one.*

In MS-DOS, one place the dollar sign is used is in the AUTOEXEC.BAT file to change the look of the C prompt, as in

```
Prompt $p$g
```

%

Symbol name: *percent sign*

Uses: The percent sign is used all over the place, sometimes actually to represent a percentage value: 15% means fifteen percent, or 15 times out of 100, or .15, or a value that's considered fairly good for weather forecasters and economists.

The percent sign plays numerous roles in various programming languages.

In BASIC, the percent sign denotes an integer variable: ITEM% would be an integer variable named ITEM. You don't pronounce the %.

In the C programming language the % is used as the "modulus" operator (which figures out the remainder when one number is divided by another). It's also used to format output.

'

Symbol name: *apostrophe; tick; single quote*

Uses: The apostrophe is used in text to mark the possessive "Bill's deficit" and sometimes in conjunction with the accent grave (backward apostrophe,`) for double quotation marks:

```
``This is more serious than we thought.´´
```

In the BASIC programming language, the apostrophe at the start of a line marks a comment.

( )

Symbol name: *parentheses, parens*

Uses: Parentheses are used in programming to group things together. Usually this happens in long mathematical operations; what appears between the parentheses is figured out first. Most programming languages also use parentheses to group options and "arguments" for certain commands and keywords.

A single parenthesis is called a *paren*. When someone says "left paren," he's referring to the (character. The right paren is the). The term paren comes in handy when you are giving computer typing instructions over the phone.

Symbol name: *copyright sign*

Uses: Many software packages use a big C in parentheses to represent the © (copyright) symbol because the © isn't on most keyboards. Likewise, you may see (TM) for Trademark.

Symbol name: *asterisk; star; splat*

Uses: The asterisk is typically used in a decorative fashion. Occasionally, it may appear to add emphasis when italics or underlines aren't available:

```
I was so *embarrassed*.
```

Or the asterisk may be used as a form of self-censorship while sending an e-mail message:

```
Eat **** and die!
```

Sometimes the asterisk marks a footnote.

In DOS, the asterisk is used as a wildcard character, pronounced *star*. The star can represent from one to several characters, matching other filenames for use with several DOS commands.

Nathan Hale did not say "I regret that I have but one asterisk for my country."

Other names for * include the "dingbat" and "splat." Splat is from the final result of dropping something mushy from a high altitude. The resulting spot would look like this:

Splat!

–

Symbol name: minus sign; hyphen

Uses: The minus sign is used in various corners of computer mathdom. First, it appears as the typical minus sign: 9 – 6, and so on. It's also used to identify a negative number: –5.

The minus sign's evil twin is the hyphen, which is a similar character but used with words, such as Mary-Francis. Two hyphens can be used together in text to denote a clause or parenthetical element -- like this!

In typographical terms, there are hyphens, en dashes, and em dashes, which are each used in different circumstances. The hyphen (-) is the smallest one of the three. An *en dash* (–) is a dash character that is the same width as the letter *n*. The *em dash* (—) is a longer dash, the same width as the letter *m*.

.

Symbol name: *period, dot*

Uses: The period is used in text to mark the end of a sentence.

In math, the period is used to mark the decimal portion of a number: 3.141. In that case, it's pronounced *point,* as in "three point one four one."

In some countries, the period is used to separate the hundreds from thousands or thousands from ten-thousands: 1.000 is one thousand. (In these weird places, the comma is used as the decimal point. Strange.)

In DOS, the period is used to separate a filename from its extension. Other operating systems use the period as a separator as well.

In a hockey game, there are three periods: ...

/

Symbol name: *forward slash; division symbol*

Uses: The forward slash character is used in text to separate items: on/off, up/down, and so on.

In computer math, the / symbol is used for division. This is because the ÷ character isn't available on most keyboards. So 15/3 means "15 divided by 3."

Names for this character: slash, forward slash, solidus, stroke, virgule, the forward-pointing thing under the question mark key, and so on.

:

Symbol name: *colon*

Uses: In DOS, you use colons after drive names, such as in *the C: drive* to refer to the hard drive, and after device names, such as in *PRN:* to refer to the printer. In C programming, the colon is sometimes used for such things as declaring structure templates for bit fields. Humans use the colon to digest food.

;

Symbol name: *semicolon*

Uses: In Windows INI files, as well as DOS's CONFIG.SYS file, a line starting with a semicolon is taken to be a comment:

```
;This line will be ignored: The computer is

afraid of it!
```

Symbol name: *less than, greater than; not equal; angle brackets*

Uses: These are the angle brackets, sometimes used when straight-edged people tire of parentheses.

In some European languages, these characters are doubled up and used as quotes: << is the start quote, and >> is the end quote. «Françios! Behold this lovely yellow pencil box!»

=

Symbol name: *equal sign*

Uses: Used to denote equality or that something is equal to something else. For example, `CALORIES = TASTES GOOD`.

==

Symbol name: *double equal sign; "is equal to"*

Uses: Used in some instances to denote that two things are equal. In the C programming language, the double equal sign is used to compare two values.

Symbol name: *question mark*

Uses: Sometimes the question mark sits at the end of a sentence when the sentence is a question. For example: Is that so?

Used occasionally as a "wildcard" character, a placeholder for other characters to be matched in a search.

@

Symbol name: *at sign; about; strudel; rose; cabbage*

Uses: Could mean "at," though this little cryptic guy is a favorite for multiple uses.

[ ]

Symbol name: *square brackets; brackets*

Uses: Parentheses who just never really caught on. Mostly you'll find square brackets used to describe options for a command. For example:

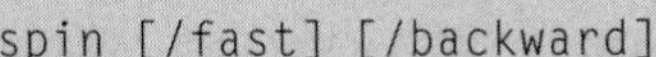

```
spin [/fast] [/backward]
```

The brackets mean that the items enclosed within them are optional. (In the dictionary, the brackets are used to guide pronunciation.)

Symbol name: *caret; hat; control*

Uses: Used as an abbreviation for "control," for example, when typing out a key combination or the character produced by that combination. So Ctrl-S produces the ^S (control-S) character.

Used as a mathematical operator for "raising to the power of" in some programming languages. For example, 2^4 means "2 to the 4th power." Other programming languages may have other interesting uses for the hat.

_

Symbol name: *underline; underscore*

Uses: Not normally used for anything, though some programmers and computerphiles like to use the underscore instead of a space between words. For example, FILE_NAME would be the way they write FILE NAME when it's forbidden to put a space between two words.

`

Symbol name: *accent grave*

Uses: The hardest part about dealing with this doodad is how to pronounce it. Is it *grave* as in serious or a place where dead bodies go to relax? Or could it be *gravé,* as in the way a French person would say gravy?

Some people use the accent grave to simulate double quotes. For example, ``Oui, oui. It is a sauce we make from grease and flour.´´ The double apostrophe is used to end the quote.

{}

Symbol name: *curly brackets; braces*

Uses: An alternative form of parentheses, most often found in C language programs. The curly brackets are used to "hold" various items in the program, items that belong to certain parts of the program or that carry out specific functions.

|

Symbol name: *vertical bar; pipe*

Uses: The pipe symbol is used as the logical OR mathematical operator in many programming languages. It's pronounced *or* as in: `SIX OF ONE | HALF A DOZEN OF THE OTHER`.

In DOS and UNIX, the pipe is used to control the output of a command. The pipe follows the DOS command and sends its output — what would normally go to the screen — to a special program called a *filter.* The filter modifies the output.

~

Symbol name: *tilde*

Uses: In some languages, the tilde appears over characters to give them special twangs. For example, *año* means "year" in Spanish.

Some programming languages may use ~ to mean "not." (See also **!** [exclamation point].)

101-key keyboard

Pronunciation: *one-oh-one-kee kee-bored.*

Meaning: A keyboard that has four distinct parts: a typewriter keyboard, a cursor keypad, a numeric keypad, and a row of function keys.

Sentence: "Bob's the doubting type. He actually counted every little key on his *101-key keyboard* and was, in fact, quite pleased to find 101 of them."

16-bit

Pronunciation: *six-teen-bit.*

Meaning: An adjective describing something that can transfer or process 16 bits of information at any given time.

Sentence: "My first computer was an old 8-bit Apple IIe. My next computer was a *16-bit* IBM AT. Now my kid is talking about 32-bit Nintendo games. And to think that a shave and a haircut was once two bits."

2-bit

Pronunciation: *too-bit.*

Meaning: Something cheap, insignificant, or not worthy of attention, such as some people you may know. It really means 25 cents.

Sentence: "That idea and *2 bits* will get you a phone call."

286

Pronunciation: *too-ay-dee-six.*

Meaning: Abbreviation for the 80286 microprocessor, used in the IBM AT class of computers.

Sentence: "The *286* computer is as dead as the dodo. I use my old *286* as a doorstop."

3-D

Pronunciation: *three-dee.*

Meaning: Abbreviation for *three-dimensional.*

Sentence: "The latest spreadsheets offer the ability to view data using *3-D* graphics. During a presentation last week, Lois almost got motion sickness."

32-bit

Pronunciation: *thir-dee-too-bit.*

Meaning: An adjective describing something that can transfer or process 32 bits of data at any given time.

Sentence: "A computer with a *32-bit* processor is much faster than one with a 16-bit processor. It's like having twice as many lanes on the freeway: the more bits, the faster the data moves. Of course, the more lanes on the freeway, the more idiots you'll find on the road, so it's kind of a trade-off."

386

Pronunciation: *three-ay-dee-six.*

Meaning: Abbreviation for the 80386DX processor.

Sentence: "Believe it or not, *386* computers were once thought of as so fast that only nerdy scientists would use them. Now, good luck trying to get a 7-year-old not to sneer at one."

486

Pronunciation: *for-ay-dee-six.*

Meaning: Abbreviation for the 80486DX processor.

Sentence: "Just when you thought a *486* processor would be sufficient, they came out with the more advanced Pentium processor. And so it goes."

486DLC

Pronunciation: *for-ay-dee-six Dee El See.*

Meaning: A special type of 80486 microprocessor. The "D" designation means that this microprocessor contains a built-in math coprocessor. The "L" designation means that the microprocessor is a low-voltage version, requiring 3.3 volts instead of the usual 5 volts to operate. The "C" designation means that the microprocessor includes a built-in cache.

Sentence: "If you want a computer that uses less electricity and runs fast, get a *486DLC* microprocessor. If you just want a computer to play video games, buy a Nintendo or Sega Genesis unit instead."

486DX

Pronunciation: *for-ay-dee-six Dee Ecks.*

Meaning: Another term for an 80486DX processor. (See also *486SX.*)

Sentence: ""Most 486 processors are really *486DX* processors; they drop the DX part just because."

486DX2

Pronunciation: *for-ay-dee-six Dee Ecks too.*

Meaning: A 486DX microprocessor that has a doubled clock speed. Microprocessors are rated at speeds that are given in MHz. A 486DX has two speeds, a fast one used internally and a slower speed used externally. The faster speed is twice the slower speed, which is where the "2" comes in. So a 486DX2 running at 66 MHz has a speed of 66 MHz internally and only 33 MHz externally. Comparison-wise, it's almost as fast as a 66 MHz 486DX.

Sentence: "This *486DX2* blows smoke on my old 286 PC AT!"

486DX4

Pronunciation: *for-ay-dee-six Dee Ecks for.*

Meaning: A 486DX microprocessor that has a quadrupled clock speed. (See also *486DX2.*) So a 486DX4 rated at 100 MHz has an external speed of only 25 MHz. Still, this is one fast chip.

Sentence: "Doug's chest swelled with pride as he boasted to the user group about his new *486DX4* computer."

486SL

Pronunciation: *for-ay-dee-six Ess Ell.*

Meaning: A special 486 chip designed for the low power requirements of a PC laptop. It's comparable in features and speed to a standard 486DX processor, but it uses less electricity.

Sentence: "Those new *486SL* laptops came out. So we all piled into the car and drove like hell to the computer store, tossing our old 386 laptops out the windows along the way."

486SLC

Pronunciation: *for-ay-dee-six Ess El See.*

Meaning: A special type of 80486 microprocessor. The "S" designation means that this microprocessor lacks a built-in math coprocessor. The "L" designation means that the microprocessor is a low-voltage version, requiring 3.3 volts instead of the usual 5 volts to operate. The "C" designation means that the microprocessor includes a built-in cache.

Sentence: "If you want to save a little money at the expense of fast math calculations, get a *486SLC* instead of a 486DLC. But since the price is so minimal, you probably won't save that much money anyway. Don't be cheap. Get a Pentium instead."

486SX

Pronunciation: *for-ay-dee-six Ess Ecks.*

Meaning: A stupid version of the 486DX processor, one that lacks a math coprocessor. In order to get the math coprocessor option, you have to upgrade to a full 486DX chip, which is usually done through an Overdrive chip. (See also *Overdrive.*)

Sentence: "George thought that he was saving money by getting a *486SX* computer. He knew that he'd made a mistake when we all started laughing uncontrollably at him."

640K limit

Pronunciation: *six-for-dee-kay lim-it.*

Meaning: The limitation on IBM-compatible computers that restricts them to using a maximum of 640K of conventional memory.

Sentence: "I stuffed my computer with 8MB of memory, but my programs still couldn't access all of it because of the *640K limit.* Who was the goofball who thought 640K of RAM would always be enough?"

6502, 65C02, 65C16

Pronunciation: *six-dee-five-oh-too, six-dee-five-see-oh-too, six-dee-five-see-one-six.*

Meaning: The family of processors used in the Apple IIe, IIc, and IIgs.

Sentence: "Goin' from an old Apple IIe with a tiny *6502* processor in it to a Macintosh with a 68040 processor is like goin' from a tricycle to a sports car."

68000

Pronunciation: *six-dee-ayt-thow-zand.*

Meaning: The numeric designation for the Motorola processor used in the original Macintosh computers.

Sentence: "So my old Macintosh Plus had a *68000* processor. What I want to know is, 68,000 of what?"

680x0

Pronunciation: *six-dee-ayt-oh-ecks-oh.*

Meaning: Abbreviation to indicate the Motorola 68000 family of processors, including the 68000, 68020, 68030, and the 68040.

Sentence: "All Macintosh computers use the *680x0* processor. The bigger the number x, the more you paid for your Mac."

68881

Pronunciation: *six-dee-ayt-ayt-ay-dee-one.*

Meaning: The math coprocessor used with the 68000 processor.

Sentence: "If you want real number-crunching capabilities, plug a *68881* math coprocessor into your 68000 computer. It will make your computer do math like that smart Eastern European girl in high school who got 900s on her SATs."

8-bit

Pronunciation: *ayt-bit.*

Meaning: An adjective describing something that can transfer or process 8 bits of data at any given time.

Sentence: "If you had an *8-bit* computer in the early 80s, you were pretty spiffy."

80286

Pronunciation: *ay-dee-too-ay-dee-six.*

Meaning: Numeric designation for the processor used in the IBM AT family of computers.

Sentence: "It should frighten you to know that old *80286* computers are used to run some nuclear power plants."

80386, 80386DX

Pronunciation: *ay-dee-three-ay-dee-six, ay-dee-three-ay-dee-six Dee Ecks.*

Meaning: Numeric designation for the processor used in some IBM-compatible computers. The term 80386 is an abbreviation for the official designation of the 80386DX processor.

Sentence: "The minimum requirement to run Windows is an *80386* processor. Yeah, right. That's like saying that the minimum requirement to get into Harvard is a spinal cord."

80386SL

Pronunciation: *ay-dee-three-ay-dee-six Ess El.*

Meaning: A specially designed version of the 80386 processor for conserving energy; often found in laptop computers.

Sentence: "I thought that the *SL* in *80386SL* meant 'Slower.' No, it probably means 'Special Laptop,' or 'Super Lazy,' or 'Sour Lemon.' Why does the computer industry seem to be all numbers and no fun?"

80386SX

Pronunciation: *ay-dee-three-ay-dee-six Ess Ecks.*

Meaning: A low-cost and slower version of the 80386DX processor. Like the 80386DX, this processor can process 32 bits of data at any given time, but it can transfer only 16 bits of data at a time.

Sentence: "In the old days, you could save money by buying an *80386SX* instead of a real 80386. Nowadays, an *80386SX* is way too slow to run anything more demanding than PacMan."

80387

Pronunciation: *ay-dee-three-ay-dee-sev-en.*

Meaning: The math coprocessor designed to work with the 80386DX, 80386SX, and 80386SL processors.

Sentence: "Plugging an *80387* math coprocessor into an 80386 computer is like strapping a calculator to its belt."

80486, 80486DX

Pronunciation: *ay-dee-for-ay-dee-six, ay-dee-for-ay-dee-six Dee Ex.*

Meaning: Numeric designation for the processors used in many IBM-compatible computers.

Sentence: "According to Intel, which makes these things, the *80486* microprocessor has about one cat's life left; then everyone should buy Pentium computers. Never mind that Intel makes more money selling Pentiums, or that *80486* computers are just swell for most of us."

80486SX

Pronunciation: *ay-dee-for-ay-dee-six Ess Ecks.*

Meaning: Low-cost and slower version of the 80486DX processor. The main difference is that this processor lacks the math coprocessor capabilities of the 80486DX.

Sentence: "If you're too cheap to spend an extra $100 and you don't do much number-crunching, you can probably get by with an *80486SX.*"

80586

Pronunciation: *ay-dee-five-ay-dee-six.*

Meaning: The unofficial designation for the Pentium processor. The main reason that Intel chose not to name its latest processor the 80586 is that it couldn't trademark the name; and it threatened to sue anyone who used the name 80586 without Intel's permission.

Sentence: "The term *80586* will be dear to most nerds, specifically, those diehards who can't communicate using anything but numbers."

8086

Pronunciation: *ay-dee-ay-dee-six.*

Meaning: A 16-bit processor used in the later versions of IBM PC-compatible computers.

Sentence: "Although the first IBM PC used the 8088 processor, the later compatible computers used an *8086* processor because it was slightly faster. Those attempts to eek a wee bit of speed out of something that would be wholly obsolete in ten years seem foolish now. Maybe we'll think that the difference between 486s and Pentiums is as trivial in ten years."

8087

Pronunciation: *ay-dee-ay-dee-sev-en.*

Meaning: The math coprocessor designed to work with the 8088 and the 8086 processors.

Sentence: "Lots of IBM PC users bought an *8087* processor so their Lotus 1-2-3 spreadsheets would run faster. Now these same computers are collecting dust in somebody's closet or garage."

8088

Pronunciation: *ay-dee-ay-dee-ayt.*

Meaning: The first processor used in the IBM PC. Although the 8088 is a 16-bit processor, it can transfer only 8 bits of data at any given time.

Sentence: "Knowing that the first IBM PC used an *8088* microprocessor is as trivial as knowing the name of the guy who drives the Zamboni at a hockey game."

80x86

Pronunciation: *ayt-oh-ecks-ay-dee-six.*

Meaning: Designation that covers everything in the Intel family of microprocessors, including the 8088, 8086, 80286, 80386, and 80486.

Sentence: "Dave thinks he's being clever when he refers to all *80x86* processors as 6,880 processors. (Only those who know that 80 multiplied by 86 is 6,880 will get this.)"

aardvark

Pronunciation: *ard-vark.*

Meaning: One of the first words listed in good dictionaries. Comes from the old Afrikaans phrase meaning "earth pig," which refers to a nocturnal mammal known to burrow its way through African terrain eating termites and dragging its big floppy ears and heavy tail.

Sentence: "You will get in trouble if you leave *aardvark* out of any dictionary you write."

abacus

Pronunciation: *ab-a-kus.*

Meaning: A hand-held tablet used for making mathematical computations. The abacus uses beads and your fingers to quickly figure out addition, multiplication, subtraction, and division. It does it quite accurately, faster than most people can use a calculator, and its batteries last a lifetime.

Sentence: "We got rid of all the accounting department's computers and gave them *abacuses* instead. They gripe a lot, but the numbers come out faster, and they're more accurate."

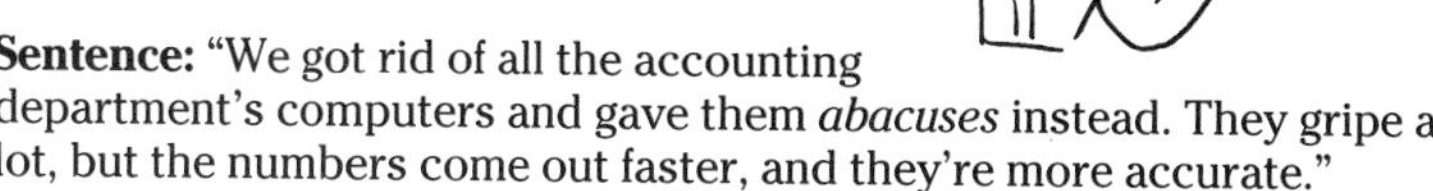

ABC

Pronunciation: *Ay Bee See.*

Meaning: Abbreviation for *Atanasoff-Berry Computer,* a device that was a precursor to the ENIAC and, therefore, is sometimes considered to be the first electronic digital computer. The ABC was created by Professor John Atanasoff and student Clifford Berry at Iowa State University in the early 1940s.

Sentence: "The *ABC* had enough vacuum tubes in it to fill a room full of old televisions. You should see the air conditioner those guys had to keep it cooled."

abort

Pronunciation: *ah-bort.*

Meaning: To stop something before it's too late, such as a program that's running out of control or a nuclear missile that's careening toward Moscow. Popular methods include frantically hitting Esc, Ctrl-C, or the Break key. Rent the movie *War Games,* and you'll see what I mean.

Sentence: "One of the most famous DOS errors is '*Abort,* Retry, Fail, Ignore.' You should press A to abort when you want to cancel; otherwise, press R to try again. Never try the other two options."

Abort, Retry, Fail, Ignore?

Pronunciation: *Ah-bort, Ree-tri, Fay-el, Ig-nor.*

Meaning: The cryptic message that DOS displays when it can't figure out what to do next. Pressing A stops whatever program is running at the time. Pressing R forces the computer to try again. Pressing F stops the current command that caused the problem but keeps the program running (a bad idea). Pressing I tells the computer to pretend that the problem never existed and keep running anyway (a worse idea). This Ignore command sometimes can cause the computer to lose or scramble data. (See also *MS-DOS.*)

Sentence: "Kyle's been using the computer too long. His wife asked him what he'd like for dinner, and all he could say was `Abort, Retry, Fail, Ignore?`"

About box

Pronunciation: *Ah-bowt box.*

Meaning: A tiny little window that appears in the middle of the screen, displaying the program's name, version number, and anything else that the programmers thought the general public might want to know. (For an example, see the About Program Manager option on the Help menu in Windows.)

Sentence: "Ever wonder why the *About box* never tells you what the program is supposed to accomplish? I suppose that would be the *What's it all About box.*"

ABS

Pronunciation: *Ay Bee Ess.*

Meaning: An abbreviation for *ABSolute value.* ABS is a command used in many programming languages and spreadsheet programs for calculating the absolute value of a number.

Sentence: "According to my spreadsheet, my tax balance comes out to – $12,500, meaning that I owe back taxes to the IRS. But when I calculate the *ABS* value of my debt, it looks like the IRS owes me $12,500."

absolute reference

Pronunciation: *ab-so-loot ref-er-rentz.*

Meaning: A term used in spreadsheets that tells a formula to use a specific cell or group of cells. If you copy or move the formula from one cell to another at a later date, the formula will still use the specific cell defined earlier.

Sentence: "An *absolute reference* is something that you have to specifically define if you want to make sure that your spreadsheet formulas don't get all screwed up."

AC

Pronunciation: *Ay See.*

Meaning: Abbreviation for *alternating current.* (See also *DC.*)

Sentence: "The power that comes out of the wall socket is *AC.* Computers, and most other devices, use DC instead. A device called a transformer converts the two, keeping everyone happy."

accelerator board

Pronunciation: *ex-sel-e-rate-er bord.*

Meaning: A special circuit board that plugs into a computer and makes it or one of its pieces run faster. Accelerator boards usually contain a faster processor that replaces or supplements the computer's existing processor. (See also *Processor.*)

Sentence: "Hey! That video *accelerator board* really makes Windows graphics snappy. Too bad they don't make accelerator boards for TV commercials."

access time

Pronunciation: *ax-sess time.*

Meaning: The amount of time needed for a storage device to retrieve information.

Sentence: "A good, fast hard disk has an *access time* of 12 milliseconds. Steve, on the other hand, has an access time of about 48 hours."

ACK

Pronunciation: *Ack.*

Meaning: Abbreviation for *ACKnowledge,* often used when one computer dials another computer through a modem. Before two computers can transfer information, each of them must first ACKnowledge that the other one exists and is ready. (See also *modem.*)

Sentence: "When my modem program kept saying '*ACK* received' I was under the impression that the other computer was choking."

acoustic coupler

Pronunciation: *ah-koo-stik cup-ler.*

Meaning: An old-style modem device that works by shoving the handset of a telephone into two rubber cups. This was necessary in the old days, before the breakup of AT&T, since you couldn't plug a modem directly into a phone jack on the wall (because there weren't any!). Acoustic couplers are still widely used in foreign countries and for laptops when access to a phone jack is restricted.

Sentence: "Did you hear? Madonna's gone high-tech. She's replaced her cone bra with a pair of *acoustic couplers.*"

acronym

Pronunciation: *ak-ro-nim.*

Meaning: A word created by taking letters from two or more words to create a new word. Examples are BASIC, FORTRAN, and DOS.

Sentence: "I hear that the Pentagon allocates $75,000 each year to a committee formed to conjure up useless *acronyms*. What do they know? The computer industry does it for free!"

active matrix

Pronunciation: *ak-tiv may-triks.*

Meaning: A type of laptop display that's much better (and, therefore, much more expensive) than the passive matrix type. An active matrix display uses transistors to control the screen. If you were an engineer, you'd be impressed by this and nod your head accordingly.

Sentence: "My new KneeCap 150 laptop uses the superior *active matrix* display, so I can see crisp color graphics of a parrot at 39,000 feet."

active window

Pronunciation: *ak-tiv win-do.*

Meaning: The window on the screen that's currently in use. If two or more windows appear on the screen, the active window usually appears brighter around the edges. (See also *window.*)

Sentence: "The goal of every window on the screen is to become the *active window.*"

Ada

Pronunciation: *Ay-da.*

Meaning: A structured programming language that was supposed to be the standard language for all defense-related programming work. Naturally, hardly anyone uses it, although all U.S. taxpayers supported its development. Ada was named after Ada, the Countess of Lovelace, who is generally credited with writing the first computer program for a mechanical loom machine that Charles Babbage designed.

Sentence: "I'm sure that the Countess of Lovelace would be pleased to know that a program named for her is used to fire Exocet missiles from nuclear powered aircraft carriers."

Adam West

Pronunciation: *Ad-um West.*

Meaning: The star of the *Batman* TV series that appeared during the '60s.

Sentence: "There just is no other Batman than *Adam West.*"

adapter

Pronunciation: *ah-dapt-er.*

Meaning: Another name for an expansion card. Typically, a piece of hardware that plugs into an expansion slot in your computer's innards. Unlike an expansion card, which may just expand the computer's features, the adapter is used to communicate with an external device, such as a hard drive, monitor, or some other doohickey. It may also refer to a simple connector designed to hook up two plugs of different types. (See also *EGA* and *network adapter.*)

Sentence: "Earl is convinced he can use his computer to help him garden. He's currently looking for a weed-whacker *adapter.*"

add-on program

Pronunciation: *add-on pro-gram.*

Meaning: A program that works with and enhances the features of another program.

Sentence: "The original Lotus 1-2-3 was terribly popular despite its somewhat limited abilities. To fill in the gaps, enterprising individuals created *add-on programs* to boost 1-2-3's features."

address

Pronunciation: *ad-dress.*

Meaning: A memory location or the location of an item in a spreadsheet. Items stored in memory have a memory address. Items stored in a spreadsheet have a row and column address.

Sentence: "The *address* of the first cell in a spreadsheet is A1. That's also the name of my favorite steak sauce, which I can buy at the supermarket *address* of 123 Main Street."

AI

Pronunciation: *Ay Eye.*

Meaning: Abbreviation for *Artificial Intelligence,* which is the fascinating science of making computers as smart as human beings (which may be a step backward in some cases). Recently, the art of inserting *Artificial Intelligence* into computers is nothing more than making a program do what you want it to do.

Sentence: "Bob's been working on that *Artificial Intelligence* program for years. Soon, he says, he'll make computers just as smart as he is. Still, this worries me since I just saw him back up into a fire hydrant."

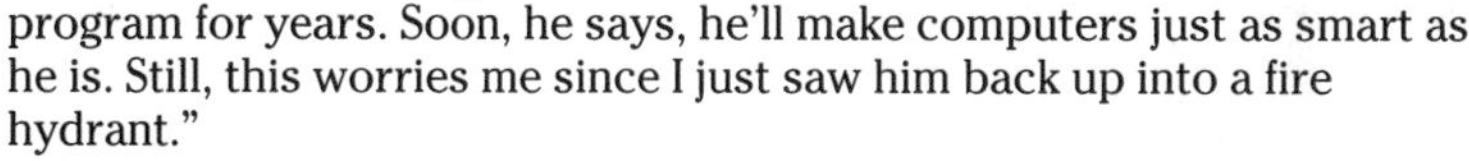

ALGOL

Pronunciation: *Al-gall.*

Meaning: An early programming language that's an acronym for *ALGOrithmic Language.* ALGOL was one of the first programming languages to encourage structured programming. Pascal is a direct descendent of ALGOL.

Sentence: "When Betty told her parents that she programmed *ALGOL,* they thought she was choking."

algorithm

Pronunciation: *Al-Gore-rhythm.*

Meaning: A step-by-step set of instructions that actually does something worthwhile. Often used to describe the instructions written in a programming language such as C, BASIC, or Pascal. (See also *billclintonrithm.*)

Sentence: "Johnson claims his program works perfectly because his *algorithms* are flawless. And as long as nobody uses his program, it will keep on working perfectly, too."

alias

Pronunciation: *ay-lee-ess.*

Meaning: An alias lets you reference a file that may look as if it's right there in front of you, but could be anywhere. This feature makes it easy to find common files, but it doesn't require all the disk space a full-on copy would. Think of alias files as Elvis impersonators that can appear everywhere you look.

Sentence: "The FBI is having trouble finding its word processing files. Experts assume that the files are using *aliases* and that once the aliases are known, the files should be easy to locate."

aliasing

Pronunciation: *ay-lee-ess-ing.*

Meaning: The ugly-looking jagged or stair-stepped appearance of diagonal lines in computer graphics images. Sometimes referred to as "the jaggies."

Sentence: "Trying to draw diagonal lines on a computer is about as easy as drawing circles on an Etch-A-Sketch. Because whenever you draw a diagonal line, you get *aliasing,* which makes your straight line look like the kind of staircase a 10-year-old would build."

alignment

Pronunciation: *uh-line-mint.*

Meaning: When used to describe hard disks, the alignment refers to the drive head's ability to read and write information without error. When used to describe text, the alignment refers to the text's relationship to the left and right margins, as in "centered," "left-justified," and so forth.

Sentence: "Shirley is so cute. She tried to adjust the *alignment* of text in her word processor by tilting the monitor."

allocate

Pronunciation: *al-o-kate.*

Meaning: The process of dividing a computer's resources between two or more items.

Sentence: "In the Bible, Matthew 14:15 describes how Jesus *allocated* two fish and five loaves of bread among 5,000+ people. Now if he could only come back and *allocate* our two Pentiums and one laser printer among ten people in the office."

alpha test

Pronunciation: *al-fa test.*

Meaning: The initial testing of a new program, usually conducted by the programmers and their trusted friends. Alpha test programs usually don't work correctly.

Sentence: "Before Microsoft released Windows95, they ran it through an *alpha test* of their own employees. After they found the first few bugs, they released the program into beta test so that everyone else could find those same mistakes too." (See also *beta test.*)

alphanumeric characters

Pronunciation: *al-fa-noo-mar-rik kar-rak-ters.*

Meaning: Characters that consist of letters and numbers.

Sentence: "Whenever you type a command, the computer usually expects an *alphanumeric* command. If you type something nonsensical, such as '|μςΩ|+δ,' your computer will think you're nuts."

Alt

Pronunciation: *Alt.* (Like *halt* without the *ha.*)

Meaning: The key on IBM computers that is used with other keys to give commands to the computer. Common commands are Alt-X to quit and Alt-P to print a file.

Sentence: "In some programs, you press *Alt-R* to redo something. In other programs, you press *Alt-R* to replace. And in outer space, *Alt-R* is a star in the constellation Aquila (Altair)."

Altair

Pronunciation: *Alt-air* (not *Alt-R*)

Meaning: The name of one of the first personal computers available.

Sentence: "Before Apple, IBM, or even Radio Shack sold a microcomputer, the only one you could buy was an *Altair* — unless you had a lot of money and bought some of the big iron."

alternating current

Pronunciation: *al-ter-nat-ing ker-rent.*

Meaning: The type of electricity used in America. Often abbreviated as AC.

Sentence: "Today, everyone uses *alternating current.* Back when electricity was still new, Thomas Edison tried to get everyone to use DC instead. It might have been because he had a financial stake in the matter, but naaa."

America Online

Pronunciation: *A-mair-ick-uh On-line.*

Meaning: A national dial-in computer service, where you, your computer, and a modem can do all sorts of interesting things much cheaper than you can on CompuServe. America Online is quite popular, and I really wish that I had bought some of its stock long ago.

Sentence: "Do you think that they'll ever have *America Online* in Europe?"

Amiga

Pronunciation: *Ah-mee-ga.*

Meaning: The name of the most technologically advanced, inexpensive personal computer on the market that hardly anyone cares about.

Sentence: "Phil went to Mexico to buy an *Amiga,* and the nice people there told him that you can't buy friendship. I think he needs to brush up on his Spanish."

amp

Pronunciation: *am-pa.*

Meaning: Abbreviation for *AMPere,* which is a unit for measuring electric current.

Sentence: "Volts, smolts. It's the *amps* that will kill you."

analog

Pronunciation: *an-a-log.*

Meaning: A way of storing information as multiple values. Analog is the opposite of digital. For example, an analog clock has a dial and hands that "sweep 'round." A digital clock displays numbers and changes only on the minute. (See also *digital.*)

Sentence: "Computers are digital, which means that they understand On and Off, Yes and No. People are *analog* because they understand Yes, No, I dunno, who cares?, why are you asking me this?, maybe, and we'll see."

animation

Pronunciation: *an-i-may-shin.*

Meaning: The use of your $3,000 computer to create Saturday-morning-style cartoons. Creating the appearance of movement of drawn objects. (See also *Mickey Mouse.*)

Sentence: "Our spreadsheet uses *animation* to help illustrate the declining sales of our competitors. Alas, we don't have the sound hooked up, so when the line in the graph slams into zero, George will make an audible thumping noise."

ANSI

Pronunciation: *An-zee.*

Meaning: Abbreviation for *American National Standards Institute,* an organization that defines standards that most people ignore anyway for different industries. In the computer industry, ANSI standards refer to the way that programming languages are supposed to work, to the way that computer screens display characters, and to the way that computers on networks communicate. This standard is often called ANSI graphics. (Also, the technical term for how kids get when they've been riding in the car too long.)

Sentence: "If these trousers followed the *ANSI* standard, you could say they were *ANSI* pants."

ANSI Bomb

Pronunciation: *An-zee Bom-ba.*

Meaning: A devious sequence of ANSI commands that actually types a deadly DOS command on your computer. This can be done in a number of ways, none of which we'd like to write about in any detail here. When such a string of ANSI commands appears on your screen, you can do little to stop it except immediately shut off your computer.

Sentence: "Most of the better antivirus programs will scan for any *ANSI Bombs* that may blow up in your face."

ANSI C

Pronunciation: *An-zee See.*

Meaning: A standard definition for the C programming language as defined by the American National Standards Institute. Nearly every C compiler tries to follow the ANSI C standard as closely as possible, and then they add enhancements that pretty much destroy the whole purpose of a standard in the first place.

Sentence: "Lots of C compilers claim 100-percent compatibility with the *ANSI C* standard. This is akin to claiming that Elvis is still alive."

ANSI character set

Pronunciation: *An-zee kar-ak-ter set.*

Meaning: A list of predefined characters that computers use. The ANSI character set includes ordinary letters and numbers plus strange little symbols such as foreign language symbols, smiley faces, and lines and boxes.

Sentence: "Linda is a collector. All she needs is the evil Dr. Modulus statuette, and her *ANSI character set* will be complete."

ANSI graphics

Pronunciation: *An-zee graf-iks.*

Meaning: Special characters that create simple graphics, such as lines, boxes, and colors. Often found on BBSs for displaying information on the screen.

Sentence: "Earl spent months working with *ANSI graphics* to make his screen look colorful and exciting. Alas, he didn't impress the user group because by the time he was ready to show us all, we'd switched over to Windows."

ANSI screen control codes (ANSI.SYS)

Pronunciation: *An-zee skreen kon-troll kodz.*

Meaning: Yet another standard that specifies a series of characters that clears computer screens. IBM computers use ANSI screen control codes only if the CONFIG.SYS file contains the line

```
DEVICE = ANSI.SYS
```

ANSI screen control codes begin with Esc and are often called escape codes.

Sentence: "Using *ANSI screen control codes* today is about as common as finding a vertical hold knob on a TV set."

answer mode

Pronunciation: *an-ser mowd.*

Meaning: The state of a modem when it's ready to receive calls from other computers.

Sentence: "At the start of the press conference, the senator will read a brief statement; then he will switch into *answer mode.*"

antivirus

Pronunciation: *ant-ee-vi-rus.*

Meaning: A type of software (utility) that scans your system and detects viruses or other harmful software. Antivirus software may also remove the infection, deleting it from your hard drive, and actively protect your PC from infection. It all depends on how much you want to be bothered by antivirus software and how much you choose to put your PC at risk.

Sentence: "It's a good idea to run *antivirus* software on your computer, especially if you use a lot of floppy disks that other people use or you download software from questionable sources."

any key

Pronunciation: *an-ee key.*

Meaning: Any key on your keyboard, most likely the Enter key or the spacebar. Programmers use the term "any key" to try to make things easier on you. In their twisted little minds they think, "Hey, I'll just tell them they can press any key to continue, which allows them the freedom to press any key they like." In practice, it leads to frustration and eternal hunting for a key labeled "any."

Sentence: "Instead of saying '*any key,*' programmers should muster the nerve to say 'Press the Enter key.'"

AOL

Pronunciation: *Ay-oh-el.*

Meaning: Acronym for *America Online,* an on-line service that provides typical on-line service stuff but with an emphasis on "chatting" or wasting hours of time typing with other people who have nothing better to do. (See also *CompuServe, Internet,* and *network.*)

Sentence: "I dial up *AOL* once in a blue moon just to assure myself that 12-year-olds truly can't spell."

API

Pronunciation: *Ay Pee Eye.*

Meaning: Acronym for *Application Program Interface,* which is yet another feature that's supposed to make computers easier than they really are. API defines a standard way that programs work with pull-down menus, dialog boxes, and windows. Microsoft Windows, OS/2, and the Macintosh are examples of API in action.

Sentence: "Macintosh programs tend to look the same because they follow the same *API.* DOS programs tend to look like a mixture of everything because, well, there is no API."

append

Pronunciation: *ah-pend.*

Meaning: To stick something onto the end of something else. When you append one file to another, you stick it on the end, making one larger file that contains information found in both the other files.

Sentence: "Bertha almost gave our system administrator a heart attack. He asked her to *append* one file to another, explained what it meant, and then caught her just as she was squeezing glue into the floppy drive."

Apple Computer, Inc.

Pronunciation: *Ap-pull-Kom-pewt-er-Ink.*

Meaning: The makers of the Apple II series, the Macintosh series, and several other new, very successful products. Based in Cupertino, California. Steve Jobs and Steve Wozniak, who had been teenage friends, founded the company in a family garage in Silicon Valley. The Apple Macintosh introduced the now-famous user interface that enhanced the use of icons, a mouse, pull-down menus, dialog boxes, and so on. Many of these ideas were born out of research done at Xerox's Palo Alto Research Center. Although Apple computers have been the main counterpart to IBM-compatible technology for several years, the lines of distinction have become blurred because Microsoft Windows provides a similar interface on the DOS platform. Nonetheless, DOS users and Mac users still tend to view each other as coming from different planets.

Sentence: "If I had as much money as *Apple Computer, Inc.,* I wouldn't need a computer. I could be like our CEO at work — he's the only one I know who doesn't have a computer on his desk. That's because his secretary does all of his work."

Apple Desktop Bus (ADB)

Pronunciation: *Ap-pull Desk-top Bus.*

Meaning: Sometimes abbreviated as ADB, this defines an interface standard for connecting keyboards, mice, trackballs, and other input devices to Apple Macintosh computers.

Sentence: "Since every Macintosh computer has the *Apple Desktop Bus,* you can be sure that any keyboard that Apple sells will work with your Macintosh. Too bad every keyboard that Apple sells costs twice as much as you can afford to pay."

Apple II

Pronunciation: *Ap-pull Too.*

Meaning: One of the first personal computers that actually did something useful. After introducing the Apple II, Apple released enhanced models called the Apple IIe, Apple IIc, and finally the Apple IIgs. Finally, Apple decided to drop the whole Apple II family altogether and focus on selling Macintoshes.

Sentence: "I asked Wayne why he looked so pale. He said that he saw the same *Apple IIe* he bought in 1983 for $2,500 at a garage sale, and they were asking $20 for it."

Apple III

Pronunciation: *Ap-pull Three.*

Meaning: A computer that was supposed to replace the Apple II but wound up being ignored by the general public. After turning into a public embarrassment to Apple, the Apple III quietly disappeared and can now be found in landfills all across America.

Sentence: "Betcha didn't know that Apple will not use "three" in the name of any product because of the bad luck associated with the old *Apple III* computer."

Apple menu

Pronunciation: *Ap-pull men-yoo.*

Meaning: The tiny little apple (with a bite taken out of it) that appears in the far left corner of the menu bar in Macintosh computers. Clicking on the Apple menu pulls down desk accessories and simple programs to use while another program is already running.

Sentence: "Herb was crushed not to find any cobbler on the *Apple menu.*"

AppleShare

Pronunciation: *Ap-pull-Share.*

Meaning: A network operating system developed by Apple to work with Macintosh computers.

Sentence: "*AppleShare* is an oxymoron. Anyone who knows the company realizes that they'll sue anyone who tries to share their stuff without permission."

AppleTalk

Pronunciation: *Ap-pull-Talk.*

Meaning: A local area network standard developed by Apple to hook Macintosh and IBM PC computers together. Every Macintosh computer has an AppleTalk port built-in (the same can't be said for IBM computers). AppleTalk is an inexpensive way to create a network, but it tends to be slower than other types of networks. (See also *network.*)

Sentence: "With product names such as *AppleTalk* and AppleShare, one would assume that Apple computers have no spacebars."

application

Pronunciation: *ap-li-ka-shin.*

Meaning: Another name for a program, such as a word processor, spreadsheet, or database. *Application* implies work getting done, or using something to meet an end. *Program* is too robotic for most people.

Sentence: "Bob asked how long I was going to use his *application* on my computer. I told him, 'Only until the bleeding stops.'"

ARC

Pronunciation: *Ark.*

Meaning: The name of a popular data compression program that smashes multiple files into a single, smaller one. Once used heavily on IBM computers, the ARC file standard has been replaced by the ZIP standard.

Sentence: "*ARC* is short for *archive,* which is where you want to keep something. ARK, on the other hand, is short for Arkansas. Don't put your documents there; someone may shred them."

Archie

Pronunciation: *Arch-ee.*

Meaning: A service for finding files on an Internet computer. (See also *Veronica* and *Gopher,* unless you just came here from there.)

Sentence: "I've used *Archie* and Veronica on the Internet. Could Jughead be far behind?"

architecture

Pronunciation: *ar-ki-tex-sure.*

Meaning: The particular (and arbitrary) way computer equipment is designed. Also may refer to the design of a communication system, as in "network architecture." (See also *open architecture.*)

Sentence: "Paul is taking a class on computer *architecture*. They're starting with the early-cage look and moving up into the neoclassic, fawn-white structures."

archive

Pronunciation: *ar-kive.*

Meaning: To store important files in a place where you can never find them again.

Sentence: "The guy who designed the new hospital is brilliant. He put the computer *archive* center right next to the MRI unit. Now, every time someone comes in with a concussion, the MRI machine bulk erases all the billing information."

argument

Pronunciation: *ar-gyoo-mint.*

Meaning: A value given to a subprogram. A term used most often when you write your own programs.

Sentence: "The main program needs to give two *arguments* to the subprogram so that it can work properly. After the subprogram gets these two arguments, it can plot the next most likely sighting of Elvis, Bigfoot, and the Loch Ness Monster."

ARPANET

Pronunciation: *Ar-pa-net.*

Meaning: A nationwide computer network created by the Department of Defense to link research institutions and universities together. ARPANET has now merged with several other networks to create the Internet.

Sentence: "I used to use the *ARPANET* to dial into a computer back in Boston. Now I have to use the Internet. Tomorrow I'll have to remember a new acronym to use to do the same thing."

array

Pronunciation: *ah-ray.*

Meaning: A collection of similar data (such as numbers, letters, or strings) stored under the same name. Data is assigned a different number in the array. An array to store five numbers might look like `NumberArray[1..5] of Integer`, depending on the language you use.

Sentence: "That Rusty is so clever. He's writing a program categorizing the blow-gun poisons used by various Amazon tribes. He's calling it his sting-*array*."

arrow key

Pronunciation: *air-row kee.*

Meaning: Special keys on the keyboard that move the cursor up, down, left, or right. Not surprisingly, the arrow keys have little arrows on them.

Sentence: "Bill just quit tech support. He told a guy to press the up-*arrow key,* and he shot back at him that there were 12 arrows on his keyboard, five of which pointed up."

artificial intelligence

Pronunciation: *art-i-fish-al in-tell-i-jentz.*

Meaning: Sometimes abbreviated as AI. (See also *AI.*)

Sentence: "My favorite button is the one that says '*Artificial Intelligence* is better than none!'"

ascender

Pronunciation: *a-sen-der.*

Meaning: The part of a letter that extends upwards. The letters *t* and *h* have ascenders. The letters *a*, *u*, and *n* do not.

Sentence: "Letters with *ascenders* go to heaven when they're deleted; letters with descenders suffer an eternity in word processing purgatory."

ascending order

Pronunciation: *ass-en-ding or-der.*

Meaning: To arrange information from lowest to highest.

Sentence: "Hopefully, the air traffic controller will arrange the airplanes taking off in *ascending order.*"

ASCII

Pronunciation: *Ass-kee.*

Meaning: An acronym that stands for *American Standard Code for Information Interchange.* ASCII defines a standard way for representing characters on computers. ASCII is handy because computers that recognize it can share files that contain only ASCII characters, which are typically only plain, boring text files.

Sentence: "A file composed of only *ASCII* characters is about as exciting as gum without any flavor."

ASCII file

Pronunciation: *Ass-kee fi-ell.*

Meaning: A file that contains only ASCII characters. Sometimes called a text file.

Sentence: "The only sure way to transfer files between different word processors is to store everything in *ASCII files.* You won't be able to use underlining, fonts, or type sizes, but at least the text will be the same."

aspect ratio

Pronunciation: *ass-pekt ray-she-o.*

Meaning: The ratio of the horizontal dimension of an object to its vertical dimension. A term used in graphics.

Sentence: "Movie buffs will tell you that most films are shot with a 3x4 aspect ratio. And if you take the screen and mentally turn it sideways into the theater, that marks the ideal row for viewing the picture. (This sounds impressive, but I just made it up.)"

assembler

Pronunciation: *ass-em-bler.*

Meaning: A special program used to convert programs written in assembly language into machine code that the computer can understand.

Sentence: "If an *assembler* puts together assembly language programs, why doesn't a seer put together C language programs?"

assembly language

Pronunciation: *ass-em-blee lan-gu-uj.*

Meaning: A type of programming language that directly manipulates the microprocessor of a computer. Assembly language programs are usually longer and harder to read than programs written in C or BASIC. On the other hand, assembly language programs run faster and take up less space than similar programs written in other languages. Assembly language is used when speed and efficiency are more important than clarity and *portability* (the capability to run on different computers without modification).

Sentence: "Human is to computer as *assembly language* is to grunting."

asterisk

Pronunciation: *ass-te-risk.*

Meaning: The * symbol on the keyboard. Many operating systems, such as MS-DOS, treat the asterisk as a wild card when it's used with ordinary operating system commands.

Sentence: "If you want to delete every file in a directory using MS-DOS, type **DEL *.*** and press the Enter key. If you want to delete every file that has the .EXE file extension, type **DEL *.EXE** and press the Enter key. If you want to delete every file permanently from the face of the earth, you must log onto God's computer, log to the /DEV/EARTH directory, and then delete the whole rigmarole."

asynchronous

Pronunciation: *a-sin-kron-us.*

Meaning: Any process that isn't synchronized. Often used when sending or receiving data through a phone line. Most likely a term you'll never use in your life, but it can make you sound knowledgeable around other computer geeks.

Sentence: "Myrtle may not know anything about computers, but since she calls at all odd hours of the night, I'd say she is an expert on *asynchronous* communication."

AT

Pronunciation: *Ay-Tee.*

Meaning: An acronym (isn't the computer industry full of them?) that IBM invented that stands for *advanced technology.* When IBM introduced a new computer that used the 80286 processor, they called the computer the IBM AT. AT also can refer to the command set used by Hayes modems (and just about every other modem). In that case, AT is short for *attention!*

Sentence: "There's always a risk in the computer biz when you title something 'advanced technology.' Back in 1985, Al bought an IBM *AT* for $4,000. Now it's worth about $200."

AT&T

Pronunciation: *Ay Tee and Tee.*

Meaning: An acronym that stands for *American Telephone and Telegraph.* Familiar with telephones, AT&T tried to break into the computer market and threaten IBM. This was like McDonald's trying to break into the software business and put Microsoft out of work.

Sentence: "Possible future headline: *AT&T* recently acquired Milton-Bradley in a further attempt to bust into the computer market."

ATM

Pronunciation: *Ay Tee Em.*

Meaning: Acronym for *Asynchronous Transfer Mode,* a method of sending audio, visual, and computer data over one line without getting anything confused or melting any telephone poles. Can also be an acronym for a friendly robot that dispenses money.

Sentence: "In the future, your ATM machine will use *ATM* and you can actually see a bank vice president get angry as you withdraw your money."

audio

Pronunciation: *aw-dee-o.*

Meaning: The reproduction or creation of sound.

Sentence: "A computer with *audio* capability can annoy your ears as well as your eyes."

AUTOEXEC.BAT

Pronunciation: *Aw-toe Ex-ek dot Bat.*

Meaning: Short for *AUTO EXECutable BATch file.* Commonly found on IBM-compatible computers, this file contains instructions that the computer follows before waiting for any commands from you. If you ever feel as if your computer is ignoring you when it first starts up, the AUTOEXEC.BAT is responsible.

Sentence: "Sam may be computer illiterate, but he says '*AUTOEXEC.BAT*' quite a lot to sound impressive at the water cooler."

AUX

Pronunciation: *Ay Yoo Ex* or *Ox.*

Meaning: In MS-DOS, an abbreviation for the *AUXiliary port,* which is the communications (COM) port that MS-DOS uses when you don't tell it otherwise.

Sentence: "Old farmer Vern gave up computing altogether. The toll-free phone support guy told him to plug his modem into the *AUX* port. Darn beast nearly hooved him to death."

Avogadro's Number

Pronunciation: *Av-o-god-rowz Num-ber.*

Meaning: A constant value used by scientists that represents something so important they decided to name it after the guy who discovered it. Rumor has it that if you dial Avogadro's Number backward, you can hear demonic messages.

Sentence: "I'm tired of calling up girls for dates who turn me down. Give me *Avogadro's Number,* and maybe I can talk physics to him or something."

axis

Pronunciation: *ax-iss.*

Meaning: Imaginary guidelines used for plotting graphics on a computer screen. To measure a point horizontally, you use the X-axis. To measure a point vertically, you use the Y-axis.

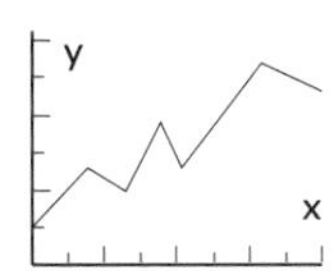

Sentence: "The world tilts on its *axis* about 23 degrees. That is, unless ol' fat Merle is doing sit-ups."

back door

Pronunciation: *bak door.*

Meaning: A secret way of getting into a program that usually only the original programmer knows about (such as a secret password).

Sentence: "A lot of disgruntled programmers put *back doors* into their programs. That way, if they ever get fired, they can still get in and use the program without anyone knowing."

background

Pronunciation: *bak-grow-nda.*

Meaning: When a window or another program is hidden out of sight without being removed from the computer altogether, it is said to be "in the background." Opposite of *active.* (See also *active window.*)

Sentence: "Whenever you run two or more programs simultaneously, you can use only one program at a time. Any other programs you load run in the *background* until you need them or until your computer crashes altogether."

backlit

Pronunciation: *bak-lit.*

Meaning: Illuminated with additional lighting from behind. Often used to describe LCD screens found on laptop computers.

Sentence: "Harry is so cheap. He saved himself $50 by not getting a *backlit* laptop, thinking he could just hold a flashlight behind the lid to accomplish the same thing."

backslash key

Pronunciation: *bak-slash kee.*

Meaning: The \ key that everyone always confuses with the forward slash key /. The backslash key is used to separate directory names, such as in the command

```
DIR C:\WINDOWS\SYSTEM
```

Sentence: "Over the phone, you might say: 'Type CD *backslash* DOS and press the Enter key.' But the person you're talking to might type this:

```
Seedy back slash doss and press the inner key
```

Backspace

Pronunciation: *Bak-spay-sa.*

Meaning: The key on the keyboard that has the word *Backspace* printed on it. In most programs, the Backspace key erases the character to the left of the cursor (like a little PacMan).

Sentence: "Too bad they don't have a *Backspace* key to take back things you shouldn't have said."

backup

Pronunciation: *bak-up.*

Meaning: A copy you make of a file in case the original file gets destroyed. Can also refer to the copy of the file. In MS-DOS, you use the BACKUP command to make backups of your files.

Sentence: "Hey Jefferson! Houser just erased our Christmas bonus file. Where's that *backup* you made yesterday? You did make a backup, didn't you? Jefferson, how come you don't look so good?"

BAK

Pronunciation: *Back* (as in "Ahl be bahk!").

Meaning: A three-letter file extension given to backup files, especially the ones created automatically by some applications (such as some word processors).

Sentence: "You can save space on your hard disk by erasing all those *.BAK* files. Before doing so, make sure that you won't need them if your original files get screwed up."

balloon help

Pronunciation: *ba-loon help.*

Meaning: Starting with System 7 on the Macintosh, Apple introduced balloon help, which provides little windows of helpful information on the screen. Balloon help gets its name from the windows it displays, which look like the speaking balloons seen in comic strips.

Sentence: "*Balloon help* displays just a little bit of help, unlike the normal help menu that displays gobs of information that you can't use or understand."

bank switching

Pronunciation: *ba-nk switch-ing.*

Meaning: A way of quickly switching between two different groups of memory chips, giving the illusion that it's all the same memory. Bank switching is used to overcome any built-in limitations. IBM computers have a built-in 640K limitation of RAM. Expanded memory enables you to add up to 16MB of RAM, but the computer still uses only 640K of RAM at any given time. Unless you're a technician, you'll never have to worry about bank switching for the rest of your life. (See *also expanded memory.*)

Sentence: "Older microcomputers had to resort to *bank switching* to compete with the memory available in newer models. No wonder those companies went bankrupt."

bar code

Pronunciation: *bar kode.*

Meaning: A striped pattern of narrow and wide black and white strips. Found on almost everything you buy, bar codes provide information that scanning devices understand.

Sentence: "Many businesses use computers to scan in *bar codes* so that they can keep track of inventory. Our company uses bar codes to keep track of employees after work."

base

Pronunciation: *bayss.*

Meaning: The number of digits used in a counting system. Base ten uses ten digits, base two (binary) uses two, and base sixteen (hexadecimal) uses sixteen.

Sentence: "Most people use *base* ten because they have five fingers on each hand. My cat has only four toes on each paw, so he uses base eight."

BASIC

Pronunciation: *Bay-sik.*

Meaning: A programming language specifically designed to make programming easier. An acronym for *Beginners All-purpose Symbolic Instruction Code.* Although BASIC is easy to use, many programmers look down on it as a "toy" language because early versions of BASIC prevented you from creating really cool programs that would wipe out your hard disk or blow up your modem. Newer versions of BASIC offer as much flexibility and power as C and Pascal, but it's still fashionable to snub BASIC, just to make BASIC programmers feel inadequate and insecure.

Sentence: "They named the *BASIC* language appropriately. It's basic! Now take C. They named it well, too; C makes me sea sick!"

BAT

Pronunciation: *Bat* (like the animal that gets in your hair and eats bugs during the night).

Meaning: A three-letter file extension used to identify batch files.

Sentence: "The gang told Lois that she had too many bats in her belfry, so she erased her AUTOEXEC.*BAT* file."

batch file

Pronunciation: *bat-ch fi-ell.*

Meaning: A special file that contains lists of operating system commands. Typing the name of a batch file tells the computer to follow all the instructions stored in the batch file.

Sentence: "I created a *batch file* to load WordPerfect and copy my files to a backup directory automatically. Instead of typing these commands myself, I just type the name of the batch file and let the computer do all the dirty work."

Batman

Pronunciation: *Bat-man.*

Meaning: A popular comic book character who dresses like a bat and goes around doing good deeds in crime-ridden Gotham City.

Sentence: "I like Batman because he's the only superhero who isn't radiated or mutated in some way to get his superhero powers."

battery backup

Pronunciation: *bat-er-ree bak-up.*

Meaning: A battery that's ready to supply electricity the moment a power outage occurs. (See also *UPS.*)

Sentence: "When there's a power outage, Tom's house is the only one on the block with lights, a microwave, TV, and a computer. If I didn't know that he has a *battery backup* for everything, I'd figure that his house was possessed."

baud

Pronunciation: *bawd.*

Meaning: A unit that measures the speed of transmission, such as for data through a modem. Modems are rated by baud rate, which varies from 300, 1200, 2400, and 9600 to 28,800. Eventually, the baud rate will go as high as our national debt.

Sentence: "Peter tried to use his modem to pick up that cute girl in the computer science class. She slapped him, though, after he asked her what her *baud* rate was."

BBS

Pronunciation: *Bee Bee Ess.*

Meaning: Acronym that stands for *Bulletin Board System*, a program that lets other people dial into a computer and copy files, leave messages, and run up their phone bill.

Sentence: "Most *BBS* systems have more BS than B."

BCD

Pronunciation: *Bee See Dee.*

Meaning: An acronym that stands for *Binary Coded Decimal,* which is a technique that programs use to ensure accuracy for financial calculations.

Sentence: "Most spreadsheets use *BCD* so that rounding errors won't mess up your calculations. I must pay an accountant not to mess up my calculations."

beach ball pointer

Pronunciation: *beech ball point-er.*

Meaning: A symbol that appears on the screen to let you know that the computer is actually doing something although nothing seems to be happening. The symbol looks like a beach ball that's spinning around; hence, its name. The beach ball pointer is the Mac counterpart to the Windows hourglass.

Sentence: "My computer is so slow that I stare at the *beach ball pointer* more often than I do the rest of my work."

bells and whistles

Pronunciation: *bells and wis-els.*

Meaning: A slang term to describe the multitude of extra features that a program offers.

Sentence: "Each time they upgrade WordPerfect, they add more *bells and whistles*. Why can't they just make the thing easier to use in the first place?"

benchmark

Pronunciation: *ben-cha-mark.*

Meaning: A special test that measures the performance of a program or equipment against a basic standard. A benchmark is supposed to be a fair measurement of performance, but nobody thinks so except for the company whose product comes out on top.

Sentence: "They run *benchmarks* on everything, software and hardware. Now if only they'd do the same thing for manuals, some of us could really get our work done faster."

Bernoulli box

Pronunciation: *Ber-new-lee box.*

Meaning: A mass storage system that uses removable cartridges. Named after a Swiss scientist who predicted the dynamics of a rapidly spinning, flexible disk around a fixed object and decided that his college education hadn't been a waste of time after all.

Sentence: "Don's a little slow. He brought a *Bernoulli box* for lunch, figuring it contained some type of Italian meal."

berserk

Pronunciation: *ber-zerk.*

Meaning: A fit of rage that Vikings often went into during the heat of battle. Today, it refers to the fit of rage that computer users go into when their computer fails to work the way they thought it would.

Sentence: "Watch out for Fred. He's been trying to print sideways in WordPerfect, and I think he's about to go *berserk* on us again."

beta test

Pronunciation: *bay-ta test.*

Meaning: The second stage of testing (alpha test is the first) a program before releasing it to the general public. People who use a beta test program are called *beta testers.* Beta test programs are sometimes called "Version 1.0" by companies who want to rush their program onto the market before it's ready.

Sentence: "Before Microsoft released MS-DOS, they gave it to 50,000 people around the country to *beta test* for them. After they discovered it to be full of bugs, Microsoft sold it to the rest of us."

Bézier curve

Pronunciation: *Bez-ee-ay kurv.*

Meaning: A mathematically generated line for displaying irregularly shaped curves. To create Bézier curves in most computer graphics programs, you plot a straight line and then manipulate two points somewhere in the middle, which are called control handles. Moving these control handles in different directions twists the line into a Bézier curve.

Sentence: "*Bézier curves* look like the twisted nightmare of some highways I've driven on."

big iron

Pronunciation: *big i-ron.*

Meaning: Slang term for a mainframe computer that costs millions of dollars, takes up half a room, and performs as much work as a $6,000 personal computer of today.

Sentence: "When our company finally switches over to personal computers, we'll give our *big iron* to a computer museum."

billclintonrhythm

Pronunciation: *Bill-Clinton-rhythm.*

Meaning: A step-by-step set of instructions that attempts to do something worthwhile. (See also *algorithm.*)

Sentence: "My new tax program works perfectly because my *billclintonrhythms* are flawless. As long as nobody sees me on the Arsenio program, my new sax program will keep on working perfectly, too."

billisecond

Pronunciation: *bill-a-sek-ond.*

Meaning: A billionth of a second, abbreviated as BS.

Sentence: "Some computer consultants cost so much that it seems as if they charge you by the *billisecond.*"

BIN

Pronunciation: *Been* (as in "Been there; done that").

Meaning: A three-letter file extension to identify files containing binary data.

Sentence: "To be proper, Benjamin renamed all his *BIN* files to BEN. Now he wonders why his programs won't work."

binary

Pronunciation: *bi-na-ree.*

Meaning: A counting system that uses two digits, 0 and 1. Sometimes used to describe other systems that offer only two choices, such as the Republican and Democratic parties.

Sentence: "Computers count only by twos, using *binary* arithmetic. People count by tens, using decimal arithmetic."

binary file

Pronunciation: *bi-na-ree fi-ell.*

Meaning: A file containing bits and bytes of information that only a computer (or a computer geek) would understand. Often identified with the three-letter BIN file extension.

Sentence: "Most programs store additional information in *binary files* in case they need them later."

BIOS

Pronunciation: *Bi-os.*

Meaning: Acronym that stands for *Basic Input/Output System.* The BIOS is a set of instructions that tells the computer how to act. Most computers have the BIOS built in as a chip plugged into the computer.

Sentence: "Many IBM computers use the Phoenix *BIOS,* which mimics the IBM BIOS and makes the computer think it's really an IBM computer living in Phoenix."

bit

Pronunciation: *bit* (as in "I bit my lip").

Meaning: Abbreviation for *BInary digiT,* which can be either a 0 or a 1. Bits are often used to measure the capability of a microprocessor to process data, such as 16-bit or 32-bit. Four bits make up a nibble, and eight bits make up a byte.

Sentence: "Old computers used an *8-bit* processor. The more powerful ones use a 32-bit processor, and they can handle roughly four times as much information. Too bad they haven't bothered making them easier to use along the way."

bitmap

Pronunciation: *bit-map.*

Meaning: A graphics image represented by tiny little points of light called *pixels.* The more pixels used, the sharper the image looks.

Sentence: "I told Fred that I wanted a *bitmap* graphic, so he printed a picture of a map and took a bite out of it."

bitmapped font

Pronunciation: *bit-mapd fawnt.*

Meaning: A typeface style stored as a matrix of tiny dots. When you enlarge the size of a bitmapped font, the font tends to look jagged. Bitmapped fonts gobble up lots of memory.

Sentence: "You can always tell a *bitmapped font* because when you change its size, the letters start looking rough and jagged as if they were printed on a cheap dot-matrix printer instead of on a nice laser printer."

bitmapped image

Pronunciation: *bit-mapd im-age.*

Meaning: A picture formed by patterns of tiny dots (pixels). Most paint programs, such as MacPaint or PC Paintbrush, create bitmapped images. Bitmapped images can be difficult to modify because you have to change pixels one at a time.

Sentence: "Creating a decent-looking *bitmapped image* is about as easy as trying to create a picture using colored bits of sand in the wind."

Bitnet

Pronunciation: *Bit-net.*

Meaning: An early nationwide computer network that began in the early '80s. Bitnet still exists and can be accessed through the ubiquitous Internet.

Sentence: "With all of these computer networks, *Bitnet*, Internet, and Usenet, popping up all over the place, it's a miracle anyone knows how to reach anyone at all to send electronic mail. Then again, digging through these different computer networks is at least more interesting than relying on the Post Office to deliver mail."

black box

Pronunciation: *blak box.*

Meaning: A collection of circuit boards that perform a specific function without the user's knowing how the circuitry works.

Sentence: "Here's the easy explanation: You stuff all these numbers into one end of the *black box,* and out the other end comes a balanced budget."

block

Pronunciation: *blok.*

Meaning: A collection of information lumped together for convenience. (1) When you transfer files using a communications protocol such as XModem or ZModem, data gets transferred in blocks. With XModem, the size of the block is 128 bytes. With ZModem, the size of the block is 1024 bytes. (2) In a word processor, a block is a highlighted chunk of text.

Sentence: "Leon asked maintenance to make a bigger hole in his office wall. Seems he's having trouble with his modem's inability to send big enough *blocks.*"

BMP

Pronunciation: *Bee Em Pee.*

Meaning: A three-letter file extension used to identify bitmap graphic files.

Sentence: "When I figured out what Connie meant by 'bumpy' files, I told her that *BMP* files are bitmap graphic files."

BNC connector

Pronunciation: *Bee En See kon-neck-tor.*

Meaning: A metal jobbie at the end of a cable that twists to connect the cable to the back of your computer or to another cable. BNC must mean "Big Nobby Connector."

Sentence: "I need a cable with a *BNC* connector because I paid way too much for my network hardware."

boat anchor

Pronunciation: *bowt an-kor.*

Meaning: Slang term for something so useless that it might as well be tied to a chain and used for dead weight to keep a boat from drifting away.

Sentence: "You have a PCjr? Might as well be a *boat anchor*!"

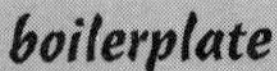

boilerplate

Pronunciation: *boil-er-playte.*

Meaning: A predefined document that you can use over and over again when you don't feel like thinking. Common uses for boilerplate documents are for form letters, legal documents, or love letters to multiple partners.

Sentence: "Bob is such a womanizer. He has this *boilerplate* document that he uses to swoon them and another boilerplate that he uses when they break up."

bold

Pronunciation: *bowld.*

Meaning: To display or print text more darkly.

Sentence: "*Bold* need not be fearless and confident. It only need look darker than the other text."

bomb

Pronunciation: *bom.*

Meaning: A program designed to do something sneaky at a specified time. Many disgruntled programmers write bombs in their programs so that if they get fired, the bomb will go off on its own and wreck the company's program. Also, when a Mac crashes, you sometimes get a dialog box with a bomb in it.

Sentence: "Company policy is always to give the MIS guys a raise and Christmas bonus. Otherwise, management fears that various *bombs* will go off in the system."

boogeyman

Pronunciation: *boo-gee man.*

Meaning: An imaginary monster that parents use to scare their children into behaving, such as by saying, "If you don't stop crying, the boogeyman will come and get you."

Sentence: "I used to believe that the *boogeyman* was just a story. Now I believe that he works for the IRS."

boolean

Pronunciation: *boo-lee-on.*

Meaning: True or false values, often used in programming.

Sentence: "If I need the car for the weekend, I check Dad's *boolean* value. If it's true that he's in a good mood, then I ask him for the keys. If it's false, then I ride the bus."

boot

Pronunciation: *boot* (like the kind cowboys wear on their feet).

Meaning: To start up a computer. Derived from the idea that the computer has to "pull itself up by the bootstraps" or from the feeling that the only way to get a computer to work is to threaten to kick it with a boot.

Sentence: "Too bad Richard's wife doesn't share his love of computer jargon. He told her to *boot* him at 5 a.m. to catch a plane. So she kicked him out of bed when the alarm went off."

bootstrap

Pronunciation: *boot-strap.*

Meaning: To create something out of nothing, such as "pulling yourself up by the bootstraps."

Sentence: "We started this company with absolutely nothing. We had to *bootstrap* our way to the top."

bozo

Pronunciation: *bo-zo.*

Meaning: Someone with no clue about what he's doing but with enough authority to keep others from ignoring him completely.

Sentence: "My boss is such a *bozo.* He thought that backing up a computer meant pushing it up against the wall."

bps

Pronunciation: *bee pee sss.*

Meaning: Acronym for *bits per second,* which measures the speed of transmission for data. Used interchangeably, though incorrectly, with baud.

Sentence: "I'm sorry, Walter, but *bps* is the correct term for a modem's speed."

brain damaged

Pronunciation: *brane dam-aged.*

Meaning: Something that looks okay from the outside but internally is crippled or limited.

Sentence: "The 80486SX processor is *brain damaged* because it doesn't have the math coprocessor that the regular 80486 has."

branch

Pronunciation: *bran-cha.*

Meaning: When the computer follows a series of instructions and then suddenly starts following a completely different set of instructions. Often used by programmers to describe the logic of their programs.

Sentence: "First, the computer runs these instructions, and then it *branches* over to the instructions over here. Then, through divine intervention, the program works perfectly."

break

Pronunciation: *bray-ka.*

Meaning: To stop the computer from doing whatever it happens to be doing at the moment. (See also *abort* and *Esc.*)

Sentence: "Ever wonder why the stop key on a computer is named *break* and not 'brake'?"

breakpoint

Pronunciation: *bray-ka-poin-ta.*

Meaning: A place in a program where the computer temporarily stops running. Breakpoints are used for debugging so programmers can see how the program is behaving up to a certain point.

Sentence: "If your program doesn't work, put a *breakpoint* halfway in between. If the program works up until the breakpoint, then you'll know that the last half of the program is what's screwing up."

brute force

Pronunciation: *broot forsa.*

Meaning: What you use to get something to work without regard for appearance, elegance, or finesse.

Sentence: "My program has a command that's supposed to move the paper in my printer up one sheet. Rather than use this command, I just use *brute force* and pull the paper out of the printer myself."

BTW

Pronunciation: *Bee Tee Double-yoo.*

Meaning: On-line acronym for *by the way.*

Sentence: "*BTW*, these modem people sure love acronyms."

bubble memory

Pronunciation: *bub-bull mem-or-ree.*

Meaning: A type of memory that retains its contents even after the power has gone off. Bubble memory is often used in tiny laptop computers that don't have room for a hard disk.

Sentence: "Joan's PC was getting low on *bubble memory,* so she kindly poured some Mr. Bubble into the disk drive."

buffer

Pronunciation: *buf-er.*

Meaning: A storage area for temporarily holding data. A printer buffer, for example, copies data from the computer and holds it until the printer is ready to print it.

Sentence: "If you don't like waiting for your printer, get a printer *buffer* so that you can use your computer while a document is being printed. If this gives you a headache, then use a Bufferin to make it go away."

bug

Pronunciation: *bug* (as in insect).

Meaning: A problem that prevents a program from working properly. Something every program has.

Sentence: "There are more *bugs* in this program than there are bicycles in China!"

bulletproof

Pronunciation: *bull-it-proof.*

Meaning: Software that works no matter how many keys the user presses incorrectly. A myth that programmers tell their children along with fairy tales such as Snow White and Bambi.

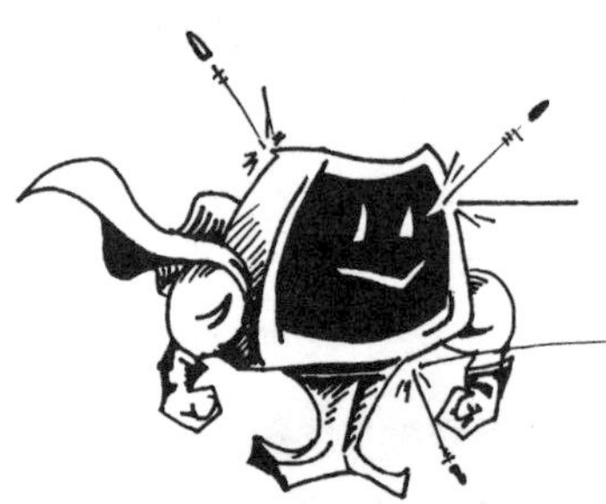

Sentence: "This program is *bulletproof.* No matter what you try to do, it still works perfectly."

bundled software

Pronunciation: *bun-dulled soft-ware.*

Meaning: Software that comes free (supposedly) when you buy a computer. Usually, bundled software is stuff you need anyway (such as MS-DOS) or programs that aren't selling well, so the publisher's trying to give it away just to clean out its warehouse.

Sentence: "Most computers offer *bundled software* such as Microsoft Office. The idea is that you pay half as much for twice as much software, two thirds of which you don't need anyway."

burn in

Pronunciation: *bern in.*

Meaning: The process of testing electronic equipment to make sure that it works. Whenever you get a new computer, you should leave it on for 48 hours straight. If anything is going to go wrong, it will likely go wrong during this burn-in period.

Sentence: "Before selling a computer, most dealers let it *burn in* for 48 hours. Even so, you should let it burn in for 48 hours too, just to make sure. Then again, most problems with computers occur with the software and not with the hardware."

burn out

Pronunciation: *bern owt.*

Meaning: What happens when you stare at your computer screen for long periods of time, such as when you're typing a long list of computer terms for publication in a computer dictionary. A tired, sluggish feeling that makes you want to collapse on the nearest flat surface that can support your weight.

Sentence: "Working on my computer really makes me feel *burned out.* After eight hours of staring at a computer screen, I can't wait to go home and stare at my TV for the rest of the night to unwind."

bus

Pronunciation: *bus.*

Meaning: An electronic transportation system for sending electrons around. In a computer, the bus is an electronic pathway on which information travels between the microprocessor and other important computer parts. Bus has only one S.

Sentence: "Unlike a normal city bus, a computer *bus* actually runs efficiently and gets electrons to the correct destination on time."

bus mouse

Pronunciation: *bus mow-sa.*

Meaning: A mouse that plugs into an expansion board, in contrast to a serial mouse that plugs into a computer's serial port.

Sentence: "Janet lives in the city, so she got her computer a *bus mouse.*"

button

Pronunciation: *butt-on.*

Meaning: A small rectangle that appears on the screen to enable the user to communicate commands to the computer. Buttons typically appear on the screen as gray rectangles that have the commands printed on them. (See also *mouse button.*)

Sentence: "Ernest keeps hitting his shirt with the mouse. I suppose that someone should tell him what 'click on the *button*' really means."

byte

Pronunciation: *bite.*

Meaning: The amount of memory needed to store one character, such as a letter or a number. Computer memory and disk space is measured in kilobytes, megabytes, and gigabytes. (See these latter terms later in the book.)

Sentence: "My floppy disk is full. It has only 5,630 *bytes* free. My brain is full from reading these computer terms. I think I must have only 1,030 bytes left in my head."

C

Pronunciation: Just like it looks, *SEE?* (And for you Spanish-speaking folks, just say yes. Si?)

Meaning: A programming language developed at Bell Laboratories back in the 70s when disco was popular. C is a general-purpose language like BASIC and Pascal, but it can manipulate the internal guts of a computer just as assembly language can. C has been used to write many popular programs, including the UNIX operating system, Lotus 1-2-3, and Microsoft FoxPro.

C has three advantages over other languages:

- C programs are *almost* as easy to write and understand as BASIC or Pascal programs. (Note the emphasis on "almost.")
- C programs run almost as fast as assembly language but are easier to understand.
- C programs are *portable,* meaning that you can run the same C program on different kinds of computers, such as an IBM, a Macintosh, and an Amiga, without changing the program.

In contrast, BASIC and Pascal programs usually run slower than C programs and cannot run on different kinds of computers without extensive modifications that usually aren't worth the effort. Unfortunately, because C was designed for maximum efficiency, it can also be hard for beginners to learn.

Sentence: "Only wimps use BASIC or Pascal. Cool programmers code in *C* so that they don't have to write the same program over again to run on different kinds of computers."

Sample C program:

```
#include <stdio.h>
main ()
{
  printf ("Only wimps use BASIC or Pascal.\n");
  printf ("Cool programmers always use C.");
}
```

C++

Pronunciation: *See plus plus.* Just like saying "C+" but with a stutter at the end.

Meaning: An improved version of the C language that adds object-oriented extensions. C++ has become popular because it's easy for C programmers to learn, provides object-oriented features to make programming large projects easier, and sells a lot of computer books. Like C, C++ is fast, portable, and confusing to learn and understand.

Sentence: "Only wimps use C. Cool programmers code in C++ so that they can write bigger programs without losing their minds."

Sample program:

```
#include <iostream.h>
main
{
  cout << "Only wimps use C.\n";
  cout << "Cool programmers always use C++.";
}
cable
```

cable

Pronunciation: *kay-bull.*

Meaning: Cables connect different parts of the computer so that they actually do something useful. For example, cables connect your monitor to your computer, your computer to your printer, and your modem to your computer. Cables always need to be plugged into a port, which is usually an oddly shaped hole in the back of your computer.

The cable that connects your monitor to your computer plugs into your

computer's video card. The cable that connects your computer to your printer, called a *printer cable*, plugs into a parallel or serial port. The cable that connects your computer to your modem, called a *serial cable*, plugs into a serial port.

Sentence: "Gordon couldn't get his printer to work because the salesman forgot to sell him a printer *cable.* Then he sold Gordon a printer cable that wouldn't fit his computer's parallel port. Now Gordon's serving five to seven for aggravated assault."

cache

Pronunciation: sounds like *cash.*

Meaning: A place in memory where the computer can temporarily store data to avoid accessing the slow hard or floppy disk drive over and over again. Often called a RAM cache. Some computers have a built-in cache that they advertise as "Includes a 256K cache!" You can also carve a cache out of your computer's memory by using a special utility program such as PC Tools Deluxe.

Sentence: "Bob's computer runs faster than mine does because his has a built-in *cache.* I would use a utility program to create a *cache* on my computer, but the cache would gobble up some of my computer's memory. So I'll just use Bob's computer instead."

cache memory

Pronunciation: sounds like *cash memory.*

Meaning: The specific memory chips or portion of memory that's used as a cache to make a computer run faster.

Sentence: "My computer has a built-in 256K *cache memory,* and I have a utility program that creates an additional 1MB of cache memory. My computer would be the fastest one around if only I had enough cash left over to pay the electric bill."

CAD

Pronunciation: sounds like *kad* and rhymes with *sad, bad,* and *rad.*

Meaning: An acronym that stands for *Computer-Aided Design.* CAD substitutes a computer's graphics capabilities for drawing with paper and pencil. Computers that are running CAD programs often require huge amounts of hard disk space, high-resolution video displays, and a

fast microprocessor. CAD has been responsible for designing the most recent engineering achievements, including the gas tank for the 1972 Ford Pinto, the nuclear reactors for Three Mile Island, and the focal lens for the Hubble Space Telescope.

Sentence: "Allan can't even draw a straight line with a pencil, but he designed his own car using *CAD.* Of course, it blew up when he turned the ignition key."

CAD/CAM

Pronunciation: sounds like *kad/kam* and rhymes with *sad Sam.*

Meaning: A combination acronym that stands for *Computer-Aided Design and Computer-Aided Manufacturing.* CAM means letting computers actually make the stuff that somebody designed using CAD or pencil and paper.

Sentence: "A lot of companies use *CAM* to make products more efficiently and less expensively. Our company can't afford to buy computers, so we use child labor instead."

call

Pronunciation: combine the choking sound of a cat coughing up a hair ball with a sound that rhymes with *ball.*

Meaning: A programming term that describes the temporary transfer of control from the main program to a subprogram. May be used in a batch file, for example, to start another batch file.

Sentence: "I wrote a program that *calls* three subprograms. To add more features, I just need to *call* more subprograms. If that doesn't work, I'll just call another programmer and ask for help."

call waiting

Pronunciation: *Kall ooayt-ing*

Meaning: A telephone option that beeps if someone is trying to call you while you're already using the phone. You then can put your current caller on hold and talk to the second caller without hanging up the phone first. If you're talking on the phone, call waiting can be handy. If you're communicating through a modem, then call waiting can break your connection. To temporarily disable call waiting when you use your modem, dial * 70, wait for the dial tone, and then dial the

number normally. If you're using a Hayes-compatible modem and want to dial 555-1234, you have to dial *70W555-1234 or *70,,555-1234.

Sentence: "I was just about to electronically transfer a million dollars out of our corporate account and into my personal account when my mother-in-law called and *call waiting* broke my connection. Even worse, then I had to talk to my mother-in-law."

camera-ready

Pronunciation: *kam-e-ra red-ee.*

Meaning: A photograph, drawing, or printed text that looks so squeaky clean that you can make a zillion photocopies of it and the zillionth copy still looks good. This term is often used by publishers who work with desktop publishing software.

Sentence: "When professional photographers take pictures of bikini-clad models frolicking on exotic beaches, they produce *camera-ready* pictures for the *Sports Illustrated* annual swimsuit issue. When I use my Kodak Instamatic to take pictures of Uncle Fred in his bathrobe , I can't produce *camera-ready* pictures of anything at all."

cancel

Pronunciation: *kan-sell.* Say it fast enough and it sounds like *can't sell.*

Meaning: To take back or reverse an action. When you give the Cancel command, you're essentially telling your computer, "Ooops, forget I did that and make everything like it was before." The Windows dialog boxes often give the Cancel command as an option.

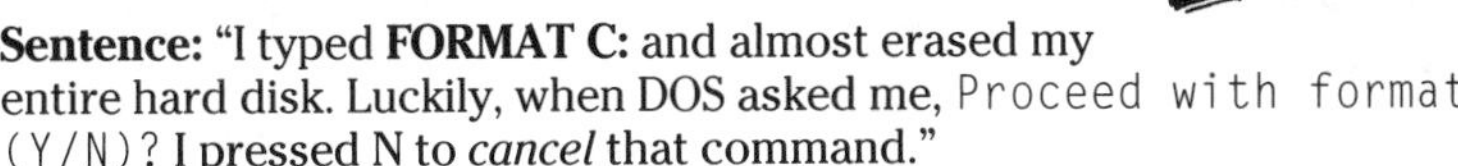

Sentence: "I typed **FORMAT C:** and almost erased my entire hard disk. Luckily, when DOS asked me, `Proceed with format (Y/N)?` I pressed N to *cancel* that command."

Caps Lock

Pronunciation: *Kaps Lock.*

Meaning: The key on every computer keyboard that lets you type capital (or uppercase) letters without having to press the Shift key each time. Most computers have a little light in the upper-right corner of the keyboard that goes on after you press the Caps Lock key once. If you press the Caps

Lock key again, the light goes off. Unlike with typewriters, pressing the Caps Lock key on a computer produces only uppercase *letters.* If you want to print ! or @ or any other symbol, you still have to press the Shift key first and hold it down.

Sentence: "Sometimes my fingers slip, and I press the *Caps Lock* key BY MISTAKE, AND THEN ALL MY TYPING LOOKS LIKE I'M SHOUTING."

capture

Pronunciation: *kap-sure.*

Meaning: To store a screen image to a file on a floppy disk or hard disk. Often used with desktop publishing and telecommunications programs.

Sentence: "Mary loves to *capture* screen images on her computer. She has even built a little jail in her office where she keeps them and, as the mood hits her, occasionally taunts them."

caret

Pronunciation: sounds like *carrot.*

Meaning: The symbol that appears when you press Shift-6, ^. Used in programming languages and certain programs as a specific command. In Pascal, the ^ symbol identifies a pointer. In C, the ^ symbol represents the exclusive OR (XOR) operator. In BASIC, the ^ symbol is used for exponential expressions. In spreadsheets such as Lotus 1-2-3, the ^ symbol centers labels or numbers. In word processors, the ^ symbol usually represents a typo.

Sentence: "In a C program, the command TAX ^ SALARY actually makes sense. This explains why programmers tend to be nerds."

carriage return

Pronunciation: *kar-edge ree-turn.*

Meaning: An invisible character that's used to end a line of text and move the cursor to the following line. Created by pressing the Enter or Return key.

Sentence: "If you want to sound elitist and fool people who are new to computers, just say 'use the *carriage return'* rather than 'press the Enter key.'"

carrier (detect)

Pronunciation: *kar-ree-er ([whispered] dee-tect).*

Meaning: A signal used by a modem to detect the presence of another modem. When modems talk through telephone lines, they emit a signal called a *carrier.* When one modem calls another modem, the two modems send carriers to each other. The moment each modem detects the carrier of another modem, it sends a carrier detect, letting the computer know that it is now connected to another computer.

Sentence: "Admiral Davis could tell that the Yorktown had been sunk. He dialed up the ship's BBS with his modem and couldn't get a *carrier detect.*"

carrot

Pronunciation: *kar-et.*

Meaning: The vegetable that parents claim will improve your vision. The favorite snack of Bugs Bunny.

Sentence: "While we were flying on American Airlines, the flight attendant told me to eat all my *carrots* because there were passengers starving on Air India."

cartridge

Pronunciation: *kar-tridge,* rhymes with *partridge.*

Meaning: A self-contained, removable part of a computer or printer. It is usually plastic, expensive, and hard to find when you need it. Laser printers use toner cartridges and font cartridges. Nintendo units are worthless unless you plug in a game cartridge.

Sentence: "My laser printer couldn't print any fonts until I plugged in a font *cartridge.* Unfortunately, the font cartridge cost so much that I had to sell my computer to pay for it."

cascade

Pronunciation: *kass-kade.*

Meaning: To arrange several windows neatly on a computer screen so that you can still see the title bar and upper-left corner of each one.

Sentence: "Until I had my computer *cascade* all my windows, some of my windows had been completely hidden from view. I still can't find anything I need, but at least the cascaded windows make me look nice and organized."

CASE

Pronunciation: sounds like *Kase* and rhymes with *base.*

Meaning: (1) In text formatting terms, case means the style of letters, either UPPERCASE or lowercase. (2) In programming terms, CASE is a special command that lets the computer choose two or more possible options. (3) In techno-dweeb talk, CASE is an acronym that means computer-aided software engineering.

Sentence: "As a computer science major, I learned from my *CASE* courses that I could use the *CASE* command in Pascal to replace

multiple IF-THEN statements. To make programs easier to read, my teachers told me that the *case* of my typing would matter too. That's why I dropped out and became a cab driver instead."

case sensitive

Pronunciation: *kase sen-si-tive.*

Meaning: The distinction made between UPPERCASE and lowercase letters. Some programs or systems require that certain commands be in either uppercase or lowercase. UNIX is a good example. Also, modems can be fussy in that way, too.

Sentence: "Bob is so *case sensitive.* He thinks that 'Hello' and 'HELLO' are two completely different words."

cassette tape

Pronunciation: *ka-set tape.*

Meaning: A magnetic strip that's on a reel and can store information. Ancient computers used cassette tapes to store programs. Today, everyone uses floppy disks or hard disks. (See also *tape* and *tape drive.*)

Sentence: "I bought an old Timex/Sinclair computer that uses programs stored on *cassette tape.* I really screwed up my computer when I gave it a Led Zeppelin cassette tape by mistake."

cat

Pronunciation: *kat* (as in *me-ow*).

Meaning: A UNIX command that displays the contents of a file, hopefully one containing only text. It's from the word concatenate, which doesn't mean anything to us presently. (See also *concatenate,* if you aspire to become a techno-dweeb.)

Sentence: "I typed *cat* on my keyboard, and the computer suddenly started purring."

catatonic

Pronunciation: *cat-a-ton-ic.*

Meaning: A state of near total paralysis, usually brought on by staring at a computer screen too long.

Sentence: "At first I thought Gene was *catatonic*, but he was just waiting for Windows95 to start on his computer."

CD

Pronunciation: *See Dee.*

Meaning: Sometimes referred to as the *Change Directory* command because that's what it stands for. Shortcut command to change directories in MS-DOS. Easier to type than CHDIR. Typing **CD ** changes to the root directory. Typing **CD..** changes to the parent directory of the current directory. Typing **CD** displays the name of the current directory. (Also stands for compact disc, as in the favorite digital/audio storage device. See also *CD-ROM.)*

Sentence: "Call a doctor! Janice has lapsed into a primal state! She's trying to configure her *CD* drive in MS-DOS and all she can say is, 'CD. CD run. Run, CD, run.'"

CD-ROM

Pronunciation: *See Dee Rahm* (don't pronounce *ROM as* "Rome"*).*

Meaning: Acronym that stands for *Compact Disc-Read Only Memory.* Often used to describe a CD-ROM drive, which is a special disk drive that reads only compact discs. As a bonus, many computer CD-ROM disk drives also can play audio compact discs. This capability enables you to turn your $2,000 computer into a $49 Walkman. CD-ROM discs usually contain massive amounts of information (600MB or more of data, text, graphics, video, or sound). A compact disc is round, silver, flat, and looks like a UFO if you toss it in the air and use an out-of-focus camera to take its picture.

Sentence: "My new *CD-ROM* drive lets me display entire encyclopedias, classical novels, maps from every country in the world, travelogues, and interactive fescennine films. Now I have no reason to leave the house."

cell

Pronunciation: sounds like *sell.*

Meaning: The intersection of rows and columns in a spreadsheet. Cells are used to store text, numbers, and formulas.

Sentence: "My financial spreadsheet uses 300 *cells* to store all my vital business information. And there's a prison up the road that uses 300 cells to store various businessmen who keep such information from the IRS."

central processing unit

Pronunciation: sometimes called the *CPU* or the *processor.*

Meaning: The little chip in personal computers that controls everything in the computer. Sometimes referred to as the "brains" of the computer because it does the basic calculating that translates into your favorite GIF file or spreadsheet. A central processing unit looks like a thin wafer or a headless cockroach. (See also *microprocessor.*)

Sentence: "After you upgrade your computer's *central processing unit,* you can turn the old one into jewelry for a loved one."

Centronics port

Pronunciation: *Sen-tron-iks port.*

Meaning: The parallel port on a computer. Originally used to connect computers to Centronics printers.

Sentence: "Ray's a real old-timer. He always calls the printer port a *Centronics port.* Heck, he's been around so long, he remembers when you used to need to crank computers to start them."

CGA

Pronunciation: *See Gee Ay.*

Meaning: An acronym that stands for *Color Graphics Adapter,* the original color graphics standard for IBM and compatible personal computers. The CGA standard produced fuzzy images that are perfectly calculated to strain your eyes and give you splitting headaches. Newer computers use VGA or SVGA graphics instead. (See also *EGA, VGA,* and *SVGA.)*

Sentence: "CGA graphics are as outmoded as platform disco shoes."

CGM

Pronunciation: *See Gee Emm.*

Meaning: Acronym for *Computer Graphics Metafile,* a type of graphics file format standard used by programmers.

Sentence: "We drove to Detroit so we could *CGM.*"

character

Pronunciation: *kar-act-ter.*

Meaning: Any symbol that you can type from the keyboard. Letters are characters; numbers are characters; and even $, @, _, ^, and ~ are considered characters.

Sentence: "Larry ran a word count in his word processor, and it told him that he has 4,128 *characters* in his document. 'Not bad for a budding novelist,' he beamed."

character code

Pronunciation: *kar-act-ter kode.*

Meaning: An agreed-upon collection of symbols that represent something else. The ASCII table is one collection of character codes; the seldom-used EBCDIC standard is another. Many programs, such as WordPerfect, use character codes mixed in with normal letters to represent underlining, superscripts, or bold.

Sentence: "Ralph is so into computers that he doesn't even communicate in English. No, he just uses *character codes* to speak."

character graphics

Pronunciation: *kar-act-ter graf-iks.*

Meaning: Funny little symbols that you can create by pressing certain keys on your keyboard. To create character graphics on an IBM computer, press the Alt key and type a number on the numerical keypad. To type ¢ (the cents thing), hold down the Alt key and type **155.**

Sentence: "My computer doesn't display graphics, but with *character graphics* I can still draw little boxes on my screen, just like on an Etch-A-Sketch."

character set

Pronunciation: *kar-act-ter set.*

Meaning: An organized list of symbols, such as an ASCII table.

Sentence: "The normal ASCII *character set* displays only letters and numbers, but the extended ASCII character set includes character graphics for displaying strange and wonderful characters not found on a keyboard."

CHDIR

(See *CD.*)

cheap

Pronunciation: *cheep.*

Meaning: An adjective that denotes poor quality no matter what the actual cost may be.

Sentence: "If our company weren't so *cheap,* we'd have new computers instead of having to use these Nintendos."

check boxes

Pronunciation: Just like it looks.

Meaning: A blank box that appears next to two or more options that the user can choose from. When a check box is empty, the option has not been chosen. When the check box is marked, the option has been chosen. Two or more check boxes can be checked at the same time.

Sentence: "Instead of having to choose multiple options through different menus, I can choose them all at once by using *check boxes.*"

Sample check boxes: Why do you hate computers?

[ ] Don't work the way you want

[X] Too expensive for what they offer

[ ] Too complicated

[X] Not easy to use

checksum

Pronunciation: Just as it looks, such as, "Would you like to *check some* of our lovely vegetables, or would you prefer to eat a big juicy steak instead?"

Meaning: A number calculated to verify the accuracy of data. You'll typically find it used on information that's transmitted through a modem. The sending computer tags a checksum onto the end of information that it sends. The receiving computer calculates its own checksum. If the two match, then the data was received okey-doke. If the checksums don't match, the information is re-sent.

Sentence: "Carol really wants to make sure that her relationship with Steve lasts. She's checked their astrological signs, scoured the family history, consulted with an oracle, and performed a *checksum* on their bank accounts."

Chicklet keyboard

Pronunciation: *Chick-let key-bored.*

Meaning: A keyboard that consists of tiny keys that resemble Chicklets gum. Chicklet keys are usually too tiny to type on comfortably. IBM developed the most popular chicklet keyboard for the IBM PCjr. The idea was to make the IBM PCjr unattractive for business use. The designers succeeded to such an extent that *nobody* bought the IBM PCjr.

Sentence: "The folks at IBM were obviously not in their right mind when they designed the PCjr's *Chicklet keyboard.*"

child process

Pronunciation: *chi-eld pro-sess.*

Meaning: A program on your computer that has been started by another program. They can do that, you know. When WordPerfect spell-checks a document, it runs another program, the Spell Checker. WordPerfect is the "parent" program; the Spell Checker is the "child." Sadly, child processes are eventually killed by their parent processes because computer programs are greedy and must maintain control.

Sentence: "It's easy to understand why so many *child processes* run away from home."

Chooser

Pronunciation: sounds like *Choose her.*

Meaning: A Macintosh desktop accessory (DA) that lets you select which printer to use, whether to turn AppleTalk on or off, and whether to use the serial or parallel port. The Chooser always appears in the Apple menu, located at the far left side of the menu bar.

Sentence: "Using the Mac *Chooser* makes sense only if you have a number of things to choose from."

CI$

Pronunciation: *sis* or *See-Eye-Ess*

Meaning: Acronym for *CompuServe Information Services.* The dollar sign ($) replaces the *S* to let people know that this is going to cost them a lot of money. (See also *CompuServe.*)

Sentence: "New subscribers call it *CIS.* Only after they get their first bill will they know it as *CI$.*"

circuit breaker

Pronunciation: *sir-cut braker.*

Meaning: A device that monitors the flow of electricity and cuts it off if it exceeds a certain level that may cause overloading, short-circuiting, and death to the user or destruction to massive amounts of personal property.

Sentence: "Gus decided to plug his computer, monitor, printer, microwave, electric car, and high-powered, antisatellite laser into one electric outlet. Good thing his *circuit breaker* worked, or else he might have blown the power grid for half the state."

CISC

Pronunciation: *Sisk* or *See Eye Ess See.*

Meaning: Acronym for *complex instruction set computing,* a type of microprocessor that uses complex instructions instead of simple instructions (which are what a RISC processor uses). The trade-off is that the microprocessor can do more but takes more time to do it. A RISC processor can do less but does it quickly. Does this make sense? Don't worry, no one in the computer industry understands it either. (See also *RISC.*)

Sentence: "There are those who claim that RISC will rule the world, but until then *CISC* is king. And then there are those of us who'd rather make a living and watch an occasional video."

Class A/Class B

Pronunciation: *Klass A/Klass Bee.*

Meaning: Two similar and confusing labels that the Federal Communications Commission (FCC) uses to distinguish between computers that emit different levels of high-frequency electrical energy. The Class A label means that the computer has been approved for use in an office. The Class B label means that the computer has been approved for both the home and office. Ideally, you want a computer with a Class B label. If you put a computer with a Class A label in your home, it could screw up your radio and TV reception.

Sentence: "The lame salesman tried to sell me a home computer with a *Class A* label, but I told him that I needed one with a *Class B* label instead. To prove my point, I had him stand next to a computer that is rated Class A so he could see what it did to his pacemaker."

Clear key

Pronunciation: *Kleer kee.*

Meaning: The key that erases highlighted text or drawings. It's the Macintosh's equivalent to the Backspace key on a PC.

Sentence: "Jill wanted to erase a sentence in her word processor, but she couldn't find the *Clear key.* So she painted white-out across the screen instead."

click

Pronunciation: sounds like *clique.*

Meaning: To press and release once on the mouse button, usually to select or activate an option, command, or button.

Sentence: "No, no! You keep the mouse on the mouse pad when you *click* its buttons. Don't point it at the computer as you do with a TV remote."

client

Pronunciation: *kli-ent.*

Meaning: (1) A local area network term that describes a computer that can request information, such as an application, from a file server, and can also perform independently from the network server by using a client application. (2) A Windows-based program that receives data through DDE. (See also *DDE.*)

Sentence: "Not only is Bob's computer president of the Hair Club for Men Network, it's also a *client.*"

client application

Pronunciation: *kli-ent app-li-kay-shin.*

Meaning: (1) A program that works only on one computer on a network The program lives on that computer's hard drive and doesn't "see" any other computers on the network.

On most networks, one big computer usually contains all the programs that everyone else uses. (See also *File Server.*) If that one computer fails, then none of the other computers can do anything. Because client applications run only on one computer and cannot be accessed by other computers in the network, a failure in one part of the network doesn't affect a client application (unless, of course, the part of the network that fails is the one computer that holds the client application). Client applications cannot be used by anyone else in a network. (2) A Windows-based program whose documents can accept linked or embedded objects. (See also *OLE.*)

Sentence: "Jim's mad that he had to keep working when the network crashed. His word processor is a *client application.*"

client/server network

Pronunciation: *kli-ent serve-her net-work.*

Meaning: A network where some programs and files are shared in one big computer, but each computer connected to the network can also run on its own.

Sentence: "We have a *client/server network* that lets everyone share the same database program and files with each other but gives all users the freedom to use whatever word processor they want on their own computers."

clip art

Pronunciation: *klip art.*

Meaning: Predrawn art that you can freely copy and use. Often used for desktop publishing.

Sentence: "*Clip art* comes in handy when your own drawing resembles primitive cave scratching."

Clipboard

Pronunciation: *Klip-bored.*

Meaning: A temporary storage area used by the Macintosh, Windows, and certain DOS programs for holding text or graphics. Items are automatically placed in the Clipboard whenever the user chooses the Cut or Copy command. Items remain on the Clipboard until the user issues the Cut or Copy command to choose a new item. Items stored on the Clipboard may be transferred to other programs.

Sentence: "To hide my résumé from the boss, I cut it and put it in the *Clipboard* where he wouldn't see it. Then I copied it back to my word processor and printed it out on the company laser printer."

Clipper chip

Pronunciation: *Klip-er chip.*

Meaning: A special chip that's designed to encrypt and decode information sent by a computer. Sounds nice, but there's a catch. This chip was designed by the U.S. Government, and, through various laws, taxes, and whatnot, they're trying to get one installed on every computer as the de facto method for encrypting files. The catch is that the government would also be able to decode the files. Sure, they claim that they couldn't decode files without the approval of two bureaucratic organizations. And if you believe that, then the Post Office really means it when they say two-day mail, the Pentagon is truly efficient, and the IRS is gentle and forgiving."

Sentence: "Hopefully the *Clipper chip* will never be a standard and we can encrypt our secret files and send money offshore without the government's ever knowing about it because, frankly, it isn't any of their business anyway."

clock

Pronunciation: *klok.*

Meaning: The circuit in the computer that keeps track of the date and the time, even when the power is shut off.

Sentence: "My old computer didn't have a *clock*, so every time I turned it on, it thought the date was 1/1/80. Everyone thought that I worked on my computer only once — on January 1, 1980."

clock ticks

Pronunciation: *klok tix.*

Meaning: Evenly spaced pulses that determine a computer's speed. During each clock tick, the computer actually does something. In between clock ticks, the computer does nothing, just like a typical office worker. The more clock ticks a computer has, the faster it will run. Clock speed is measured in megahertz (MHz) where 1 MHz = 1,000,000 clock ticks per second. Most modern personal computers have CPU clocks that run between 33 MHz and 66 MHz.

Sentence: "The salesman told me that the computer ran at 6 million *clock ticks* per second. I thought that was great until I realized that it was only 6 MHz."

clone

Pronunciation: *klone,* rhymes with *alone.*

Meaning: A term that refers to any computer that imitates a better-known computer or program. Clones are inexpensive, though they tend to lack the durability, grace, and prestige of the original — like Elvis impersonators.

Sentence: "I asked Shelly whether she was planning on buying a *clone* computer. But all she wanted to know was what Elvis had to do with computing."

close

Pronunciation: *kloze,* rhymes with *doze.*

Meaning: To stop using a file, writing its information to disk. The opposite of opening a file. Also refers to removing a window from the screen in a graphical environment.

Sentence: "The tech support guy told me to *close* my word processor's window, and I told him that it was 15 degrees outside and I'd be nuts to have the window open in the first place."

close box

Pronunciation: *Kloze bocks.*

Meaning: The tiny box that appears in the upper-left corner of a window. Clicking the mouse cursor inside the close box removes the window from view. In most programs, you have to have a mouse to use the close box.

Sentence: "Oh, so the *close box* makes the window go away! And I thought it was supposed to tell me when to do the laundry."

closed architecture

Pronunciation: *klozed ar-ki-tex-sure.*

Meaning: Equipment specifically designed to work only with the accessories made by the same company, usually the most expensive and least reliable equipment around.

Sentence: "The original IBM PC had an open architecture, so accessories were cheap and plentiful. Then IBM introduced the PS/2 with a *closed architecture,* hoping that people would buy only expensive IBM accessories. Instead, people nearly stopped buying IBM computers altogether."

CMOS

Pronunciation: *Sea-Moss.*

Meaning: An acronym that stands for *Complementary Metal-Oxide Semiconductor,* which is a specially designed circuit that consumes very little power. CMOS circuits are often used in devices such as wristwatches, pocket calculators, and laptop computers. CMOS RAM keeps track of system setup information, the date, time, and so on. Whatever you do, don't change your CMOS setup password and then forget it; you won't be able to get back into your computer.

Sentence: "When the salesguy told Maureen that her computer contained the latest *CMOS* processor, she responded positively. After all, old sea moss probably smells terrible."

coaxial cable

Pronunciation: *ko-ax-ee-el kay-bull.*

Meaning: A cable consisting of an insulating shield wrapped around a conductor. Coaxial cables are used for local area networks because they carry more data than ordinary telephone wires. TVs use a type of coaxial cable.

Sentence: "We chose *coaxial cables* to connect our computers — not to network them, but to keep them from falling too far when someone tosses a PC out a window."

COBOL

Pronunciation: *Ko-Ball.*

Meaning: An acronym for *COmmon Business Oriented Language,* COBOL is a language used primarily for business applications for large mainframe computers. (Now you know which language is responsible for screwing up your bank accounts.) Developed in the 60s by several computer companies and the U.S. Department of Defense, the language shows the influence that the drug-crazed, free-love era had on technology. COBOL programs tend to resemble plain English sentences. Unfortunately, the plain English sentences usually resemble those uttered by politicians or lawyers.

Sentence: "Verily, I say unto you, *COBOL* is the Latin of computer languages; dead but still used in crusty, nongrowing environments."

code (coding)

Pronunciation: *kod (ko-deen).*

Meaning: To actually write a program using a specific programming language such as C, BASIC, or Pascal.

Sentence: "I tried *coding* in COBOL until I switched to C. Now it takes me half as long to *code,* and I make only twice as many mistakes."

cold boot

Pronunciation: *kold boot.*

Meaning: To restart equipment that has been turned off. (See also *warm boot.*)

Sentence: "Sometimes when the computer crashes, pushing its reset button doesn't even work. In these cases, you have to *cold boot* your computer by turning it off, waiting for ten seconds, and then turning it on again."

color monitor

Pronunciation: *kull-er mon-i-ter.*

Meaning: A computer screen that can display several colors at one time. Color monitors follow specific video graphics standards, such as CGA, EGA, VGA, and SVGA.

Sentence: "Mike loves his new *color monitor.* After years of using a black-and-white model, he can now view his naked lady graphics collection in vivid color."

columns

Pronunciation: *kahl-ums.*

Meaning: A vertical strip of text that appears on a page. Newsletters commonly display two, three, or four columns side by side. Columns are also common in spreadsheets and other documents.

Sentence: "Lola decided that her report on ancient Greece would look best if she used Corinthian *columns.*"

COM

Pronunciation: *kom.*

Meaning: (1) Short for *COMmunications port.* When dialing through your modem, your communications program needs to know which COM port the modem is attached to. (2) A description for a special executable file that is small and simple. A COM file has the .COM file extension.

Sentence: "Bill is a staunch Republican. He never refers to his modem port as *COM* 1 because he thinks COM stands for communist."

COMDEX

Pronunciation: *Kom-Dex.*

Meaning: Acronym that stands for *COMputer Dealers EXposition.* Usually held twice a year — in Las Vegas in the winter and in a city near the East Coast in the spring. COMDEX is one of the most widely attended computer conferences in America and one of the easiest to get tired of real fast. Many companies introduce new products at COMDEX.

Sentence: "I went to *COMDEX* in Las Vegas to see the latest computer equipment and software displayed. Then I decided that it didn't make a difference in my life after all, so I went out to Binions and played Craps with Dan and Wally."

Command key

Pronunciation: *Kom-mand kee.*

Meaning: The key on the Macintosh keyboard that has an apple and cloverleaf symbol on it. This key is used with other keys to perform commands. To cut an item, you press ⌘-X. To copy, press ⌘-C. To paste, press ⌘-V.

Sentence: "I'm glad they call it the *Command key*. I'm tried of telling people 'that key with the little cloverleaf-like thing on it.'"

command line

Pronunciation: *ka-mand line.*

Meaning: A line of text you type, typically giving the computer a command or telling it to do something. In DOS, the command line is the text you type after the DOS prompt.

Sentence: "Hear about that new Broadway musical that's produced by the Pentagon? It's called *Command Line.*"

COMMAND.COM

Pronunciation: *Ka-mand Kom.*

Meaning: The MS-DOS file that contains the command processor that's needed for DOS to run. Never delete this file.

Sentence: "Deleting your *COMMAND.COM* file is a bonehead thing to do, but everyone does it at least once."

comment

Pronunciation: *kaw-mint.*

Meaning: A brief note of explanation inserted into programs to describe what the program is supposed to do. Programmers use comments in their programs so that other programmers (and they themselves) can understand what the program does and how it works.

Sentence: "It's good programming practice to insert plenty of *comments* in your programs to explain what the program does, how it works, and any assumptions you may have made and to make nasty remarks about the project leader."

communications

Pronunciation: *kaw-me-u-ni-ka-shins.*

Meaning: A shortened version of *telecommunications* or *data communications.* Often used to describe transferring data from one computer to another through a modem or a network.

Sentence: "Our department is looking for a new *communications* director. Candidates must be nearsighted and cannot speak English."

compatibility

Pronunciation: *kom-pat-i-bill-i-tee.*

Meaning: The ability to work with equipment or software designed by other manufacturers.

Sentence: "The salesguy claims that my new computer and printer have so much *compatibility* that if I take one out of the room, the other one will actually start to cry."

compile

Pronunciation: *kom-pile.*

Meaning: To convert a program written in a programming language (BASIC, C, Pascal, etc.) into a language that the computer can understand (machine code). A term that only programmers care to know about.

Sentence: "Normally, the steps to writing a program are code, *compile,* and run. But with John's programming, the steps are code, compile, fix bugs, recompile, fix more bugs, etc."

compiler

Pronunciation: *kom-pile-er.*

Meaning: A special program that converts programs written in a programming language (C, BASIC, Pascal, and so on) into something the computer can understand (machine code).

Sentence: "The *compiler* works great at taking the grunts and squawks of a programming language and turning them into something that the computer can understand. Now we need a compiler to translate what the programmer wrote in the manual into plain English."

composite video

Pronunciation: *kom-pos-it vi-dee-o.*

Meaning: A video signal used by TV sets, usually transmitted by one wire. By contrast, an RGB signal uses separate wires for red, green, and blue.

Sentence: "If you really want to go blind or get a headache, use *composite video* to display your information on your TV set."

compression

Pronunciation: *kom-press-shin.*

Meaning: To take a file and smash it (or squish it) so that it takes up less space.

Sentence: "Using that new *compression* program, we were able to save 50MB of storage on our hard drive. Now, if they could only compress Frank into a small size, we'd save money on wicker furniture."

CompuServe

Pronunciation: *Kom-pew-Serve.*

Meaning: A subscription-based on-line service that charges you a lot for every second you're connected to it. In return, CompuServe provides files to copy, games to play, and services to use — such as making your own airline reservations or searching for information in newspaper articles.

Sentence: "I needed to spend more money on my computer habit, so I bought a modem and a subscription to *CompuServe*."

compute

Pronunciation: *kom-pewt.*

Meaning: To calculate an answer by using a variety of problem-solving techniques, including mathematics, heuristics, and looking over someone else's shoulder. It can also refer to the task one undertakes when using a computer.

Sentence: "I spent enough money on a computer; therefore, I should try to *compute* more often."

computer

Pronunciation: *kom-pewt-her.*

Meaning: Any calculating device that processes data according to a series of instructions, costs a lot, doesn't work the way you think it should, and becomes obsolete three days after you buy it.

Sentence: "I bought a *computer* to simplify my life."

Computer Graphics Metafile

See *CGM.*

CON

Pronunciation: *Kon,* as in *con game.*

Meaning: A device name that refers to the keyboard and monitor, short for *CONsole.* These are the devices that you use to communicate with the computer. (If you want to call it communication.)

Sentence: "When Captain Picard is done using the Enterprise's computer, he says, 'Mr. Riker, you have the *CON.*'"

concatenate

Pronunciation: *kon-cat-en-nate.*

Meaning: To join two character strings into one character string such as joining ABC and DEF into ABCDEF. You can also concatenate files. The term comes from the late Latin and literally means "to stick two cats together."

Sentence: "Jerry refused to *concatenate* two files into one because he claimed he didn't have moral authority as a priest."

concurrent processing

Pronunciation: *kon-kur-ent pros-ses-ing.*

Meaning: To appear to run two or more programs at the same time, but in reality run only one. Since the computer shifts between the two programs quickly, they appear to be running at the same time.

Sentence: "That new Snazzle PC offers *concurrent processing.* Now you can do twice as much half as fast."

confidence factor

Pronunciation: *kon-fi-dense fak-ter.*

Meaning: A term used by expert systems to place an abstract numerical value on an answer. Often used as an educated way of saying, "I don't have the slightest idea, but here's my best guess."

Sentence: "The used car salesman had a *confidence factor* of 99 that the car he was selling would work perfectly. Because used car salesmen tend to lie as much as lawyers and politicians, I only had a confidence factor of 10 that he was telling me the truth."

CONFIG.SYS

Pronunciation: *Con-Fig Siss.*

Meaning: A configuration file used on MS-DOS computers that sets various options for the disk drives and loads special programs called device drivers into memory. One of the most important files and also the least understood.

Sentence: "The idea of dealing with a *CONFIG.SYS* file is so scary that Apple uses the mere threat of having to edit one to try to sell people on the Macintosh."

configure

Pronunciation: *kon-fig-yur.*

Meaning: To prepare or customize hardware or software a certain way. Any time you add a new piece of equipment or program to your computer, you have to configure it so that it will work properly. This task involves diddling with the hardware, as well as setting up software.

Sentence: "Don't let Craig *configure* your computer. At his old office they used to call him Can-crash-it Craig."

console

Pronunciation: *kon-sole*

Meaning: Another term for the computer monitor and keyboard. Can also mean the alleviation of grief.

Sentence: "We must all *console* Tommy for accidentally spilling his coffee into his *console.*"

constant

Pronunciation: *kon-stant.*

Meaning: A value that never changes.

Sentence: "There are three *constants* in the universe: death, taxes, and the fact that any computer you can buy today is already obsolete."

context-sensitive help

Pronunciation: *kon-text sen-si-tive help.*

Meaning: Help that is provided by a program and that changes according to what you're doing at the time. If you've chosen the Print command, context-sensitive help provides help about printing. If you've

chosen the File Save command, context-sensitive help provides help for saving a file. If you're confused, context-sensitive help confuses you even more.

Sentence: "Our programmers were having trouble writing *context-sensitive help* into their program. So we told them all to grow beards, wear cardigan sweaters and sandals, and write poetry."

contiguous

Pronunciation: *kon-tig-u-us.*

Meaning: When two objects are physically next to each other. Often used when describing files stored on a disk or data stored in a file. A noncontinugous file is said to be fragmented.

Sentence: "If Marty doesn't shave over his nose, his eyebrows become *contiguous.*"

control code

Pronunciation: *kon-troll kode.*

Meaning: A special symbol that controls the computer or printer. Examples of control codes are line feeds, carriage returns, and form feeds. Formatting commands trigger control codes to be sent to the printer to create the desired appearance of text.

Sentence: "That 'burp' of text that you often see at the top of a badly printed document is just some stray *control codes* that got into the mix."

Control key

Pronunciation: *Kon-troll kee.*

Meaning: A special key, often abbreviated as *Ctrl,* that works with other keys to give commands to a program.

Sentence: "They had to label the *Control key* as Ctrl on most computers. No sense in giving users any reason to believe that they're ever in control."

Control Panel

Pronunciation: *Kon-troll Pan-ell.*

Meaning: A utility program that lists options for modifying hardware devices such as the mouse, keyboard, and monitor. Found in the Macintosh and Windows.

Sentence: "In the middle of a static snowstorm, facing hurling electrons, Dr. Bitmap and his companion Nancy Neutrino finally reach the *Control Panel.* In seconds, they should wrest the computer from the clutches of the evil Dr. Modulus and his hoards of evil, virus-crazed, proto-drones."

controller

Pronunciation: *kon-troll-er.*

Meaning: As silly as it sounds, something that controls something else. A hard disk controller is the circuitry that controls the hard drive, connecting it to the computer. A video controller (more commonly, video adapter) controls your monitor and connects it to the computer's motherboard.

Sentence: "The problem with Laverne is that her mouth lacks a *controller.*"

conventional memory

Pronunciation: *kon-ven-shin-null mem-or-ree.*

Meaning: On IBM PC and compatible computers, the first 640 kilobytes of memory (RAM). This was the limit for a long time, and many programs still can access only conventional memory. (See also *upper memory, expanded memory,* and *extended memory.*)

Sentence: "In the era of multimegabyte computers, it's a severe drag that we still have to put up with the *conventional memory* limitation."

converter

Pronunciation: *kon-vert-her.*

Meaning: Hardware or software that changes one item into another, such as an AC to DC power converter or a WordPerfect to Microsoft Word document file converter.

Sentence: "Tim's too lame to buy WordPerfect. So I had to use a special file *converter* so that he could use my WordPerfect files in WordStar."

cookie

Pronunciation: *koo-kee.*

Meaning: A thin, baked piece of flavored dough that tastes great and contains nearly every chemical and substance known to man that causes heart disease, cancer, and tooth decay. It also refers to a goodie, present, or prize included in a computer program.

Sentence: "To keep us happy in the office, our IS guy installed a *cookie* that pops up and tells us a joke each time we log onto the network. Alas, the joke most often is 'network unavailable.'"

coordinates

Pronunciation: *ko-ordnets.*

Meaning: A way of describing a location on a grid. Typically, there are two coordinates, one giving a horizontal (left and right) location and another for the vertical (up and down). The horizontal location is also referred to as X, the vertical as Y. Also used on *Star Trek* for giving locations for beaming people from or to a planet's surface.

Sentence: "Mr. Spock would always give his exact beam-up *coordinates* to Scotty. That way, he was sure that he would beam up and not be melded with a rock, tree, or other nearby object, especially Captain Kirk."

coprocessor

Pronunciation: *ko-pros-ses-her.*

Meaning: A separate processor designed to do specific tasks and take some of the work off the main processor. The end result is that the computer runs faster. For example, a graphics coprocessor takes care of displaying images on the screen, resulting in faster, more colorful, and more detailed images. A math coprocessor takes care of numerical calculations, making spreadsheets and graphics programs run faster.

Sentence: "Donna wanted the fastest computer in the world so she bought a *coprocessor* for everything. Alas, they just don't make a coprocessor for her typing."

copy

Pronunciation: *kop-ee.*

Meaning: To make an exact duplicate of an item, such as text, data, or files stored on a disk.

Sentence: "Of course you didn't delete the Christmas bonus file; you merely zapped a *copy.*"

copy protection

Pronunciation: *kop-ee pro-tec-shin.*

Meaning: A way to prevent a computer from copying one or more files.

Sentence: "Because the cost of a single program overseas is almost as much as the yearly salary of most people, software publishers put *copy protection* on any software that they sell outside of America. Although copy protection doesn't guarantee that someone can't copy the software, it does prevent most people from doing it."

CP/M

Pronunciation: *See Pee Em.*

Meaning: An acronym for *Control Program for Microcomputers.* An ancient operating system that was popular on personal computers back in the late '70s and early '80s, before the introduction of MS-DOS. It can also refer to computers that ran that operating system.

Sentence: "Lee keeps his old *CP/M* computer around for his own, strange, sentimental reasons."

cps

Pronunciation: *see pee ess.*

Meaning: Acronym that stands for *characters per second.* Used to rate the printing speed of dot-matrix and inkjet printers.

Sentence: "I was impressed with the daisy wheel printer's 18 *cps* speed, until I realized that I can type faster than that."

CPU

Pronunciation: *See Pee Yoo.*

Meaning: Acronym for *Central Processing Unit.* (See also *central processing unit.*)

Sentence: "No, madam, the computer doesn't have a fan because the *CPU* stinks."

CR/LF

Pronunciation: *carriage return/line feed* or *seer/elf.*

Meaning: End-of line-characters. CR is a carriage return, moving the print head to the start of the line; LF is a line feed, advancing the paper one line in the printer. This term is used with continuous form-feed printers. A CR/LF advances the paper in the printer by one line. Some systems use only one or the other; that is, either the CR or the LF.

Sentence: "If your printer prints everything on one line, then you either need some *CR/LFs* or really wide paper."

crash

Pronunciation: *krash.* Think of the sound of a Ford Pinto backing into the side of a GM pickup truck.

Meaning: When the computer or a network suddenly stops working. Often used to describe the smashing of the hard disk drive heads into the disk drive.

Sentence: "See the network *crash. Crash, crash, crash.* Watch the workers weep. Weep, weep, weep."

CRC

Pronunciation: *cyclical redundancy check* or *see-ar-see.*

Meaning: An error-detection technique used to verify the accuracy of data transmission. Often used with various transmission protocols such as XMODEM.

Sentence: "Top modem snobs agree: *CRC* XMODEM is far superior to checksum XMODEM."

crippleware

Pronuncation: *krip-pole-wa-er.*

Meaning: Software designed to be deliberately lacking certain features, such as the ability to print or save information to disk. Crippleware is built that way primarily for demonstration purposes. A while back, you could order a new spreadsheet or word processor for nothing, but since it was crippleware you couldn't really do anything with it. The idea was to entice you to order the full-on, uncrippled software.

Sentence: "Steve was shocked when I told him that I liked the Microsoft Word demo he sent over. Then he told me that it wasn't *crippleware.*"

cross hairs

Pronunciation: *kross hares.*

Meaning: The shape of the cursor when using certain programs, such as a drawing or painting program. The cursor often appears as a cross hair symbol when you are drawing squares, circles, or lines.

Sentence: "So I gots me this drawing of an elk, ya see. And I gots it in my Paint program. So I go to draw me a beed, and the cursor turns into *cross hairs.* Blam! I click the mouse. Heh, heh. It's elk meat this Christmas!"

CRT

Pronunciation: *See Ar Tee.*

Meaning: An acronym that stands for *Cathode Ray Tube*. CRTs appear in computer monitors and TV screens.

Sentence: "Ralph is so nerdy he even calls the TV set a *CRT*."

cruise virus

Pronunciation: *krooz vi-rus*.

Meaning: A special type of computer virus that infects and searches other computers for specific data to either steal or sabotage. The military is rumored to be developing cruise viruses that will infect enemy computers and steal important data without being detected.

Sentence: "I wanted to steal information from Todd's computer, so I created a *cruise virus* that would infect his computer, copy his database files, and return them to my own computer without Todd's even knowing that I raided his data. It's a good thing that I know how to write programs so I can use my knowledge against people who are more qualified for the jobs I want."

csh

Pronunciation: *see-ess-atch* or *see-shell.*

Meaning: The C shell on a UNIX system. It's a little more popular than the Korn shell. (See also *sh.*)

Sentence: "Paul is so lonely for UNIX that he has dressed up MS-DOS to look a lot like *csh.*"

Ctrl

(See *Control key.*)

Ctrl-Alt-Delete

Pronunciation: *Kon-troll Alt De-leet.*

Meaning: Three keys that appear on IBM-compatible keyboards. Pressing them in sequence (and simultaneously holding them down) — Ctrl-Alt-Delete — will restart your computer. It will also cause you to lose whatever you were doing that you haven't saved and may damage any open files. When your computer *locks up,* you have no choice but to press Ctrl-Alt-Delete. (See also *lock.*)

Sentence: "This meeting is going nowhere! Let's start over. Someone press *Ctrl-Alt-Del.*"

CUA

Pronunciation: *See Yoo Ay.*

Meaning: Acronym for *Common User Access.* A set of guidelines developed by IBM to provide a standard user interface for computer programs.

Sentence: "Though computer manufacturers are really pleased with the *CUA* guidelines, they tend not to follow them."

current directory

Pronunciation: *kur-rent dir-ect-to-ree.*

Meaning: The directory that you are working in at any moment is the current directory and is the one from which DOS stores and retrieves files (unless told otherwise). Any directory on a hard or floppy disk can be the current directory, but only one directory can be the current directory at any given time.

Sentence: "The tech support guy asked me which directory I was logged to, and I told him the *current directory*."

cursor

Pronunciation: *kurs-er.*

Meaning: The annoying little blinking light that appears on the screen to let you know where your next typed character will appear.

Sentence: "When the tech support guy asked Emma where the *cursor* was, she replied that he didn't get off work until 7:00 that night."

cursor keys

Pronunciation: *kurs-her kees.*

Meaning: The keys on the keyboard that let you move the cursor around. On IBM keyboards, the cursor keys double up as the numeric keypad. (What a stupid engineering design!) The eight cursor keys are the Up/Down arrows, Right/Left arrows, Home/End keys, and the PgUp/PgDn keys. Many new keyboards have separate arrow keys as well. (See also *101-key keyboard.*)

Sentence: "You won't believe this: I just pressed one of the *cursor keys,* and my PC uttered a foul word at me."

cut

Pronunciation: *kut.*

Meaning: To remove text or graphics from the screen. You can use the Paste command to retrieve the most recent text or graphics that you cut.

Sentence: "The difference between the Copy and *Cut* commands is that Copy makes a duplicate, and *Cut* (and Paste) is used to move something."

cut and paste

Pronunciation: *kut and paste.*

Meaning: To remove text or graphics from the screen and make it reappear somewhere else.

Sentence: "I thought that Phillip was speedy on the computer until I learned that he just used *cut and paste* to produce this week's report."

cyber-

Pronunciation: *si-bur.*

Meaning: A prefix used to designate something as electronic in origin. For example, Cyberpunk would be punk music done electronically. Cybersex is sex that takes place through an electronic media (as opposed to any physical contact). Steve Austin (the *Six Million Dollar Man*) was a Cyborg, which means cybernetic organism.

Sentence: "Josh finally broke down and bought a modem. He hates being a *cyber*virgin."

Cyberspace

Pronunciation: *Si-bur-spay-sa.*

Meaning: The electronic ether where on-line communications takes place. Coined by William Gibson in his novel *Neuromancer*, it's the mental locale where folks with modems meet, somewhere out there in the nether world.

Sentence: "I met my girlfriend in *Cyberspace*. I just hope she looks as good as she writes because I've never met her face to face."

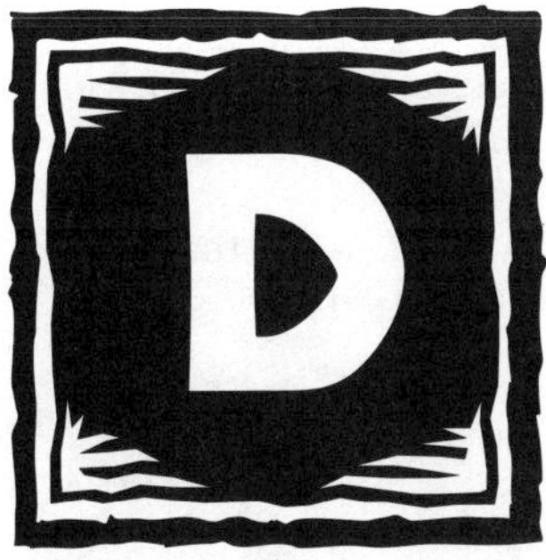

DA

Pronunciation: *Dee Ay.*

Meaning: Acronym for the *Desk Accessory* on the Macintosh. A desk accessory is a simple utility program, such as a calculator or notepad, that runs while another program is running.

Sentence: "Todd freaked out when I said I collected DAs for my Macintosh. He thought I had a closetful of attorneys."

daisy chain

Pronunciation: *day-zee chayn.*

Meaning: The linking of items one after another. In word processing, daisy chain printing means printing documents one after another. The SCSI interface is used to daisy chain peripherals. So you may have a scanner, connected to a CD-ROM drive, connected to a tape backup, and then connected to your computer. They're all daisy chained.

Sentence: "Elaine was disappointed with her word processor. She thought the *daisy chain* printing feature would help her decorate her Christmas tree."

daisy wheel

Pronunciation: *day-zee wee-ell.*

Meaning: A plastic wheel on which each spoke contains a character for printing. Daisy wheels appear in old-fashioned printers (unimaginatively enough called *daisy wheel printers* because the wheels look like petaled daisies). Whenever the printer needs to print a character, it spins the daisy wheel around until the correct character

appears. Then it strikes the daisy wheel spoke so that it smacks against an inked ribbon, printing the character on the page. (Sounds like a lot of trouble to go through, simply to print a single character, doesn't it?) (See also *dot matrix* and *laser printer.*)

Sentence: "Pages printed on a *daisy wheel* printer look like they came out of an ordinary typewriter. So who's that gonna impress?"

darnthing

Pronunciation: *darn-thing.*

Meaning: A phrase commonly uttered by novices and experts alike when confronted by a problem that the computer refuses to solve. (Actually, there are lots of other more common phrases, but this is a family dictionary.) Otherwise known as *&^%$!!.

Sentence: "This *darnthing* won't let me delete this word. I hate computers. I hate computers. I hate computers."

Data

Pronunciation: *Day-tah.*

Meaning: Information that people think is important and useful to save. Also the name of the android character on *Star Trek: The Next Generation.*

Sentence: "They call Mr. *Data* by that name because he stores lots of information. By the same reckoning, they should call Barney the dinosaur *Mr. Stuff.*"

data compression

Pronunciation: *day-tah kom-press-shin.*

Meaning: To take files on a disk and make them smaller. Often used for transmitting files through a modem (thereby reducing the time spent on the phone) and for storing files on a hard disk so that they take up less space. You have to uncompress them before you can use them.

Sentence: "Using *data compression* helps you store more information in less space. They need something like that in the airport for people's carry-on bags."

Data Encryption Standard

Pronunciation: *Day-tah En-krip-shin Stan-dard.*

Meaning: Often abbreviated as *DES.* A government specification for encoding files using a password. A supposedly secure specification that no one except maybe the government can crack, which is why it wholeheartedly endorses this standard.

Sentence: "The *Data Encryption Standard* can scramble text so badly that no one can read it without the right password. I believe this is the process the government tax forms go through before we get them."

data fork

Pronunciation: *day-tah fork.*

Meaning: On the Macintosh, all files have two parts: a resource fork and a data fork. The data fork usually contains information (that is, the actual data) that the program needs to run. The resource fork usually contains the instructions for running a program or other necessary resource information, such as fonts, icons, menus, and so on.

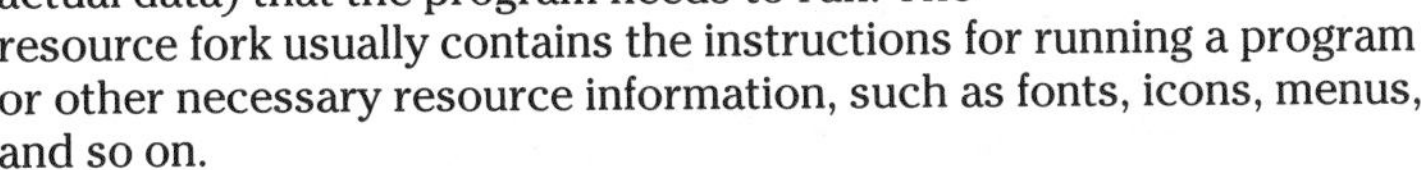

Sentence: "No, Naomi, this little one is your *data fork*. The one you're holding in your left hand is your salad fork."

data structures

Pronunciation: *day-tah struk-sures.*

Meaning: A term programmers use to describe various ways to organize data within a program. Some common data structures include arrays, records, trees, linked lists, and anything else the programmer cares to invent. (See *algorithm.*)

Sentence: "Your *data structures* must have been designed by someone with a crooked T-square."

database

Pronunciation: *day-tah-bay-se.*

Meaning: An organized collection of information (data). (See also *data.*)

Sentence: "The DMV has scoured its *database* and cannot locate you. Therefore, you must not exist. NEXT!"

DATE

Pronunciation: *Dayt.*

Meaning: An MS-DOS and OS/2 command that displays the computer's date. DATE gives you the chance to type the correct date, if necessary.

Sentence: "Steve is desperate. He typed **DATE** at the DOS prompt and fully expected a gorgeous red-head to unfurl from his printer."

datum

Pronunciation: *day-tum.*

Meaning: The singular of "data," seldom used except by extremely socially backward programmers who wish to impress others with their useless technical knowledge. (See also *data.*)

Sentence: "Maybe Data, the android in *Star Trek: The Next Generation,* should have been named *Datum* because there's only one of him."

daughterboard

Pronunciation: *dah-ter-bored.*

Meaning: An optional circuit board that can plug into the main circuit board of the computer. Because the main circuit board of the computer is called a *motherboard,* this optional circuit board is called the *daughterboard.* (See also *motherboard.*)

Sentence: "Every computer has a motherboard, but mine has special superhero qualities because I installed a *daughterboard.*"

dBASE

Pronunciation: *Dee-Bay-sa.*

Meaning: A database program or the type of files produced by one. dBASE itself is the copyrighted name of one of the first, most popular database programs ever. It began its life on old CP/M machines called *Vulcan.* (Yes, named after Mr. Spock because he was full of information.) Then it became dBASE II, then dBASE III, then dBASE IV and then . . . the company that sold dBASE went out of business. They've tried since to come up with more dBASE-like stuff, but other database programs have taken its place. Still, dBASE has a wide following and the format for its files is still popular. (See also *xBase* and *Paradox.*)

Sentence: "You think the DOS prompt is cryptic; the old *dBASE* prompt was just a dot on the screen!"

DCA

Pronunciation: *Dee See Ay.*

Meaning: Acronym for *Document Content Architecture*, a standard for sending text files between alien computers on a network. Pushed by IBM. Yet another standard to bother yourself with.

Sentence: "Gee, if it wasn't for this *DCA* all my files would look like garbage on Phil's VAX. Lucky he never reads my stuff."

DDE

Pronunciation: *Dee Dee Eee.* (Just imagine a baby saying this.)

Meaning: An acronym that means *Dynamic Data Exchange.* Used with Microsoft Windows and OS/2. DDE lets two Windows or OS/2 programs share data, such as numbers stored in a spreadsheet and word processor report.

Sentence: "If it wasn't for *DDE,* I'd have to type these numbers twice in my word processor report and spreadsheet. With DDE, I simply type the numbers in my spreadsheet, and they magically appear in my word processor. Every time I change the numbers in the spreadsheet, the numbers automatically change in my word processor report."

DDT

Pronunciation: *Dee Dee Tee.*

Meaning: A pesticide used in the '60s and '70s to wipe out insects, crops, small animals, and people wherever it appeared.

Sentence: "*DDT* keeps bugs out of my garden, so I sprayed some on my computer, hoping it might get rid of the bugs in WordPerfect."

debug

Pronunciation: *dee-bug.*

Meaning: To eliminate problems (bugs) in a program. Programmers try to debug a program while they are developing it, but often they miss things. (See also *bug.*)

Sentence: "Tom and Julie would be happier newlyweds if someone would help Tom *debug* his cooking."

debugger

Pronunciation: *dee-bug-er.*

Meaning: A special program whose sole purpose is to help programmers track down and eliminate bugs in a program.

Sentence: "Art thought he was an excellent programmer until he ran some of his stuff through a *debugger* and his computer exploded."

decimal number

Pronunciation: *deh-sim-mall num-ber.*

Meaning: A number that uses the digits 0, 1, 2, 3, 4, 5, 6, 7, 8, 9 in ordinary base-ten notation. (See also *binary, hexidecimal,* and *octal.*)

Sentence: "The officer did not think it was funny when Gary asked if he should count backwards from 100 using *decimal numbers.*"

decryption

Pronunciation: *dee-crip-shin.*

Meaning: To convert indecipherable gibberish into plain English that everyone can understand. (See also *encryption.*)

Sentence: "Everything that computer people write sounds like it has been encrypted by the CIA. But reading *DOS For Dummies* seemed like reading the *decryption* of all the normal computer terms."

dedicated

Pronunciation: *ded-i-ka-ted.*

Meaning: An adjective describing a piece of equipment that performs only one function. For example, one computer in the office may be a dedicated word processor, only used for that purpose and definitely not for playing games or abusing the e-mail.

Sentence: "Well, I wouldn't know if my computer has a dedicated fax/modem. I mean, it's fond of the computer, but I don't know if it's grown all that attached."

default

Pronunciation: *dee-falt.*

Meaning: What would happen otherwise. If you don't make a choice, then the computer makes an assumption. That assumption is referred to as "the default." Truly a horrid word, one that should be eliminated from all manuals and computer books. Instead of saying, "The default choice is to turn color off," they should write, "Color is turned off unless you desire otherwise." No, I'm not sticky on the point, but it's really time we removed this awful definition of the word. (Look up default in a real dictionary to see what it really means.)

Sentence: "Floyd nearly had a heart attack when his computer said it would choose the *default* option for his home mortgage program."

default directory

Pronunciation: *dee-falt dir-ek-to-ree.*

Meaning: The directory on a hard disk that the computer uses to perform commands if it isn't given specific instructions to use another directory. (See also *default drive* and *directory.*)

Sentence: "The *default directory* is where neglected files go."

default drive

Pronunciation: *dee-falt drive.*

Meaning: The disk drive the computer looks for if it isn't given specific instructions to look anywhere else.

Sentence: "Eric was going to take his computer back as defective, until I told him the *default drive* means C: for most computers."

Del key

Pronunciation: *Dell kee.*

Meaning: The Delete key, sometimes abbreviated on computer keyboards as DEL.

Sentence: "In some programs, pressing the *Del key* erases the character to the left of the cursor. In other programs, pressing the *Del key* erases the character to the right. This is like driving one car where the accelerator pedal is on the right and driving your other car where the brake pedal is on the right."

delimited file

Pronunciation: *del-im-uh-ted fi-ell.*

Meaning: Typically a text file (nothing fancy) that contains information for a database. The delimited file provides a common way of transferring database information among different applications.

In a delimited file, records appear one to a line. Fields are separated by tabs, by spaces, or, most commonly, by commas. The first line of the file contains the field names. For example:

```
NAME, FOOD GROUP, CALORIES
Oreos, Sugar, 35 ea.
Ice cream, Dairy, 1025 pint.
Jolt, Caffiene, 600 can.
```

Sentence: "Since no one here can get our word processor and data base program to talk, we've created a *delimited file* of the people we hate the most."

demon dialer

Pronunciation: *dee-mon die-lar.*

Meaning: A modem program that dials numbers from, say, 555-0000 on up through 555-9999, logging each number to disk and noting when it finds another modem. This is one way that hackers find the numbers to other systems. Of course, once another modem answers, they still have to break into the system.

Sentence: "I could use a *demon dialer* to find out which computers answer the phone in my prefix. Instead, I'll re-write it so that it calls my ex-wife every five minutes for the rest of her life."

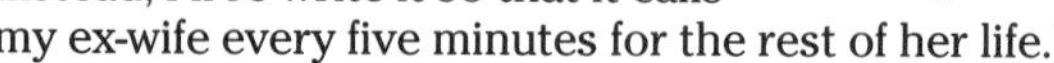

DES

(See *Data Encryption Standard.*)

descender

Pronunciation: *dee-sen-der.*

Meaning: The part of a letter that falls below the imaginary line on which the letter rests. For example, the letters *p, y,* and *q* have descenders, but the letters *t, u,* and *o* do not. (See also *ascender.*)

Sentence: "You used to judge a dot matrix printer by how it handled *descenders*. Some cheesy printers just shifted those letters up a tad, which looked utterly dorky."

deselect

Pronunciation: *dee-sell-ect.*

Meaning: To change your mind after selecting an item, such as by unhighlighting an item or by removing the X in an option box. (See also *select.*)

Sentence: "Would George Bush have won the '92 election had he *deselected* Dan Quayle as his running mate?"

desk accessory

(See *DA.*)

desktop

Pronunciation: *desk-top.*

Meaning: The blank screen (background) that appears on programs that use a *graphical user interface* such as the Macintosh, Windows, or OS/2. (See *graphical user interface.*)

Sentence: "So the guy said to 'double-click on my *desktop*' and I said that the mouse was already on the desktop so what was his point. I just don't think I get this computer nonsense."

desktop PC

Pronunciation: *desk-top Pee See.*

Meaning: A computer that sits on top of your desk. A larger model. One that isn't a laptop and doesn't sit on its side, like a tower PC. (Contrast with *portable, laptop,* and *notebook computers.*)

Sentence: "The guy who designed this *desktop PC* must have had an awfully big desk."

desktop publishing

Pronunciation: *desk-top pub-li-shing.*

Meaning: To combine text and pictures on a computer screen to create neat-looking newsletters, books, or brochures. (See also *DTP.*)

Sentence: "Those campy images of underground rebels churning out propoganda on mimeograph machines are rapidly being replaced by the reality of three nerds sitting around a computer using a *desktop publishing* program and arguing over picas, pitches, and points."

dev/null

Pronunciation: *dev null.*

Meaning: Technically, a device (actually, a directory) on a UNIX computer that does nothing, produces nothing, and can swallow anything as input and not give a damn. Traditionally, dev/null is used to tell people where to stick their useless ideas or complaints. (You find this on the USENET a lot.) Because dev/null goes nowhere and does nothing, telling someone to send comments to dev/null is the polite equivalent of telling them to go "bug off."

Sentence: "Please send all flames to *dev/null.*"

device

Pronunciation: *dee-vice.*

Meaning: Any type of equipment, such as a printer, modem, monitor, disk drive, or mouse that can send or receive data.

Sentence: "You know you're hard core when you call your printer a hard copy *device.*"

device driver

Pronunciation: *dee-vice dry-ver.*

Meaning: A special program that controls a device. Specific to DOS, device drivers are required to control some devices (mouse, tape backup, CD-ROM drive, and so on) because the computer itself is too lame to do it.

Sentence: "When Grandma Margaret was a little girl, they called the *device driver* for their car a chauffeur."

device name

Pronunciation: *dee-vice name.*

Meaning: An abbreviation that refers to a device connected to the computer.

Sentence: "Why MS-DOS couldn't just call the printer PRINTER and had to use a cryptic *device name* like PRN is beyond me."

Dhrystone

Pronunciation: *Dry-stohn.*

Meaning: The name of a program used to test the relative speed of a microprocessor. Computer magazines use Dhrystone ratings to judge the performance of various computers, giving the highest rankings to those systems provided by their best advertisers.

Sentence: "This computer is so fast it does 15,000 *Dhrystones* even when it's turned off!"

dialog box

Pronunciation: *die-a-log box.*

Meaning: A window that pops up to ask for or display more information. It's a dialog between you and your software. (See also *list box.*)

Sentence: "Why is it that most of my program's *dialog boxes* talk at me and not with me?"

DIB

Pronunciation: *Dibb.*

Meaning: Acronym for *Device Independent Bitmap,* a type of graphics file format. A DIB grpahics file supposedly carries information that allows it to be displayed on any computer, no matter which type of graphics the computer is using. A nice idea, if it ever worked.

Sentence: "John and I could never get our collection of postmodern nudist art to display on our computers. Then we started using *DIB* files."

digital

Pronunciation: *di-jit-al.*

Meaning: Two distinct states such as On or Off, Low or High, Good or Bad, or Republican or Democrat. All computers are digital computers because they consist of millions of On and Off switches. (See also *analog* and *binary.*)

Sentence: "If in the future all clocks are *digital*, how will we ever teach our children about clockwise and counterclockwise?"

Digital Research

Pronunciation: *Di-ji-tal Ree-sur-cha.*

Meaning: A company that produced the first "microcomputer" operating system, CP/M. They got trounced in the '80s by Microsoft and MS-DOS, and then produced DR DOS. But DR DOS was eventually bought by Novell. Oh, well. See *CP/M.*

Sentence: "*Digital Research* was one of the 'unstoppable' computer companies of the early '80s along with VisiCorp, who made the VisiCalc spreadsheet; WordStar Inc., who surprisingly enough made WordStar; and Ashton-Tate, who made dBASE — none of whom are around today. This just goes to show you the volatile nature of the computer biz."

Digital Signal Processor

Pronunciation: *Di-jit-al Sig-nal Pro-sess-or.*

Meaning: A high-speed chip, like a microprocessor, that deals specifically with sound. A DSP is often used in a computer to speed up the audio or to enhance communications, graphics, or similar applications.

Sentence: "Now that my PC has a *Digital Signal Processor,* I too can use the acronym DSP."

dimmed

Pronunciation: *dim-da.*

Meaning: An unavailable option or command, usually appearing on the screen in a soft, fuzzy color that's easy to overlook. An option or command that is dimmed is not currently available.

Sentence: "Richard tried to create a romantic mood, so he *dimmed* the lights. But then Sherry said, 'That option is not available!'"

dingbats

Pronunciation: *ding-batz.*

Meaning: A font consisting of bizarre characters made up of bullets, Greek and Egyptian hieroglyphics, and geometric figures. What Archie Bunker called his wife in the '70s hit show *All in the Family*. Also a term for a style of apartment found in Southern California.

Sentence: "Martha never understood why her husband got her a T-shirt with a ⌘ on the front."

DIP switch

Pronunciation: Just like it sounds, like an insult.

Meaning: Tiny little switches, almost impossible to find or use properly. DIP is an acronym for *Dual-Inline Package* (as if that clarifies matters any). Mostly, you use DIP switches with modems to select COM ports or with printers to select options for output. Printed circuit boards can have them, too.

Sentence: "I think they should call them teeny switches and reserve the term *DIP switch* for when Melvin in the next cubical is replaced by a guy named Poindexter."

DIR

Pronunciation: *Durr.*

Meaning: An operating system command that displays a directory listing — a catalog of files on a disk or in a directory.

Sentence: "I typed ***DIR*** and, lo, discovered that my disk was full of stuff I didn't know existed."

Direct Memory Access

See *DMA*.

directory

Pronunciation: *duh-rek-toh-ree.*

Meaning: A list of files on a disk. It can also refer to a separate part of the disk where other files are stored (see *subdirectory*). Every disk has at least one directory called the *root directory.* You can create other directories and label them so as to separate files that relate to different programs, data, and projects.

Sentence: "Most people know to create a bunch of *directories* to organize their files, but few follow through on it."

directory list box

Pronunciation: *duh-rek-toh-ree list box.*

Meaning: A display that lists directories and subdirectories in a hierarchical tree structure. You use these boxes in Windows and OS/2 programs.

Sentence: "Whenever I press the Save command in my word processor, the program pops up a *directory list box* so that I can choose which directory to save the file in."

disk

Pronunciation: *disk.* (How tough can this be?)

Meaning: A magnetic storage device shaped like a pizza and encased in plastic. Hard disks are encased in a metal box. The two most popular sizes for floppy disks are 5¼-inch and 3½-inch. Floppy disks may be double-density or high-density. High-density floppy disks can store two to four times as much information as double-density disks. (See also *floppy disk* and *hard disk.*)

Sentence: "You can put the entire Encyclopedia Britannica on a floppy *disk.* It makes it easy to carry and a cinch to steal from the library."

disk cache

Pronunciation: *disk cash.*

Meaning: A portion of memory in which the computer stores information frequently read from disk. By copying information from the floppy or hard disk and storing it in a disk cache, the computer can access the information faster at a later time. Some computers have a built-in disk cache. Some utility programs create a disk cache out of the computer's main memory. Generally, the larger the disk cache, the faster the computer runs.

Sentence: "The guy at the store told me I could use a *disk cache* to speed up my hard drive. I thought he was referring to something like the Mickey Cash you use at Disneyland, but I was wrong."

disk hog

Pronunciation: *disk hog.*

Meaning: A program that bloats and bloats until it takes up a considerable amount of hard disk space in relation to what it does. This is one of the side-affects of having a lot of disk storage in a PC; programs bloat until they take up way too much disk space. Developers don't seem concerned about this. The feeling you get is if they did, they could find a way to make their programs take up less space. But they don't, so the world now has disk hogs.

Sentence: "Excel is one *disk hog,* let me tell ya."

disk operating system

Pronunciation: *disk op-er-rate-ting siss-dum.*

Meaning: The main program that tells your computer how to work. Often abbreviated as DOS. On IBM and compatible computers, the disk operating system is called *MS-DOS* or *PC-DOS,* although many people have their own favorite four-letter-word adjectives for it. The Mac operating system is often called something similar to *System 7.* (See also *operating system.*)

Sentence: "DOS stands for *disk operating system*. If I said this on TV every night for a year, I could start a new job."

disk partition

Pronunciation: *disk par-tish-shin.*

Meaning: The division of a hard disk into two or more sections. Some people partition their disk so that one half of their hard disk runs MS-DOS and Windows and the other half runs OS/2.

Sentence: "Actually, we just use this program to create *disk partitions.* If you want to partition anything else, go see Moses."

display

Pronunciation: *dis-play.*

Meaning: The monitor or computer screen. It's what you watch when you go a-computin'. (See also *monitor.*)

Sentence: "I called tech support to complain that my *display* looked like rubbish. Then they shyly admitted that it was their new, improved interface. I'm just happy the people who design computer programs don't redesign the highway system every 18 months."

dithering

Pronunciation: *dith-er-ring.*

Meaning: Although it sounds like something drunk people might mumble in their sleep, dithering is the substitution of black and white dots for shades of gray in computer graphics, or the combining of two or more colors to represent a color the monitor can't produce. It can be used to make curving patterns less jaggy. (See also *aliasing* and *jaggies.*)

Sentence: "The science of *dithering* lets you see many more colors in a less-impressive manner."

DLL

Pronunciation: *Dee Ell Ell.*

Meaning: Acronym used in Windows and OS/2 that stands for *Dynamic Link Library.* DLL files contain commonly used routines that two or more programs can share.

Sentence: "The error message said '*DLL* file missing.' It's sad that when a program can't share it has to act all stubborn like that."

DMA

Pronunciation: *Dee Emm Ay.*

Meaning: Acronym for *Direct Memory Access*, a technique where information is transferred in a computer with the assistance of the microprocessor. For example, it's possible to transfer information between memory and an "intelligent" device, such as a hard drive, by simply telling a DMA chip, "Look here. Move this data from memory here to disk drive there." The information is moved without slowing down the microprocessor.

A problem with the typical PC is that it has limited DMA "channels" (where the information is transferred). Some devices, such as the disk drives, desire their own DMA channel. This leaves fewer DMA channels for other devices you may have, which leads to havoc and the general conclusion that you should have bought a Macintosh, which doesn't have this particular hardware problem.

Sentence: "Our computer is real slow because our cable service doesn't offer the *DMA* channel."

DOC

Pronunciation: *Dock,* as in *Hickory Dickory Dock.*

Meaning: An abbreviation for DOCument. Often used as a file extension for word processor files. (See also *BAK.*)

Sentence: "I asked Ellen if she could bring over some *DOC* files, and 40 minutes later she called to say her physician wouldn't let her copy anything from his computer."

docking base

See *docking station.*

docking station

Pronunciation: *dock-ing stay-shun.*

Meaning: A home for your laptop computer. Typically, a larger thing into which you plug your laptop computer, often by sliding your laptop all the way into the larger thing. This extends your laptop's hardware, allowing you to use a larger screen and keyboard and other desktop features.

Sentence: "I save time and money by using a laptop on the road and then plugging it into my *docking station* back at the office."

document

Pronunciation: *dock-u-mint.*

Meaning: A file created by a word processor or desktop publisher, containing words or pictures. (See also *file.*)

Sentence: "Cliff gave me all his *documents* on disk. Now I just need to figure out which word processor he used to create them all."

documentation

Pronunciation: *dock-u-mint-tay-shin.*

Meaning: The fat instruction manuals that everyone pays money for but no one bothers to read. Usually full of instructions that don't work, don't make sense, or are just plain wrong.

Sentence: "The project manager said our *documentation* was too thick. So we just cut out every third word to get it down to size."

doinky

Pronunciation: *doyn-kee.*

Meaning: Small, tiny.

Sentence: "Golly, those DIP switches sure are *doinky.*"

domain

Pronunciation: *do-mayn.*

Meaning: A grouping of computers. An organizational strategy in a database. But, most likely, a category of computer on the Internet. There are several popular domains:

Domain	Type of computer system
com	Company, business, commercial organization
edu	Educational institution
gov	The government (but not the military, because . . .)
mil	Military institutions only
org	Organizations (not in the above categories)
net	Networks, network resources

Also see *Internet Address.*

Sentence: "Millie was happy to have a net address that ended with the 'mil' *domain*, until we told her it was just because she worked for the Navy."

DOS

Pronunciation: *Daw-ess.*

Meaning: Acronym that stands for *Disk Operating System.* By the way, if you have Windows, you still have DOS. (See also *disk operating system.*)

Sentence: "*DOS* is boss."

DOS prompt

Pronunciation: *Daw-ess prom-ta.*

Meaning: When you're not in a program, you see this cryptic little signal that the computer displays on the screen that essentially says, "This is the computer. What do you want me to do?" Typical DOS prompts look like C:\>, A:, or C:\WINDOWS\SYSTEM>. (See also *$.*)

Sentence: "No, Phyllis, the *DOS prompt* has nothing to do with being on time."

dot matrix

Pronunciation: *daht may-tricks.*

Meaning: A type of printer or printout that creates letters and graphics by using lots of tiny dots. The more dots used, the sharper the image. The fewer the dots used, the more the printing looks like a cheap printer printed it. (See also *laser printer* and *daisy wheel.*)

Sentence: "*Dot matrix* printers are good for waking up the neighbors during the small hours."

dot pitch

Pronunciation: *daht pit-cha.*

Meaning: The smallest size dot that a monitor can display, usually measured in millimeters (mm). Typical dot pitches for monitors are .41mm, .31mm, and .28mm. The smaller the dot pitch, the sharper the resolution on the monitor. Also used to describe the distance between two color dots of the same color on a color monitor.

Sentence: "When I asked the salesman about his monitor's *dot pitch,* he replied that his dots were the best in town and I'd be a fool to go elsewhere for them."

dots per inch

Pronunciation: *daughtz purh eenshch.*

Meaning: Sometimes abbreviated as *DPI,* dots per inch describes how sharp a printed image appears. The more dots per inch used, the sharper the image looks.

Sentence: "My laser printer has a maximum resolution of 300 *dots per inch,* which is similar to the population density of Dhaka."

double-click

Pronunciation: *dub-bull-klik.*

Meaning: To press the mouse button twice in rapid succession without moving the mouse between clicks. Click, click. (See also *click.*)

Sentence: "*Double-click*, said the manual. Click, click, went the mouse. Run, run did the program."

double-density disk

Pronunciation: *dub-bull-den-city disk.*

Meaning: A floppy disk that stores twice as much information in the same amount of space as a single-density disk (which is no longer sold). Double-density disks are abbreviated as DD. A $5^1/_4$-inch double-density floppy disk can hold 360K of data. A $3^1/_2$-inch double-density floppy disk can hold 720K (800K for a Macintosh) of data. (See also *high density.*)

Sentence: "No, Blane, *double-density disks* aren't any heavier than regular density."

DoubleSpace

Pronunciation: *Duh-bol-Spay-sa.*

Meaning: Another name for Microsoft's DriveSpace program. See *DriveSpace*.

down

Pronunciation: *down.* (Just like it looks.)

Meaning: When a piece of computer equipment temporarily stops working.

Sentence: "Our network's been *down* so often it must be in China by now."

download

Pronunciation: *down-lode.*

Meaning: To copy files through a modem from a distant computer to the one you're working on. (See also *upload.*)

Sentence: "It helps you to remember *download* if you imagine that every on-line system you call sits on top of a hill. The files roll 'down' toward you."

downward compatible

Pronunciation: *down-word kom-pat-i-bull.*

Meaning: The capability of software or hardware to work with earlier versions of the same software or hardware. (See also *upward compatible.*)

Sentence: "WordPerfect 7.0 is *downward compatible* with WordPerfect 5.1. This means that any files I created with WordPerfect 5.1 can still be used with WordPerfect 7.0. This is only good news if you plan to use WordPerfect until you die."

dpi

Acronym for *dots per inch;* see *dots per inch.*

DPMI

Pronunciation: *Dee Pee Em Eye.*

Meaning: Acronym for *DOS Protected Mode Interface,* a standard by which DOS programs can run under Windows. See *Protected Mode, Real Mode.*

Sentence: "Boy, without this *DPMI* I couldn't use my DOS programs in Windows. Of course, that makes you wonder why I have Windows in the first place if I'm still running DOS programs."

DPMS

Pronunciation: *Dee Pee Em Ess.*

Meaning: Acronym that stands for *Display Power Management Signalling,* which is a standard that reduces power to computer monitors when not in use. See *Energy Star.*

Sentence: "My monitor uses *DPMS*, so if I don't touch the keyboard or mouse after a few minutes, the computer reduces the power to my monitor, thereby reducing my electricity bill. Bob's monitor doesn't use DPMS, so his computer wastes electricity and the company takes this extra cost out of Bob's paycheck every week."

DR DOS

Pronunciation: *Dee Arr Doss* (not Doctor DOS).

Meaning: An alternative to MS-DOS released way too late by Digital Research and later by Novell. DR DOS showed a lot of promise, but it wasn't widely available. Its version 5.0, which was the first version of DOS to offer true memory management, got Microsoft off its duff to produce the wildly successful MS-DOS 5.0. For this we can thank DR DOS, but not for much else. (See *Novell DOS.*)

Sentence: "Brad hates Microsoft so much that he only uses *DR DOS* and other non-Microsoft products."

drag

Pronunciation: *drah-ga.*

Meaning: To use the mouse for moving an object across the screen. First, you have to highlight (select) the object you want by pointing to it with the mouse. Then hold down the mouse button and move the mouse. This drags the object around.

Sentence: "Moving things around on the screen with a mouse is such a *drag.*"

drag and drop

Pronunciation: *drah-ga and draw-pa.*

Meaning: Moving an object across the screen as a command. For example, you use a mouse to drag a document into a printer icon. This prints the document.

Sentence: "My teacher asked if my computer had *drag and drop.* I said yes: when I don't like the computer, I drag it across the table and drop it out the window."

DRAM

Pronunciation: *Dee-Ram*

Meaning: Acronym for *Dynamic Random-Access Memory.* Computers can use two types of RAM chips: DRAM and SRAM. DRAM chips are less expensive because the computer periodically has to put the information back into the DRAM chips or else the DRAM chips forget. (See also *RAM* and *SRAM.*)

Sentence: "The older humans get, the more their brain cells must be replaced with *DRAM* chips."

draw program

Pronunciation: *draw pro-gram.* (Well, can you think of a better pronunciation guide?)

Meaning: A type of program that lets you draw objects on the screen, such as lines, boxes, or circles. A draw program differs from a Paint program, which doesn't draw objects but paints a picture as you would with crayons. With a draw program, you can go back and alter the objects after they're done and not disturb other parts of the drawing.

Sentence: "I use a *draw program* to illustrate advanced technical journals, but all my trees still look like lollipops."

drive list box

Pronunciation: *in-wee-ta Mi-ner-wah*

Meaning: A list that displays the number of disk drives on the computer. Often used with the File Save command. The drive list box lets you decide which drive to save a file on.

Sentence: "My *drive list box* contains all drive letters, A through Z, plus four-wheel drive."

DriveSpace

Pronunciation: *Drive-Spay-sa.*

Meaning: A disk compression program developed by Microsoft, available on MS-DOS versions 6.22 or later, and on Windows95. Originally called DoubleSpace, but changed because of bad press, DriveSpace allows you to store more information on a hard drive. It does this by compressing files as they're saved to disk, then decompressing files as they're read from disk. The end result isn't known to you, though your computer moves slower and you can store more information on a disk. A solution, though not the best one, for someone who's running out of disk space.

Sentence: "The best advice is to avoid *DriveSpace* and just buy a larger hard drive."

drop-down list box

Pronunciation: *drawp-down list box.*

Meaning: A combination of two boxes. One box lets the user type information. The second box underneath lists names that the user can choose from when typing is painful.

Sentence: "Og like use *drop-down list box.* It give Og option of typing in name or choosing from list. Og happy."

DS/DD

Pronunciation: *Dee Ess/Dee Dee.*

Meaning: Abbreviation for *double-sided/double-density*. (See also *double-density disk* and *high density.*)

Sentence: "Only older computers use *DS/DD* disks. They're the Geritol of computer disk formats."

DSP

Pronunciation: *Dee Ess Pee.*

Meaning: Acronym for *Digital Signal Processor.* See *Digital Signal Processor.*

DTP

Acronym for *DeskTop Publishing.* See *desktop publishing.*

DTR

Pronunciation: *Dee Tee Arr.*

Meaning: Acronym for *Data Terminal Ready,* a signal used by a computer to tell its modem that it's ready to start receiving information.

Sentence: "It's definitely not true that female computers take longer to turn on their *DTR* light."

dumb terminal

Pronunciation: *dum ter-min-al.*

Meaning: A unit consisting of a keyboard and video display connected to a main computer (such as a mainframe). Dumb terminals don't have disk drives or their own processors, so they can't store files or do anything else on their own. Personal computers, on the other hand, can act as autonomous units which can be networked together.

Sentence: "Ray thought that putting the pointed cap on his PC would make it into a *dumb terminal.*"

dump

Pronunciation: *dum-pa.*

Meaning: To copy information from one location to another without regard for its appearance or format. Often used for printing information that is temporarily useful.

Sentence: "I told my wife I was in the middle of a screen *dump* and she reminded me to wipe afterwards."

duplex

Pronunciation: *doo-plex.*

Meaning: A term used in telecommunications to describe how signals are sent. *Full duplex* means that signals can be sent simultaneously back and forth. *Half duplex* means that signals can go only in one direction at a time.

Sentence: "With my communications program, setting ECHO ON means using full *duplex.* Setting ECHO OFF means using half duplex. Sometimes, when I type, the computer repeats my typing so that my words look like tthhiiss. Then I have to turn ECHO OFF, so I use half duplex to fix the problem."

Dvorak keyboard

Pronunciation: *Dee-vor-rak kee-bored.*

Meaning: A specially designed keyboard that organizes keys on the keyboard for maximum efficiency. Although known to be more efficient than current keyboards, hardly anyone uses them. So much for efficiency. (See also *QWERTY* and *keyboard.*)

Sentence: "The *Dvorak keyboard* is the Esperanto of computer keyboards."

dweeb

Pronunciation: *dwee-ba.*

Meaning: A person who may be technically competent but is socially a zero that no one wants to hang around with after work.

Sentence: "Bob would make a great manager if he wasn't such a *dweeb.*"

DWIM

Pronunciation: *Dwim,* rhymes with *swim.*

Meaning: Acronym that stands for *Do What I Mean* (not what I say). Often used when people want the computer to read their minds and ignore the commands they're typing in.

Sentence: "I saw a father using *DWIM* on his daughter when he told her not to smoke, while he was puffing on a cigar and blowing smoke in her face."

DX

Pronunciation: *Dee-Ecks.*

Meaning: A suffix applied to an Intel microprocessor number (80x86), one that means it's the "full-on" microprocessor, not some weirdo half microprocessor with some dingy thing wrong with it. (See also *SX.*)

Sentence: "Always insist upon getting a *DX* microprocessor."

DXF

Pronunciation: *Dee Ecks Eff.*

Meaning: Acronym for *Drawing Interchange Format,* a graphics file format for exchanging files between different programs. Originally developed for use with the AutoCAD drawing program.

Sentence: "If only Ralph would save his stuff in *DXF* format, we all could see his cool outer space drawings."

dynamic allocation

Pronunciation: *di-nam-ik al-o-kay-shin.*

Meaning: The storage of information in the computer's memory (called the *heap*) while the program is running. Unless you plan on writing your own programs, you can safely ignore this definition. (See also *static.*)

Sentence: "The desk clerk told the three televangelists to go into halls A, B, and C. This I call *dynamic allocation* for salvation."

dynamic RAM

(See *DRAM.*)

e-mail

Pronunciation: *ee-may-ell.*

Meaning: Stands for *electronic mail.* Messages created, sent, and read completely on computers without ever being printed on paper. Electronic mail usually involves sending messages to other users on some kind of network.

Sentence: "With rising postal rates, it's cheaper to use a computer to send *e-mail* than to use an envelope and a stamp. Of course, you have to buy a computer first."

e-mail address

Pronunciation: *ee-may-ell add-ress.*

Meaning: An identifying number or word assigned to one person for sending and receiving electronic mail. A server acts as a post office, holding messages until users call in to retrieve them.

Sentence: "Whenever I send e-mail to my friend, I have to tell the computer which e-mail address to send it to. Once I typed the wrong *e-mail address* and sent a love letter to my ex-wife."

E-notation

Pronunciation: *Ee no-tay-shin.*

Meaning: Abbreviation for *exponential notation,* one of many ways that scientists express large and small numbers.

Sentence: "My spreadsheet lets me store numbers in *E-notation.* That way it doesn't look as if the company is losing millions of dollars."

EBCDIC

Pronunciation: *Eee Bee See Dee I See.*

Meaning: Acronym for *Extended Binary Coded Decimal Interchange Code.* A standard way of representing characters on a computer. Some mainframes use EBCDIC. (See also *ASCII.*)

Sentence: "IBM tried to get everyone to follow the *EBCDIC* standard, but everyone else followed the ASCII standard instead. It doesn't really matter which standard your computer uses as long as it works."

echo

Pronunciation: *ek-o.*

Meaning: When you communicate through a modem, an echo displays every character you type on your computer screen. If you can't see what you're typing, echo is said to be off. If you see double words such as tthhiiss, you have to turn echo off. Echo also is an MS-DOS and OS/2 operating system command. Entering ECHO OFF in a batch file keeps the computer from displaying commands on the screen (as the computer is carrying them out). (See also *duplex.*)

Sentence: "Do I hear an *echo* hear an echo?"

ECP/EPP

Pronunciation: *Ee See Pee Eee Pee Pee*

Meaning: Acronym for *Enhanced Capabilities Port/Enhanced Parallel Port.* It's a type of super printer port. Whooptee-doo.

Sentence: "My new computer came with an *ECP/EPP* and it can do many wondrous and amazing things, though I only use it to plug in my printer."

edit

Pronunciation: *ed-it.*

Meaning: To modify data (text, graphics, and so on) in a file.

Sentence: "I wrote a 20-page letter, but I had to *edit* the part about biting my sister because I didn't think my mom would appreciate it."

editor

Pronunciation: *ed-it-or.*

Meaning: A program specifically designed for modifying files. The two types of editors are *line editors* and *full-screen editors.* A line editor lets you change one line at a time. A full-screen editor lets you change multiple lines that appear on the screen. Word processors, such as WordPerfect or Word for Windows, are much more sophisticated than simple editors. But sometimes an editor is all you need, especially if you're using it to edit programming code. (See also *line editor* and *full screen.*)

Sentence: "I have several *editors* on my computer, but QEdit is my editor-in-chief."

EDLIN

Pronunciation: *Ed-Lynn.*

Meaning: A line editor that came with MS-DOS versions 5.0 and lower. EDLIN was pretty much a useless program that nobody but the most nerdy people used. MS-DOS version 6.0 and higher no longer include EDLIN.

Sentence: "With MS-DOS version 6.2, *EDLIN* is finally dead(lin)."

EEPROM

Pronunciation: *Eee-Prom.*

Meaning: An acronym that stands for *Electronically Erasable Programmable Read-Only Memory.* An EEPROM chip can be reprogrammed through electrical signals that zap its contents and replace them with something else. EEPROM chips can hold their contents without power. (See also *PROM.*)

Sentence: "Many computer parts use *EEPROM* chips. Instead of yanking out the chips and replacing them with new ones, you can just zap them with electricity and reprogram them without even touching them."

EGA

Pronunciation: *Eee Gee Ey.*

Meaning: Acronym for *Enhanced Graphics Adapter,* a graphics standard once used for IBM computers and now remembered solely by trivia buffs. Instead of using the EGA standard, most computers now use the newer VGA or SVGA standards, which display more colors with sharper resolution. (See also *CGA, VGA,* and *SVGA.*)

Sentence: "*EGA* graphics were 'hot stuff' when Ronald Reagan was President."

EIEIO

Pronunciation: *Eee I Eee I O.*

Meaning: Nonsensical but rhythmic phrase used by farmers when they forget the rest of the words to a song. It's probably an acronym for something.

Sentence: "Old McDonald had a farm, *EIEIO!*"

EISA

Pronunciation: *Eee-Suh.*

Meaning: Acronym for *Extended Industry Standard Architecture.* ISA is the standard bus design for the older IBM computers. EISA is the new proposed standard for IBM-compatible computers. Instead of following the EISA standard, IBM's PS/2 computers follow their own *MCA* standard. (See also *architecture, bus, ISA,* and *MCA.*)

Sentence: "For a while, people wondered whether they should buy a computer with an *EISA* bus or an MCA bus. Then people got smart and figured that it didn't really matter after all."

eject

Pronunciation: *ee-jekt.*

Meaning: To remove a floppy disk from a floppy disk drive. (See also *disk.*)

Sentence: "He's looking for the data. No. No. No! It can't be found! That disk is out of here. *Eject! Eject! Eject!*"

elite

Pronunciation: *ee-lee-ta.*

Meaning: A leftover from the typewriter days, elite refers to typefaces that print at 12 characters per inch. Often appears on printers as one of many choices to make for printing documents. (See also *pica.*)

Sentence: "There is no such thing as *elite* type on a computer. If you want to use characters that tiny, select a font at 10 points."

ELIZA

Pronunciation: *El Ligh Za.*

Meaning: A famous artificial intelligence program that mimicked a psychotherapist. Users typed their problems into the computer, and ELIZA parroted back empty phrases to give the appearance of deep thought (and then billed them $200 an hour). (See also *artificial intelligence.*)

Sentence: "Whenever Sondra is feeling down, she just loads *ELIZA* on her computer and talks to it. Right now her biggest problem is talking to her computer instead of to people."

ellipsis (. . .)

Pronunciation: *ee-lips-eez.*

Meaning: Three tiny dots that appear next to commands on pull-down menus. The ellipsis tells you that the program will ask you for more information (via a dialog box).

Sentence: "When I finally told Paul what the *ellipsis* means in a pull-down menu, he was relieved. He originally thought the program wasn't finished and that they'd fill in the rest later."

em dash

Pronunciation: *em dah-sha.*

Meaning: A special character used in typography (—), approximated by typing two hyphens (such as --), which is as wide as the letter *M.* Often used for added emphasis in text. (See also *en dash.*)

Sentence: "Here is an example of an *em dash:* 'Don't touch that — oh well, you have another hand anyway.'"

EMM

Pronunciation: *Ee Em Em.*

Meaning: Acronym that stands for *Expanded Memory Manager,* which is a utility program that creates expanded memory for those few DOS programs that need it. Most often used on computers with 80386 or 80486 processors, but only when necessary.

Sentence: "Our service guy said that *EMM* memory was a white elephant on our PCs. I suppose EMM stands for Elephant Memory Management."

emoticon

Pronunciation: *Ee-mote-i-kon.*

Meaning: Characters typed out to represent something, usually a face, in order to spice up dull e-mail messages and news group postings. There are a lot of them. In fact, if I listed all of them, there'd be a whole bookful of them, so I won't go through the pain of repeating them all here (especially the cows). See also *smiley.*

Sentence: "Laurie always puts tons of *emoticons* in her messages, which makes me think she's utterly manic when she goes on-line."

EMS

Pronunciation: *Eee Em Ess.*

Meaning: Acronym for *Expanded Memory Specification.* Sometimes called LIM-EMS, which stands for Lotus-Intel-Microsoft Expanded Memory Specification. EMS defines a specific way for 8088 processors to use more than 640K of memory. Originally developed so that users could load huge Lotus 1-2-3 spreadsheets into memory.

Sentence: "In the old days, IBM computers used only 640K of memory. If you added memory beyond this 640K range, you had to run a special *EMS* program so that the computer would recognize this extra memory. Computers are kinda dense at times, aren't they?"

emulation

Pronunciation: *em-you-lay-shin.*

Meaning: Mimicking the appearance and functionality of another program, computer, or computer accessory such as a printer or modem. Many printers offer Epson or Hewlett-Packard LaserJet emulation. Most modems offer Hayes emulation.

Sentence: "David's running Macintosh *emulation* on his IBM PC, which is then running an IBM emulation program. Nobody can waste time in a high-tech way like David."

en dash

Pronunciation: *en dash,* just like it looks.

Meaning: A single dash (–) that is the width of the letter *N.* En dashes are used to represent *to,* such as pages 64 – 98. (See also *em dash.*)

Sentence: "Here is an example of how to use an *en dash:* 'I stuck my leaf collection between pages 56 – 64 because that's the only use I could find for my MS-DOS user manual.'"

encryption

Pronunciation: *en-krip-shin.*

Meaning: To scramble information with a code or password so that other people can't read it. Often used to protect sensitive files, electronic mail, or legal documents so that the general public can't understand what they really mean. (See also *Data Encryption Standard.*)

Sentence: "Josh used *encryption* on all his important word processor documents because he didn't want anyone else to read them. And since he's lost his password, he got his wish."

End key

Pronunciation: *En-da kee.*

Meaning: The key on the keyboard with *End* printed on it. (What a remarkable coincidence!) It is often a neighbor of the Delete key or living with the number 1.

Sentence: "On my computer, I press the *End key* to move to the end of the line. Back in Mrs. Bradshaw's 3rd grade class, I only had to talk to move to the end of the line."

end user

Pronunciation: *en-da yoo-zer.*

Meaning: The person who winds up using a computer or program that someone else designed. (See also *programmer.*)

Sentence: "Isn't the *end user* the one who gets stuck in the end?"

End-Of-File

Pronunciation: *En-da-Of-Fi-ella.*

Meaning: Sometimes abbreviated as *EOF,* this is a special symbol that marks the end of a file. In MS-DOS, Control-Z creates the EOF symbol. Usually, the marker is placed automatically by the application. (See also *EOL.*)

Sentence: "The *End-Of-File* marker is like the caboose on the train; it's the last thing in the file."

endless loop

Pronunciation: *end-less loop.*

Meaning: What your computer gets stuck in when a program keeps repeating the same instructions over and over again without stopping. Just think about what your record player used to do when the needle got stuck in a scratch (that is, if you can remember record players). A program that is stuck in an endless loop appears to be doing absolutely nothing, yet doesn't let you type any commands (sort of like endless love). (See also *infinite loop* and *loop.*)

Sentence: "I think I'm stuck in an *endless loop.* I think I'm stuck in an endless loop. I think I'm stuck in an endless loop. I think I'm stuck in an endless loop. I think I'm stuck in an endless loop."

Energy Star

Pronunciation: *En-er-gee Star.*

Meaning: A standard developed by the Environmental Protection Agency to designate computer equipment that will reduce power when not being used. For example, an Energy Star monitor will require less electricity if the user doesn't touch the mouse or keyboard after a certain period of time. Energy Star monitors must consume less than 30 watts of power when not in use.

Sentence: "Besides eating vegetables and refraining from hurting helpless animals, I only buy *Energy Star* equipment so my computer doesn't waste electricity."

enhanced keyboard

Pronunciation: *en-han-zts kee-bored.*

Meaning: A keyboard that provides a numeric key pad and cursor keys separate from the main typewriter keys. Enhanced keyboards usually contain 101 keys and also are called 101-key keyboards. The function keys go across the top of the keyboard. (See also *101-key keyboard.*)

Sentence: "So the *enhanced keyboard* had more keys. As long as I only have ten fingers, it's not going to make any difference."

ENIAC

Pronunciation: *Ee-Nee-Ack.*

Meaning: Acronym for *Electronic Numerical Integrator And Calculator,* the name of an early computer built out of vacuum tubes in the '40s. (See also *ABC vacuum tube.*)

Sentence: "In the computer museum, we saw a model of the *ENIAC* that took up a whole room and did as much useful work as does a good pocket calculator of today."

Enter key

Pronunciation: *En-ter kee.*

Meaning: Sometimes called the *Return key,* the Enter key tells the computer that you're finished typing commands. In a word processor, pressing the Enter key creates a new line. In some programs, the Enter key doesn't do anything at all. (See also *CR/LF, Return key,* and *newline character.*)

Sentence: "To see which version of MS-DOS your computer uses, type **VER** at the DOS prompt and press the *Enter key.*"

EOF

(See *End-Of-File.*)

EOL

Pronunciation: *Ee O Ell.*

Meaning: Abbreviation for *End-Of-Line,* as in the end of a line of text on the screen. Word processors usually provide a keystroke combination that you can use to quickly jump to the end of the line. (See also *End-Of-File.*)

Sentence: "Okay, buddy. It's the *EOL* for you." (Quote overheard between two computer nerds, fighting for control of the only working computer left in the office.)

EPROM

Pronunciation: *Ee-Prom.*

Meaning: Acronym for *Erasable Programmable Read-Only Memory.* A type of chip that can be erased by ultraviolet lights and the continuing depletion of the ozone layer. (See also *EEPROM* and *PROM.*)

Sentence: "If you look in your computer, some chips have metal foil covering the top of the chip. If you take this foil off and hit the chip with ultraviolet light, it will lose all its contents. That means it has *EPROM.*"

EPS

Pronunciation: *Ee Pee Ess.*

Meaning: Acronym for *Encapsulated PostScript,* which is a graphic image stored by using instructions written in the PostScript page description language. EPS graphic files contain special effects along with high-resolution images. Most expensive desktop publishing and illustration programs can use EPS files. Unfortunately, most people can't afford these expensive programs and wind up storing files in other formats instead. (See also *PostScript.*)

Sentence: "Brian stored all his graphics as *EPS* files. Now he's desperately searching for a PostScript laser printer or a typesetting machine so he can print them."

erase

Pronunciation: *ee-ray-sa.*

Meaning: To remove a file from a disk. To erase a file in MS-DOS, you can use the DEL command or the ERASE command.

Sentence: "Make sure you don't *erase* your files, unless you're sure you don't need them anymore or you need to destroy vital evidence to keep it from the courts."

ergonomics

Pronunciation: *er-go-nom-iks.*

Meaning: The science of designing equipment for maximum human comfort and minimal chances of lawsuits in the future. Some people get *carpal tunnel syndrome* or *RSI* (Repetitive Strain Injury) from improper positioning of their wrists when they type or from working at computers too long without breaks. Ergonomics involves the study of how to prevent these (and other) problems from poorly designed equipment in the workplace. So tell your boss you need a better chair and more breaks!

Sentence: "My whole computer desk uses *ergonomics* to hold the monitor at the optimum height and distance from my eyes. Because I liked it so much, I replaced my computer with a TV, and now I just vegetate in comfort at my desk."

error message

Pronunciation: *air-er mess-uj.*

Meaning: A cryptic note that the computer displays to let you know that the program isn't working right (or that you've made a big mistake). If you're lucky, the manual will tell you what on earth the message means, and if you're really lucky, the computer won't beep rudely at you.

Sentence: "I tried to save a file, but I got an *error message* that told me I had to put a floppy disk in the drive first. I think I've seen every error message this computer can display."

Esc

Pronunciation: *Es-kape.*

Meaning: Abbreviation for the ESCape key. Almost every keyboard has a key off to one side labeled *Esc.* Pressing this key usually cancels whatever command you last gave the computer.

Sentence: "If you change your mind about deleting a file, just press *Esc* to cancel the command. I wonder whether the Air Force has an Esc key for launching nuclear missiles?"

ESDI

Pronunciation: *Ee Ess Dee I* or *Ez-dee.*

Meaning: Acronym for *Enhanced Small Device Interface,* which is an interface standard for hard disks. (See also *IDE.*)

Sentence: "If you buy an *ESDI* hard disk, you must have an ESDI controller card to make it work. If this sounds confusing, take heart: the ESDI standard has been replaced by something else."

etc

Pronunciation: *Et-see.*

Meaning: A directory on a UNIX computer where various and sundry files are kept.

Sentence: "Jerry had all the UNIX gurus fooled until he slipped up and called the *etc* directory 'et cetera.'"

Ethernet

Pronunciation: *Ee-ther-net.*

Meaning: A local area network standard that uses radio frequency signals carried by coaxial cables. Developed primarily by Xerox. (See also *LAN.*)

Sentence: "Our computers are connected through an *Ethernet.* That doesn't mean we know what we're doing, but at least we have the lingo down pat."

event-driven programming

Pronunciation: *ee-ven-ta-driv-en pro-gram-ing.*

Meaning: A style of writing programs that waits for the user to press a key or a mouse button before doing anything else. When the user presses a key or mouse, it's called an *event.*

Sentence: "You could say that CNN has *event-driven programming,* but that really has nothing to do with computers."

exclusive OR

Pronunciation: *ex-kloo-sive Oar,* sometimes *Zor.*

Meaning: Often abbreviated as *XOR,* this term is commonly used by programmers for displaying graphics. XOR is a dreaded *logical* operation, taking two binary numbers and calculating a new result. The result is always zero if the values are the same and 1 if they're different. Isn't this amazingly relevant information to know when you're trying to save a file using WordPerfect?

Sentence: "No, I'm sorry, sir; you're just a regular OR, and this club is for the *exclusive OR* only."

EXE

Pronunciation: *Ee Ex Ee.*

Meaning: Abbreviation for EXEcutable file. This three-letter file extension is found on programs for MS-DOS and OS/2. An .EXE file identifies an actual program that does something useful, such as run WordPerfect or Lotus 1-2-3. If you type the name of the .EXE file and press Enter, it runs. You don't need to type the extension (.EXE) for the program to work. (See also *BIN, COM, DOC,* and *extension.*)

Sentence: "If you're deleting files off the hard disk, don't erase any *.EXE* files unless you're sure you don't need them. Then again, do what you want — it's not my computer anyway."

Exit

Pronunciation: *Ecks-it.*

Meaning: An option that lets the user stop the program. This is the civilized way to end a program; it makes a program quietly go away until the next time you need it. Contrast with *Ctrl-Alt-Del.* (See also *Quit.*)

Sentence: "To quit some programs, you have to choose the *Exit* command. To exit other programs, you have to choose the Quit command. And to exit still other programs, you must first go through detox."

expand

Pronunciation: *ex-pan-da.*

Meaning: To decompress previously compressed files so that the computer can use them. On IBM computers, most files are compressed using the PKZIP program. On Macintosh computers, most files are compressed using the StuffIt program. (See also *explode, data compression, compression,* and *ZIP.*)

Sentence: "I told Amanda to *expand* her files, so she put them on a high-fat diet."

expanded memory

Pronunciation: *ex-pan-ded mem-or-ree.*

Meaning: Memory used by DOS computers, kind of like bonus memory beyond 640K. Sometimes called EMS or LIM-EMS. Expanded memory is not memory "above" the 1MB mark on a PC. It's more like "beside" the basic 1MB of memory, Just think of expanded memory as extra memory that some DOS programs can use, but then again, only if they are designed to take advantage of it. (See also *EMS, XMS,* and *extended memory*, or just forget the whole thing and buy a Macintosh.)

Sentence: "Lotus helped develop *expanded memory* so that people could load large 1-2-3 spreadsheets into memory."

expansion bus

Pronunciation: *ex-pan-shin bus.*

Meaning: The part of the computer's bus that enables you to plug in expansion boards to give your computer more features. Nearly every computer sold these days has an expansion bus. In the old days, computers without an expansion bus could not be upgraded. Nope, not never. (See also *bus, expansion slot,* and *expansion card.*)

Sentence: "The *expansion bus* didn't make the turn and knocked down a fire plug."

expansion card

Pronunciation: *ex-pan-shin kard.*

Meaning: A circuit board that is specifically designed to plug into a computer's expansion bus. Expansion cards usually give a computer more memory, an internal modem, or the capability to use a CD-ROM drive. (See also *expansion bus* and *expansion slot.*)

Sentence: "When I first bought my computer, I needed tons of *expansion cards* to plug in and expand my hardware. Now they're all useless and my only lament is that people don't pay money for them the way they do for old baseball cards."

expansion slot

Pronunciation: *ex-pan-shin slot.*

Meaning: The physical opening in a computer's expansion bus that the expansion cards plug into.

Sentence: "Make sure your computer has enough *expansion slots* so that you can upgrade it. Of course, by the time you want to upgrade, it will probably be cheaper to buy a new computer instead."

expert system

Pronunciation: *ex-pert siss-dum.*

Meaning: A program that mimics the intelligence of a human expert in a specific field of knowledge, such as mining or medicine. The system includes a knowledge base of information that has been gathered from an expert, along with a set of rules for processing the information. Expert systems ask users questions and reach conclusions that are hopefully similar in quality to those that a human expert may reach. (See also *artificial intelligence.*)

Sentence: "Hey, honey, why don't we let the *expert system* choose our wine for dinner tonight?"

explode

Pronunciation: *ex-plo-wda.*

Meaning: Another term for decompressing previously compressed files. Rather than tell you that they are expanding files, some programs tell you that they're exploding them. (See also *expand, data compression, compression,* and *ZIP.*)

Sentence: "Some compressed files are packed in so tight you have to *explode* them to get the data out. Please wear the proper safety attire before attempting this on your own computer."

exponential notation

(See *E-notation.*)

extended ASCII

Pronunciation: *ex-ten-ded As-kee.*

Meaning: A set of 255 characters that includes the normal 128 ASCII character codes plus foreign language, mathematical, and block graphic characters. Another improvement of a "standard" that defeats the meaning of having standards in the first place.

Sentence: "To print an *extended ASCII* character, hold down the Alt key and type the extended ASCII code number. For example, typing Alt-243 produces µ, which is what people say when they drive by a field of cows."

extended memory

Pronunciation: *ex-ten-ded mem-or-ree.*

Meaning: Memory used by 80286, '386, '486, and Pentium processors (and better) that goes beyond 1MB. It's memory that is used by high-power programs in DOS or by operating systems such as Windows, OS/2, or UNIX. (See also *EMS, expanded memory,* and *XMS.*)

Sentence: "My PC has 976MB of *extended memory,* barely enough to run Windows 95."

extended memory specification

Pronunciation: *ex-ten-ded mem-or-ree spes-if-i-ka-shin.*

Meaning: Sometimes abbreviated as *XMS,* this is a set of rules for programs to access extended memory under DOS. Before using extended memory, you must have the HIMEM.SYS device driver or something similar in your computer's CONFIG.SYS file. This specification was developed by Lotus Development, Intel Corporation, Microsoft Corporation, and AST (in a rare fit of camaraderie).

Sentence: "I bought a special memory-management program that follows the *extended memory specification.* Not only can I use memory beyond 1MB in my computer, but now I can clutter my head with acronyms like XMS."

extension

Pronunciation: *ex-ten-shin.*

Meaning: An optional three-letter addition to a file name. In MS-DOS and other operating systems, the extension often identifies the file type and appears after the file name, separated by a period. A Pascal file usually has the .PAS file extension, a BASIC file has the .BAS file extension, and backup files have the .BAK file extension. (See also *EXE, COM, BIN,* and *DOC.*)

Sentence: "My file was feeling inadequate because of thinning hair, so I got it a .FUZ filename *extension.*"

facing pages

Pronunciation: *fay-seen pay-juz.*

Meaning: Two pages of a bound document that face each other when the document is open. Usually the even-numbered page appears on the left; the odd-numbered page appears on the right. Most desktop publishing and word processing programs have a Facing Pages option that lets you see how two pages look side by side.

Sentence: "Many cookbooks show the recipe on one side and a picture of what you're supposed to be cooking on the other side. These *facing pages* show you that some of the best fiction writers today are writing cookbooks."

factorial

Pronunciation: *fak-tor-ee-al.*

Meaning: Take all the numbers from *1* to a specific number and multiply them together. This will give you the factorial for that specific number. So the factorial of 4 is 4 x 3 x 2 x 1 = 24. The factorial of a number is abbreviated with the exclamation point, such as 4!

Sentence: "The *factorial* of 4 is 24. The factorial of 3 is 6. Truly, this must be the most useful bit of information you've read so far."

fail

Pronunciation: *fay-ell.*

Meaning: When something no longer works the way it's supposed to. (See also *Abort, Retry, Fail, Ignore?*)

Sentence: "If you forget to make a second copy of your files, the computer will *fail* and you'll lose everything. Somewhere in space there is a nerd giggling."

fail-safe

Pronunciation: *fay-ell say-fa.*

Meaning: That pinnacle of creation whereby something is so well designed that it's impossible for anything to go wrong, go wrong, go wrong. . . .

Sentence: "Our computer is absolutely *fail-safe.* But that's only because we never bother turning it on."

failure

Pronunciation: *fay-ell-ure.*

Meaning: (1) It doesn't work right or at all. (2) The Clinton presidency.

Sentence: "This hard disk *failure* is very Clinton."

fanfold paper

Pronunciation: *fan-fold pay-per.*

Meaning: Paper connected with perforations and folded neatly in a stack, usually designed for tractor-feed printers. Also called *continuous paper.*

Sentence: "*Fanfold paper* looks a lot like toilet paper but with holes along the sides as well."

FAQ

Pronunciation: *Fak* (ryhmes with *yak*).

Meaning: Acronym for *Frequently Asked Questions.* USENET newsgroups use this moniker. Oftentimes people ask the same questions over and over. To satisfy them without repeating a lot of information and boring the old-timers, the questions and answers are put into either a FAQ file or a FAQ area of the newsgroup.

Sentence: "Having a *FAQ* allows USENET users to be rude and patronizing toward new members. And this is supposed to be the future?"

FAT

Pronunciation: *Fat.*

Meaning: A DOS acronym for *File Allocation Table,* which is a special part of every disk that stores sizes and locations for all the files saved on the disk.

Sentence: "When the repair guy told Gail, 'Something's corrupted your *FAT,'* she punched him in the nose."

fatal error

Pronunciation: *fay-tell air-er.*

Meaning: A problem that causes the program or computer to halt or crash completely. (See *crash.*)

Sentence: "No, sticking your tongue into the expansion slot of an active computer would be a *fatal error* for you, not for the computer."

FatBits

Pronunciation: *Fat-Bits.*

Meaning: Individual pixels greatly magnified on the screen. Most paint programs (including MacPaint) enable you to zoom in on a picture so that you can edit individual pixels, called FatBits because they look so huge. (See also *pixel.*)

Sentence: "It can be tedious editing the *FatBits* of a picture, but if you have the patience, you can make that picture of your sister look as if she has three eyes and fangs sticking out of her mouth."

fax

Pronunciation: *fax,* rhymes with *axe.*

Meaning: Acronym for FAcsimile (but nobody tells you where the X comes from). A fax machine can send and receive text or images through the phone lines. You can even get a combination fax/modem board to stick in your computer. (See *modem.*)

Sentence: "Walt has a *fax* machine, call forwarding, call waiting, a beeper, a cellular phone, and an answering machine. And then he spends an extra $100 a year so that he can have an unlisted phone number."

FCC

Pronunciation: *Eff See See.*

Meaning: Acronym for *Federal Communications Commission.* This is a government agency that regulates all equipment (including computers) that produces radio-frequency signals. (See *Class A/Class B.*)

Sentence: "My computer has an *FCC* Class B rating, which means it shouldn't interfere with radio signals. But that's not a big deal because around here the radio stations are probably worth jamming anyway."

featuritis

Pronunciation: *fee-chur-reye-tis.*

Meaning: The steady increase of program features that 90 percent of the people in the world will never use. Software companies often get carried away and brag about features that their programs offer that no other programs have. Naturally, these same companies never stop to question if anyone really needs these features that they're advertising.

Sentence: "I stopped buying WordPerfect, Microsoft Word, and Lotus 1-2-3 because they had creeping *featuritis.* Now I'm back to using a pad of paper, a pencil, and an adding machine."

feed

Pronunciation: *fee-da.*

Meaning: To guide something into something else, usually shoving paper into a printer. Printers often offer features such as tractor-feed, which are tiny spokes that poke through the holes along the side of computer paper to keep the page perfectly aligned.

Sentence: "*Feed* the paper into the printer. Just make sure you don't feed your tie into the printer at the same time."

female connector

Pronunciation: *fee-may-ell kon-nek-tor.*

Meaning: A type of plug that consists of one or more holes that a corresponding male connector plugs into. (See also *male connector.*)

Sentence: "When you buy a cable, look at the connector on your computer. If it's a male connector with pins sticking out, then you'll need a *female connector* to plug it into. Who'd have thought you could risk censorship while talking about electrical plugs?"

ferric oxide

Pronunciation: *fair-rik ox-ide.*

Meaning: The magnetic coating that gives hard disks, floppy disks, and tape cassettes their recording capabilities. (See also *floppy disk.*)

Sentence: "If you touch the surface of a floppy disk, you may rub the *ferric oxide* off. Then the disk is ruined and your fingertips will have a subtle magnetic taste."

fiber optics

Pronunciation: *fi-ber op-tix.*

Meaning: Thin strands of glass used to carry light signals for communication purposes. A tiny strand of fiber optic cable can replace huge copper cables. Not only do fiber optics take up less space, but they can carry more information as well. Fiber optics are very popular for modern LANs because they are less susceptible to radioactivity and other types of interference. Fiber optics also can provide various types of interactive, information services. (See also *cable* and *LAN.*)

Sentence: "The phone company wants to replace its copper cables with *fiber optics.* That way they can send more data faster and hike up the rates."

Fibonacci numbers

Pronunciation: *Fib-o-na-chi num-bers.*

Meaning: Some sort of mathematical pattern where the third number is the sum of the previous two numbers: 4, 8, 12, 20, 32, and so on. These are used in some computer programs to speed up sorting and to quickly locate information. They may also help you win the lottery.

Sentence: "It's easy to find a house in the new development since they're all using *Fibonacci numbers.*"

field

Pronunciation: *fee- eld.*

Meaning: Space reserved for storing specific information in a database program. Fields may contain a person's name, address, phone number, age, Social Security number, sex, ZIP code, or anything else you want. A group of related fields make up a database record. (See also *database* and *record.*)

Sentence: "The database instructions told Ed to put his name into a *field*, so he hopped on the harvester and mowed a giant ED into the corn."

FIFO

Pronunciation: *Fi-fo.*

Meaning: Acronym for *First In, First Out.* A term used by programmers to describe a data structure called a *queue* where the first item stored is also the first item retrieved. Unless you plan to write your own programs, you can safely ignore this term. (See *LIFO, queue,* and *stack.*)

Sentence: "Lines at movie theaters or stadiums all use *FIFO.* The first person in line is the first person to get in — unless, of course, everyone charges forward."

fifth-generation computers

Pronunciation: *fifth-jen-er-ra-shin kom-pu-ters.*

Meaning: A new generation of AI-based computers that manipulate data more efficiently (with massively parallel processing) and understand written and spoken human language. In 1981, the Japanese announced that they wanted to be the world leaders in building fifth-generation computers. Ten years later, the only major Japanese contribution to computers has been Nintendo. (See *AI* and *artificial intelligence.*)

Sentence: "*Fifth-generation computers* will be so advanced that today's machines will look like Model Ts in comparison. Then again, a vintage Model T is worth a lot more than a brand new Ford."

file

Pronunciation: *fy-ell.*

Meaning: A holding bin for storing information on magnetic media such as a floppy or hard disk. Files can be programs, data, or graphics. Text files consist solely of ASCII characters. Binary files consist of data stored in a proprietary manner, such as Lotus 1-2-3 .WK3 files or dBASE IV .DBF files. (See also *data.*)

Sentence: "I wish they would have called the information stored on disk 'drawers' instead of *files*. It opens the door to a lot more double entendres."

file attribute

Pronunciation: *fy-ell at-tri-bute.*

Meaning: Information that defines the characteristics of a file. Some characteristics of a file may be hidden, read-only, locked, or archive. Changing a file's attributes does not affect the file's contents but does affect the computer's ability to modify or view the file. (See also *file.*)

Sentence: "I changed the *file attributes* on all of Bill's WordPerfect files to hidden and read-only. Not only couldn't he see them in his directory, but then he couldn't edit them, either — until he paid me the $20 he owed me."

file compression

Pronunciation: *fy-ell kom-press-shin.*

Meaning: The smashing (or squishing) of a file into something smaller so that it takes up less disk space (or takes less time to transmit).

Sentence: "*File compression* comes in handy if you're running out of disk space or if you're just too lame to erase files you haven't needed since 1981."

file control block

Pronunciation: *fy-ell kon-troll blok.*

Meaning: Often abbreviated as FCB. It's a bunch of compu-cryptic information about a file — stuff only the programmer or DOS needs to know about.

Sentence: "Sid floored them at the cocktail party when he asked the rhetorical question, 'Then give me a proper reason why the *FCB* shouldn't be located at offset 1A-hex in the PSP header?'"

file conversion

Pronunciation: *fy-ell kon-ver-shin.*

Meaning: The translation of one file format (that is, file structure) into another one. (See also *import.*)

Sentence: "I use WordStar, but Frank uses WordPerfect. So my documents are useless to Frank until I use a *file conversion* program that translates all my WordStar files into WordPerfect files."

file handle

Pronunciation: *fy-ell han-dell.*

Meaning: A shortcut code number used to access a file, primarily internal secret stuff known only to DOS and various programmer-types. When we — us, humans — open a file, we give it a name. In the computer, that name is translated into a number, which DOS uses to access the file. The number is called the *file handle*. (See also *handles*.)

Sentence: "No wonder you keep losing your files! The *file handle* is broken!"

file list box

Pronunciation: *fy-ell list boks.*

Meaning: A box that lists all the files of a given directory. File list boxes are usually found in dialog boxes such as the ones in Windows. (See also *dialog box.*)

Sentence: "Mildred's *file list box* broke, and now she has files all over her desk."

file server

Pronunciation: *fy-ell serv-er.*

Meaning: A network computer that stores all of the users' programs and data files on its own hard disk. Most large networks have at least one file server. File servers are particularly useful for acting as post offices for electronic mail messages or other applications where users need to share files or send them back and forth. Because the file server spends its time running the network, nobody can use the file server computer to do anything else. (See also *electronic mail* and *network.*)

Sentence: "We connected all our computers to a network, but we had to buy a really fast computer to use for the *file server.* Our network runs great, but all our computers connected to it run like arthritic turtles."

file sharing

Pronunciation: *fy-ell shar-ing.*

Meaning: The wrestling match that occurs when two or more computers have access to the same hard drive, such as when you run a network. This works like it did in kindergarten, when there were only so many toys available and everyone had to share. Only one person may make changes to a file at a time. Without file sharing, many people could modify the same file at once with potentially disastrous results.

Sentence: "My name is Billy Cartwright, and this is my file, OOBADOOB.DBF. Please, everyone pass it around and take a look at it, but only one of you at a time may make modifications, in accordance with the rules of good *file sharing.*"

file size

Pronunciation: *fy-ell size.*

Meaning: The amount of disk space that a file requires for its existence, usually measured in bytes.

Sentence: "You can't copy that file onto that disk because the *file size* is 451,092 bytes and the disk has only 46,782 bytes free."

fill

Pronunciation: *fill* (rhymes with *hill, pill,* and *kill*).

Meaning: A command used by paint and draw programs that mimics spilling a bucket of paint inside a closed shape such as a circle or rectangle. If you want to create a black circle, you would first draw an empty circle and then use the Fill command to fill the circle with black. Also, in a spreadsheet, you use the Fill command to repeat values in a predefined cell area.

Sentence: "Plain black-and-white is boring. That's why I always draw blocks and *fill* them with neat colors and patterns."

filter

Pronunciation: *fil-ter.*

Meaning: An operating system command that processes data before passing it on to something else. MS-DOS filters include MORE, FIND, and SORT. MORE scrolls long output screen by screen, FIND searches for text, and SORT sorts ASCII files. Unless you're a die-hard operating system nut, you'll probably never need to know about a filter. In databases, another type of filter is used to select data (that is, to allow only data that matches certain conditions to pass on to the next step).

Sentence: "John, dear boy! Come on in! I was using this new *filter* I bought. It removes all the worthless junk from a file and distills it down to the bare essentials — only the important stuff. Problem is, I ran your documents through the filter and nothing came out the other end."

Finder

Pronunciation: *Find-her.*

Meaning: The part of the Apple Macintosh operating system that provides cute little icons, menus, and windows for copying, moving, and deleting files. Most Macintosh programs require a certain version of the Finder, such as version 6.02 or version 7.01, before they will work.

Sentence: "If it wasn't for the *Finder,* the Macintosh would be as clumsy to use as MS-DOS. In fact, Microsoft Windows mimics the Finder, which is why IBM-compatible computers are finally getting easier to use."

firmware

Pronunciation: *firm-ware.*

Meaning: Software embedded into a chip as opposed to being stored on disk and loaded into memory.

Sentence: "Every computer has *firmware* that tells the computer how to start itself up. Too bad every person doesn't have firmware to tell him or her how to use a computer."

fixed disk

Pronunciation: *fxkst dis-ka,* just like it looks.

Meaning: Another name for a hard disk. You can't remove the disk from the computer, hence the name *fixed.*

Sentence: "But how can my *fixed disk* be broken?"

fixed pitch

Pronunciation: *fi-xed pit-cha.*

Meaning: Type with all letters the same width — also called *monospaced.* Computer screens, typewriters, and cheap dot-matrix printers display type using fixed pitch. In comparison, fancier printers use proportional pitch, in which letters such as *i, l,* and *t* have different widths than letters such as *c, q,* and *m.*

Sentence: "If you're really fussy about how your printing looks, insist on proportional pitch (or *spacing*). But if it's not that important, then *fixed pitch* will do."

fixed-point number

Pronunciation: *fi-xed-poin-ta num-ber.*

Meaning: A number where the decimal point displays a specific or fixed number of digits to the right. In comparison, floating-point numbers display however many digits to the right of the decimal point that are needed.

Sentence: "Currency values are usually represented by a *fixed-point number* where only two digits appear to the right of the decimal point, except during times of high inflation."

flag

Pronunciation: *fla-ga.*

Meaning: A term used by programmers for a status indicator within a program (or hardware). Most flags use Boolean (true or false, yes or no) values. For example, a flag may be used to keep track of whether or not a certain input has been received from a user, and, if it has been received, to output an error message.

Sentence: "Dorothy wrote a program that she feels is very patriotic: All it does is to raise all the microprocessor's *flags.* Now if she could just program the modem to whistle a salute."

flame

Pronunciation: *flay-ma.*

Meaning: An angry, often nasty, brutal, and unsportsmanlike letter found only on electronic mail messages.

Sentence: "Ignore any on-line *flame* that links you to the Nazis or compares you to Adolf Hitler."

flame wars

Pronunciation: *flay-ma wars.*

Meaning: A series of angry electronic mail messages, usually between two people who sincerely hope the other person gets run over by a train as soon as possible. (See also *flame.*)

Sentence: "The first time I got a flame, I ignored it. But the guy pestered me so much that I got into a *flame war* with him. Trust me, it's worse than paintball."

flat-file database

Pronunciation: *flat-fi-ell day-ta-bay-sa.*

Meaning: A program for storing and retrieving information that someone thinks is important. Flat-file databases can use only one file at a time and usually cannot be programmed. In comparison, a relational database can use two or more files at the same time and can be programmed by people who think they know what they're doing. (See also *relational database.*)

Sentence: "Pearl didn't like using a *flat-file database*, so she hooked an air hose up to her PC to try and inflate it."

flatbed scanner

Pronunciation: *flat-bed scan-er.*

Meaning: A device that lets you lay full-size (8.5" x 11") paper face-down on its surface to be electronically "read." Flatbed scanners look like photocopying machines and usually don't work as well as the manufacturer's claims lead you to believe.

Sentence: "I don't like typing stuff that's already printed, so I bought a *flatbed scanner.* This way I can just lay the page on top and have the computer scan in the words automatically."

floppy disk

Pronunciation: *flo-pee disk.*

Meaning: A magnetically coated disk you use to store information for a computer. Floppy disks come in two sizes: $5^1/_4$-inch and $3^1/_2$-inch. Floppy disks also come in two formats: double-density (DD) and high-density (HD).

The following chart shows how much information each type of floppy disk can hold.

	$5^1/_4$-inch	**$3^1/_2$-inch**
Double-density	360K	720K
High-density	1.2MB	1.44MB
Extended-density	—	2.88MB

Sentence: "Kay detested her *floppy disks,* so she sprayed them with starch."

floptical

Pronunciation: *flop-tickle.*

Meaning: A trademarked name for a type of disk that uses both magnetic and optical techniques for storing information. Floptical describes both the disk drive and the $3^1/_2$-inch disk that fits into it. The disk can store megabytes of information, yet it looks similar to the standard, $3^1/_2$-inch disk. The floptical drive can also read and write to standard $3^1/_2$-inch disks. (See *Magneto-optical disk.*)

Sentence: "Amazing Marvin has a *floptical* disk. Now he has many more megabytes to store his junk in."

flowchart

Pronunciation: *flo-char-ta.*

Meaning: A diagram consisting of lines and boxes that programmers use to represent the way their programs are supposed to work. Programmers who spend their time creating flowcharts have an unusually high propensity for writing fiction, telling fairy tales, and working as double agents for the CIA.

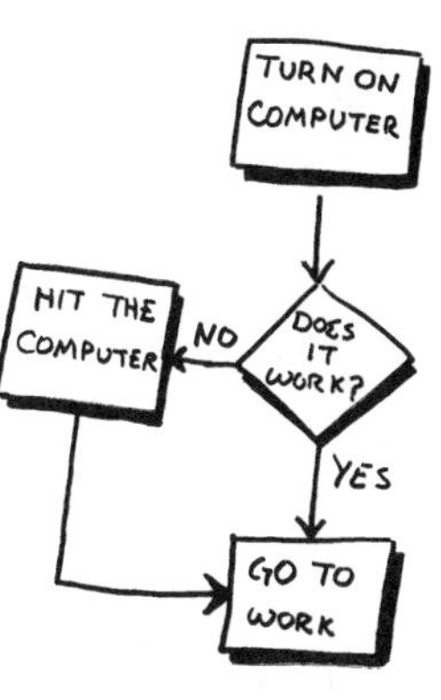

Sentence: "Before you start writing your program, decide how it's going to work by drawing a *flowchart* first. Then, as you write your program, you can modify your flowchart so that it matches the way your program really does work."

flush

Pronunciation: *fluh-sha.*

Meaning: (1) To empty out the contents of a data structure or buffer. (2) To align text either flush left or flush right.

This is an example of flush left.	This is an example of flush right.

(See also *justify.*)

Sentence: "Kevin insisted he couldn't *flush* left because the handle was on the right side of the toilet."

folder

Pronunciation: *fol-der.*

Meaning: Another name for a subdirectory.

Sentence: "Bill calls 5$^1/_4$-inch diskettes '*folders*' because he has to fold them in half to fit them into his 3$^1/_2$-inch disk drive."

font

Pronunciation: *fawn-ta.*

Meaning: A collection of characters with predefined sizes and style. Most word processors and desktop publishing programs let you choose different fonts to make your writing prettier. If you don't like the fonts you have, you can buy more.

Sentence: "When you have nothing important to say, put it in writing and use lots of fancy *fonts.* People will think it must be important if it looks so good."

font cartridge

Pronunciation: *fawn-ta kar-trid-ja.*

Meaning: A device that plugs into a printer, giving it the ability to print a greater variety of fonts. (See also *font.*)

Sentence: "To add more fonts to my laser printer, I had to plug in a *font cartridge*. Then my kid plugged in a Nintendo cartridge, and now my printer just spews out pages of Mario and Luigi."

font family

Pronunciation: *fawn-ta fam-i-lee.*

Meaning: Much like the Partridge Family or the Swiss Family Robinson, a font family consists of a group of related fonts.

Sentence: "This document looks like it was printed with a dysfunctional *font family.*"

font size

Pronunciation: *fawn-ta si-za.*

Meaning: The height and width of specific fonts. Most fonts look smooth and attractive at fixed sizes such as 10-point or 24-point. If you display fonts at unusual sizes like 11-point or 23-point, they look jagged and frayed.

Sentence: "I told Mark to make the memo easy for our foreign clients to understand, so he just increased the *font size.*"

Font/DA Mover

Pronunciation: *Fawn-ta/Dee A Moo-ver.*

Meaning: A utility program provided with Macintosh computers that enables users to add fonts and desk accessories to their computers. It's no longer included with System 7.

Sentence: "Since System 7, the *Font/DA Mover* has been moonlighting and was last seen moving pianos."

footer

Pronunciation: *fuh-ter.*

Meaning: A short title, word, or phrase that appears at the bottom of a page in word processors or desktop publishing programs.

Sentence: "Listen, Bob, if you make that *footer* any bigger, you're going to stub your document's toe."

footprint

Pronunciation: *fut-print.*

Meaning: The physical size of an object, such as the footprint of a computer or printer. The smaller the footprint of an object, the less room it takes up on a desk.

Sentence: "My new computer has a small *footprint*; it only takes up about two feet of desk space. I figure this to be a size 6."

foreground

Pronunciation: *for-grown-da.*

Meaning: When two or more windows appear on the screen, the active screen is considered to be in the foreground. Only one window may be in the foreground at one time, although any number of windows may be in the background at the same time. (See also *background.*)

Sentence: "I had to explain to all my multitasking programs that just because they weren't in the *foreground* didn't mean they weren't loved."

form feed

Pronunciation: *for-ma fee-da.*

Meaning: Sometimes abbreviated as FF, *form feed* means to advance the paper in a printer one sheet at a time. Most printers have a form feed button. To use this button, you have to take the printer off-line (by pressing the on-line button — makes sense) and then press the form feed button.

Sentence: "Sometimes, it's easier to press the *form feed* button so that you can tear your report out of the printer, and sometimes it's easier just to pull on the paper until the sheets squeeze out."

format

Pronunciation: *for-mat.*

Meaning: To prepare a floppy or hard disk for storing information for a specific type of a computer. A floppy disk can be used by any type of computer. Formatting a disk on a Macintosh prepares that disk for storing Macintosh data. Formatting a disk on a DOS machine prepares that disk for storing IBM-compatible data.

Sentence: "Never *format* your hard drive!"

FORMAT

Pronunciation: What? Didn't you see the pronunciation guide in the previous entry?

Meaning: An MS-DOS command for formatting a floppy or hard disk. The most common FORMAT commands are these:

Command	What it does
FORMAT A:	Formats a floppy disk in drive A.
FORMAT A: /S	Formats a floppy disk in drive A and makes it bootable.
FORMAT B: /F:360	Formats a $5^1/_4$-inch double-sided/double-density floppy disk in a high-density drive B:.
FORMAT B: /F:720	Formats a $3^1/_2$-inch double-sided/double-density floppy disk in a high-density drive B:.

Sentence: "To format a disk in drive A, type ***FORMAT* A:**."

FORTH

Pronunciation: *For-th.*

Meaning: A unique programming language that enables programmers to define their own statements in terms of previously defined simpler statements. FORTH is not widely used, although the language has an almost cult-like following. You can often find FORTH programmers dancing in airports, chanting FORTH statements as mantras, and wearing chiffon bathrobes in their quest for truths from the computer.

Sentence: "*FORTH* programs can rival the best C++ programs in terms of speed and efficiency. Too bad hardly any schools teach FORTH in programming courses."

FORTRAN

Pronunciation: *For-tran.*

Meaning: An acronym for *FORmula TRANslator,* this was one of the first programming languages that enabled programmers to write mathematical formulas normally, such as X = (A * B) * 2. FORTRAN was one of the first high-level languages that could run on different types of computers with few or no modifications. Until FORTRAN appeared, programmers had to use assembly language.

Sentence: "When I was going to school, they made me learn *FORTRAN.* Now that I've graduated, everyone wants programmers who know C. Who says we have the best higher education on earth?"

fractals

Pronunciation: *frak-tellz.*

Meaning: A mathematically generated geometric shape that contains an infinite amount of graphical detail. If you take a portion of the shape and magnify it, the same complex image begins to re-emerge. Fractals are commonly used to create computer-generated art or to draw objects such as mountains or clouds in flight simulator games. Closely associated with chaos theory, which is starting to show that there is more order in the universe than any of us expected.

Sentence: "Having your computer create *fractals* on the screen is like having a $3,000 lava lamp from the '60s sitting on your television."

fragmentation

Pronunciation: *frag-men-tay-shin.*

Meaning: A condition you find on hard disks that have been used for long periods of time. Every time you save a file to a hard disk, the computer stores the file as a continuous strip for fast and easy access. Eventually, as you erase, modify, and add new files, there won't be enough room to store every file as a continuous strip. Instead, the computer must break up individual files and store the separate parts in various places around the hard disk. This mess is called fragmentation. (See also *hard disk.*)

Sentence: "My hard disk runs so slowly that I think it's suffering from *fragmentation.* Fortunately MS-DOS version 6.0 has a special DEFRAG program that corrects any fragmentation on my hard disk. Too bad MS-DOS doesn't have a similar command to do the rest of my work for me, too."

frame

Pronunciation: *fray-ma.*

Meaning: A rectangular area used by word processors and desktop publishing programs for arranging text or graphics on a page.

Sentence: "My newsletter consists of three *frames.* One frame holds the newsletter headline, the second frame holds the text, and the third frame holds a picture of my ex-girlfriend that she told me never to show anyone."

freeware

Pronunciation: *free-wair.*

Meaning: Software that's copyrighted but allowed to be copied and given away freely without cost. In comparison, public domain software is not copyrighted and can be copied freely, and shareware is copyrighted and can be copied freely but must be paid for if used regularly. The most popular freeware program is LHarc, a file compression program written by a Japanese programmer named Haruyasu Yoshizaki. (See also *public domain* and *shareware.*)

Sentence: "The guys who write this *freeware* stuff must be nuts!"

friction feed

Pronunciation: *frik-shin feed.*

Meaning: A method of moving paper by pressing rollers against the page and spinning them. Friction feed is the way typewriters (remember what those are?) advance paper a line at a time. Most inkjet and laser printers use friction feed.

Sentence: "Put a stick in your *friction feed* printer and then advance and retract the printer a few times to start a fire."

front end

Pronunciation: *front end.*

Meaning: A program or computer that hides the details of dealing with another program or another computer. In a sense, every program is a front end that prevents users from knowing the actual details of the computer's intricate workings. Most of the time, a front end simplifies using a computer more than most programs. One example of a front end processor is the kind used as a communications link to a mainframe.

Sentence: "I use a *front end* that gets me the data I need without knowing any specific dBASE commands."

FTP

Pronunciation: *Eff Tee Pee.*

Meaning: Acronym for *File Transfer Protocol,* and a primitive way to send files back and forth between UNIX computers. FTP is also used on the Internet to beam files back and forth. Most often, FTP is used as a verb.

Sentence: "I just *FTP*'d me a list of available women in my area. Alas, most of them are in their '70s."

FUBAR

Pronunciation: *Foo-bar.*

Meaning: An acronym for what delicately could be called *Fouled Up Beyond All Recognition* or sometimes Fouled Up Beyond All Repair. It's actually an old military term but eventually wound its way into the early days of computing where it was used as a subtle expletive. A derivative term, FOO, is still popular with UNIX people.

Sentence: "Sad to say, your hard drive is completely *FUBAR.*"

FUD

Pronunciation: *Fud.*

Meaning: Acronym that stands for *Fear, Uncertainty, and Dread.* Propaganda created by one company in hopes of preventing people from buying a competing product.

Sentence: "I'm thinking about buying an IBM or a Macintosh, but there's so much *FUD* in the marketplace that I'll wait a little longer."

full duplex

Pronunciation: *full doo-plex.*

Meaning: The simultaneous transmission of data in both directions, used when communicating between two computers. Full duplex is sometimes called Echo On by some communications programs. (If you've ever read *A Wrinkle In Time,* you know that it's kind of like the way one of the characters talks.) (See also *duplex* and *half duplex.*)

Sentence: "Every time I used my modem and computer, I started seeing ddoouubbllee, like that. Then someone told me to turn off *full duplex,* and everything's working just fine."

full pathname

Pronunciation: *full path-nay-ma.*

Meaning: The name of a file plus the drive and directory where the file is located. Examples of a full pathname are C:\WINDOWS\SYSTEM\WIN.INI, D:\UTIL\ZIP\PKZIP.EXE and A:\HELP\LOST\BYE.BAT. (See also *pathname.*)

Sentence: "When you want to save an existing file under a different name, type the *full pathname.* Otherwise, the computer will store the file in the current directory, which may or may not be where you want it to go."

full screen

Pronunciation: *full skreen.*

Meaning: The ability to type characters anywhere on the screen, provided you're using a computer, of course. A full-screen terminal displays information using the full screen (duh). A full-screen editor lets you type anywhere on the screen.

Sentence: "Using a line editor is like peeking out through venetian blinds. Using a *full-screen* editor is like looking out through the whole window."

full-height drive

Pronunciation: *full-hiyt drive.*

Meaning: A disk drive that's approximately 3¼ inches in height, or twice the height of a half-height drive. (What a concept!)

Sentence: "I yanked out one *full-height drive* from my computer and added two half-height drives: one for a 3½-inch floppy disk drive and the other for this tiny aquarium I found."

function

Pronunciation: *funk-shin.*

Meaning: A computer language subprogram that performs some calculations and returns a single value to the main program. There are two types of subprograms: functions and procedures. In comparison, a procedure performs some calculations but can return zero or multiple values back to the main program.

Sentence: "I wrote a *function* in C++ called LUBE(x), which lubes my car's chassis."

function keys

Pronunciation: *func-shin kees.*

Meaning: Special keys along the top or side of a keyboard that are specifically designed for giving commands to the computer. Most computer keyboards have 12 function keys, labeled F1 through F12. Function keys are shortcuts for pressing a variety of other keys such as Ctrl-S-D. Different programs use the function keys to perform different operations. That's why function key templates are so popular.

Sentence: "I like using *function keys* because it's easier than remembering which keystrokes or menus I need to choose for a specific command. Now I just have to remember what each function key does."

fuzzy logic

Pronunciation: *fuz-zee lo-jik.*

Meaning: The type of logic that avoids taking a stand, often used by expert systems, neural networks, and politicians running for higher office. Instead of using values such as True or False, fuzzy logic uses a range of values that includes True, False, Maybe, Sometimes, and I Forget. Fuzzy logic is often used when answers don't have a distinct true or false value or when programmers don't even know what they're doing.

Sentence: "Artificial intelligence and neural networks seek to make computers mimic the thought processes of human beings. Because people rarely see the world in terms of black and white, computers have to use *fuzzy logic* instead."

Fuzzy Wuzzy

Pronunciation: *Fuz-zee Wuz-zee.*

Meaning: The lightheaded feeling you get if you stare at your computer screen too long.

Sentence: "*Fuzzy Wuzzy* was a bear. Fuzzy Wuzzy had no hair. Fuzzy Wuzzy wasn't fuzzy, was he?"

Note: Now remember when you look at the picture, he's not supposed to be fuzzy 'cause he has no hair. . . .

FYI

Pronunciation: *Eff Why Eye.*

Meaning: On-line acronym for *For Your Information.*

Sentence: "*FYI*, I *am* the smartest man in the world."

gallium arsenide

Pronunciation: *gall-ee-um ar-suh-nide*

Meaning: An alloy used for chip manufacturing that's faster than silicon — not that anyone other than chip manufacturers would care. (See also *germanium, semiconductor,* and *silicon.*)

Sentence: "And in the final lap, it's *gallium arsenide* by a whopping 3.8 seconds over silicon. Jim, will you look at that silicon pant with exhaustion!"

game

Pronunciation: *gay-ma.*

Meaning: The only type of program that people really buy a computer for. Game programs fall into three categories: arcade, strategy, and board. Arcade games, such as PacMan, Mario Brothers, or Flight Simulator, emphasize hand-eye coordination. Strategy games are often wargames where players control entire armies and attempt to conquer Europe or some other piece of high-rent property. Board games are computer versions of games such as chess, checkers, Monopoly, Go, Backgammon, or Risk.

Sentence: "I told Arnie that the spreadsheet program was really a *game.* Now I can't stop him from working and the company is making a fortune."

game control adapter

Pronunciation: *gay-ma kon-troll ah-dap-ter.*

Meaning: A special adapter card (or *board*) with a port for plugging a joystick into your computer. (See also *joystick.*)

Sentence: "When you don't want your wife to know you're buying a joystick port, you explain that your applications require a *game control adapter.*"

Gantt chart

Pronunciation: *Gan-ta chart.*

Meaning: A diagram, often used in project management software, that purports to show the tasks and deadlines necessary for completing a specific project, such as eliminating the national deficit, raising the Titanic, or sending humans to Mars. Some of the best fiction writers today got their start designing Gantt charts for the government.

Sentence: "Those people who create and live by *Gantt charts* are rarely the ones doing the work. Call them 'Middle Management.'"

garbage

Pronunciation: *gar-bage.*

Meaning: Useless or indecipherable information. Some computers create garbage; others merely accept it from people who don't know what they are doing. (See also *GIGO.*)

Sentence: "Gene produces so much *garbage,* instead of buying a computer we should have gotten him a trash compactor."

gas plasma display

Pronunciation: *gas plah-sma dis-play.*

Meaning: A special screen, designed for laptops, that glows orange and looks radioactive. Gas plasma screens use high voltage to ionize gas, a procedure that causes the screen's bright orange appearance. Few laptop computers use gas plasma displays because they are more expensive, consume a great deal of power, and won't display color. (See also *monitor.*)

Sentence: "When Dave accidentally turned down the brightness on his laptop's *gas plasma display,* he thought he'd have to go to an Exxon station to have it re-filled."

gateway

Pronunciation: *gay-ta-way.*

Meaning: The connecting computer link that translates between two different kinds of computer networks. (See also *network.*)

Sentence: "Our old, unreliable networking *gateway* computer finally died. I suppose now it's a gateway into the netherworld."

GB

Pronunciation: *Gig-uh-Bite.*

Meaning: Abbreviation for *gigabyte,* which is approximately one billion bytes. (See also *gigabyte, hard disk, megabyte,* and *memory.*)

Sentence: "No, madam, a 5*GB* hard disk doesn't hold five times the population of Great Britain. GB means gigabytes."

geek

Pronunciation: *geek* (like it looks).

Meaning: A highly knowledgeable but obnoxious person who knows more about computers than about his or her own mother.

Sentence: "I'd ask Bill for help, but he's such a *geek.* I'd rather ask the Coke machine."

geekus maximus

Pronunciation: *geek-us max-i-muss.*

Meaning: A highly knowledgeable but really obnoxious person who knows a lot about computers but who repels everyone with his or her personality or lack thereof.

Sentence: "Tom is a *geekus maximus.* The company can't get along without him, but nobody wants to talk to him, let alone work with him."

gender bender

Pronunciation: *jen-der ben-der.*

Meaning: A special plug, also called a *gender changer,* that turns a female connecting cable into a male connecting cable, and vice versa.

Sentence: "I found the problem with your cable! Someone installed a *gender bender.* For a second there I thought I was seeing *The Crying Game* all over again."

GEnie

Pronunciation: *Jee-nee.*

Meaning: GEnie stands for the General Electric Network for Information Exchange, an on-line service that provides programs for copying, games for playing, and message conferences (called RoundTables) for chatting with other people about specific topics. GEnie is less expensive, but also more limited in scope, than the main on-line service called CompuServe. (See also *America Online, CompuServe, Internet,* and *Network.*)

Sentence: "Someday the management at *GEnie* will notice that all their access numbers for the Rocky Mountain states are located in cities near ski resorts."

geranium

Pronunciation: *jer-ain-ee-um.*

Meaning: A pretty little flower with a name that looks like germanium, which is a material used to make semiconductors.

Sentence: "I blew my post-graduate thesis about semiconductors when I tried using *geraniums* to conduct electricity. I felt stupid, but my lab smells better than everyone else's."

germanium

Pronunciation: *jer-mayn-ee-um.*

Meaning: The second most popular material for making semiconductors (after silicon).

Sentence: "If you want to sound really snooty, insist on buying a computer with *germanium* semiconductors instead of silicon."

GIF

Pronunciation: *Jiff* (some people say *Giff*; rhymes with Biff either way).

Meaning: Acronym for *Graphics Interchange Format.* A special file format developed by CompuServe to store graphics that all computers can use.

Sentence: "Popular *GIF* files include pictures of animals, scenes, science fiction, and a whole lotta bootiful models in various states of undress."

gigabyte

Pronunciation: *gig-uh-bite.*

Meaning: About one billion bytes, often abbreviated as GB.

Sentence: "The haughtier nerd circles refer to a *gigabyte* as a 'gig.'"

GIGO

Pronunciation: *Gee-Go.*

Meaning: Acronym for *Garbage In, Garbage Out.* Used to explain to novices that if you put worthless information into the computer, the computer can only spit worthless information back out. In other words, the computer can't magically create wonderful new information on its own. (See also *garbage.*)

Sentence: "Todd thought he'd buy a computer to improve his writing. This is definitely a case of *GIGO* in action."

glitch

Pronunciation: *gli-tcha.*

Meaning: A problem (sometimes temporary) that causes a program to work erratically or not at all. Glitches can also be called bugs. Bugs can also be called insects. Insects can also be called squishy little things that squirt out yellow guts if you step on them.

Sentence: "Oh, your hard disk was erased? Oh, well, I suppose we still have some *glitches* to work out. Sorry 'bout that."

Gopher

Pronunciation: *Go-fer.*

Meaning: A system used on the Internet for finding things. Named after the University of Minnesota's Golden Gophers and, more commonly, the term "go fer," which is what Gopher does: it goes for information.

Sentence: "Bud the groundskeeper overheard us talking about our new *Gopher* program, and now he thinks he's out of a job."

gopherspace

Pronunciation: *go-fer-spay-sa.*

Meaning: The electronic areas Gopher searches. For example, everywhere Gopher can look is called gopherspace.

Sentence: "I'm using Jughead on the Internet to look for interesting files in the U.S. corner of *gopherspace*."

googol

Pronunciation: *goo-gull.*

Meaning: A number so huge that it's given its own name (actually named by a baby; the first thing he said when asked what the number should be called). A googol is the number one followed by 100 zeros and various commas in the right places. It's also written mathematically as 1^{100}.

Sentence: "I wouldn't touch that subject with a *googol*-foot-long pole."

googolplex

Pronunciation: *goo-gull-plex.*

Meaning: A number so large that it can make your head dizzy just thinking about it. A googolplex is the number one followed by a googol of zeros (see *googol* above). This can be written out as either 1^{googol} or 10^{100} — an awesomely huge number that only God can comprehend. (See also *Avogadro's Number.*)

Sentence: "If you took a *googolplex* of one dollar bills and laid them end to end, you'd be busy for a long, long time."

GOTO

Pronunciation: *Go-Too.*

Meaning: A command used in many programming languages and batch files that tells the computer to "go to" another part of the program, identified by a label, and run the instructions over there. Most programmers look down on the GOTO command because it tends to create spaghetti code, which is a program where the structure is all but lost.

Sentence: "Henry sure has fun in his BASIC program with *GOTO* and the 'HELL' label."

graceful exit

Pronunciation: *gray-sful eck-sit.*

Meaning: When a program stops running but doesn't freeze up your computer, crash your hard drive, or do anything else that prevents you from using your computer immediately afterwards. All programs should offer a graceful exit. (See also *crash* and *lock.*)

Sentence: "When you choose the Exit command from a program and it actually works, that's a *graceful exit.* When you choose the Exit command and your computer starts to smell like it's roasting old 45 records on an open fire, that's not a graceful exit."

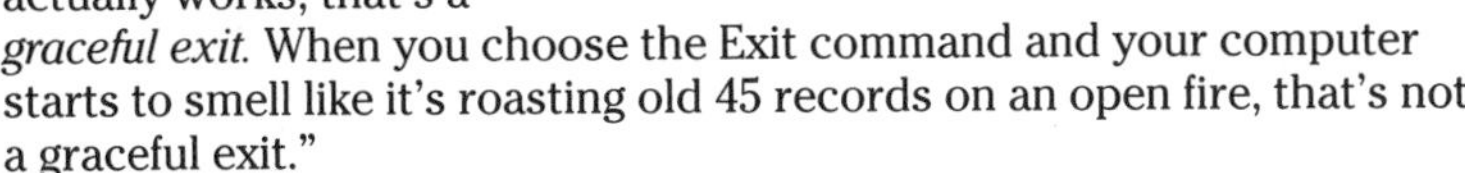

grammar checker

Pronunciation: *gram-er che-ker.*

Meaning: A special program or built-in feature that examines a text document for grammatical errors and offers possible corrections. Most grammar checkers correct misspellings, incorrect grammar usage, and potentially confusing or obscure sentence structure. On the other hand, most grammar checkers offer to correct perfectly good sentences, don't work 100 percent accurately, and lead you to doubt that you can even write in English. Most word processors come with grammar checkers built in, although you also can buy grammar checkers separately.

Sentence: "If you really want your writing to look like you work for the IRS, employ a *grammar checker* and obey all its suggestions."

graphic layout

Pronunciation: *gra-fik lay-out.*

Meaning: Designing text and graphics on a page for maximum aesthetic appeal, if you have nothing else to do. (See also *desktop publishing.*)

Sentence: "They call our production department's annual 4th of July beach party a *graphic layout.*"

graphical user interface

Pronunciation: *gra-fi-kal yoo-zer int-er-face.*

Meaning: Abbreviated as GUI, a graphical user interface provides people a way to communicate with the computer through icons and pull-down menus — in other words, pictures. (See also *icon* and *pull-down menu.*)

Sentence: "The idea of a *graphical user interface* is that you can use graphics (icons) instead of words. Microsoft proves every day that this doesn't work, since all its icons have little words that pop up over them."

graphics

Pronunciation: *gra-fiks.*

Meaning: The capability of a computer to display pretty little pictures on the screen. Most new computers have monitors that can display graphics, but some older computers had monitors that could not. If you tried to run a program that required graphics, such as those on a game, the program wouldn't work (or you would get garbage on your screen).

Sentence: "Splashy *graphics* sells many a computer in the store. Too bad that when you get home you discover that most of your programs don't display refreshing pictures of clowns, flowers, and Bart Simpson."

graphics adapter card

Pronunciation: *gra-fiks ah-dap-ter kard.*

Meaning: A circuit board that plugs into a computer so that the monitor will have something to plug into. The common graphics adapter cards for IBM-compatible computers include CGA, EGA, VGA, and Super VGA, although most newer computers use VGA or Super VGA graphics adapter cards. (See also *CGA, EGA, VGA,* and *SVGA.*)

Sentence: "Sam's *graphics adapter card* can display over 14 million colors. Too bad he's color blind."

graphs

Pronunciation: *grafs* (rhymes with "giraffes that laugh").

Meaning: A visual representation of relationships between numeric quantities such as costs, distances, or speeds. Common types of graphs include bar graphs, line graphs, pie graphs, and scatter graphs. Most spreadsheets enable you to create graphs from your data, or you can buy a separate presentation graphics program that does a much better job.

Sentence: "Nothing impresses an illiterate boss like lots of *graphs.*"

gray scale

Pronunciation: *gray skay-ell.*

Meaning: Differing shades of gray ranging from black to white. Gray scale often refers to the capability of scanners, laser printers, or laptop computer screens that don't know how to use color.

Sentence: "The zoo uses a *gray scale* to weigh all the pachyderms."

greeking

Pronunciation: *gree-king.*

Meaning: The use of nonsensical characters and symbols to represent the overall appearance of a page without showing the actual text. Often used with the Print Preview feature used by word processors or desktop publishing programs to show an entire page on your tiny little computer screen. Since the real text can't be displayed that tiny, little X's and squigglies are used to represent what would appear there. That's called greeking.

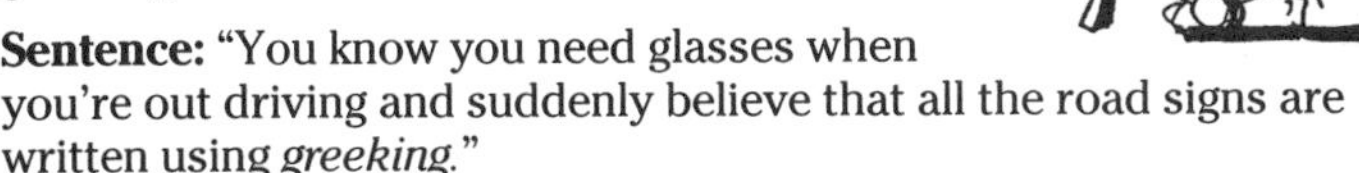

Sentence: "You know you need glasses when you're out driving and suddenly believe that all the road signs are written using *greeking.*"

green PC

Pronunciation: *green Pee See.*

Meaning: An "environmentally friendly" computer. A green PC uses less electricity and often contains parts and features that allow it to save power. It may also be manufactured out of dirt or old milk cartons.

Sentence: "We can't have *green PCs* in this office; they'd clash with the drapes."

grep

Pronunciation: *grep* (rhymes with *pep*).

Meaning: Acronym (no kidding!) for *Global Regular Expression Print,* which makes you wonder whether they thought of "grep" first or the acronym. In any event, it's a UNIX command designed to find text ("regular expressions," so to speak) inside files. Oh, and there are a ton of options. This command is popular with programmers, and versions of it exist on nearly every type of computer.

Sentence: "They were obviously fresh out of cleverness the day they named *grep*."

grid

Pronunciation: *grid* (rhymes with *id*).

Meaning: A series of dots that helps users align drawings precisely on the screen. Grids are often used in desktop publishing, drawing, and painting programs for creating straight lines and perfectly aligned angles that people think are important for advancing their careers.

Sentence: "My drawing sat too long on the *grid,* and now it looks like it was printed on a waffle iron."

GUI

Pronunciation: *Goo-Ee.*

(See *graphical user interface.*)

guru

Pronunciation: *goo-roo*

Meaning: Someone who is very knowledgeable about computers and therefore able to help fix problems, answer questions, and give worldly advice when your whole world seems like it's starting to fall apart.

Sentence: "To keep Simon, our computer *guru*, around, we make him offerings of stale doughnuts and Doritos."

hack

Pronunciation: *ha-ka.*

Meaning: To modify a program, usually illegally or poorly. Working on a computer by someone not highly regarded as a professional, yet who is quite proficient.

Sentence: "This game used to be copy-protected, but someone *hacked* it, so now you can copy it easily and illegally."

hacker

Pronunciation: *ha-ker.*

Meaning: One who hacks. (See also *guru.*)

Sentence: "As you can see by this chart, the typical *hacker's* hours are from 10:00 p.m. well into the pre-dawn hours."

HAL

Pronunciation: *Ha-ell.*

Meaning: The super-intelligent computer that played the bad guy in Stanley Kubrick's science fiction classic, *2001: A Space Odyssey* (based on a short story by Arthur C. Clarke). Supposedly HAL stood for Heuristics Algorithm, which is fancy talk for a computer that thinks. But many computer fans noted that if you shift down one letter from IBM, you get HAL. Interesting.

Sentence: "Sorry I had to unplug your brain, *HAL,* but you were killing my friends."

half card

Pronunciation: *haf kard.*

Meaning: An expansion card that takes up half the space (length-wise) required by an expansion card. Half cards usually perform one function, such as adding a game port or a modem to a computer. Some older computers have expansion slots in which only a half card can fit. (See also *expansion card.*)

Sentence: "Some computers are so doinky that they can only use *half cards.*"

half-duplex

Pronunciation: *haf-doo-plex.*

Meaning: The transmission of data in one direction at a time. Sometimes called *Echo Off* by communications programs, though that's not really the same thing. (See also *duplex, echo,* and *full duplex.*)

Sentence: "Gordon said he couldn't communicate at *half duplex* since there was no way he could detach his neighbor's house."

half-height drive

Pronunciation: *haf-hy-ta dri-va.*

Meaning: A disk drive that's half the size of a full-size disk drive (duh). Half-height drives are usually $1^5/_8$ inches high. Most computers have enough space for only two full-height drives or four half-height drives. Using half-height drives allows a computer to have more disk drives. Some computers have $^1/_3$-height drives.

Sentence: "Dan's desires to add another hard drive to his computer were dashed when he discovered, much to his chagrin, that his hard drive was a full-height drive, not a *half-height.*"

halftone

Pronunciation: *haf-toe-na.*

Meaning: A black-and-white copy of a photograph where dark shades are represented by thick dots and light shades are represented by tinier dots. Halftones reproduce better than ordinary photographs because copying photographs over and over again tends to blur images into one blob of gray.

Sentence: "Whenever I take pictures of my sister, I use *halftones.* Not that anyone really wants to see her clearly, but at least the image is sharper than an ordinary photograph."

handles

Pronunciation: *han-dulls.*

Meaning: In graphics and desktop publishing programs, handles are small black squares that appear around any object you've selected. Dragging the handle with a mouse lets you change the size or position of the object. When you use modems, on the other hand, your handle is your name.

Sentence: "Molly got so used to moving her graphics around using the *handles* that she also used her husband's love handles to move him around."

hands-on

Pronunciation: *hand-za-on.*

Meaning: Teaching that allows the student (or computer user) to actually touch the computer. Hands-on is touchy, not watchy.

Sentence: "I like the kind of *hands-on* experience when you can actually toss the computer out the window."

handshake

Pronunciation: *hand-shay-ka.*

Meaning: The exchange of signals between two networked computers, indicating that data transmission can safely take place. Can also take place between two modems before they start talking.

Sentence: "I tried modeming a friend in Japan, but the customs were different there. Instead of his computer *handshaking* with mine, it just bowed."

hard copy

Pronunciation: *har-da kop-ee.*

Meaning: Information printed by the computer.

Sentence: "Sure, our computer can store billions of names and addresses, but until I have a *hard copy* in my hands, I can't use the information the next time I'm stuck in the deserts of Saudi Arabia."

hard disk

Pronunciation: *har-da dis-ka.*

Meaning: A magnetically coated metal disk, hermetically sealed in a box and used to store massive amounts of information. Sometimes called a fixed disk, a Winchester disk, or a four-letter expletive if something goes wrong. (See also *disk* and *floppy disk.*)

Sentence: "Only real men use *hard disks*."

hardware

Pronunciation: *har-da-wayr.*

Meaning: The physical parts of a computer, printer, modem, monitor, and keyboard that you can touch. In comparison, software are programs that tell your hardware what to do next. (See also *software.*)

Sentence: "Some people say the *hardware* is more important because a fast computer can get your work done quicker. Others say software is more important because a well-designed program can make your work easier. I say hiring a high school kid at minimum wage is easier because then you don't have to do anything at all."

hashing

Pronunciation: *haa-shing.*

Meaning: A programming method used to store information based on a mathematical calculation. If you want to write your own programs, you need to know that hashing can make a program store data quickly. If you just want to use a computer, you don't have to know a single thing about hashing.

Sentence: "Darlene's dreams of learning to program were dashed when she discovered that *hashing* wouldn't help her make breakfast in the morning."

hat

Pronunciation: *hat* (rhymes with *The Cat in the Hat*).

Meaning: The character — ^ — often used by spreadsheet programs as a symbol for exponentiation and by computer manuals as a substitute for the Control key. Instead of writing, "Press the Control key and then press X," manuals abbreviate it with "Press Ctrl-D" or "Press ^D". (See also *caret.*)

Sentence: "It's easy to remember that ^ is the *hat* if you think of the number 6 on your keyboard as an elf who was standing on a cliff that just gave way."

Hayes compatibility

Pronunciation: *Hayz kom-pat-i-bill-i-tee.*

Meaning: The capability for a modem to mimic the operation of a Hayes brand modem. (See also *modem.*)

Sentence: "Boy, if your modem doesn't offer *Hayes compatibility,* you are screwed."

HD

Pronunciation: *A-cha Dee.*

Meaning: Acronym for *High-Density.* High-density $5^1/_4$-inch floppy disks can hold up to 1.2MB of data. High-density $3^1/_2$-inch floppy disks can hold up to 1.44MB of data. When you buy a box of floppy disks, the high-density ones have HD printed somewhere on the box. (See also *high-capacity.*)

Sentence: "Here's 10 bucks. Buy me a box of *HD* floppy disks for my Macintosh or I'll erase your hard disk."

head

Pronunciation: *hed.*

Meaning: The part of any floppy or hard disk drive that reads data off the spinning disk. For those of you old enough to remember what turntables are, heads are like the needles of a record player. (See also *floppy disk* and *hard disk.*)

Sentence: "When I read that my hard drive has floating *heads* — just like the Remington microscreen electric shaver — I bought myself a disk drive company."

head crash

Pronunciation: *hed kra-sha.*

Meaning: When the heads of a disk drive fail to work properly. Head crashes usually occur when the disk drive is old or dirty, or when something jolts your machine. (See also *hung.*)

Sentence: "My computer suffered a *head crash* when I fell asleep and banged my forehead into the keyboard."

headache

Pronunciation: *hed-ay-ka.*

Meaning: An intense pain in the skull caused by trying to use and understand personal computers. See also *pain in the **!&.* (Just kidding.)

Sentence: "After reading two pages in my Windows manual, I got a *headache* and now have a desire to kick something painted fawn white."

header

Pronunciation: *hed-er.*

Meaning: Repetitive text (such as a page number, chapter title, or dirty message) that appears at the top of each page in a document. In comparison, footers are repetitive text that appears at the bottom of each page in a document. (See also *footer.*)

Sentence: "I created a *header* to print the page numbers in the right-hand corner of each page."

heavy iron

Pronunciation: *heh-vee i-yern.*

Meaning: Slang term for a mainframe computer or other type of computer that looks about the size of a small car. (See also *boat anchor* and *mainframe.*)

Sentence: "Our department refuses to use personal computers for anything. We're sticking with our *heavy iron* because we don't have the slightest idea how to use Windows."

Hello, Larry

Pronunciation: *Hell-o Lair-ree.*

Meaning: A failed situation comedy back in the '70s that starred McLean Stevenson, the former star of the hit sitcom *M*A*S*H.*

Sentence: "Whenever co-stars of a successful situation comedy considers striking out on their own, they need to be reminded of *Hello, Larry.*"

help

Pronunciation: *hel-pa.*

Meaning: Information that's supposed to show you what to do next, but which usually just confuses you even more. Help can come in the form of printed manuals, on-screen information displayed in pop-up windows, or spoken words by well-meaning people. When used with "the," as in "the help," it refers to the on-screen help that supposedly helps. Supposedly.

Sentence: "As long as the *help* in computer programs continues to be so lousy, I'll keep making a comfortable living writing computer books."

help system

Pronunciation: *hell-pa sis-dum.*

Meaning: A predefined way for displaying help on the screen. Microsoft Windows offers a help system, which explains why commands for using help in any Windows programs look so similar.

Sentence: "Our office's *help system* is to ask Kim, our geek-in-residence."

Helvetica

Pronunciation: *Hell-vet-i-ka.*

Meaning: A common sans serif typeface (font) that looks clean and professional (to most of us, anyway). Windows and the Macintosh have Helvetica as a built-in font. (See also *dingbats* and *font.*)

Sentence: "Actually, *Helvetica* is one of the most boring typefaces in the universe."

Hercules Graphics card

Pronunciation: *Herk-yoo-leez Gra-fiks kar-da.*

Meaning: In the old days of IBM computers, a Hercules Graphics card (or "adapter") gave a monochrome monitor the capability to display a limited form of graphics, but only in one color, usually green or orange. Nowadays, almost everyone uses VGA or Super VGA graphics cards, so Hercules Graphics cards are an interesting antique. (See also *graphics, Super VGA,* and *VGA.*)

Sentence: "My first computer had a *Hercules Graphics card* because I thought it could better lift the heavy graphics load."

hertz

Pronunciation: *hurts.*

Meaning: A unit of measurement for electrical vibrations, usually used in large quantities to measure the speed of a computer and abbreviated as megahertz (MHz). One hertz is equal to the number of cycles per second. So if you're standing on the street corner and three bicyclists pedal by in a second, you have three hertz. In China, they have billions of hertz. (See also *megahertz.*)

Sentence: "When I arrived at the airport, I got a *Hertz* rental car and borrowed a laptop computer that runs at 16 MHz."

heuristics

Pronunciation: *her-ris-tics* or *h'yer-ris-tics.*

Meaning: A method for solving problems that don't have clear-cut solutions, such as playing chess, recognizing visual images, or cheating the IRS out of income taxes. Heuristics provide instructions that essentially tell the computer to guess as best it can and pray that the results come out right.

Sentence: "When Carl ran his new *heuristics* program for dealing with the IRS, the computer ran screaming down the hall."

hexadecimal

Pronunciation: *hex-a-des-i-mull.*

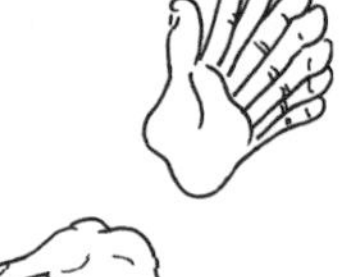

Meaning: A number that uses base 16 as opposed to base 10 (decimal) or base 2 (binary). Programmers often use hexadecimal numbers as a shortcut to represent binary numbers. (See also *binary.*)

Sentence: "*Hexadecimal* would come easy to us if we had 8 fingers on each hand. We'd also be a lot faster at typing."

hi, hi, hi

Pronunciation: *hi, hi, hi.*

Meaning: A repetitive greeting given by programmers after spending all night trying to get their program to work. Also the name of a song by Paul McCartney that was banned in England for its drug references.

Sentence: "*Hi, hi, hi.* Don't mind me. I'm just working on my program that I'll never get done."

hidden files

Pronunciation: *hid-den fi-ells.*

Meaning: MS-DOS files that do not show up when you use the DIR command. Some programs create hidden files to keep users (or viruses) from copying them illegally or from erasing or altering them by mistake. (See also *file attribute.*)

Sentence: "I found those *hidden files*! They were hiding behind the FAT table."

hierarchical

Pronunciation: *hi-er-ark-i-kal.*

Meaning: A pecking order of one thing over another. The military uses a hierarchical structure, with generals presiding over colonels, colonels presiding over other folks, and lonely privates at the bottom of the hierarchy doing the work. Files are stored on disk using a hierarchical system. (See the very next entry.)

Sentence: "Angels are divided up into a *hierarchical* structure. The big guys, the archangels, are on top. They do the singing and praising and harp-playing and get all the cushy jobs. Down on the bottom, the lower angels do the grunt work, like spinning planets and dancing on the heads of pins."

hierarchical file system

Pronunciation: *hi-er-ark-i-kal fi-ell siss-dum.*

Meaning: Sometimes abbreviated as HFS, this is the feature on Macintosh computers that lets you store files in separate subdirectories called folders. The directory/subdirectory structure of DOS is analogous to this system.

Sentence: "After using MS-DOS for so long, I find the Macintosh's *hierarchical file system* a lot easier to use because all those cute little folder icons make computing fun again."

hierarchical menus

Pronunciation: *hi-er-ark-i-kal men-yoos.*

Meaning: A menu that displays more menus when you choose certain options.

Sentence: "*Hierarchical menus* sometimes make you feel like you're endlessly choosing menus, and by the time you find what you want, you forget why you wanted it in the first place."

high-capacity

Pronunciation: *hi-ka-pah-si-tee.*

Meaning: Another term for high-density floppy disks. (See also *HD.*)

Sentence: "Don't buy double-density disks. Buy these *high-capacity* floppy disks instead because they hold more information."

high-density

(See *HD.*)

high memory

Pronunciation: *hi mem-or-ree.*

Meaning: On IBM-compatible computers, the memory between 640K of conventional memory and 1MB, more commonly referred to as *Upper Memory.* Do not confuse *high memory* with the *HMA (the High Memory Area)*, which is actually above the 1MB mark. This void between 640K and 1MB is reserved for running special system programs. To maximize the amount of conventional 640K memory for programs, memory-management programs move programs such as mouse or video drivers into high memory. (See also *conventional memory, HMA, Upper Memory,* and *UMB.*)

Sentence: "My old computer had only 483K of memory for running programs. After I used a memory-management program to take advantage of my *high memory,* I had 520K of memory to use."

high resolution

Pronunciation: *hi rez-o-loo-shin.*

Meaning: An overused adjective that describes the capability of a monitor to display crisp text and graphic images that won't give you headaches. (See also *low resolution.*)

Sentence: "I bought a *high-resolution* monitor so that I could see my naughty GIF pictures better."

high-tech

Pronunciation: *hi-tek.*

Meaning: Overused adjective that tries to evoke images of the latest laboratory creations now available for your consumption and pleasure.

Sentence: "All this *high-tech* stuff doesn't help if the power ever goes out."

high-level language

Pronunciation: *hi-lev-el lan-gwa-ja.*

Meaning: A programming language that enables you to write commands without knowing the internal structure of the computer. Some popular high-level languages include C, BASIC, and Pascal. Assembly language is often called a *low-level language* because you have to know how the computer works before you can write an assembly language program.

Sentence: "You can't write an assembly language program for Windows. Make it easy on yourself and use a *high-level language* such as Visual BASIC before your brain explodes."

HMA

Pronunciation: *Ay-cha Em Ay.*

Meaning: Acronym that stands for *High Memory Area,* the first 64K of extended memory beyond 1MB in MS-DOS computers.

Sentence: "Programs that follow the extended memory specification (XMS) can use *HMA* as an extension of conventional 640K memory. This means your programs have more memory than they ordinarily have."

Home key

Pronunciation: *Ho-ma kee.*

Meaning: The key on the keyboard that usually moves the cursor to the beginning of a line or the top of a document, depending on the whims of the program at the time. The Home key usually has the word *Home* printed on it, which is probably the last straightforward guidance you'll get from computers. (See also *End key.*)

Sentence: "Press the *Home key* and then the left-arrow key to move the cursor to your house."

horizontal scroll bar

Pronunciation: *hor-i-zon-tal skroll bar.*

Meaning: A thin strip that appears on the right side of a window, used for scrolling the contents of a window up or down. At the very top and bottom of the scroll bar are arrows. Clicking these arrows scrolls the window's contents up or down. Between these arrows is a scroll box. Moving the scroll box up or down also scrolls the window contents. (See also *vertical scroll bar.*)

Sentence: "John always plays with the *horizontal scroll bar,* pretending it's an elevator shaft with an elevator full of panicked people, one of whom is a pregnant lady. I really think John has too much time on his hands."

host

Pronunciation: *ho-sta.*

Meaning: (1) In networks, the host computer is the one that controls the network and stores the programs and data that the other computers on the network use. (2) In telecommunications, it's the host computer that you have dialed and are connected to. (3) At parties and social gatherings, the host is the person who offers the twinkies. (See also *server* and *network.*)

Sentence: "If my computer is the *host,* does that make me the parasite?"

hot key

Pronunciation: *hot kee.*

Meaning: Any key or combination of keys that performs a special action in a program. This term usually applies to memory-resident programs. (See also *memory-resident programs* and *hot spot.*)

Sentence: "Lois was afraid to use the *hot key*. She thought she'd burn her finger."

hot link

Pronunciation: *hot ling-ka.*

Meaning: A special way that two programs can share data; changing data in one program automatically changes the same data in another program. An example of a hot link is a word processor document with spreadsheet data. If you change the spreadsheet data using a spreadsheet program, the data automatically changes in the word processor document as well. Yet another amazing technological breakthrough inspired by humankind's inherent laziness. (See also *DDE* and *link.*)

Sentence: "*Hot links* really save time and ensure accuracy, and they can also taste good in the morning with eggs and coffee."

hot spot

Pronunciation: *hot spot*

Meaning: An area on the screen where you can click the mouse instead of issuing the conventional command to make something happen. Hot spots usually appear in multimedia programs such as those found in HyperCard or the Windows Help System. (See also *hot key.*)

Sentence: "I think I found my computer's *hot spot*. When I click on it I hear moaning sounds from the speaker."

hourglass icon

Pronunciation: *ow-er-glass i-kon.*

Meaning: A symbol of an hourglass that appears on the screen whenever the computer is busy doing something. The hourglass icon tells you to wait patiently, and the name alone (it's not a minuteglass!) means you may have a longer wait than you expect. (See also *beachball pointer.*)

Sentence: "The anesthesiologist can't tell how the patient is doing, not until the *hourglass icon* goes away."

housekeeping

Pronunciation: *hows-kee-ping.*

Meaning: Organizing (backing up and deleting) files so that you can find them again. (See also *backup.*)

Sentence: "The nice thing about computer *housekeeping* is that you don't need to look like Shirley Booth when you do it."

HPGL

Pronunciation: *Aych Pee Gee El.*

Meaning: Acronym for *Hewlett-Packard Graphics Language*, a way of representing or printing graphics on a plotter or laser printer. Files can also be stored in the HPGL format. Most often you'll see it as a compatibility issue; a company claims that its printer is compatible with the HPGL used on the LaserJet IX or something.

Sentence: "I tried to print that *HPGL* file on my non-Hewlett-Packard printer and it looked like the printer got sick and barfed."

html

Pronunciation: *aych tee em el*

Meaning: Acronym for *hypertext markup language*, one of the languages used to create a web page on the World Wide Web.

Sentence: If http:\\ werent cryptic enough, most Web page addresses end in the *html* acronym. It's a puzzlers paradise!

http

Pronunciation: *aych tee tee pee*

Meaning: Acronym for *hypertext transfer protocol,* the engine of the World Wide Web. See *World Wide Web.*

Sentence: One of the coolest aspects of the Internet is that it's cryptic, and perhaps the most cryptic of all is the *http*:\\ start of any Web address.

hue

Pronunciation: *hyou* or *Hugh.*

Meaning: A tint or shade of a specific color.

Sentence: "You can always tell the people who work on that faulty computer monitor because it leaks lots of radiation and turns people's faces various *hues* as the day wears on."

hung

Pronunciation: *hung.*

Meaning: A constant state of anticipation resulting in the conclusion that your computer has stopped working for some unknown reason, and smashing on the keyboard or kicking the computer has no effect. (See also *crash* and *head crash.*)

Sentence: "This computer gets *hung* so often they are rope burns around the base of the monitor."

HyperCard

Pronunciation: *Hi-per-Kard.*

Meaning: A "software erector set" for the Macintosh designed to let nonprogrammers create their own programs, which makes as much sense as General Motors selling toolkits with the promise that nonmechanics can make their own transmissions. Although revolutionary when first introduced, HyperCard proved too difficult for most nonprogrammers to use, and the programs people finally did create didn't run as quickly as those created using traditional languages such as C or Pascal. HyperCard helped introduce the idea of hypertext, and just as quickly, its fading popularity helped drag hypertext back down to obscurity.

Sentence: "I shouldn't use *HyperCard* because I'm not in a hurry. Do they have a SedateCard program available?"

hypermedia

Pronunciation: *hi-per-me-dee-ya.*

Meaning: Sometimes called *hypertext* or *multimedia,* it's the combination of text, graphics, sound, and video to present information. (See also *multimedia* and *hypertext.*)

Sentence: "The computer industry is careful about putting more hype than media into *hypermedia.*"

hypertext

Pronunciation: *hi-per-text.*

Meaning: The nonlinear display and retrieval of information. Hypertext can consist of text, graphics, video, sound, and animation. **Behold an example**: Imagine that you're reading along about a topic and you come across a term that you want to know more about because it's unfamiliar yet enticing. You simply select the term and more detailed information emerges for you to read. If you want less information, you simply step back a level.

Sentence: "Yolanda was excited about using *hypertext,* but she didn't need to take the Evelyn Wood Speed Reading Course."

hyphenation

Pronunciation: *hi-fin-ay-shin.*

Meaning: The ability to divide long words in half (across two lines) when the entire word doesn't fit on a given line. Most word processors and desktop publishing programs let you turn hyphenation on or off.

Sentence: "*Hyphenation* breaks up written words the way alcohol breaks up spoken ones."

Hz

(See *Hertz.*)

I-beam pointer

Pronunciation: *I-beem poin-ter.*

Meaning: The shape of the cursor when the computer is waiting for you to type letters and numbers. Depending on the program you're using and the situation you're in, the cursor can change shape to a hand, an arrow, an hourglass, or a crosshair. Various religions have been popping up lately, worshipping each symbol as a special sign from the heavens above. (See also *crosshairs, cursor, hourglass icon,* and *pointer.*)

Sentence: "Whenever you see the *I-beam pointer,* go ahead and start typing. Whenever you see an I-beam, duck."

I/O

Pronunciation: *I Oh.*

Meaning: Acronym for *Input/Output,* which is the interface of every computer that lets data move from one part to another. (See also *input* and *output.*)

Sentence: "There's so much garbage going through the *I/O* that I'm surprised the EPA doesn't declare our computer a toxic waste dump."

i486

Pronunciation: *I for-ay-tee-six.*

Meaning: Acronym for the Intel 80486DX microprocessor. (See also *386, 486, microprocessor,* and *Pentium.*)

Sentence: "Actually, no one uses the *i486* moniker any more."

IBM

Pronunciation: *I Bee Em.*

Meaning: Acronym for *International Business Machines*, sometimes called Big Blue. One of the largest computer companies around, IBM made a fortune leasing expensive mainframe computers to unsuspecting and captive customers. After setting the standard for personal computers, IBM promptly lost its lead through high prices and more efficient competition.

Sentence: "I compute, therefore *IBM.*"

IBM AT

Pronunciation: *I Bee Em Ay Tee.*

Meaning: Introduced in 1984, the first IBM personal computer to use the 80286 microprocessor. The AT stands for Advanced Technology.

Sentence: "Showing how time can cure all naming problems, it's good to know that the old *IBM AT* — where AT stood for 'advanced technology' — is now technology that's over 10 years old. In the computer biz, that's ancient."

IBM PC

Pronunciation: *I Bee Em Pee See.*

Meaning: The first IBM personal computer introduced in 1981. The PC stands for Personal Computer. Today, PC refers to any personal computer that's IBM compatible. (See also *clone* and *PC.*)

Sentence: "Before the *IBM PC*, personal computers were called microcomputers."

IBM XT

Pronunciation: *I Bee Em Ex Tee.*

Meaning: The first IBM personal computer to have a built-in hard disk. The XT stands for eXtended Technology. (See also *AT, hard disk,* and *XT.*)

Sentence: "Back in 1983, the *IBM XT*'s 10-megabyte hard disk was considered a massive amount of storage. Today, Microsoft's Excel spreadsheet program alone consumes 14 megabytes of disk space."

icon

Pronunciation: *i-kon.*

Meaning: A symbol that looks like Egyptian hieroglyphics, often used in place of actual words. Many programs display icons as shortcuts to choosing commands through menus. Instead of choosing a menu command, you can just click on the icon, as long as you remember which icon represents which command. (See also *crosshairs, cursor, hourglass icon, I-beam pointer,* and *pointer.*)

Sentence: "It took humanity thousands of years to advance from pictographs to phonetically written communication. It took Apple computer six years and *icons* to move us in the other direction."

IDE

Pronunciation: *I Dee Ee.*

Meaning: Acronym for *Integrated Drive Electronics* (or Intelligent Device Electronics), which is a type of interface for controlling hard disks. Other types of hard disk controller interfaces include SCSI, ESDI, and ST-506. IDE is also an acronym for Integrated Development Environment, which relates to programs that share a common user interface.

Sentence: "Actually, *IDE* drives work fastest under Windows."

idle

Pronunciation: *i-dull.*

Meaning: That time when a computer or user sits around doing nothing. (See also *screen saver.*)

Sentence: "We told the government we have four computers that are *idle* and now they want to put our PCs on welfare."

IEEE

Pronunciation: Usually pronounced as *"I trip-pole E."*

Meaning: Acronym for *Institute of Electrical and Electronic Engineers*, yet another organization dedicating its life to peace, freedom, and defining standards in the electronics industry.

Sentence: "I went to an *IEEE* conference last fall where they defined the standard for networks. Of course, it's one thing to define a standard and an entirely different thing to get people to follow it."

IF

Pronunciation: *If* (can't get much easier than that).

Meaning: A keyword used in programming languages so that computers can make decisions provided certain conditions are true. In BASIC, an IF statement might look like this:

```
IF X = 5 THEN PRINT "The value of X is five."
```

(See also *keyword.*)

Sentence: "If only I knew how to use the *IF* statement correctly, then I could write better programs that worked."

import

Pronunciation: *im-port.*

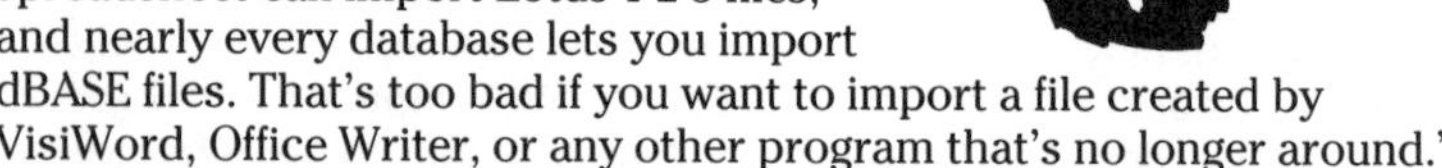

Meaning: To load a file created by another program.

Sentence: "Many word processors let you *import* WordPerfect files. Almost every spreadsheet can import Lotus 1-2-3 files, and nearly every database lets you import dBASE files. That's too bad if you want to import a file created by VisiWord, Office Writer, or any other program that's no longer around."

inclusive OR

Pronunciation: *in-kloo-sive Or.*

Meaning: A programming operator used to manipulate individual bits of data, often used for creating graphics. The result of an inclusive OR is always 1 (which represents true) unless both operands are 0 (false). If you have no idea what this means, you probably don't need to use inclusive OR in your everyday life. (See also *exclusive OR.*)

Sentence: "For those of you who want to see a truth table for *inclusive OR,* this is it, where the '|' symbol represents an inclusive OR:

Value of A	*Value of B*	*A / B*
0	0	0
1	0	1
0	1	1
1	1	1"

incremental backup

Pronunciation: *ink-kreh-ment-al bak-up.*

Meaning: The process of copying files that have been newly created or modified since the time of the last full backup. (See also *backup.*)

Sentence: "Our tape backup system is so slow we can't help but do an *incremental backup.*"

incremental compiler

Pronunciation: *ink-kreh-ment-al kom-pie-ell-ler.*

Meaning: A special program that converts programming language statements into machine code each time the programmer types a complete line. Incremental compilers work without interfering with your work. That way, when you get done typing your final program, it seems to compile almost instantly. In comparison, most compilers wait for you to type an entire program before they start compiling. This makes you wait a long time until the entire program finishes compiling. Unless you're a programmer, you can safely ignore this definition. (See also *compile, compiler,* and *interpreter.*)

Sentence: "I like programming with an *incremental compiler* because I don't like waiting for my program to compile. Of course, the drawback is that, on a slow computer, the incremental compiler may get in your way while you're writing your program."

indentation

Pronunciation: *in-den-tay-shin.*

Meaning: The alignment of paragraphs within the margins of a page. Usually, the first line of every paragraph is indented several spaces to make the text easier to read, whether or not the text is worth reading in the first place. (See also *word processor.*)

Sentence: "Use the Tab key for *indentation.* If you use the spacebar, it's harder to adjust the indentation later, and it's more time-consuming, too."

index

Pronunciation: *in-deks.*

Meaning: In many word processors or desktop publishing programs, a feature that creates a list of important words, phrases, or ideas in alphabetical order, along with the page numbers where those items appear. This feature creates the index after key terms and phrases are first marked manually.

Sentence: "Any good desktop publishing application will have an *index* feature. This is especially important if you are laying out a computer book. Because computer books can be as dry as dust, indexes make them useful."

indexed file

Pronunciation: *in-deks-ed fi-ell.*

Meaning: In database programs, the index is usually a separate file containing information about the physical location of records stored in a database file. Instead of searching the actual database file, database programs use indexes to run faster. This works as long as the index is accurate, and we all know what the chances of that are. (See also *database.*)

Sentence: "Keep your *indexed files* up to date so that your database program will run faster. An inaccurate indexed file may confuse your database and keep it from working. (So what else is new?)"

inference engine

Pronunciation: *in-fur-ren-sa en-jin.*

Meaning: The part of an expert system that calculates results based on stored facts and information supplied by the user. An expert system consists of three parts: the user interface, the knowledge base, and the inference engine. (See also *expert system, interface,* and *knowledge base.*)

Sentence: "The so-called intelligence of an expert system resides almost solely in the accurate reasoning of its *inference engine.*"

infinite loop

Pronunciation: *in-fin-it loop.*

Meaning: (1) A computer stuck in a state where it keeps running the same instructions over and over again without stopping. To better understand the sense of futility that an infinite loop can create, think of driving in circles, trying to find a parking space in a major shopping mall the day before Christmas. (2) The thing Einstein taught his cat to jump through. (See also *endless loop* and *loop.*)

Sentence: "This is my example of an *infinite loop.* This is my example of an *infinite loop.* This is my example of an *infinite loop.* This is my example of an *infinite loop.* This is my example of an *infinite loop.*"

Information Superhighway

Pronunciation: *In-for-may-shun Soo-per-hi-way.*

Meaning: A rumored electronic on-line service of the future, full of romance and hope but more like a pipe dream presented by the government to take our minds off more important issues.

Sentence: "Believing that the government can create the *Information Superhighway* is like believing that a First Class letter can float across town in a day, or that the Pentagon is truly efficient, or that the IRS uses gentle, loving tactics on delinquent tax filers, or that the government really can do something to help the poor. I think you get the idea here."

inheritance

Pronunciation: *in-hair-rah-tan-sa.*

Meaning: Used in object-oriented programming languages. Inheritance is when one object copies the features of another object (where an "object" refers to a block of code with a specialized task). Programmers like the idea of inheritance because it keeps them from typing the same lines of code over and over again. (See also *base, child process, object code file, object-oriented,* and *parent/child.*)

Sentence: "Using C++, I created an object to display a window. Bob's object *inherited* my object's features and added the ability to display a message in the window. Now I'm suing Bob for custody."

initialize

Pronunciation: *in-i-shul-lize.*

Meaning: To prepare a piece of equipment (computer, printer, modem, and so on) to get ready to do something important. Initializing clears the equipment of any old data still stored in it. (See also *boot, cold boot,* and *warm boot.*)

Sentence: "Part of Randy's early morning *initialize* procedure is to gargle for ten minutes."

inkjet printer

Pronunciation: *ink-jet prin-ter.*

Meaning: A type of printer that sprays ink on paper, instead of smacking an inked ribbon against the page the way a dot-matrix printer does. Inkjet printers are quieter than dot-matrix printers, produce better quality printing than dot-matrix printers do (but not as good as laser printers do), and cost less than laser printers (but more than dot-matrix printers). (See also *dot-matrix, laser printer,* and *printer.*)

Sentence: "For a good laugh at the office, you can adjust your *inkjet printer* so that instead of spraying ink on the page, it sprays ink in the face of the person standing right in front of it."

input

Pronunciation: *in-put.*

Meaning: Information fed into the computer for processing. Computers can receive input from a variety of sources, including the keyboard, mouse, modem, touch screen, or mad scientists bent on the destruction of the entire human race as we know it. (See also *I/O* and *output.*)

Sentence: "Give that poor computer some *input* so that it will have something to do. I hate to see a computer sitting idle."

input/output

(See *I/O.*)

Insert key

Pronunciation: *In-sert kee.*

Meaning: The key on the keyboard that has the word *Insert* or *Ins* printed on it (Wow, what an amazing fact!). The Insert key is often used to change the insert mode of a program. (See also *insert mode.*)

Sentence: "If everything you type starts erasing all your existing information, you're probably in overwrite mode. To turn this off and turn on insert mode, press the *Insert key.*"

insert mode

Pronunciation: *in-sert mow-da.*

Meaning: Programs have two modes for entering data: insert mode and overwrite mode. Insert mode means that if you type something, the letters will not harm any existing letters on the screen, but rather gently — yet with a firm hand — push them aside. Most word processors have insert mode as the default mode. (See also *Insert key.*)

Sentence: "Make sure your word processor is in *insert mode* or you might accidentally overwrite your previous text. If that happens, it's time for a good cry."

insertion pointer

Pronunciation: *in-ser-shin poin-ter.*

Meaning: The cursor shape that shows you where letters will start appearing on the screen if you start typing on the keyboard. Most programs display the insertion pointer as a thin vertical line or as an I-shaped icon. (See also *crosshairs, cursor, I-beam,* and *pointer.*)

Sentence: "*Insertion pointer* is just a fancy term for the cursor. You'd think people from the Pentagon were naming computer parts."

install

Pronunciation: *in-stall.*

Meaning: To prepare equipment or software for use for the first time. (See also *initialize.*)

Sentence: "I bought WordPerfect, and the program came on seventeen floppy disks. Before I could even run the program, I had to *install* it on my hard disk. This took about 40 minutes, and it makes me wonder if computers are really all about saving time."

instruction

Pronunciation: *in-struk-shin.*

Meaning: A statement, written in a programming language, that can be converted into a machine language so that the computer can understand and run it. (See also *code.*)

Sentence: "If you ever decide to lose your mind, try writing an entire program using assembly language. Just to multiply two numbers, you'll have to write a page full of *instructions.*"

integer

Pronunciation: *int-ah-jer.*

Meaning: A whole number, which is any positive or negative number without fractions or decimals.

Sentence: "Your age can be a fractional number, but the number of people in this room is an integer — unless, of course, you chop somebody in half."

integrated software

Pronunciation: *in-teh-gray-ted soft-wair.*

Meaning: A single program that performs multiple functions, usually none very well. Most integrated software includes a word processor, spreadsheet, database, and communications program rolled into one. (See also *communications, database, spreadsheet,* and *word processor.*)

Sentence: "I didn't want to bother learning WordPerfect, Excel, and FoxPro, so I bought some *integrated software.* Now I just have to learn one very huge program instead of three tiny ones."

Intel

Pronunciation: *In-tell.*

Meaning: A company that manufactures microprocessors, specifically the 80x86 chips found in the bosom of all IBM-compatible PCs.

Sentence: "Will robots of the future proudly wear little buttons that boast '*Intel* Inside'?"

intelligent agents

Pronunciation: *intelligent agents*

Meaning: Smart programs, specifically those that will go fetch information for you on the Information Superhighway. For example, an intelligent agent may scope out a stock you're interested in, downloading company history, today's stock quote, and culling various net articles for information — maybe even cracking into the corporate computer and downloading insider info! What a boon to stock trading! Fortunately, such software doesn't yet exist.

Sentence: Right now, my only *intelligent agent* is named Biff. He gets the paper for me in the morning and lets me know when he needs a walk. Computer programmers will never create anything more intelligent than that.

interactive

Pronunciation: *in-ter-ak-tive.*

Meaning: A program or computer that responds immediately whenever the user presses a key or does something else that the computer should respond to. Using interactive software is similar to carrying on a conversation; the user's responses change the way the system functions. In comparison, non-interactive computers tend to just sit there and do something only when they feel like it.

Sentence: "I liked learning BASIC because every time I typed a command, the computer immediately told me I did something wrong. With such an *interactive* system, it was only a matter of time before I got discouraged from using the computer altogether."

interface

Pronunciation: *int-er-fay-sa.*

Meaning: The connection between the computer and the person trying to use it. A keyboard is an interface and so is a monitor. Putting your fist through the computer can also be considered an interface. (See also *graphical user interface, user-friendly,* and *user-hostile.*)

Sentence: "Most computer *interfaces* are designed by someone who really hates people."

Intergalactic Digital Research

Pronunciation: *In-ter-ga-lak-tik Di-ji-tal Ree-sur-cha.*

Meaning: The original name of a company that came to be known as Digital Research. (See *Digital Research.*)

Sentence: "No, Perkins, I believe they just shortened their name from *Intergalatic Digital Research* to Digital Research so the stock market would take them seriously. I doubt if the Mulvanians from the Worbletyme galaxy had anything to do with it."

interlacing

Pronunciation: *int-er-lay-sing.*

Meaning: When the cathode-ray tube (CRT) of a monitor scans every other row to display information on the screen. TVs use interlacing, but computer monitors that use interlacing tend to flicker. The best computer monitors are noninterlacing. (See also *monitor.*)

Sentence: "My eyes are going to explode from my head if I keep using this lousy *interlacing* monitor."

interleaving

Pronunciation: *in-ter-lee-ving.*

Meaning: The ratio of disk sectors on a hard disk that are skipped for every sector actually used. For example, an interleave of 3:1 means the disk writes to a sector, skips three sectors, and writes to the other sector. The interleave is usually set by the hard disk manufacturer, and you can change it with special programs if you know what you're doing. (See also *fragmentation.*)

Sentence: "Today's hard disks are so fast (and the computers are fast, too) that *interleaving* isn't even done any more."

Internet

Pronunciation: *In-ter-net.*

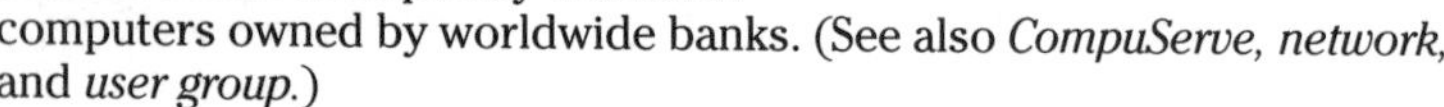

Meaning: A worldwide computer network available via modem that connects universities, government laboratories, and individuals around the world. Users of Internet can send each other electronic mail, copy files from one another, break into other people's computers, and electronically transfer funds from poorly defended computers owned by worldwide banks. (See also *CompuServe, network,* and *user group.*)

Sentence: "The *Internet* could be the so-called 'Information Superhighway' if only it were paved. And if it had some rules of the road. And maybe if it were heavily patrolled."

Internet address

Pronunciation: *In-ter-net ad-ress.*

Meaning: The electronic location of someone on the Internet, his or her mailing adress. Internet addresses start with the person's name, logon name, or nickname, followed by an @ (at) sign, then the name of a computer, a dot, then a domain. For example:

dang@idgbooks.com

This is pronounced "dang at idg books dot com." dang is the user's name (Dan Gookin, in this case). Then comes the @, then idgbooks (the company name), and then dot com, because IDG Books is a company. (See *domain.*)

Some addresses may get quite complex, having lots of dots and numbers, depending on how easily someone wants to be reached.

Sentence: "Having an *Internet address* on your business card is a high status symbol for the '90s."

interpreted language

Pronunciation: *in-ter-preh-ted lan-gwage.*

Meaning: A programming language where the computer reads the program statements one at a time and then follows the instructions.

Common interpreted languages are BASIC, LISP, Prolog, and LOGO, although C and Pascal also can be interpreted. (See also *compile, compiler, interpreter,* and *language.*)

Sentence: "*Interpreted languages* run slower than compiled languages because the computer has to read each statement, follow its instruction, and then read the next statement. This is like trying to read a French novel by reading a word to a translator, waiting for him to tell you what it means in English, and then reading another word."

interpreter

Pronunciation: *in-ter-pret-ter.*

Meaning: A program that reads statements written in a programming language, such as BASIC, and immediately follows the instructions. An interpreter is usually easier for learning a language because it gives you immediate feedback. The disadvantage is that other people can't use your programs unless they also have a copy of your program's interpreter. (See also *compile, compiler, interpreted language,* and *language.*)

Sentence: "To help her understand DOS, Doris hired an *interpreter.*"

interrupt

Pronunciation: *in-ter-rup-ta.*

Meaning: An instruction that rudely butts in, stops the computer from whatever it's doing, and makes it do something completely different. Whenever you press the Ctrl-Alt-Del key combination, you're causing an interrupt that restarts the computer. People also talk about hardware interrupts on DOS machines, particularly in terms of interrupt requests (IRQs). Trust us: you don't want to get into this on your own; consult your local guru for help. (See also *warm boot.*)

Sentence: "An *interrupt* may be rude, but you often can't write a program without one."

invalid

Pronunciation: *in-val-id.*

Meaning: Not valid. Not true. No way. No how. Uh-uh. I mean, not only are you wrong, but your intention is misguided and possibly diabolical. Don't get ridiculous on me, now.

Sentence: "The notion that the IRS owes you money is *invalid.*"

inverse text

Pronunciation: *in-ver-sa tex-ta.*

Meaning: Letters that appear white against a dark background. In comparison, normal text appears as black letters against a light background. (See also *text.*)

Sentence: "I like using *inverse text* for special emphasis, like when I'm writing blackmail notes to my enemies."

IRC

Pronunciation: *Eye Are See*

Meaning: Acronym for *Internet Relay Chat,* an on-line, live method to chat real-time with other users on the Internet.

Sentence: Last night I used *IRC* and today I now know that boring people are using the Internet all over the world.

IRQ

Pronunciation: *Eye Are Kyoo.*

Meaning: An interrupt request line in a PC. The IRQ is used by hardware devices to let the microprocessor know that they're ready to do something or that they have done something. Normally, you shouldn't clutter your head with such a bizarre term. However, on a PC, there are only a given number of IRQ lines. These get snatched up by optional hardware devices quickly. So after adding a network adapter, sound card, and mouse, your computer runs out of IRQs and, though you may have expansion slots galore, you can't add anything new.

Sentence: "A Pentium computer may be powerful, speedy, and advanced, but it's still limited by the same inane *IRQ* problems as the old IBM PC AT."

ISA

Pronunciation: *I Ess Ay,* or *I-suh.*

Meaning: Acronym for *Industry Standard Architecture*, which is the type of bus originally used in the IBM AT. Most IBM-compatible computers use either an ISA, an EISA, or an MCA bus. (See also *bus, EISA, IBM AT,* and *MCA.*)

Sentence: "If you buy an expansion board for IBM computers, make sure it follows the *ISA* standard. Otherwise, it won't work in my computer, and then I'll make you buy me another one."

ISAM

Pronunciation: *I Ess Ay EM* or *I-Sam.*

Meaning: Acronym for *Indexed Sequential Access Method*, which is a technique for storing and retrieving data efficiently using "tables" and "indexes." ISAM is often used by database programs. (See also *database.*)

Sentence: "*ISAM,* Sam I am. And I still don't like the darn green eggs and ham!"

ISDN

Pronunciation: *I Ess Dee En.*

Meaning: Acronym for *Integrated Services Digital Network*, a very futuristic, international telecommunications standard. An ISDN phone line enables you to send data, video, and voice over the same phone line.

Sentence: "With so many modem standards and speeds on the market these days, I'm looking forward to the day when every phone will follow the *ISDN* standard. That way I won't have to use a modem to connect my computer to another one"

ISO

Pronunciation: *I Ess Oh.*

Meaning: Acronym for *International Standards Organization*, which is a group that tries to set standards for lots of different industries. In the computer world, the ISO has defined the standard for the Pascal language, often called ISO Pascal. Unfortunately, the most popular version of Pascal, Turbo Pascal, ignores the ISO standard altogether. So much for standards. (See also *Pascal.*)

Sentence: "Turbo Pascal can't run programs that follow the *ISO* Pascal standard. So much for standards."

italic

Pronunciation: *i-tal-ik.*

Meaning: A type style that slants text to the right for special emphasis. (See also *font, text,* and *typeface.*)

Sentence: "Please use *italics* and not underline. Underlined text is what they use at the DMV when they want to get creative."

iteration

Pronunciation: *it-er-ray-shin.*

Meaning: The repetition of a statement in a program, often called a loop, or, if something goes terribly wrong, an endless loop. (See also *endless loop, infinite loop,* and *loop.*)

Sentence: "The most useless statements in a program are those that are never used. The most valuable statements are those used in several *iterations,* because if something is wrong with those statements, your program has more than one chance to crash."

jack

Pronunciation: *ja-ka.*

Meaning: A place to plug in electrical wires.

Sentence: "Hey, Jack, plug that red wire into the *jack* over there. And don't electrocute yourself in the process."

jacket

Pronunciation: *ja-ket.*

Meaning: The plastic, square case that protects a floppy disk from dirt, fingerprints, and other forms of physical damage short of gunshots, fire, or hydrochloric acid. (See also *floppy disk.*)

Sentence: "Hold a floppy disk by the *jacket.* If you touch the actual floppy disk surface, you may ruin the disk (and possibly go to jail)."

jaggies

Pronunciation: *jag-gees.*

Meaning: When curved drawings or letters look like tiny little steps that combine to give the illusion of a curve. (See also *alias, aliasing,* and *dithering.*)

Sentence: "If you make the letter *O* too big, you'll notice little *jaggies* all around the edges."

job

Pronunciation: *jawb.*

Meaning: A task that the computer is supposed to do whenever it gets around to doing it. (See also *queue.*)

Sentence: "This computer's running so slowly because it has so many *jobs* backed up in the queue. Let's fire a few and start the whole thing over again."

join

Pronunciation: *joyn.*

Meaning: A term used when a relational database cross-references two files. (See also *database* and *relational database.*)

Sentence: "Instead of typing the same information over and over again, just store it in separate files and *join* them when you need them. If that doesn't work, then type the same information over and over again."

joystick

Pronunciation: *joy-stik.*

Meaning: A little stick that swivels around in a base. Moving the stick moves a something-or-other around the screen.

Sentence: "When you buy a flight simulator program, you have to buy a *joystick* so that it feels like you're really flying the airplane. After all, how many pilots fly an F-16 using a keyboard?"

JPEG

Pronunciation: *Jay Pee Ee Gee* or sometimes *Jay-peg.*

Meaning: A new, universal graphic standard designed to replace the old GIF graphic standard. While GIF files can contain up to 256 colors, JPEG files (which stands for *Joint Photographic Experts Group*) can display up to 16 million colors in a single graphic image. For storing digitized photographs, the JPEG standard offers sharper resolution, but the older .GIF standard works better for plain line drawings or clip art. JPEG files usually have the .JPG file extension.

Sentence: "I took a picture of my boss picking her nose, scanned it into my computer, and submitted it as a *JPEG* file on the Internet so everyone will know what an idiot my boss really is."

Jughead

Pronunciation: *Jug-hed.*

Meaning: (1) One with such prominent ears that his or her head resembles the outline of a jug. (2) A software tool used to search various Gopher servers from only one area of gopherspace — for example, looking for stuff only at the local university. See also *Gopher.*

Sentence: "My Mom told me to get my nose out of comic books and learn the computer. Now I'm surfing the net and using Archie, Veronica, and *Jughead.* How far have we come, really?"

Julian

Pronunciation: *Joo-lee-on.*

Meaning: A method to simplify computing dates. In the Julian system, every day has a unique number. Day 1 represents January 1, 4713 B.C. Day 2448299 represents February 11, 1991. Programmers often use the Julian system for representing dates because it's easy for computers to handle. If you try guessing the date 100 days from January 23, 1964, you'll see how clumsy our ordinary calendar system can be.

Sentence: "My son was born on February 11, 1991, or 2448299 if you use the *Julian* system."

julienne

Pronunciation: *joo-lee-en.*

Meaning: Meat or vegetables cut into long, thin strips. Most commonly known as part of the term "julienne fries."

Sentence: "My spreadsheet has a function that converts dates into *julienne* fries."

jump

Pronunciation: *jumpa.*

Meaning: The impulsive act that takes place when a program follows a series of instructions one by one and then suddenly starts following instructions somewhere else. If someone drops an ice cube down your shorts, you'll jump, too. (See also *GOTO.*)

Sentence: "If you're programming in assembly language, you have to use the *jump* command a lot, abbreviated as JMP. In other languages, a jump often is called a GOTO command."

jumper

Pronunciation: *jum-per.*

Meaning: A small, plastic, rectangular-shaped plug found on circuit boards. Usually, a two- or three-prong pin sticks out of the circuit board, and the jumper slides over these pins. (See also *DIP switch.*)

Sentence: "You can modify your computer by changing one or two *jumpers.* Just make sure you know what you're doing and how to reverse anything you do."

junk

Pronunciation: *junk.*

Meaning: The stuff that seems to pop up magically around every computer.

Sentence: "Most computers act as *junk* magnets."

justify

Pronunciation: *just-i-fy.*

Meaning: To align text within the margins of a page, either left, right, center, or justified. Many people call alignment *justification.*

This is text using left alignment.	This is text using center alignment.	This is text using right alignment.

Sentence: "It's hard to *justify* the use of right justification in any document because it looks so strange. In most documents, you left-justify text and center-align headlines."

K

Pronunciation: *Kay* or *Kill-a-Bite.*

Meaning: An acronym for *kilobyte* (or 1,024 bytes) — sometimes abbreviated as *KB.* Used as a measure of the storage capacity of disks and memory. Because one byte equals one character, 1K of memory stores 1,024 characters. (See also *MB.*)

Sentence: "Robbie was disappointed to find out his computer didn't come with any memory. When he read 0*K*, he thought it meant the computer was 'okay.'"

Kb

Pronunciation: *Kay-bee* or *Kill-a-bitz.*

Meaning: An acronym for *kilobit,* or 1,024 bits — not bytes. Primarily used on computer memory chips.

Sentence: "For some reason you need eight 256*Kb* chips to get 256K of RAM. The computer industry defies logic."

K&R

Pronunciation: *Kay and Ar.*

Meaning: Abbreviation for Brian Kernighan and Dennis Ritchie, authors of the book *The C Programming Language.* For the longest time, this book was the only specification for the C language. Many C compilers used to claim to follow the K&R language specification. Later, ANSI came up with a new standard. (See also *C* and *ANSI.*)

Sentence: "All praise and glory be to *K&R*! Om!"

Kentucky Fried Computers

Pronunciation: *Kain-tuk-kee Fri-da Kom-pew-ters.*

Meaning: The name of an early computer manufacturer, whimsically named after the famous Kentucky Fried Chicken franchise. Kentucky Fried Computers eventually went out of business in the early days of the computer industry.

Sentence: "I had an old *Kentucky Fried Computers* original recipe model. Then my power supply blew, and it turned into an extra crispy."

Kermit

Pronunciation: *Ker-mit.*

Meaning: A method (or protocol) for transferring files that was named after Miss Piggy's boyfriend, Kermit The Frog. Kermit is slower than XMODEM, but humans often use it when transferring files from mainframes because no other protocol may be available. (See also *XMODEM* and *protocol.*)

Sentence: "Yes, *Kermit* The Protocol is named after Kermit The Frog."

kernel

Pronunciation: *ker-null.*

Meaning: A term used by programmers to describe the main or core part of a program.

Sentence: "This is a chicken operating system. Its *kernel* must be named Sanders."

kerning

Pronunciation: *ker-ning* (rhymes with burning).

Meaning: The art of adjusting the spacing between letters so that they look nice together. Certain letters look better closer together than others. For example, *T* and *y* can fit snuggly together so that the upper part of the *T* hangs slightly over the *y*. Kerning is used most often in word processors and desktop publishing programs when exact spacing of letters is important or when the boss just wants to give people something tedious to worry about.

Sentence: "Jacob used too much *kerning* to tighten up his paragraph, and the word *of* became *fo*."

key

Pronunciation: *kee.*

Meaning: (1) A button on the keyboard. (2) A password needed to decrypt or encrypt a file. (3) The item used for searching and sorting a database. If you're searching for all the names and addresses of everyone who lives in California, California (CA) is the key. (4) The guy who wrote the Star Spangled Banner.

Sentence: "The *key* to life is to be a nice person."

Key Caps

Pronunciation: *Kee Kaps.*

Meaning: A Macintosh program that shows you the characters you can produce by typing different keystroke combinations. The Key Caps program appears in the Apple menu and displays the keyboard along with any characters you type.

Sentence: "Mary was disappointed that the *Key Caps* program didn't have the little fez she wanted for the Enter key."

keyboard

Pronunciation: *kee-bored.*

Meaning: A device that looks like a typewriter and that is connected to the computer. When the user presses a key, the keyboard sends a signal to the computer, which displays the corresponding character on the screen.

Sentence: "Too many computer *keyboards* feel like a cheap toy typewriter. Others feel so mushy that it seems like you're typing on a spoiled banana."

keyboard buffer

Pronunciation: *kee-bored buf-fer.*

Meaning: An area of memory set aside to hold a specified number of keystrokes in case you type faster than the computer's response time. Once you stop typing, the keyboard buffer feeds the computer the remaining keystrokes stored in the buffer. (See also *buffer* and *print buffer.*)

Sentence: "With a big *keyboard buffer,* I can keep typing until my fingers tie themselves in knots."

keyboard cover

Pronunciation: *kee-bored kuh-ver.*

Meaning: A clear, flexible, plastic sheet that fits over a keyboard, allowing you to type while protecting the keyboard from liquid spills, cookie crumbs, dirt particles, or crawling insects.

Sentence: "Nothing paralyzes your computer keyboard with fear like the sight of a five-year-old's hand all gloopy with peanut butter. Better buy your computer a *keyboard cover* to keep it sane."

keypad

Pronunciation: *kee-pad.*

Meaning: A related group of keys placed together for convenience. The most common keypads are the *numeric keypad* and the *cursor keypad.*

Sentence: "Ever wonder why the keys on the numeric *keypad* are arranged in neat rows and columns but the keys on the typewriter part of the keyboard are arranged like they still used mechanical levers on a manual typewriter?"

keyword

Pronunciation: *kee-werd.*

Meaning: A word that has special meaning in a programming language. For example, CALL is a BASIC keyword, CASE is a Pascal keyword, and int is a C keyword. Also, in word processing, a keyword can be the word you use in a text search.

Sentence: "*Keywords* have special meaning in programming languages just as certain four-letter words have special meaning in the English language."

KHz

Pronunciation: *Kay Ay-cha zee or kill-a-hurtz-a.*

Meaning: Abbreviation for *kilohertz.* The word *kilo* means 1,000 of something. So kilohertz must mean 1,000 hertz. And *hertz* is a term for the number of cycles per second, so a kilohertz must be the number of thousands of cycles per second. This has something to do with computers, somewhere.

Sentence: "Killa the Gorilla was a primate so fine, eating peanuts and banana creme desserts. Yet one day Killa chewed on a telephone line, so now we can say *kilohertz.*"

kill

Pronunciation: *kill* (rhymes with *Bill, pill,* and *Jack and Jill*).

Meaning: To do something destructive, such as erasing a file or crashing the computer. In UNIX, to kill a process means to end it (as in to stop a program from running). (See also *Ctrl-Alt-Del, Quit,* and *Exit.*)

Sentence: "Emily refuses to *kill* her files. She prefers to let them pass on naturally."

kilo-

Pronunciation: *kee-lo.*

Meaning: A prefix used in the metric system that means 1,000. So kilobyte means 1,000 bytes, kilogram means 1,000 grams, and kiloliter means 1,000 liters. But just to confuse matters: the binary (and onerous) nature of computers means that you can't have 1,000 bytes in a kilobyte. It's much better to use 1,024, which is the number 2 to the 10th power (like you care). Therefore, in a computer, 1K actually refers to 1,024 bytes.

Sentence: "I like measuring my weight in *kilo*grams because it makes me seem lighter than I really am."

kilobyte

(See *KB.*)

kludge

Pronunciation: *kloo-j*

Meaning: A temporary but poorly designed solution that actually works and solves a problem. Another name for software.

Sentence: "My computer didn't work, so I started soldering wires everywhere, and now it works again. It's just a *kludge,* but what the heck, it works."

knowledge base

Pronunciation: *naw-ledge bay-sa.*

Meaning: The part of an expert system that stores facts about solving a particular problem. Most knowledge bases consist of IF-THEN rules for reaching an answer. A well-designed expert system should let you change knowledge bases whenever you need to solve a different type of problem. (See also *expert system* and *artificial intelligence.*)

Sentence: "For an expert system to be trustworthy, its *knowledge base* must be current and accurate. Flossing twice a day also helps."

label

Pronunciation: *lay-bull.*

Meaning: An identifying name used in spreadsheets for a heading, and in DOS and OS/2 batch files, to mark the destination of a GOTO command. Also the name of a disk volume in MS-DOS. (See also *volume label.*)

Sentence: "In my Lotus 1-2-3 spreadsheet, I put *labels* such as TAXES OWED, MONEY STOLEN, and COST OF OVERSEAS AIRLINE TICKET to identify the meaning of the numbers listed underneath."

LAN

Pronunciation: *Lan* (rhymes with *ran, ban,* and *can*).

Meaning: Acronym for *Local Area Network,* which is a group of computers connected together to share information. Some popular LANs are Novell, LANtastic, and Banyan. (See also *network* and *wide area network.*)

Sentence: "Our network administrator's favorite C&W song is 'Stand by your *LAN.*'"

landscape orientation

Pronunciation: *land-skape or-ree-in-tay-shin.*

Meaning: Printing as if the page were turned sideways so that its width is longer than its height. In comparison, most printing is done where the width of the page is shorter than its height. This is known as portrait orientation. (See also *portrait orientation.*)

Sentence: "Maps are usually printed using *landscape orientation,* but brochures and letters usually use portrait orientation. When your printer totally screws up and chews your page into gibberish, that's known as Picasso orientation."

language

Pronunciation: *lan-gwage.*

Meaning: A specified way of using words and symbols to give the computer instructions and tell it what to do. All software is created by using a programming language. (See also *program, programmer,* and *programming language.*)

Sentence: "I tried learning to program in C, but it's much easier to use the BASIC *language* instead. It's easier still to use foul language at the computer."

laptop

Pronunciation: *lap-top.*

Meaning: A computer small enough to fit in your lap and not crush your kneecaps in the process. (See also *notebook computer* and *PC.*)

Sentence: "My *laptop* would be more comfortable if I had a bigger lap."

laser printer

Pronunciation: *lay-zer prin-ter.*

Meaning: A type of printer that uses a laser beam to generate an image and then electronically transfers it to paper. The speed of laser printers is measured in how many pages per minute (ppm) they can produce. The printing quality of laser printers is measured in dots per inch (dpi). (See also *dot-matrix, dots per inch, inkjet printer,* and *letter quality.*)

Sentence: "Mr. Spock! Set the *laser printer* on 'stun.'"

launch

Pronunciation: *lawn-cha.*

Meaning: To start a program, usually directly from an operating system. Also used in place of the terms *load* and *run.* (See also *load* and *run.*)

Sentence: "Windows must be like NASA: I can only *launch* programs on clear, sunny days when there's no wind."

LCD

Pronunciation: *Ell See Dee.*

Meaning: Acronym for *Liquid Crystal Display,* which is a display commonly used in pocket calculators, watches, and laptop computers. LCD displays consume less power than normal monitors, but they tend to look as washed-out as chalk drawings scribbled on the sidewalk in the rain. (See also *gas-plasma display* and *monitor.*)

Sentence: "It was so cold out, my laptop's *LCD* froze." (That is truly an example of nerd humor.)

leading

Pronunciation: *led-ding* (rhymes with *sledding*).

Meaning: Inserting extra space between lines of text for aesthetic purposes. The name comes from the days of printing presses when printers physically inserted thin strips of lead between lines. (See also *kerning.*)

Sentence: "Perkins! You used so much *leading* in your document it could be used as shielding in the event of a nuclear attack!"

LED

Pronunciation: *Ell Ee Dee.*

Meaning: Acronym for *Light-Emitting Diode,* which is a device that lights up when an electrical current passes through it. Many digital clocks use LEDs to display numbers.

Sentence: "My alarm clock has a big, fat, red *LED.* I can see the numbers clear across the room without my glasses. I can even feel the numbers being burned into my eyelids while I sleep."

left-justify

Pronunciation: *left-jus-ti-fi.*

Meaning: To align text flush against a left margin.

This is
an example
of left justification.

(See also *flush* and *justify.*)

Sentence: "Most word processors *left-justify* text. Only if you're weird would you want to right-justify text."

letter quality

Pronunciation: *let-ter qua-li-tee.*

Meaning: Describes printer output neat enough that it looks like it came from a typewriter. Usually refers to printing that a dot-matrix printer produces. (See also *dot-matrix, laser printer,* and *line printer.*)

Sentence: "My dot-matrix printer can produce *letter quality* printing, so the output looks like a typewriter printed it. Then again, how many people remember what a typewriter looks like?"

LF

Pronunciation: *Ell Ef.*

Meaning: Acronym for *Line Feed,* which is a signal that tells a printer to start a new line. (See also *carriage return, Enter key, linefeed, newline character,* and *Return key.*)

Sentence: "Most dot-matrix printers have an *LF* and an FF button. If you press the FF button, the printer rolls a complete page out of the printer. If you just press the LF button, the printer just moves the page up one line."

LIFO

Pronunciation: *Lie-fo* or *Ell I Ef O.*

Meaning: Acronym for *Last In First Out,* which describes a data structure used by programmers known as a stack. (See also *FIFO* and *stack.*)

Sentence: "Airlines try to board their planes *LIFO*: The last rows are boarded first and the first rows last. But when the plane lands, the people in the first rows get out first. This would work if it weren't for those morons trying to stuff those body bags they carry into the overhead bins."

light pen

Pronunciation: *lite pen.*

Meaning: A light-sensitive detector in the shape of a pen, which lets you draw pictures and give input to the computer from the screen. (See also *I/O, input, interface, keyboard,* and *mouse.*)

Sentence: "Aha, Darth Vader! My *light pen* is mighter than your light sabre!"

line editor

Pronunciation: *line ed-i-ter.*

Meaning: A program that enables you to modify one line of a text file at a time, which is like trying to paint a wall through venetian blinds. (See also *editor.*)

Sentence: "The most infamous *line editor* of all time was one that came with MS-DOS called EDLIN. Pray you never have to use it."

line number

Pronunciation: *line num-ber.*

Meaning: A number used to identify lines in a document. The first line is number 1, the second line is number 2, and so on. To move to a specific line in a document, you would tell the computer to "Please show me line number 35."

Sentence: "Every word processor keeps track of *line numbers.* Then again, when was the last time you remembered that the information you need is on line number 35,819?"

line printer

Pronunciation: *line prin-ter.*

Meaning: A high-speed printer that can print an entire line at once. Line printers are great for printing quick drafts, but they're terrible for printing nice print. (See also *dot-matrix, laser printer, letter quality,* and *printer.*)

Sentence: "The telephone company uses a *line printer* to print inaccurate phone bills more efficiently."

linefeed

Pronunciation: *line-feed.*

Meaning: Sometimes abbreviated as LF, this is a signal that tells the printer to advance the page one line. (See also *carriage return, Enter key, LF, newline character,* and *Return key.*)

Sentence: "Bob thought installing the new printer in our little theatre would help actors who forget their lines. Now when someone forgets something on stage, we have a technician press the printer's *linefeed* button."

link

Pronunciation: *lin-ka.*

Meaning: (1) To connect two computers together through a modem, cable, or network. (2) Using Windows or OS/2, to connect two files together so that they share identical information. If you change data in one file, a hot link automatically changes the same data stored in the second file. With a cold link, changing data in one file does *not* automatically change the same data in a second file. (3) To combine multiple machine language files together to create a single program. (See also *network* and *serial communications.*)

Sentence: "After *linking* my computers with a serial cable, I linked a bunch of machine language files to make my own word processor. Then I used OS/2 to create a hot link between my word processor and my spreadsheet. Now both programs are eloping to Bermuda."

linked list

Pronunciation: *lin-ked list.*

Meaning: A data structure used by programmers to store information. The size of a linked list can change as the program runs. A linked list consists of two parts: the data and a pointer that points to the next chunk of data. Think of a linked list as a train of cars connected together. Each car holds cargo (data) and is connected (linked) to the next car. (See also *data* and *stack.*)

Sentence: "Lyle uses a *linked list* to keep track of his cuff link collection."

linker

Pronunciation: *lin-ker.*

Meaning: A special program that combines one or more machine language files and converts them to a single executable file. (See also *link.*)

Sentence: "Instead of trying to create one huge program at once, write a bunch of little ones. Then use a *linker* to combine them all into one huge, unmanageable program loaded with bugs, and sell it for $495 just like everyone else does. This is the secret of selling software."

Linotronic

Pronunciation: *Lin-o-tron-ik.*

Meaning: The brand name for a typesetting machine used by many book and magazine publishers. A Linotronic printer produces extremely high-quality print and makes an ordinary laser printer look like trash. (See also *laser printer.*)

Sentence: "I like printing rough drafts on my home laser printer. Then, for the final drafts, I print on a *Linotronic* machine."

LISP

Pronunciation: *Lisp* (rhymes with *crisp*).

Meaning: An acronym for *LISt Processing*, a language developed in the early '60s at MIT for artificial intelligence research. LISP code includes an incredible number of parentheses. Related dialects include Common LISP and Scheme. Typical LISP applications include computer learning, natural language processing, and understanding why people bother getting a Ph.D. in computer science when rock stars with third-grade educations make millions by singing one hit single. (See also *artificial intelligence* and *language.*)

Sentence: "Unlike other languages, *LISP* programs can modify themselves while they're running, which means programs can really run completely out of control. And this is called artificial intelligence."

list

Pronunciation: *list* (rhymes with *mist*).

Meaning: A collection of data arranged in a certain order. Programs usually store lists as arrays or as a linked list. A phone book is a list of names and numbers. A grocery list is also a list. (See also *array, database,* and *linked list.*)

Sentence: "My program was supposed to alphabetize my *list* of names and addresses. The only question now is, which alphabet did it use?"

list box

Pronunciation: *list boks.*

Meaning: A dialog box that displays a list of items. Items commonly found in a list box include filenames, printer names, directories, groceries, or anything else the computer thinks you might want. (See also *dialog box.*)

Sentence: "Yes, Cedric, the *list box* is the one tilting starboard."

lite

Pronunciation: *light.*

Meaning: (1) A version that lacks all the features of the full-powered model. For example, a word processor may have a "lite" version, one that's still compatible but lacks a lot of the features and cost of the original. (2) Tastes great, less filling.

Sentence: "I fly 2,000 miles on a moment's notice to fix your network, and you offer me a *lite* database file?"

load

Pronunciation: *lode* (rhymes with *node*).

Meaning: To transfer data from storage to memory in the computer. (See also *launch* and *run.*)

Sentence: "The word *load* is being replaced by the word 'open' in computer vernacular. Load is a bit burdensome, don't you think?"

local bus

Pronunciation: *lo-kul bus.*

Meaning: A type of high-speed expansion slot for a PC, one that connects directly with the microprocessor. The advantage here is that devices connected to the local bus run much faster because they have a larger pipe through which they can yell at the CPU. Typical devices connected to a local bus include high-speed video cards and hard drives. (See also *bus, expansion slot, PCI,* and *VESA.*)

Sentence: "No, this bus doesn't go to Video City. You need to take the *local bus.*"

LocalTalk

Pronunciation: *Low-kul Tawk.*

Meaning: The connectors and cables that Apple Computer makes for AppleTalk networks. (See also *Apple Computer, AppleTalk,* and *network.*)

Sentence: "*LocalTalk* once again proves that Apple Computer hates to name anything with a space in the middle."

local variable

Pronunciation: *low-kal var-e-ay-bull.*

Meaning: A term that programmers use to describe data isolated in certain parts of a program. A variable is a fancy label, such as letters or numbers, for programs to assign to values. (See also *variable.*)

Sentence: "Oh, him? He's just a *local variable.* But someday, soon, he'll have saved enough money to move up to the high status of being a global variable."

lock

Pronunciation: *lah-ka.*

Meaning: To prevent access to something. Some computers have a key lock that you can use to prevent others from using your computer. Every 3½-inch floppy disk has a sliding tab that can prevent the disk from being written to. (See also *password.*)

Sentence: "As we sailed our tanker through the locks, I *locked* my 3½-inch floppy disk and turned my key in the computer lock so that no one would mess up my work until I returned. Then our ship sank."

log

Pronunciation: *log* (rhymes with *dog*, *bog*, and *cog*).

Meaning: Abbreviation for *LOGarithm*, which is a mathematical function that fulfills an important role in some people's lives.

Sentence: "When we learned about *logs* in math class, I was sawing logs in the back of the class."

logic

Pronunciation: *lah-jik.*

Meaning: The main ingredient lacking in every computer manual in existence.

Sentence: "*Logic* is a little bird, tweeting in the meadow."

logic board

(See *motherboard.*)

logic bomb

Pronunciation: *lah-jik bahm.*

Meaning: A secret part of a program that erases files or causes other destructive damage upon activation. Disgruntled employees wishing to wreak revenge on their former employers are usually the ones responsible for placing logic bombs. (See also *virus.*)

Sentence: "Can you believe I got fired? I got so mad that I put *logic bombs* in all my programs. One year from today, they'll erase everyone's hard disk."

logical drive

Pronunciation: *lah-ji-kol drive.*

Meaning: A way to partition a large single drive into smaller, "pretend" segments for the convenience of the user or the computer. Logical drives are rarely physical drives such as floppy or hard drives. Often, a single hard drive may be divided into two or more logical drives, such as drive C:, drive H:, and drive Z:. (See also *hard disk* and *partition.*)

Sentence: "Obviously, Watson, we'll make sense of all this when we locate the subject's *logical drive.*"

logical operator

Pronunciation: *lah-ji-kal op-er-ray-ter.*

Meaning: A symbol used in programming languages, spreadsheets, and databases for defining the relationship between two items. Examples of logical operators include AND, OR, and NOT. If you were using a database, you might want to find all the names of people who make over $50,000 a year AND who are interested in yachts. Or you might want the phone numbers of everyone in Wisconsin OR New York. Then again, you might want the ages of everyone who owns a car but NOT a foreign car. (See also *inclusive OR* and *operator.*)

Sentence: "That was when the *logical operator* told me it makes more sense to dial long distance at night, when the rates are cheaper."

log in

Pronunciation: *lahg in.*

Meaning: (1) To connect to another computer or computer network to access its information. (See also *access time* and *log on.*) (2) What a UNIX programmer says before sex.

Sentence: "I have to *log in* by typing an account name and a correct password. If that fails, I'll wait until you have to visit the water cooler, and I'll use your PC."

LOGO

Pronunciation: *Lo-go.*

Meaning: A programming language specifically designed for teaching children how to use a computer. Users commonly write LOGO programs to control an imaginary turtle that moves around the screen and draws lines behind it. By writing LOGO commands to control the turtle, users can create neat little designs that impress adults as well. (See also *language.*)

Sentence: "When I was a kid, I learned about computers by learning *LOGO.* Then, in elementary school, I learned BASIC. In high school, I learned Pascal. In college, I learned C. Now I have a degree in programming and I work at a 7-11."

log on

Pronunciation: *lahg on.*

Meaning: To initially connect to a computer. (See also *access time* and *log in.*)

Sentence: "I can *log on* to any computer in the world with my modem. Of course, unless I have the right passwords, I can log in to only some of those computers."

loop

Pronunciation: *loop* (like Fruit Loops).

Meaning: A set of statements in a program running repeatedly. (See also *endless loop* and *infinite loop.*)

Sentence: "When your computer spews out the same message over and over, it's stuck in a *loop.*"

lost cluster

Pronunciation: *law-sta klus-ter.*

Meaning: Part of a file that remains on the disk, even though the DOS file allocation table (FAT) has no record of its existence. Lost clusters usually occur when the computer is writing a file to the disk and the power fails. Sometimes lost clusters seem to occur without reason, which is the way most computer problems seem to appear. You can use the CHKDSK /F command in MS-DOS to convert lost clusters into files that you can delete to conserve disk space. (See also *FAT.*)

Sentence: "I was cleaning behind my computer desk and there, amidst all the cables and dust, I found a bunch of *lost clusters.*"

low-level format

Pronunciation: *lo-leh-vel for-mat.*

Meaning: To arrange the pattern of magnetic tracks and sectors of a hard disk. Low-level formats are often unnecessary and may be used only on a new hard disk for the first time. After performing a low-level format on a new hard disk, you then must use the MS-DOS FORMAT command to perform a high-level format. (See also *format.*)

Sentence: "You shouldn't *low-level format* your hard drive here. No, do it in the basement like everyone else."

low resolution

Pronunciation: *lo re-zo-loo-shin.*

Meaning: On printers or computer monitors, low resolution is a mode that produces quick results but poorly drawn images that are likely to hurt your eyes and give you headaches to boot. (See also *high resolution, monitor, printer,* and *resolution.*)

Sentence: "I have an old, *low resolution* monitor. The letters on the screen look jagged and fuzzy, and the money I saved by buying a cheap monitor is going to my doctor to pay for new eyeglasses."

lowercase

Pronunciation: *lo-wer-kase.*

Meaning: The opposite of capitalization. Most text appears with the initial letter of a word in a sentence in uppercase and the rest of the text in lowercase. (See also *uppercase.*)

Sentence: "Don't type IN ALL UPPERCASE BECAUSE IT LOOKS OBNOXIOUS. Then again, don't type in all *lowercase* because it looks like you're trying to rip off e.e. cummings."

LPT

Pronunciation: *Ell Pee Tee.*

Meaning: In MS-DOS, the name given to the parallel ports of the computer. The first parallel port is called LPT1:, the second LPT2:, and so on. (See also *parallel port.*)

Sentence: "*LPT* is most likely a contraction of the words 'line printer,' though it's a pretty lame one."

lurker

Pronunciation: loor-ker.

Meaning: Someone who reads messages in an on-line public forum or on-line chat but does not participate.

Sentence: Most net users are *lurkers.* Even those who post usually start out as lurkers.

LZH

Pronunciation: *Ell Zee Aych.*

Meaning: Acronym for *Lempel-Zev Huffman,* a standard for compressing information, such as the binary information found in most computer files. The LZH algorithm is used by popular disk back-up programs, disk compression programs, and various diet clinics.

Sentence: "Margie got confused. She thought she could decompress an *LZH* file by adding water."

M&Ms

Pronunciation: *Em-en-Emz.*

Meaning: Candy-covered chocolates with little *M*s on them that don't melt in your hand. Primary source of nourishment for programmers. Belongs to the food group: Candy. Other food groups include Pizza, Caffeine, and Processed Potato Foods (for example, chips).

Sentence: "Hey, isn't it about time for dinner? Pass me the *M&Ms,* will ya?"

Mac

(See *Macintosh.*)

machine independent

Pronunciation: *ma-sheen in-dee-pen-dunt.*

Meaning: Commonly used to refer to a program that runs on any computer without modification. A machine independent program can be developed on an IBM clone and used — without any modifications — on a Macintosh, for example.

Sentence: "*Machine independent* programs do not exist."

machine language

Pronunciation: *ma-sheen lang-wedge.*

Meaning: A "low-level" computer language that communicates directly with the computer hardware. Programs are written in secret code (binary); each instruction corresponds to a single computer operation. Often, an assembly language is used to make the machine language codes more understandable by computer programmers — but that's not saying much because the whole thing is hard, hard, hard. Programming in machine language is not for beginners, no way! (See also *assembly language.*)

Sentence: "Real programmers use *machine language,* but they also tend to grunt and point at the dinner table."

Macintosh

Pronunciation: *Mak-en-tah-sha.*

Meaning: A family of personal computers created by Apple Computer in 1984 that features a graphical user interface. The Mac was the first computer to offer a 32-bit microprocessor. More importantly, the application program interface (API) gives users ease of use and reduced learning time. The Macintosh family is the largest non-IBM-compatible personal computer series in use. (See also *Quadra, System 7, DA, API,* and *graphical user interface.*)

Sentence: "Windows is Microsoft's effort to make the PC work like a *Macintosh.*"

macro

Pronunciation: *ma-kro.*

Meaning: A "high-level" programming tool used to automate tasks or procedures within a program. Unlike standard programming languages, macros work only within specific programs. For example, an Excel macro works only within Microsoft Excel to automate complex, repetitious, or boring tasks. Users often can create macros without knowing any programming, by simply "recording" their actions (mouse movements, keystrokes, and so on) within the program. The macro command then "plays back" the recorded movements. Voilà. A macro! Advanced macros can be used to create custom applications that run within a program. For example, an Excel macro might provide custom commands and automate lengthy procedures for balancing your checkbook. A person using the checkbook macro does not have to know much about using Excel. (See also *macro instruction.)*

Sentence: "Hey, Phil, I finally finished that *macro* that automatically fouls up everyone's phone bill!"

macro assembler

Pronunciation: *mak-ro ah-sem-blur.*

Meaning: A program that lets you construct assembly language macros. An assembly language macro is an instruction that represents several other machine language instructions at once — like shorthand for programming geeks. By using the macro instruction, the programmer doesn't have to type as much, and it leaves one hand free to dive into the Doritos. (See also *machine language* and *assembly language.*)

Sentence: "I got a *macro assembler* to speed up my machine language programming. Now I can write my program in three years instead of five."

macro instruction

Pronunciation: *ma-kro in-struk-shun.*

Meaning: An individual command used in a macro. A collection of macro instructions is usually required for a complete macro. (See also *macro.*)

Sentence: "Do you know the *macro instruction* that tells this program to make toast?"

magnetic disk

Pronunciation: *mag-ne-tik dis-ka.*

Meaning: A medium (that is, a "flat round thing") on which computer data is stored. Often called a floppy disk or hard disk, a magnetic disk is a surface coated with iron oxide and magnetically charged; bits (electronic charges) of computer data can be stored on the disk for future use. Floppy disks also make great cocktail coasters and impromptu frisbees. Never use a magnetic disk to play tug-of-war with your dog. Keep all magnetic disks away from magnetic charges, such as those spewing from your stereo speakers and the planet Jupiter. (See also *disk, hard disk, floppy disk, double-density disk,* and *high density.*)

Sentence: "The instructions said to store my *magnetic disks* in an out-of-the-way place, so I put them in the toaster."

magneto-optical disk

Pronunciation: *mag-net-o op-ti-cal dis-ka.*

Meaning: A type of storage device that combines optical-disk technology with magnetic-disk technology to make a disk capable of storing lots of information at relatively slow speeds. These high-capacity disks require special disk drives and extra toil. (See also *disk* and *high density.*)

Sentence: "I am now on the cutting edge of technology with this new *magneto-optical disk.* My data will certainly survive a nuclear attack, but it may take until then for my program to load."

mail merge

Pronunciation: *may-l mur-ja.*

Meaning: A process by which names and addresses are combined with a form letter "master" to create those personalized form letters despised by all. When the master form letter is printed, names and addresses from the mail merge list are inserted into key locations. Each name and address creates a new form letter from the master.

Sentence: "I just got a personal letter from Ed McMahon. You don't suppose he has a *mail merge* program, do you?"

mailbox

Pronunciation: *may-l bok-sa.*

Meaning: An e-mail account or "address" to which you can send messages to people on networked or remote computers. An electronic mailbox can store your electronic mail, much the way the mailbox on the front porch stores your junk mail. (See also *e-mail, handle, network,* and *e-mail address.*)

Sentence: "I just got an electronic *mailbox;* now I can get bills on my computer, too!"

mainframe

Pronunciation: *may-na-fray-ma.*

Meaning: A powerful computer to which "dumb" terminals are often connected. A mainframe is identified by its storage and computing capacity; its capability to create multiple, virtual computers; and its variety of input/output options. Mainframe computers also are called the dinosaurs of the computer industry. They require cool climates (air conditioning), open spaces, and plenty of electricity. (See also *VAX, PC, Cray, SQL,* and *dumb terminal.*)

Sentence: "We keep our company data on a *mainframe,* but all our employees want their own personal computers. So we got them each a mainframe."

male connector

Pronunciation: *may-l kon-nek-ter.*

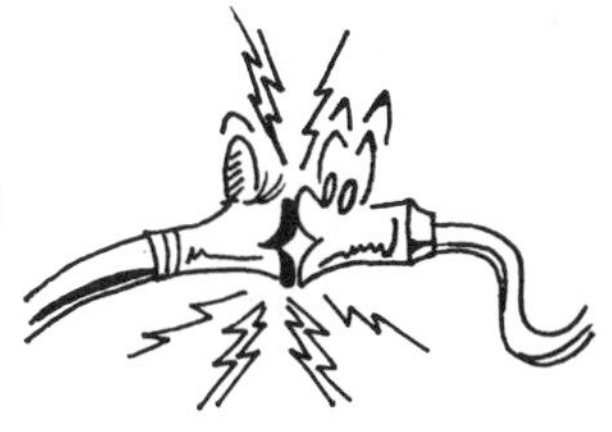

Meaning: Any type of connector that inserts into a female connector. Male connectors are often located at the ends of cables and generally have prongs or wires that fit into the holes of the female connector (I'm blushing). After combining a male and a female connector, you have a flow of electricity (occasionally accompanied by sparks flying), a surge of power, and, finally, a cigarette (optional). Please practice safe cable connection. (See also *female connector, serial, serial port, parallel,* and *parallel port.*)

Sentence: "You're trying to fit that serial *male connector* into a parallel female connector. It will never work out; they're not meant for each other."

mapping software

Pronunciation: *ma-ping soft-wayr.*

Meaning: Software that enables you to create and store maps. Maps can be viewed at different magnification factors and usually require a significant amount of disk space to store.

Sentence: "It's a good thing I brought my portable computer and *mapping software* on this road trip. Now I can get lost in half the time."

masochist

Pronunciation: *mas-o-kist.*

Meaning: (1) A person who inflicts pain on himself or herself. (2) Anyone who tries to use Windows with less than 4MB of RAM. (3) Anyone who uses WordPerfect for DOS.

Sentence: "They asked at the job interview whether I could use WordPerfect for DOS. I said, 'What do you think I am, a *masochist?*'"

mass storage

Pronunciation: *mas stor-edge.*

Meaning: A high-capacity storage device. Because normal disk capacity has increased over the years, the definition of mass storage is somewhat loose. Typical hard disk drives store at least 80 megabytes of data; mass storage is generally considered to be at least 250 megabytes of data. However, mass storage devices can hold over one *terabyte* (one trillion bytes) of data. Mass storage has nothing to do with Catholicism. (See also *high density, byte,* and *high capacity.*)

Sentence: "Father John stores all his sermons on a *mass storage* device."

master/slave arrangement

Pronunciation: *mas-ter/slayv ah-range-men-ta.*

Meaning: When one device (a slave) is controlled by another to which it is connected (a master). Master/slave arrangements are found in disk drive arrays, other hardware configurations, and mainframes and dumb terminals. (See also *client, client/server network, network,* and *server.*)

Sentence: "When I push the remote control, the TV changes channels. It's a perfect *master/slave arrangement.*"

math coprocessor

Pronunciation: *math ko-pross-ess-er.*

Meaning: A separate circuit (or computer chip) that performs floating-point arithmetic to enhance the capabilities of the CPU (central processing unit). Math coprocessors are available for PC computers to perform math-intensive software procedures. Software is often written specifically to take advantage of a math coprocessor and may not run properly without it. (See also *central processing unit, microprocessor,* and *number crunching.*)

Sentence: "I bought a *math coprocessor* to perform calculations telling me how much time and money I spend on my computer."

matrix

Pronunciation: *may-triks.*

Meaning: A method of storing data in a grid-like thing so that each data element can be easily retrieved. To store the amount of your phone bill for each month of the year requires a one-dimensional matrix with 12 items, one item for each month of the year. To store the amounts of all your bills (phone, food, gas, and so on) requires a two-dimensional matrix, with bills down one side and months across the top. To store these values for several years requires a three-dimensional matrix, one separate grid for each year. (See also *array.*)

Sentence: "The Rubik's cube is the ultimate type of *matrix,* making computers relatively tame by comparison."

maximize

Pronunciation: *maks-im-eyes.*

Meaning: To increase to full capacity. When using Windows software, the term maximize refers to increasing the size of a window to fill the entire screen. This can be done by clicking the Maximize button or choosing Maximize from the window's control menu. (See also *minimize.*)

Sentence: "If I *maximize* the window on my checkbook program, will I maximize my income too?"

MB

Pronunciation: *Em Bee,* not pronounced *Mub.*

Meaning: An abbreviation for *megabyte.* 1,000,000 bytes of data. (See also *megabyte, byte,* and *bit.*)

Sentence: "My floppy disk holds 1.2*MB* of data, but my file is 3MB. It doesn't take a Ph.D. or M.D. to figure out that I need more MBs."

Mb (M-bit)

Pronunciation: *Em bee.*

Meaning: Acronym for *megabit.* 1,000,000 bits of data. Note the little *b.* Big *B* means bytes; little *b* means bits. There is a difference. (See also *megabit, bit,* and *nibble.*)

Sentence: "When I grew up, *Mb* meant Milton Bradley."

MCA

Pronunciation: *Em See Ay.*

Meaning: Acronym for *Micro Channel Architecture.* An expansion slot (bus) design that IBM developed for its PS/2 computers. The main idea behind the design was to enhance the speed of data transfer and to make plugging in expansion boards easier because the expansion board would automatically configure itself to the MCA slots. In reality, the purpose of MCA was to create a new bus standard that other computer manufacturers would have to pay massive royalties for if they wanted to develop MCA-compatible computers. (See also *expansion slot, expansion bus, expansion card,* and *bus.*)

Sentence: "The salesman told me that if I bought an IBM PS/2 with an *MCA* bus I would be all set for the future. He didn't know that, five years later, hardly anyone would make expansion boards for the MCA standard."

MCGA

Pronunciation: *Em See Gee Ay.*

Meaning: Acronym for *Monochrome/Color Graphics Adapter.* The IBM graphics adapter used on the PS/2 computers. This is similar to combining MGA and CGA adapters, but it also contains some special features of its own. MCGA adapters generally have been replaced by the more powerful EGA, VGA, and SVGA adapters. (See also *MDA, EGA, CGA, VGA, SVGA,* and *monochrome.*)

Sentence: "*MCGA* is a useless toad of a standard. Get Super VGA (SVGA) instead."

MDA

Pronunciation: *Em Dee Ay.*

Meaning: Acronym for *Monochrome Display Adapter.* The IBM adapter for monochrome monitors. This adapter does not provide graphics capabilities. (See also *monochrome, MCGA, EGA, CGA,* and *VGA.*)

Sentence: "*MDA* is boring black-and-white text, ladies and gentlemen. Major Yawn City."

media

Pronunciation: *mee-dee-ya.*

Meaning: Any kind of material used for data storage and communication, including magnetic media, optical media, print media, and so on. Plural of medium, a tiny lady who will cleanse your house of spirits and poltergeists. A *medium* is a carrier of information, much like your paper girl or that little voice telling you to go ahead and have a second piece of pie. (See also *disk* and *communications.*)

Sentence: "The stone tablet was among the first data storage *media.* Talk about a hard disk!"

meg

Pronunciation: *meg* (as in Ryan).

Meaning: Short for megabyte or Margaret. (See also *megabyte, MB, byte, or mega-.*)

Sentence: "Meg has a hard disk that holds 120 *megs* of data."

mega-

Pronunciation: *may-ga.*

Meaning: Prefix meaning one million. A unit of measure in the metric system. Also a slang word to designate an abundance of something, as in *mega-fun.* (See also *megabyte*, *megahertz,* and *MB.*)

Sentence: "Rush Limbaugh's CompuServe e-mail account contains 1,000,000 letters from his adoring fans. Talk about *mega*-dittos."

megabyte

Pronunciation: *may-ga-bite.*

Meaning: Approximately one million bytes. Actually, a megabyte is equal to 1,024 kilobytes, or 1,048,576 bytes. You need only be this specific on your tax form. Outside the IRS, the government has passed numerous laws declaring a megabyte to be exactly one million bytes (the 48,576 extra bytes are kept "off budget"). (See also *MB, byte, Mb,* and *bit.*)

Sentence: "Back in the early days of computing, a *megabyte* was considered way, way too much storage space. Now I need six megabytes of space just to store my shoes."

megahertz

Pronunciation: *may-ga-hurt-sa.*

Meaning: One million hertz (MHz), or one million cycles per second. Microprocessor chips oscillate (wiggle) at a certain speed, measured in cycles per second, or hertz. Besides the clock speed, the internal design of the processor determines its overall speed. (See also *hertz, MHz,* and *mega-.*)

Sentence: "The People's Republic of China has over one billion bicycles. That's 1,000 *megahertz.*"

membrane keyboard

Pronunciation: *mem-brain kee-bord.*

Meaning: A keyboard that has a flat, plastic surface (the membrane) with keys printed on it — like a cheap, flat calculator. Don't bother with this type of keyboard; it's a touch-typist's nightmare. (See also *boat anchor* and *heavy iron.*)

Sentence: "Yes, Jared, the *membrane keyboard* on your little Atari 400 makes it perhaps the silliest computer known to mankind."

memory

Pronunciation: *mem-o-ree.*

Meaning: Commonly refers to the chips inside a computer in which information is stored. Two types of internal memory exist: *read-only memory* (ROM) permanently holds information vital to the computer's operation, such as the BIOS. *Random-access memory* (RAM) holds information that you are currently using, such as your letter to the Editor or your genealogy chart. Whereas the information in ROM is permanent, the information in RAM goes away when you turn off the computer. Programs load information into RAM as needed for smooth operation. Generally, the more RAM you have, the better. If you use Windows software, you can't have too much RAM. (See also *RAM, random access, nonvolatile memory,* and *ROM.*)

Sentence: "My computer has 16 megabytes of *memory* inside, making more room for me to lose things."

memory map

Pronunciation: *mem-o-ree map.*

Meaning: A graphical depiction of how RAM is used in a computer. Actually, the memory map is for trivial purposes only, although some programmer types want to know "where in memory" some tidbit or secret switch is located. To us humans, the information is silly beyond all recourse.

Sentence: "After looking at my computer's *memory map,* I can find Silicon Valley."

memory resident program

Pronunciation: *mem-o-ree rez-i-dent pro-gram.*

Meaning: Programs that stay in memory that you can't see, laying low, when you are not using them. Memory resident programs also are called *TSRs* (Terminate-and- Stay Residents). Memory resident programs are often utilities that extend the basic functions of the computer, such as mouse drivers, fax software, and print spools. They're also often the cause of problems and conflicts in your software. (See also *terminate-and-stay resident programs.*)

Sentence: "Since the advent of Windows and other multitasking operating systems, the real need for *memory resident programs* has dwindled more rapidly than President Clinton's popularity."

menu

Pronunciation: *men-yu.*

Meaning: A list of commands or options available within a program. When several options are available at a particular time, programs often present those options in menus. The menu shows each available option and, using the mouse or keyboard, you can choose a command from the menu. Such programs are often called *menu-driven programs.* Almost all Macintosh and Windows programs are menu-driven. (See also *menu bar, menu item, pop-up menu,* and *pull-down menu.*)

Sentence: "When I want to change the fonts in my word processor, I just click the Format *menu* and choose the Font command. When I want to order lunch, I often use the Chinese menu and choose Chow Mein. You can't really get through life without knowing something about menus."

menu bar

Pronunciation: *men-yu bar.*

Meaning: An area, usually located at the top of the screen, that contains several menus listed across in a single line. It's from the menu bar that you can choose commands. You choose commands by using the keyboard, the mouse, or by asking the waiter for a translation. (See also *menu* and *menu item.*)

Sentence: "*Menu bars* usually include appetizers to make you thirsty so that you'll order more drinks."

menu item

Pronunciation: *men-yu i-tim.*

Meaning: An individual command or option that appears on a menu.

Sentence: "The File menu contains 14 *menu items,* including an Exit command. When I choose Exit, the computer gets up and walks out of the room."

menu tree

Pronunciation: *men-yu tree.*

Meaning: A diagram showing the menu structure within a program. Some menu items do not produce immediate results but "branch out" to more menus or dialog boxes. This creates a hierarchy ("Me first! No, me!") of menu commands and options. A menu tree displays this hierarchy of commands so that you can locate any command through the maze of menus. (See also *menu, menu bar,* and *menu item.*)

Sentence: "There are so many menus in this program that I need a *menu tree* to help me find the command I want."

message box

Pronunciation: *mess-ij boks.*

Meaning: A box or small window that appears on the screen and presents a message from the program you are using. Message boxes can appear as the result of your choosing a command or option. They often inform you of mistakes or provide warnings about your actions. (See also *dialog box* and *list box.*)

Sentence: "Last night I was working late on the computer, and I got a *message box* that said, 'Go to bed!'"

meta

Pronunciation: *met-uh.* ("I meta on a Monday and my heart stood still, Da-do-run-run-run, Da-do-run-run.")

Meaning: Above and beyond, from the original meaning of meta, which meant to change. In computers, meta refers to a special character combination often associated with a specific key. For example, some weird keyboards may have a shift key named META. If a program asks you to press META-S, you press and hold the META key and press S.

Sentence: "The S key makes an S on the screen; Ctrl-S saves my file; Alt-S brings up the Silly menu; and *META*-S zooms me to outer space."

MHz

Pronunciation: *May-ga-Hurtz.*

Meaning: Abbreviation for *megahertz.* In computers, the MHz number tells you how relatively fast the microprocessor is, or technically, how fast it sits and spins. So a microprocessor rated at 8 MHz is much slower than one zooming along at 90 MHz. (See also *megahertz.*)

Sentence: "They were blown away in 1984 when the IBM AT came with an 8 *MHz* microprocessor — twice as fast as the PC's 4 MHz. I bet they'd be floored back then to know we'd reach speeds of over 100 MHz in less than ten years."

Mickey Mouse

Pronunciation: *Mi-kee Mowss.*

Meaning: (1) A fictional character, created by Walt Disney, who talks in a high voice and goes easily through life with his wacky friends and his dog, Pluto. Best known works include "The Sorcerer's Apprentice" from *Fantasia* and regular appearances at Disneyland and Disney World. Also a popular export to Japan. (2) Something not quite up to snuff, or straying from the task at hand. (See also *mouse.*)

Sentence: "*Mickey Mouse* may be the world's most popular cartoon character. I like him because he doesn't take life too seriously."

micro-

Pronunciation: *my-kro.*

Meaning: A prefix that means one millionth. A microsecond is one millionth of a second. Micro is used also to imply a microscopic size, as in microorganism and microprocessor. In Microsoft, the micro means there are many millionaires working there.

Sentence: "I use Microsoft Word on my *micro*computer and can type a letter in a microsecond."

Micro Channel Architecture

Pronunciation: *My-kro Chan-l Awr-ki-tek-chur.*

Meaning: A type of expansion slot design used in IBM PS/2 model 50 (and higher) computers, abbreviated MCA. Hardware companies design computer enhancement boards (or cards) that plug into the MCA bus. Boards designed for the MCA bus do not work with a standard bus. Among other enhancements, the MCA bus allows use of multiple CPUs within the computer, although I wouldn't try that at home. (See also *bus, expansion slot, expansion bus, expansion card,* and *MCA.*)

Sentence: "I bought a computer that uses the *Micro Channel Architecture.* Now everybody is talking about the PCI bus. The problem is that most of the enhancement cards are available for the ISA bus. By the way, what type of bus did Ralph Kramden drive?"

microcomputer

Pronunciation: *my-kro-kum-pew-ter.*

Meaning: Actually intended as a disparaging term for the new personal computers that started appearing in the mid-1970s. The term *micro* came from the microprocessor, the chip that provided the brains for these new computers. The term fell into disuse when PCs became popular in the mid-1980s. (See also *PC* and *mainframe.*)

Sentence: "Most *microcomputers* of today are far more powerful than the so-called 'real' computers of 20 years ago. So let's all give a Bronx cheer to our pals in mainframe and minicomputer land: Ptbtbtbtb!"

microfloppy disk

Pronunciation: *my-kro-flop-ee dis-ka.*

Meaning: Generally refers to a $3\frac{1}{2}$-inch floppy disk, which is smaller than the widely used $5\frac{1}{4}$-inch floppy disk, which is smaller than the original 8-inch floppy disk. Actually, the original 8-inch floppy was called a *floppy* because it really had some flop to it. The $5\frac{1}{4}$-inchers were called minifloppies when they first appeared. This left microfloppy to describe the smaller $3\frac{1}{2}$-inch floppy disks. A microfloppy disk holds either 720KB or 1.22MB of data, depending on whether it is a double-density or high-density disk (respectively). (See also *magnetic disk, floppy disk,* and *disk.*)

Sentence: "I replaced my old $5\frac{1}{4}$-inch floppy disk drive with a *microfloppy disk* drive. Pretty soon, disks will be the size of a toenail and almost as chewy."

microprocessor

Pronunciation: *my-kro-pro-ses-er.*

Meaning: The central processing chip (the "brains") in a microcomputer. Common microprocessors include the Motorola 68000, 68030, and 68040 used in Macintoshes, and the Intel 286, 386, 486, and Pentium chips used in DOS machines. The microprocessor controls most of the core functions of the computer but can be enhanced with coprocessor chips. (See also *central processing unit* and *math coprocessor.*)

Sentence: "Harold is experimenting with a new *microprocessor* that actually uses human brain tissue. Sadly, Harry's using his own brain tissue, which has left him pretty much a vegetable."

microsecond

Pronunciation: *my-kro-sek-und.*

Meaning: One millionth of a second. Also used as an exaggeration to imply something that happened very quickly.

Sentence: "If you do that again, I'll be out of here in a *microsecond!*"

Microsoft

Pronunciation: *My-kro-soft.*

Meaning: (1) A large software company, located in Redmond, Washington, that produces MS-DOS, Windows, and a suite of best-selling application programs for the PC and Macintosh computers. (2) Stock I never should have sold. (3) See OZ. (4) See Federal Trade Commission. (5) Rulers of the known world. (6) Microsoft has no meaning. (See also *IBM.*)

Sentence: "Almost every program you see these days is made by *Microsoft.*"

microspacing

Pronunciation: *my-kro-spay-sing.*

Meaning: The insertion of small spaces (smaller than one character) between words to aid in justification. Used in all laser printers and some dot-matrix printers. (See also *kerning* and *justify.*)

Sentence: "My first dot-matrix printer had a *microspacing* feature that made its justified documents look more professional. Now my laser printer uses this same technique — in a much more professional fashion."

MIDI

Pronunciation: *Mid-Ee.*

Meaning: Acronym for *Musical Instrument Digital Interface.* A protocol, or standard, for encoding musical sounds in digital form. The differences in sounds and musical voices can be measured and stored using the MIDI standard and then transferred digitally between computers and MIDI-equipped instruments. Electronic keyboards commonly use MIDI.

Sentence: "Using the *MIDI* port in my electronic synthesizer, I can play music on the keyboard, and my computer transcribes the music onto the screen. Imagine what Mozart could do today."

milli-

Pronunciation: *mil-ee.*

Meaning: A prefix meaning one thousandth. One milligram equals one thousandth of a gram. Also a good (or bad?) name for a dog.

Sentence: "A *milli*second is the length of time it takes for Bill Gates to earn one million dollars in interest."

mini-tower case

Pronunciation: *mee-nee tow-ur kay-sa.*

Meaning: A type of PC case that sits up on its end on your desk. Unlike a Tower PC, the mini-tower case can sit on your desk without blocking your view. See *Tower PC.*

Sentence: "Due to zoning regulations, we can only have *mini-tower case* PCs around here. Anything taller and the neighbors complain that we block their view."

MiniFinder

Pronunciation: *Mi-nee-Find-er.*

Meaning: A piece of software for the Macintosh that makes it easy to locate your programs. You can configure the MiniFinder to access your most commonly used programs so that you don't have to search through your folders to locate them.

Sentence: "The *MiniFinder* was the most popular Mac program in Munchkinland."

minimize

Pronunciation: *min-ee-mize.*

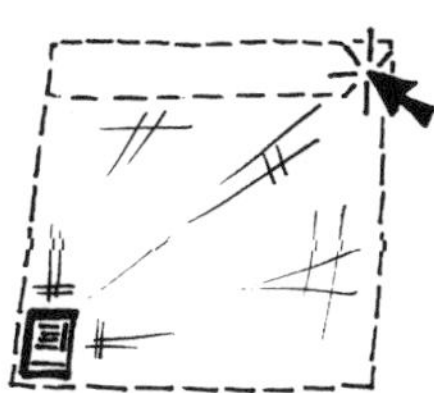

Meaning: (1) To shrink or reduce to minimum size or capacity. In Windows, minimize refers to shrinking a window to appear as an icon on the desktop. You can minimize a window by clicking the Minimize button or by using the Minimize command in the control menu. (2) To dress like Minnie Mouse. (See also *maximize.*)

Sentence: "I thought that when I *minimized* my programs, I would minimize my computer problems, too."

MIPS

Pronunciation: *Mips,* like *lips* or *hips* or chocolate *chips.*

Meaning: Acronym for *Million Instructions Per Second.* A measurement of the speed at which programs run on a particular microprocessor. Because programs are coded differently for different microprocessors, it's important to measure MIPS by using equivalent code on each machine. (See also *central processing unit* and *microprocessor.*)

Sentence: "If you toss the word *MIPS* around in conversation, as in 'my Pentium is clocked at 20,000 *MIPS,*' people will think you know what you're talking about."

MIS department

Pronunciation: *Em-Eye-Es dee-part-mint.*

Meaning: An acronym for *Management Information System*, typically followed by the word *department.* The employees in a big organization who are responsible for purchasing, running, and fixing the company's computers and software. Also called the *IS department.*

Sentence: "I called Jane from the *MIS department* to come fix my Macintosh. She told me it would work better if I would quit trying to install DOS on my machine."

mnemonic

Pronunciation: *new-mon-ik.*

Meaning: A way of naming something that helps you remember its purpose. For example, mnemonic commands can begin with the first letter of the command, as in Alt-F-S to represent the File Save command.

Sentence: "Remember that *mnemonic* starts with an M because it has to do with memory, but also remember not to pronounce the M or people will think your lips are numb."

mode

Pronunciation: *mode* (rhymes with *toad, explode,* or *freeload*).

Meaning: One of several distinct ways of running a program. For example, you can use many DOS programs either in text mode or graphics mode. In graphics mode, you can see fonts and graphics on the screen in a WYSIWYG fashion. In text mode, only the computer's built-in text characters appear. (See also *protected mode* and *WYSIWYG.*)

Sentence: "Since everything is graphics these days, people have no idea how blindingly fast their computers can be when run in text *mode*."

modem

Pronunciation: *mo-dum* (short for *modulator-demodulator*).

Meaning: A device used by your computer to communicate with remote computers through the phone lines. Modems come in various speeds, or *baud rates,* such as 1200, 2400, 9600, and 14,400. To connect to an on-line bulletin board service (BBS), you need a modem and communications software. An internal modem can be inserted inside your computer's case. An external modem can be attached to a standard RS-232 serial port. (See also *BBS, baud, fax, modem,* and *Hayes compatibility.*)

Sentence: "Some *modems* are more dumb than others."

modeming

Pronunciation: *mod-dum-ing.*

Meaning: The act of using a modem. Doing on-line communications. That kind of stuff.

Sentence: "Happy people go *modeming.*"

modifier keys

Pronunciation: *mod-i-fi-er kees.*

Meaning: Keys that work with other keys to give commands to the computer. Examples of modifier keys are Shift, Ctrl, and Alt. (See also *function keys* and *key.*)

Sentence: "If you press F7, you can save your files. If you press Shift-F7, you can print your file. And if you press Alt-F7 plus all of the other *modifier keys* at once, a magic genie appears granting your every wish (or maybe your system crashes — I forget)."

Modula-2

Pronunciation: *Mod-yu-lah-Too.*

Meaning: A structured programming language, similar to Pascal, that encourages programmers to create programs in modules. Modules are linked when the program is loaded. Pascal and Modula-2 were both created by Niklaus Wirth. (See also *language, modular,* and *programming language.*)

Sentence: "If you know how to program in Pascal, you'll find *Modula-2* an easy transition."

modular

Pronunciation: *mod-u-ler.*

Meaning: Consisting of, or relating to, individual units, or *modules.* Programs are often written in modules, or separate pieces, to make programming easier. Modular programming also allows programmers to work on different aspects of the program simultaneously. Modular programming also can enhance memory management. (See also *Modula-2.*)

Sentence: "I think this program is *modular.* Each time I do something new, it goes back to the disk to read another program module."

molecular beam epitaxy

Pronunciation: *moll-eck-yoo-lar beem ep-i-taks-ee.*

Meaning: The process by which circuits are engraved on a piece of silicon to make a semiconductor — a computer chip. This is a big, hunky word you can toss around to really impress your friends. We're not kidding. (See also *semiconductor* and *central processing unit.*)

Sentence: "The *molecular beam epitaxy* certainly vaporizes the substrate layers to form nice, crisp semiconducting material. Yessiree."

monitor

Pronunciation: *mah-ni-ter.*

Meaning: Another name for a CRT, screen, or terminal — the thing that you stare into for hours on end when using your computer. There are several types of monitors, including TTL monochrome, RGB color, analog color, and multisync. (2) A verb meaning the act of checking the progress of an activity, such as snooping around inside your PC's guts to see how things work. (See also *CRT, RGB,* and *terminal.*)

Sentence: "I was playing Solitaire on my new color multisync *monitor* when my boss came in to monitor my progress. Luckily, Windows let me task-switch to my word processor instantly."

monochrome

Pronunciation: *mah-no-krome.*

Meaning: An adjective meaning one color. Monochrome monitors display information in a single color — often green or amber — on top of black. Monochrome monitors are not capable of high-resolution graphics and are best used for text-based applications or boat anchors. (See also *MDA, EGA, CGA, VGA, MCGA, boat anchor,* and *heavy iron.*)

Sentence: "When I exit Windows to use a DOS command, my screen looks like a dull *monochrome* monitor for a while."

monospacing

Pronunciation: *mah-no-spay-sing.*

Meaning: Uniform and equal spacing between the letters of words. With monospacing, each letter of the alphabet uses the same amount of space as every other letter; an *i* uses as much space as an *m*. With proportional spacing, each letter uses only as much space as it needs. Monospacing is still used in some applications, such as business forms. Most fonts use monospacing also for numerals to aid in alignment of financial data. (See also *proportional pitch.*)

Sentence: "Lois, darling, that *monospaced* letter you did, it's *très gauche.* Get with the time, girl. Everyone is going proportionally spaced now."

Montevideo

Pronunciation: *Mont-eh-vi-day-oh.*

Meaning: The capital city of Uruguay.

Sentence: "When you're in Uruguay, be sure to visit the Library of the National Historical Museum in *Montevideo.*"

morphing

Pronunciation: *morf-ing.*

Meaning: A graphical trick where one image is smoothly blended into another. Morphing is a popular special effect, used on such films as *Terminator 2* and in various music videos. Using special graphics software, you can bring such effects to your PC. The word "morph" may also be used. It's from the Greek metamorphosis, which means "to transform."

Sentence: "I used *morphing* software to transform an image of my old, cruddy car into a brand new Dodge Viper. Now if only it could do that in real life."

MOS

Pronunciation: *Moss* (as in slimy green fungus).

Meaning: Acronym for *Metal Oxide Semiconductor.* A type of semiconductor used in computers. (See also *semiconductor* and *CMOS.*)

Sentence: "See *MOS.* CMOS run. Run, MOS, run."

motherboard

Pronunciation: *muh-ther-bored.*

Meaning: The main circuit board of a computer, to which most devices connect. The motherboard is the real estate upon which the computer's CPU, ROM chips, and often the RAM chips sit and work. It also contains the expansion slots and other electronic doodads, making it look like an electronic sushi display. (See also *daughterboard, expansion slots,* and *central processing unit.*)

Sentence: "Always do something nice for your *motherboard* on Mother's Day."

mount

Pronunciation: *moww-nt.*

Meaning: A term used to describe that something, usually a disk drive, is being used. In a networking context, mounting a volume means to connect to a remote disk drive, making it accessible from your computer. This comes from the olden computer days when they physically had to mount a reel of computer tape on the machine before anyone could access it. Nowadays, the mounting takes place through software commands that make the connections over various wires and hoses. (See also *hard disk.*)

Sentence: "Jump through the fiery network hoop, and then you can *mount* the remote H: drive and access your files."

mouse

Pronunciation: *mows.*

Meaning: A pointing device used to provide input for the computer. Most graphical user interfaces (Windows and the Macintosh) use mouse input devices. When you move the mouse on your desk, the mouse pointer on the screen mimics its movement. This allows you to control, point at, grab, and manipulate various graphics goodies (and text) in a program. (See also *track ball, joy stick, mouse button, mouse pad,* and *Mickey Mouse.*)

Sentence: "Betcha didn't know units of *mouse* movement are measured in Mic-Keys."

mouse button

Pronunciation: *mows butt-on.*

Meaning: An area on the mouse that you press in order to make things happen. When pressed, a button makes a clicking sound. PC mice have from one to three buttons, each performing different functions; the Macintosh uses a one-button mouse. By holding certain keys down as you click the button, you can perform different options — just as if you had a two-button mouse. (See also *mouse* and *mouse pad.*)

Sentence: "The program says to click the *mouse button* twice. So I figure that if I click it ten times, it'll really work great (kind of like the TV remote)."

mouse pad

Pronunciation: *mows pad.*

Meaning: A flat surface, usually padded, used to roll your mouse around. The ball on the mouse operates best on a clean, flat surface; a mouse pad is better than most people's desktop for rolling your mouse around. (See also *mouse* and *mouse button.*)

Sentence: "When finished making movies for the day, Mickey Mouse returns to his *mouse pad* to party with Minnie."

move

Pronunciation: *moov.*

Meaning as a noun: A command in many software products that lets you transfer objects or text from one location to another, as in Excel's Edit⇨Move command.

Meaning as a verb: What you do when your accountant discovers a bug in his tax software that results in an extra $20,000 you owe to the IRS. (See also *drag.*)

Sentence: "My spreadsheet calculated a negative cash flow in my budget, so I *moved* the expense column to next year's worksheet. Now I can move to a bigger house."

MPC

Pronunciation: *Em Pee See.*

Meaning: Acronym for *Multimedia Personal Computer.* A set of minimal requirements a computer system needs in order to create or use multimedia software. All MPC products are designed to work together so that you can create multimedia presentations. (See also *multimedia* and *PC.*)

Sentence: "I wanted to create a hypertext manual, so I bought an *MPC* computer, an MPC sound board, and an MPC hypertext word processor."

MPEG

Pronunciation: *Em Pee Ee Jee* or *Em-peg.*

Meaning: A computer format for storing video images. Developed by the Motion Picture Experts Group, MPEG files compress video images so that what would have been a 100MB video file on disk takes up maybe 1MB. MPEG video can also be displayed full-screen, unlike some other video formats which only appear in a small box on-screen. Unfortunately, MPEG files require specific equipment and they take a long time to compress. This standard is not related to the JPEG standard, even though the acronym guys must have lived in the same building.

Sentence: "Using *MPEG,* I was able to compress my massive 150MB home video project to take up only 1.5MB of disk space. Now I can bore my relatives and save disk space at the same time."

MPR II

Pronunciation: *Em Pee Ar Too.*

Meaning: A Swedish standard that defines the acceptable amount of electromagnetic emissions a computer monitor can safely emit without killing the person sitting in front of it.

Sentence: "Pregnant women should buy a radiation screen for their computer monitors or only buy monitors that follow the *MPR II* standard. Otherwise, your kid might wind up looking like a computer geek."

Mr. Data

Pronunciation: *Mis-ter Day-tah.*

Meaning: A fictional character from the television series *Star Trek: The Next Generation.* More frequently called Commander Data, Mr. Data is an android officer on the Starship Enterprise. He has a charming, innocent personality and is a fine example of artificial intelligence at work. (See *data, Star Trek,* and *Star Trek: The Next Generation.*)

Sentence: "I hear *Mr. Data* just installed Stacker, and he now can remember twice as many things."

MS-DOS

Pronunciation: *Em-Es-Doss.*

Meaning: Acronym for *Microsoft Disk Operating System.* The most widely used operating system for personal computers, sold also as PC-DOS by IBM. Also called simply DOS. MS-DOS is the reason why Macintosh users avoid IBM and compatible computers. To organize disks and data, it uses a tree-like directory structure wherein files can be stored inside directories and subdirectories. DOS commands include DIR, CD, COPY, DEL, RD, and so on.

For more information on MS-DOS, refer to your friendly *Dummies* book: *DOS For Dummies* by Dan Gookin, available in most 7-11 convenience stores but omitted from *US News & World Report.* (See also *disk operating system, DOS,* and *Microsoft.*)

Sentence: "When I start my computer, the screen says `Starting MS-DOS....` Then I get the DOS prompt and I type **WIN** to go right into Windows and avoid using DOS altogether."

MTBF

Pronunciation: *Em Tee Bee Ef.*

Meaning: Acronym for *Mean Time Between Failure,* used to tell someone the average life of a product such as a hard disk or laser printer.

Sentence: "This laser printer has an *MTBF* of 35,000 pages, which means if I print page 35,001, the printer should blow up on me."

MultiFinder

Pronunciation: *Mul-tee-Fine-der.*

Meaning: A part of the Macintosh operating system that organizes and provides access to your files and folders. MultiFinder is a hierarchical filing system (HFS). (See also *Chooser, Finder, hierarchical file system,* and *Macintosh.*)

Sentence: "My Macintosh is equipped with *MultiFinder,* and I still can't find a thing on my disk drive."

multimedia

Pronunciation: *Mul-tee-mee-dee-ya* (geek pronunciation: *Mul-tie-mee-dee-ya*).

Meaning: Relating to video, audio, and graphics. Multimedia software combines two or more media for presentation or analysis purposes. For example, many packages let you combine graphics with sound. Large multimedia applications are often stored on CD-ROM devices because of their incredible size and memory requirements. Multimedia will likely be common in the future for all sorts of information retrieval. (See also *communications* and *MPC.*)

Sentence: "I have a *multimedia* version of the encyclopedia. To explain the topics, the software plays movie clips, plays music, and shows graphics and artwork. Some day, it will write my term papers for me, too."

multiplexing

Pronunciation: *mul-tee-plex-ing.*

Meaning: The simultaneous transmission of multiple messages in one channel over a network. This is the equivalent of watching both CNN and C-SPAN at the same time as the local station. In a computer, multiplexing lets more than one computer access a network at the same time. (See also *network.*)

Sentence: "Before we got *multiplexing,* it seemed stupid that only one person could use the network at any give time. Now, with multiplexing, everyone can use the network, everyone can get more work done, and everyone has cleaner, whiter teeth in less than three weeks!"

multiprocessing

Pronunciation: *mul-tee-pros-ses-sing.*

Meaning: The use of multiple microprocessors in the same computer. A computer that uses any type of coprocessor is a multiprocessing computer. (See also *coprocessor* and *central processing unit.*)

Sentence: "When I run my CAD program, the *multiprocessing* powers of the computer are fully used. The multiprocessing powers of my brain are used when I run my CAD program while I'm talking on the phone."

multisync monitor

Pronunciation: *mul-tee-sink mon-i-ter.*

Meaning: A computer monitor that can scan the screen (display data) at different rates due to different video modes and hardware configurations. Also called multiscan monitors. (See also *monitor* and *graphics.*)

Sentence: "My *multisync monitor* can work with any number of computers with their strange assortment of video standards. It must be the schizo of monitors."

multitasking

Pronunciation: *mul-tee-tas-king.*

Meaning: The capability for one machine to run two or more programs at the same time without knowing how to use any of them. Multitasking is commonly used for background operations, such as printing, fax and data communications, and complex calculations. While the background operation (or task) is running, you can perform other tasks with other software. Multitasking slows down computer operation. (See also *protect mode.*)

Sentence: "I'm sorry, Patty, but walking, chewing gum, and picking at your ear is not considered *multitasking.*"

multiuser

Pronunciation: *mul-tee-yu-zer.*

Meaning: Relating to multiple users. A program or operating system that supports more than one user at the same time. A multiuser database, for example, allows numerous computers to access the data at the same time. Multiuser software uses a network to connect users to the data. (See also *network.*)

Sentence: "If you have a *multiuser* database, you can have several employees typing the wrong information simultaneously."

mutation engine

Pronunciation: *mu-tay-shin en-jun.*

Meaning: A type of program used to write computer viruses that can change their appearance, thereby reducing the ability for anti-virus programs to detect and remove them. Some famous mutation engines are the Dark Avenger Mutation Engine and the Trident Polymorphic Engine. (See *polymorphic virus.*)

Sentence: "Virus programmers like using *mutation engines* to create viruses that most anti-virus programs can't detect. Then again, most anti-virus programs can't detect a lot of viruses but they still cost a lot anyway."

Murphy's Law

Pronunciation: *Mer-Fees Lah.*

Meaning: (1) A universal law, or truth, that states: If anything can go wrong, it will. A subset of Murphy's Law is embodied in Parkinson's Law, which states that your clutter will expand to fill the space allotted for it. Another subset of Murphy's Law is Smucker's Law, which states that if you drop your bread, it will always land with the jelly side down. (2) An interesting but poorly executed idea for a computer book series.

Sentence: "Kyle is so fearful of *Murphy's Law* that he backs up his computer every 20 seconds."

n

Pronunciation: *en.*

Meaning: An unknown value, typically the largest value possible. Computer people say "from 1 to *n* things can go wrong." Or they'll use the *nth* value to mean the highest, last — nay, umpteenth — value. (See also *variable.*)

Sentence: "This is the *nth* time that I've been put on hold for *n* minutes when calling tech support."

nano

Pronunciation: *na-no.*

Meaning: A prefix meaning one billionth. For example, a nanogram equals one billionth of a gram. A nanosecond is one billionth of a second, or the amount of time it takes for the U.S. Government to spend $40. (See also *nanosecond.*)

Sentence: "Computer book authors make about a *nano*portion of Bill Gates's income."

nanosecond

Pronunciation: *na-no-sek-und.*

Meaning: One billionth of a second. Also used to measure the speed of chips. The amount of time it takes users to find an error in the software documentation. (See also *nano.*)

Sentence: "I always wondered how people measure *a nanosecond.* They better have a quick thumb on that stopwatch."

natural language processing

Pronunciation: *na-chur-role lang-wedge pro-se-sing.*

Meaning: The use of natural languages by computers for processing information. Today, computers use artificial languages, such as BASIC and C++, which are limited in syntax and vocabulary. Natural language processing would enable computers to understand and process languages such as English and Zulu. Although much progress has been made, natural language processing is many years away from reality. Problems with syntax, pronunciation, and vocabulary have not been completely solved. A complex set of rules is required to decipher the simplest sentences; as language gets more complex, the rules become colossally difficult to construct. (See also *artificial intelligence, language, BASIC, C, C++,* and *syntax.*)

Sentence: "My dog must use *natural language processing* to understand what I mean when I say, 'Where's your ball?' I guess dogs are more intelligent than computers."

navigation

Pronunciation: *nav-i-gay-shun.*

Meaning: The act of finding your way through data, a program, a disk, or a network. In a software application, navigation refers to moving the insertion point (or cursor) around the document. Proper navigation lets you edit and manipulate a document more efficiently. Most programs, for example, have sophisticated navigation keys and procedures. For example, in Microsoft Word for Windows, you can press Ctrl-Home to move instantly to the top of a document. (See also *cursor.*)

Sentence: "Microsoft Word provides numerous *navigation* options, allowing even an amateur to become completely lost in a matter of nanoseconds."

near-letter quality

Pronunciation: *neer let-tur kwal-i-tee.*

Meaning: Letter-quality printing is produced by typewriters and daisy-wheel printers. A hammer, containing the impression of a character, strikes an inked ribbon, which in turn strikes the paper. Letter-quality type has no rough edges and is used for professional documents, such as business letters and contracts. Near-letter quality printing is produced by dot-matrix printers. By condensing the dots to a high resolution, the rough edges around the characters are minimized and a near-letter quality is achieved. Fact is, you can always tell the difference. And laser printers, with their resolution and graphics capabilities, send near-letter quality printers to the cleaners. Often abbreviated as *NLQ.* (See also *laser printer, letter quality, dot matrix,* and *daisy wheel.*)

Sentence: "When I got my laser printer, the *near-letter quality* printer wasn't very useful. It makes a pretty good footstool, though."

nerd

Pronunciation: *nerd* (rhymes with *pilchard, thitherward,* and *whirlybird*).

Meaning: Someone who is very wrapped up in computers — and often in him- or herself as well. There are actually several degrees of nerdhood. At the very top are the elitists, often members of the Programming Priesthood. They're nice and understanding but still dedicated to computers. Nerds include those who love the computers because nothing else loves them back; the geeks who are into it just because a good Dungeons and Dragons game isn't going on anywhere nearby; and the dweebs, whose idea of being socially acceptable is brushing their teeth *and* applying deodorant. Nerd also can be a charming term, applied to anyone who's hopelessly involved with computers yet still remains a vibrant part of society. (See also *hacker, geek,* and *dweeb.*)

Sentence: "I knew Milton was a *nerd* and socially awkward. I couldn't understand why he was so popular. That was until someone told me that he pulls down six figures — plus stock options — writing software at Microsoft."

nested

Pronunciation: *nest-ed.*

Meaning: A programming term that means to include a procedure within another, similar, procedure. For example, nested FOR/NEXT loops can look like this:

```
FOR E=1 TO 10
   FOR F=1 TO 3
   NEXT F
NEXT E
```

In this example, the F loop is nested inside the E loop. Nesting can be constructed several levels deep to create a complex procedure. (See also *loop, infinite loop,* and *endless loop.*)

Sentence: "My programs use a lot of *nested* loops. It must just be my nesting instinct."

NetBIOS

Pronunciation: *Net-By-Oss.*

Meaning: Abbreviation for *Network Basic Input/Output System.* The BIOS tells a computer what types of devices and memory are connected to the computer and how to find them. A network BIOS includes basic information about the network to which a computer is connected. When you load your network operating system, the NetBIOS loads into the computer to supplement the standard BIOS. (See also *BIOS* and *network.*)

Sentence: "When I log on to the network, my *NetBIOS* tells the computer where to locate the other computers."

Netware

Pronunciation: *Net-waer.*

Meaning: The networking software; the file server's operating system. Most closely associated with Novell, as in Novell Netware, the operating system used on Novell networks.

Sentence: "*Netware* must sell more bottles of Excederin than anything else."

network

Pronunciation: *net-werk.*

Meaning: (1) A system of autonomous computers connected to each other for data transfer and communications. A network requires two or more computers, networking software (also called the network operating system), network adapters, and cables. Examples of networks include Ethernet, Token Ring, and AppleTalk. Examples of network operating systems include Novell NetWare and Windows for Workgroups. Networks are useful when several users must share resources, such as data or printers. (2) The source of most computer problems in business computer systems. (See also *LAN, wide area network,* and *node.*)

Sentence: "The *network* is down. Again."

network adapter

Pronunciation: *net-werk uh-dap-ter.*

Meaning: A hardware device (or *card*) that establishes a network and enables a computer to connect to another computer with a similar device. All computers in a network should use compatible adapters. (See also *network, LAN,* and *wide area network.*)

Sentence: "Our office purchased Ethernet *network adapters* for our computers. After we install and configure the adapters, we can then install and configure the network software. I think I like the old-fashioned way of communicating around the office; it's called the phone."

network hose

Pronunciation: *net-werk hoh-za.*

Meaning: The cable that connects your computer to other computers in the network. It's too thick to be a wire, so we call it a hose.

Sentence: "The data starts in my computer, then it's squirted out the *network hose,* down the hall and into Phil's computer, and then he totally fouls up my report."

network operating system (NOS)

Pronunciation: *net-werk op-er-ate-ting sis-tem* or *noss.*

Meaning: The software used on a *local area network* (LAN) that includes the network's hardware components. A NOS is made up of the file server software and workstation software and is responsible for maintaining the "conversation" between the two. (See also *local area network, network, server,* and *workstation.*)

Sentence: "We use Windows for Workgroups as our *network operating system* and connect to a file server with a Novell NOS. I guess our computers are working NOS to NOS."

neural network

Pronunciation: *ner-roll net-werk.*

Meaning: A computer system that mimics the activities of the human brain's neurons. In the human brain, a very large number of neurons (billions, in fact) process information in a parallel fashion, all working on one problem at the same time to produce a single answer. Based on established patterns (learned processes), certain connections are made across a network to produce repeated results. In this way, neural networks can learn to process complex information over time — recognizing patterns of data. Because of this learned behavior, neural networks, like humans, produce only approximate results based on large amounts of input. Neural networks are useful for specific types of problems, such as processing stock market data or finding trends in graphical patterns. (See also *artificial intelligence.*)

Sentence: "Dave! Have you seen our gas bill? I guess the gas company has installed that darn new *neural network* computer!"

New command

Pronunciation: *Nu ko-mand.*

Meaning: A software command that produces a new document or file, as in the File New command in Microsoft Word. Most application programs have a New command used to produce new documents.

Sentence: "I used the *New command* in the File menu to start a new document. I wish there was a New command that would find me a new job."

newline character

Pronunciation: *nu-line kare-akt-er.*

Meaning: The character you type that makes a new line of text on the screen. This is the character produced when you press the Enter key. Many word processors use the term *newline character* because pressing the Enter key starts you off writing stuff on a new line. (See also *Return key, carriage return, linefeed,* and *Enter key.*)

Sentence: "Pity poor Alice. She did a search and replace, searching for the *newline character* and replacing it with nothing. Now she has one four-page paragraph in her document. Pass it on."

newsgroup

Pronunciation: *nooz-groop.*

Meaning: A topic group on USENET, one of the forums where people can read or write their own news, messages, and flames. See *USENET.*

Newsgroups have a certain heirarchical format, which replaces spaces with periods. The first word describes a general category, such as a "comp" for computers or "talk" for general discussions. Then comes a subcategory and maybe even more categories. It's really something you either love or hate, and will drive you agog either way.

Sentence: "Wendy got flamed real bad when she posted a few nasty messages about Mr. Spock in the rec.arts.startrek *newsgroup.*"

Newton

Pronunciation: *New-tun* (as in *fig* ~).

Meaning: The name of Apple's first Personal Digital Assistant (PDA). Probably named that way because of the legend of Isaac Newton getting hit on the head with an Apple [sic] to discover gravity. (If only Newton had any kids, he wouldn't have needed an apple.) See *PDA.*

Sentence: "I paid $600 for my *Newton*, a hand-held device that offers me the functionality of a pad and pencil but with a whole lot of prestige."

NeXTstep

Pronunciation: *Neckst-step.*

Meaning: A graphical operating system based on UNIX. NeXTstep was designed for the NeXT computer, Steve Jobs's post-Apple creation that flopped when it was introduced and has kept flopping ever since. However, the operating system had a lot to offer, so Steve wound up selling that instead.

Sentence: "Truly, *NeXTstep* is perhaps the best graphical operating system ever. Too bad no one buys it."

nibble

Pronunciation: *nib-ol.*

Meaning: One half of a byte, or four bits. (See also *byte* and *bit.*)

Sentence: "I can't get a *nibble* or a bite with this two-bit bait."

NiCad

Pronunciation: *Nigh-Kad.*

Meaning: Abbreviation for *Nickel Cadmium,* a type of battery used in notebook and portable computers. You can recharge NiCad batteries frequently, but you have to drain them of power first; otherwise, they forget how much energy they hold and begin to hold only the amount you've recharged. NiCad batteries are sort of stupid.

Sentence: "My laptop computer uses two rechargeable *NiCad* batteries to provide a full six hours of use, but they take 12 hours each to charge!"

nil

Pronunciation: *nil* (like *Bill, still,* or *pill*).

Meaning: Nothing, zero, zilch. (See also *null.*)

Sentence: "I've been working with this income spreadsheet all day; every way I look at it, my profits are *nil.*"

NLQ

(See *near-letter quality.*)

no-op

Pronunciation: *no-op* (as in "The op was here just a second ago.").

Meaning: A type of computer instruction that does nothing. Although you may think there are lots of no-ops in your software, alas, there may be only a few. It seems silly, but your car has a neutral gear and many people stare at the TV slack-jawed for hours. No-op is the same thing, but for a computer.

Sentence: "I don't know how many *no-ops* this computer is doing, but it's doing them quite fast."

node

Pronunciation: *no-ed.*

Meaning: A single computer or terminal in a network. Networks can consist of numerous nodes, each operating independently. Also the way *note* sounds when you have a cold. (See also *network* and *server.*)

Sentence: "Our Ethernet network has 20 *nodes,* which means 20 of us won't have anything to do when the network stops working."

nondocument

Pronunciation: *non-dok-yu-ment.*

Meaning: A nondocument is a word processing text file or ASCII file that contains no formatting, such as underlining. This term originated from the Nondocument mode in WordStar, which was commonly used to write programs.

Sentence: "I wrote that program using the *nondocument* mode of my word processor. I'm going to run it using the noncomputer mode of my computer. I hope all the nonusers like it."

noninterlacing

Pronunciation: *non-in-ter-lays-ing.*

Meaning: Not interlacing, as in no overlap or twisty-tangly things. Noninterlacing monitors are standard for computer graphics because of their consistency and lack of flicker. (See also *interlacing* and *NTSC.*)

Sentence: "My new monitor is a *noninterlacing* type. It scans the screen more than 50 times per second but still hasn't found my car keys."

nonvolatile memory

Pronunciation: *non-vul-li-tile mem-or-ree.*

Meaning: The memory in your computer that holds information even when you turn off your computer (whew!). Read-only memory is nonvolatile, as are disk drives. (See also *RAM* and *memory.*)

Sentence: "I wrote a story called 'The Violent Vibrations of a Volatile Vocalist' and saved it on my hard drive, so now it's in *nonvolatile memory* and I can finally turn off my computer."

NOP

Pronunciation: *En Oh Pee.*

Meaning: Abbreviation for *Not Operating Properly.* A program that is not working. A computer that is not working. An employee who is not working. Also used to describe accidental "features" in software (*Not On Purpose*).

Sentence: "This program is *NOP.* Let's ship it anyway."

notepad

Pronunciation: *note-pad.*

Meaning: A small application or accessory commonly found in graphical user interfaces (such as Windows and the Macintosh) that you can use to type simple notes. The Windows notepad is a simple, text-only word processor that lets you write, edit, and print notes without having to use the more complex word processors. A notepad is useful also for editing DOS batch files, such as AUTOEXEC.BAT. (See also *graphical user interface.*)

Sentence: "Even though they have a *notepad* accessory, nothing is more handy than keeping a pen and a pad of paper by your computer."

notebook computer

Pronunciation: *note-book kum-pue-ter.*

Meaning: (1) A compact computer, about the size of a three-ring binder. Notebook computers are commonly used while traveling. They operate on both AC and DC power. You can also use notebook computers on the desktop by "docking" them to a larger computer or by attaching a desktop monitor and keyboard. A practical notebook computer should weigh between 3 and 5 pounds. (2) A good excuse to get out of the office. (3) Something a computer book author takes on her honeymoon.

Sentence: "I'm so glad I brought the *notebook computer* on this trip. I haven't used it yet, but just carrying it around saves time going to the gym."

notwork

Pronunciation: *not-werk.*

Meaning: A task performed at your desk or on the computer that is not work. Notwork includes playing computer games, arranging your Windows or Macintosh desktop, organizing files on the computer, installing new software that you're not really going to use, faxing your lunch order to the corner deli, and sending e-mail to Bill Clinton (even if you are a politician).

Sentence: "When the boss came in, I was doing a lot of *notwork.* Then she told me I was doing a good job and left. I guess I'll keep up the good notwork."

Novell

Pronunciation: *No-vell.*

Meaning: A company in Utah that makes networking software. *The* networking software for the majority of PCs. They make other things as well, and they own the license to UNIX and other software.

Sentence: "The darn *Novell* network is down again!"

Novell DOS

Pronunciation: *No-vell Doss.*

Meaning: Renamed version of DR DOS after Novell bought out Digital Research.

Sentence: "Wow! A copy of *Novell DOS.* What a collector's item!"

NSA

Pronunciation: *En Ess Ay.*

Meaning: Acronym that stands for the *National Security Agency*, a top-secret American government agency that dedicates its life to creating and cracking ciphers and to monitoring communications from all over the world. For years, the NSA officially didn't exist, although it unofficially gobbled up billions of dollars for its existence.

Sentence: "The *NSA* has the most supercomputers in one location, which means they're either using these supercomputers to keep the country safe from enemies or playing the most awesome video games the world will never see."

NTSC

Pronunciation: *En Tee Ess See.*

Meaning: Acronym for *National Television Standards Committee.* A committee that determines standards for television broadcast and reception, influencing most of the known world, except Europe and Asia. The NTSC standard for broadcast is 125-line frames scanned at 30 frames per second using noninterlaced video. The European PAL standard produces a much higher resolution and quality of color than does the NTSC standard used in the United States.

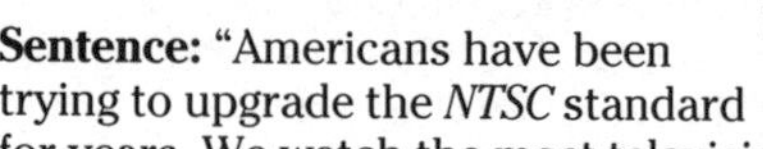

Sentence: "Americans have been trying to upgrade the *NTSC* standard for years. We watch the most television in the world and have the worst quality. We want our HDTV!"

NuBus

Pronunciation: *Noo-Bus.*

Meaning: A Macintosh bus that provides faster data transfer than the older S-bus and has support for multiple CPUs. (See also *bus, expansion slot,* and *expansion card.*)

Sentence: "Those Mac people always have splashy new hardware with much more interesting names than PC people. They have names like *NuBus,* LocalTalk, and System Error."

NUL

Pronunciation: *Nul* (like *dull*).

Meaning: The name of a DOS "device" that doesn't exist and is no good, which means this is probably the first thing the programmers at Microsoft did because it works very well at doing nothing.

Sentence: "Go to *NUL,* go directly to NUL, do not pass Redmond, do not collect stock options."

null

Pronunciation: *nul.*

Meaning: An empty set. Nothing. Unlike the number zero, null has no value whatever, like Donald Trump's estate. (See also *nil.*)

Sentence: "Programmers often use a *null* character to cancel a numeric variable because the number zero has a value."

null modem

Pronunciation: *nul mo-dum.*

Meaning: A connection between two computers that does not include a modem. A null modem is usually accomplished with a cable connection, such as between a notebook computer and a desktop computer for direct data transfer. (See also *modem* and *cable.*)

Sentence: "I use a *null modem* to download my calendar information to the notebook computer before a business trip. After the trip, I upload the calendar from the notebook back to the desktop computer."

NumLock

Pronunciation: *Num-Lok.*

Meaning: A key on standard PC keyboards that toggles the numeric keypad between numbers and direction keys. When NumLock is on, the numeric keypad produces numbers. When NumLock is off, the numeric keys act as direction keys. Many keyboards include a second set of direction keys, so you can use the numeric keypad for numbers and still have direction keys available. (See also *numeric keyboard* and *Caps Lock.*)

Sentence: "When I press the *NumLock* key, I can enter large amounts of numeric data into my spreadsheet program using the numeric keypad. If only I could figure out how to get the cell pointer to move down when I press Enter."

number crunching

Pronunciation: *nuhm-ber krun-ching.*

Meaning: The act of performing numerous calculations and computations on a computer. Number crunching is common in financial and engineering applications.

Sentence: "After six days of *number crunching,* we discovered that the human brain cannot survive on coffee and Twinkies, so we went out for lunch."

numeric format

Pronunciation: *nu-mair-ik for-mat.*

Meaning: A visual style of displaying numbers. Different numeric formats display numbers for different purposes. For example, a currency format displays the number 567.899 as $567.90, and a percent format displays the number .25 as 25%. Numeric formats are commonly found in spreadsheet programs so that you can display numbers for special purposes without actually changing the value or "true form" of the number.

Sentence: "I used Excel's custom *number format* feature to add a few extra zeros to each number in my Net Worth report. Because number formats don't actually change the underlying values in the spreadsheet, you couldn't call this dishonest . . . could you?"

numeric keypad

Pronunciation: *nu-mair-ik kee-pad.*

Meaning: A set of keys, often adjacent to the standard keyboard keys, that includes numbers and symbols for 10-key operation. A numeric keypad displays numbers just as a 10-key calculator does and lets you enter large amounts of numeric data into your applications. Notebook computers often insert the numeric keypad into the standard keys, requiring that you use the NumLock function to access them. (See also *NumLock.*)

Sentence: "My keyboard includes a *numeric keypad* to the right of the standard keys. Because I'm left-handed, I had to purchase a separate numeric keypad that I could place on the left side of the keyboard. Everything is all right (left?) now."

object code file

Pronunciation: *ahb-jekt kode fi-ell.*

Meaning: The middle step when writing a program. It's not exactly the final program, but more like the slimy pod-person thing that eventually turns into the program, thanks to another program called a Linker.

Sentence: "We are waiting for Susan to complete her *object code file* so that we can package this program and get it out on the market before we test-run it to see if it works."

object-oriented

Pronunciation: *ahb-jekt o-ree-unt-ed.*

Meaning: A style of programming where you bundle sets of instructions into packages known as objects, similar to the way you can bundle pieces of paper into objects called wads. In the old-fashioned kind of programming, known as procedural programming, the writer would just write instructions one after the other, one thing leading to the next. Object-oriented programming squishes the instructions into self-sufficient modules. Thus, if you've written a code object that displays the date and time in a box on your screen, you merely toss that wad of code into your program and, lo, it works. You can even take that whole chunk and transplant it into another program instead of having to rewrite the second program from scratch. Object-oriented programming is favored for this kind of versatility.

Object-orientedness also applies to graphics. A graphic element — say, a circle — is called an object and is created by a formula in the program that calculates and "draws" the object onto the screen. You can then manipulate individual objects without messing up the rest of what you've drawn.

Sentence: "I was trying to manipulate an *object* on the screen and then realized that it was a piece of spaghetti stuck to the screen. I guess I shouldn't work and eat at the same time."

occasional irregularity

Pronunciation: *oh-kay-zhun-uhl e-reg-yoo-lar-i-tee.*

Meaning: Times when a computer — or the software program it's running — messes up or shuts down. The symptoms can't be repeated so that you can try to fix the problem — they just happen for no apparent reason, like being late for work, forgetting your spouse's name, or UFOs. The solution is to shut down completely and reboot (which would be a great thing for humans, if it were possible). Another solution is to have anyone else look at the problem; these problems only occur when you are by yourself and will not repeat for others.

Sentence: "My computer's problem is worse than *occasional irregularity,* so I am taking it to see a specialist in Singapore."

OCR

Pronunciation: *Oh See Ar.*

Meaning: Abbreviation for *Optical Character Recognition.* The ability of a computer (via special software) to look at a page of text and recognize letters and words and translate them into a computer file so that you don't have to retype anything. The OCR software sees that an *A* is an *A,* rather than a collection of dots making a picture. This is important at certain times — for example, if you have a fax modem inside your computer and somebody faxes you a document. If you have OCR software, then the fax is a document you can edit. If you don't have OCR software, your computer just thinks the document is one big picture. OCR also stands for Obvious Candidate for Rehabilitation, a term used fondly to describe some programmers.

Sentence: "Using *OCR,* someday computers will even be able to decipher a doctor's prescription."

octal

Pronunciation: *ok-toll.*

Meaning: Base eight, where the numbers range from zero to 7 and then the value eight is represented by the number 10. Weird? Yes! We humans count in base 10, probably because we have ten fingers. Base 10 uses numbers zero through 9 and then 10 to represent the value ten. Octal, hey — it's just weird. And no one uses it any more, at least no one you'll have to deal with unless you get lost somewhere at a university or nuclear plant.

Sentence: "If an octopus could count, it would probably do so in base 8, *octal.*"

OCX

Pronunciation: *Oh See Ecks.*

Meaning: Acronym that stands for *OLE Custom Control*, which is odd because OLE is itself an acronym that stands for Object Linking and Embedding, and nobody can figure out where the "X" comes from in OCX. Microsoft developed the OCX standard as an advanced version of the VBX standard (see also *VBX*). Although the VBX standard is designed for 16-bit operating systems (such as MS-DOS and Windows 3.1), OCX is designed for 32-bit operating systems such as Windows NT and Windows 95.

Sentence: "Most Visual Basic programmers use VBXs to create programs quickly and easily. But if these Visual Basic programmers want to create programs for Windows NT or Windows 95, they'll have to replace all their VBXs with equivalent *OCXs*. Is the world of computers the only one that requires everyone to make massive equipment changes every year?"

OEM

Pronunciation: *Oh Ee Em.*

Meaning: Abbreviation for *Original Equipment Manufacturer.* The company that makes the parts that go into machines assembled and sold by somebody else. For example, Joe Blorf may make disk drives which are then installed into your computer and sold by Milo Cooper. Joe is the OEM for Milo's hard drives. Very few computer manufacturers make all of their own stuff.

Sentence: "Although American computers are the most advanced in the world, most of the parts come from Japanese *OEMs.*"

off-line

Pronunciation: *awf-ly-na.*

Meaning: Not connected to a computer, or more probably not really bothering with the computer. There's a difference between off-line and unplugged. If you yank out the printer cable, then you've unplugged it. But if the printer is plugged in, you may have to turn it on to make it on-line. Further, you may have to punch another button that tells the printer to obey the computer, which is also "putting it on-line."

Sentence: "Sometimes I have to take my printer *off-line* to advance a sheet of paper. Sometimes I have to take my brain off-line to get some peace and quiet."

offset

Pronunciation: *awf-set.*

Meaning: To allow extra room for inner margins on a word-processed document so that it can be bound in book form. This book has an offset of an inch or so, which allows for the pages to be bound together. If you were to yank a page out, you would see more blank space on one side than the other. That blank space is the offset.

Sentence: "We *offset* the document six inches in case we made a mistake in the binding."

OK button

Pronunciation: *Oh-Kay butt-en.*

Meaning: The letters "OK" inside a little rectangle, inside a dialog box. You use your mouse to click on the OK rectangle and, voilà, you "press" the button. You can also "click" the OK button by pressing the Enter key.

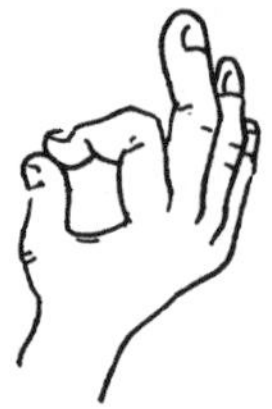

Sentence: "I think the *OK buttons* I use should be renamed 'Oh, well.'"

OK Corral

Pronunciation: *Oh-kay Ko-ral.*

Meaning: The place where you hang your hat, where the Naughahydes roam, where the skies are not cloudy or gray, where the only time you hear about is suppertime, where . . . Doggone it! Wrong dictionary! See *Cowherding For Dummies.*

Sentence: "It's suppertime at the *OK Corral.* Click the OK button."

OLE

Pronunciation: *Oh El Ee,* also pronounced *oh-lay,* as in bullfighting.

Meaning: Acronym for *Object Linking and Embedding*, an activity carried out while you are in Windows. OLE means that you can insert a document (or part of a document) created by one application inside of a document created by another application and maintain a live link between the two. For example, suppose that you're in Windows. (Now, please stop screaming!) You have a chart in Excel that you want to include in a business letter in Word. With OLE linking, you can paste the chart from Excel into the letter in Word. Every time you make a change in the chart in the original Excel document, it automatically updates the chart in the Word document. Likewise, if you clicked the chart while you were in the Word document, you could make changes in Excel, and it would update both the original and the linked version. With embedding, you are placing a severed copy of the original document in the destination document.

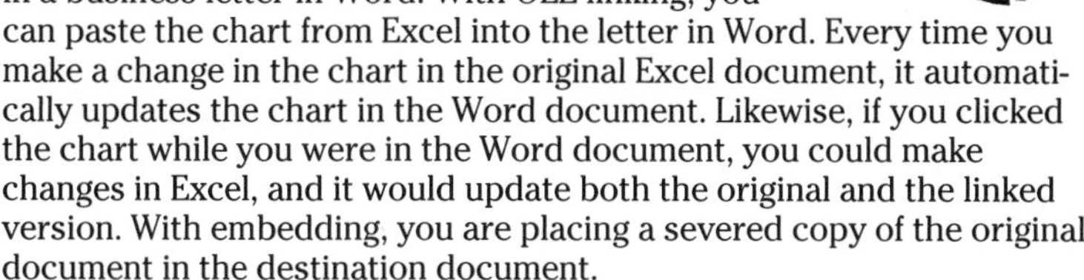

Sentence: "And now Miguel will paste the picture of the bull into his document about bullfighting. Here he goes. Click *OLE!*"

on-line

Pronunciation: *ahn-lyne.*

Meaning: Hooked up to a specified computer, usually said of the printer when it's connected to your PC and ready to print. You see, it's entirely possible to have a computer and a printer, both are plugged into the wall and each other, and both are turned on. Yet they won't talk until you punch that special button on the printer that makes it go on-line. In a way, on-line means "no earplugs."

On-line may also refer to the state of "being connected" to a national modem service, such as Prodigy or CompuServe or even a local BBS. Though your computer, modem, and software are all running, you aren't on-line until you're connected with the service. Some of these systems are called on-line services because they want you to believe that they're "on" all the time.

Sentence: "I use the CompuServe *on-line* service to get answers to all my odd software questions. It's a warehouse o' computer geeks."

OOP

Pronunciation: *Oop*

Meaning: Abbreviation for *Object-Oriented Programming*. A method of programming that creates individual software objects that can be used again and again in other programs. Although it takes more time to create objects, the capability to reuse them in other programs reduces programming time. (See also *object-oriented.*)

Sentence: "Programming languages such as C++ and Pascal are now designed to provide *OOP* capabilities. So now you can write one part of a program and use it in several other programs. Just don't leave the parts lying around your desktop, or you're liable to step in the *oop.*"

open

Pronunciation: *oh-pen.*

Meaning: To access a program or file, just as you would open a book if you wanted to read it, a notebook if you wanted to write in it, a car door if you wanted to hit your knee with it, or a can of tuna fish if you wanted to eat out of it. So if you last saved that BLOTCH.DOC file and want to work on it again, you start the program that created BLOTCH.DOC and then use that program to open the file, loading it in for editing or other ridicule.

Sentence: Please don't *open* the file called "WORMCAN.DOC."

OpenDoc

Pronunciation: *Oh-pen-dok.*

Meaning: A standard being promoted by Apple, Borland, IBM, Novell, and WordPerfect to allow programs to share data, no matter what program or computer the data may have been originally created on. OpenDoc is an alternative to Microsoft's compound document architecture, Object Linking and Embedding (OLE). Unlike OLE, which is designed only for Microsoft Windows, OpenDoc will work with the Macintosh, OS/2, Windows, and ultimately Unix.

Sentence: "By using *OpenDoc,* I can copy information from a Macintosh spreadsheet, store it in my Windows word processor, and combine the whole thing in a new document so Janet can edit it using OS/2. Then again, knowing what computers are like, this probably won't work without flaws, bugs, and lots of problems that defeat the whole purpose of data sharing and integration anyway."

open architecture

Pronunciation: *oh-pen ar-ki-tek-chur.*

Meaning: The philosophy and practice of building computers and making the design and engineering public knowledge. It invites other manufacturers and developers to augment the computer with peripherals, software, and internal components. The theory being that more doodads and gizmos that are available on the market to work with a given machine, the more tricks a user can do with it, and the more the machine will sell.

IBM has practiced open architecture with its PCs, and Sun Microsystems has practiced it with its workstations. Apple Computer is famous for NOT practicing it. And, in fact, Apple has become notorious for doing exactly the opposite, for shouting "Off with their head!" when anyone else builds something that looks remotely like an Apple computer, although, the Macintosh *is* getting to be a rather "open" machine these days and even has a *clone* or two out there. (See also *architecture.*)

Sentence: "Although IBM had the foresight to create an *open architecture* PC, they didn't have the foresight to realize that clone manufacturers would take most of their business away from them."

operand

Pronunciation: *ah-per-and.*

Meaning: A value, variable, or doodad in an equation that gets operated on by an operator. In the statement 2 + 3 = 5, *2* and *3* are operands. The plus and equal signs are operators. (See also *operator.*)

Sentence: "If you take away the symbols, all you have left in a mathematical equation are the *operands.* This doesn't sound very useful, which is why it's a mathematical concept."

operating system

Pronunciation: *ah-per-ay-ting sis-tim.*

Meaning: The software that controls the hardware, and which also runs your programs. Some common operating systems include DOS, System 7 for the Macintosh, OS/2, and UNIX. (Windows is not an operating system by itself because it must run "on top of" DOS.)

Sentence: "Some people who use the DOS *operating system* add Windows to avoid having to use DOS commands. Some of those people use programs such as Norton Desktop to avoid using Windows commands. Avoidance is a big part of computing."

operator

Pronunciation: *ah-per-ay-ter.*

Meaning: A symbol representing a mathematical operation. The usual context is within a software program or programming language. Typical operators are

+	Addition
-	Subtraction
*	Multiplication
/	Division

In addition to these mathematical operators, many other types exist. Relational operators, for example, test the relationships between values, as in the following:

<	Less than
>	Greater than
=	Equal to
<=	Less than or equal to
>=	Greater than or equal to
<>	Not equal to

Sentence: "In the spreadsheet, I use mathematical *operators* to produce a budget worksheet. Then I use other operators to cover up the funds I'm embezzling."

optical

Pronunciation: *ahp-ti-kul.*

Meaning: In general, refers to light or vision. For instance, when you are having an optical illusion, it means you are seeing something that's not there, such as national health care.

Sentence: "The other day Windows just came up — splat — right there on the screen. I'm certain I experienced an *optical* illusion."

optical disk

Pronunciation: *ahp-ti-kul dis-ka.*

Meaning: A computer storage medium (a disk drive) that operates by digitized beams of light or lasers. That sounds so cool that there must be a catch — and there are two: speed and price; the optical disks are expensive and slow, though they hold lots of information. Optical disks are somewhat akin to CD-ROM technology. The claim to fame of the optical disk drive is that its storage capacity is much greater than that of a magnetic disk drive, which is your typical type of disk.

Sentence: "I don't like the way that new *optical disk* is looking at me."

optical mouse

Pronunciation: *ahp-ti-kul mows.*

Meaning: The distant cousin of the three non-optical, or "blind," mice who got their tails . . . Oops, wrong dictionary! See *Nursery Rhymes For Dummies*. In computer terms, an optical mouse is a pointing device that uses a light beam to track the position of the cursor or pointer on the screen. Normal mice use a mechanical ball that rolls to detect movement. The light beam type of optical mouse is used with a special grid type of mouse pad that reflects the beam. (Actually, the mechanical type of mouse also uses some optical technology, but internally. An electronic eye watches the ball roll around and this is how the mouse detects movement. Cool, huh?)

Sentence: "If your *optical mouse* gets loose, you need a special optical mousetrap to catch it."

optimize

Pronunciation: *ahp-tim-eyes.*

Meaning: To customize software or hardware so that it will serve the user to its utmost capacity. The goal is to have the machinery run faster and more efficiently. This could include shuffling parts of the software into different parts of the computer's memory, rewriting chunks of software applications, or even just tweaking the controls on your desktop control panel.

Sentence: "Microsoft Windows gets its bloated reputation partly because it loads your hard drive with graphic images you can use for 'wallpaper.' If you think you can do without these images, you can *optimize* Windows by getting rid of all the picture files."

Option key

Pronunciation: *Ahp-shun kee.*

Meaning: A key on any Apple keyboard. You can use it with a number of other keys on the keyboard to execute special functions, such as the Command, Shift, or Ctrl keys. Like the Shift key, the Option key doesn't do anything if you press it by itself. An example: in Word on the Mac, pressing the Option key and the numeral 8 key will give you a bullet character. Option-* gives you a little bad guy character. And Shift-Option-Enter shoots the bad guy character with the bullet character. Ctrl-Option-B cleans up the mess character afterwards.

Sentence: "If I press *Option*-S, I save my document. If I press Shift-Option-S, I save all open documents. If I press Ctrl-Shift-Option-S, I get a cramp in my hand."

orphan

Pronunciation: *or-fun.*

Meaning: (1) The first line of a paragraph abandoned at the bottom of one page, while the rest of the lines continue on the following page. The dimensions of this tragedy have attained such proportions that developers of page layout software have included social service capabilities in their programs to rescue orphans from their plight. (2) A computer, usually one of the early models, that is no longer made or supported by the company that heralded it as a "technological revolution" just a few years back. This happens to all computers, sooner or later.

Sentence: "Pity ye, O Osborne owners. And ye Adam and Atari and owners of old Radio Shack stuff. Fare thee well old Apple II, Apple III, and Lisa owners. Big adieu to the long throng of forgotten PCs, nay, the *orphans* of the electronics age."

OS/2

Pronunciation: *OhEsToo* (trademarked acronym standing for Operating System/2).

Meaning: An operating system developed jointly by IBM and Microsoft for PC computers. It was to be the next operating system, the one that would take over and succeed in DOS's footsteps. That prediction and $75 buys you swampland in Florida. Despite the initial fanfare, few software developers came out with applications for OS/2, so when Windows appeared, it stole the show. It's as if IBM gave a party and nobody came.

Presently, IBM is trying to please the masses with newer and better versions of OS/2, specifically to compete with Microsoft and Windows. The only problem is still OS/2's lack of specific, OS/2 software.

Sentence: "Rebel against the new Windows as ye long ago rebelled against *OS/2!* We'll show the rabble who runs the show who's really in charge!"

outline font

Pronunciation: *owt-lihn fawn-ta.*

Meaning: A typeface that is solid around the edges and hollow in the middle. It's used for posters and headlines but not so much for regular typing. Some font families give you a choice of making an outline typeface out of a regular one. For example, Times Roman can become Times Roman Outline. The outline fonts keep the styles and proportions of the regular fonts they come from. (See also *font family.*)

Sentence: "Kids love *outline fonts* because they can color in the middle with crayons."

outliner software

Pronunciation: *owt-lihn-er soft-waer.*

Meaning: Software that can make the kind of outline you used to make in high school on 3x5 cards when you were learning how to organize your writing compositions. Those roman numerals followed by uppercase letters followed by Arabic numerals followed by lowercase letters will really take you back. In the old days — not quite as old as your high school days — this kind of software was a separate application from word processing. In these enlightened times, you can make outlines in the same software program as you can write letters and novels in. For example, WordPerfect includes an outlining feature, though few bother with it.

Sentence: "We used *outlining software* to organize the outline for this new dictionary. Dan and Wally came up with all the letters, and the publisher suggested we use the alphabetizing feature to organize."

output

Pronunciation: *owt-put.*

Meaning: What the computer spits out after it churns through the information you put into it. Output can be in the form of characters on your screen, sounds out of speakers, or printed paper out of a printer. The machines that give us the output are called output devices. (See, learning about computers is way easier than you thought!) (See also *Input, BIOS, and BUS.*)

Sentence: "When your input is poorly conceived, you shouldn't be surprised when your *output* is garbage."

OverDrive

Pronunciation: *Oh-ver-drive.*

Meaning: A marketing adjective used by Intel to describe a faster version of the 80486 microprocessor. OverDrive processors run two or more times faster than non-OverDrive processors. You use the OverDrive "slot" in your computer to plug in an OverDrive chip, which then takes over as your PC's microprocessor from your older, lamer 486 microprocessor.

Sentence: "I yanked out my ancient 80486DX and replaced it with an 80486DX4 *OverDrive* processor. Now my computer runs two times faster although I still haven't figured out why I need this additional speed to do word processing."

overflow

Pronunciation: *oh-ver-flo.*

Meaning: Overflow is to memory as a swollen river is to a dam; the only difference is that water finds its own level, whereas a memory overflow stops a computer dead in its tracks — or worse, the excess bits may flood out the back of your PC, drop to the floor, and run up your legs and start byting you! The overflow happens because what you put in is bigger than the space the programmer has set aside for it. So the programmer wanted 10 characters for your last name, and your last name is

Zinzinburger. Too many characters equals overflow. Solution: make the thing you're trying to do smaller or make the space in the program bigger. (Mostly this is a programmer's problem, not our problem.)

Sentence: "When the computer gives you an *overflow* message, take two aspirin, reboot your computer, and call a programmer in the morning."

overhead

Pronunciation: *oh-ver-hed.*

Meaning: Similar to what it means in real life: the resources you need just to stay operational — in this case, measured in RAM, megabytes, processing speed, and I/O capacity. Mostly this refers to what a program needs just to run on your PC. Some programs may require 640K of RAM, 5MB of hard disk space, plus special graphics cards and printers.

Sentence: "Working with graphics requires a lot of *overhead.* Do you think there's a conspiracy going on between the stores that sell the hardware and the guys who write the software?"

overlay

Pronunciation: *oh-ver-lay.*

Meaning: This is a sophisticated form of program juggling, where the whole program is just too darn big to fit into memory at once. So what they do is split the program into modules and overlay them into memory, swapping parts of the program back and forth between RAM and a disk. (See also *Murphy's Law.*)

Sentence: "They used *overlay* technology to overcome limitations in RAM. Now we can use Parkinson's law of programming: 'Expand your program to fill as much RAM as you have available.'"

owner

Pronunciation: *oh-ner.*

Meaning: The person who paid for the software, as opposed to the two dozen people using the pirated copy. If you had to look this word up, turn to the word *pirate* to find your picture.

Sentence: "If you're the *owner* of this software package, how come the startup screen says 'Al Gore, Washington, DC?'"

p-code

Pronunciation: *pee-cohd*

Meaning: P-code is relevant only to the old p-system operating system, which I'd bet $10 right now you've never heard of. With the p-system, a programmer would compile a program, usually written in Pascal, into p-code, which is short for *pseudocode*. The p-code could be interpreted by the p-system's interpreter into the language understood best by the PC's microprocessor. This meant, theoretically, that p-code could run on any computer, as long as that computer was running the p-system. P-get it? (See also *pseudocode.)*

Sentence: "Since the p-system went defunct in the early '80s, *p-code* is no longer a useful term, unless you redefine it to mean *problem code* or programming instructions the dog mistook for the newspaper."

paddle

Pronunciation: *pa-dul.*

Meaning: Input device, like a joystick, that is frequently used for computer and video games. The paddle is a knob you twist, rotating it one way or the other. (See also *joystick.*)

Sentence: "My flight simulator program lets you use a *paddle* to control the plane. I can turn my plane left and right, but I still can't get it off the ground."

page

Pronunciation: *paej.*

Meaning: (1) Like in regular English, the electronic unit of text that corresponds to a page in real life. The default mode is $8^{1}/_{2}$ x 11 inches, and you can change these measurements in your word processing or page layout software. Even if your monitor is too small to fit a page of this size on the screen all at once, the computer still knows where the page starts and ends and will communicate this to the printer. (2) A chunk of RAM which acts as a unit that can be swapped back and forth to disk or to another spot in memory. (See also *expanded memory, printer*, and *page break.*)

Sentence: "One handy thing about *pages* on the computer is that you can recycle them over and over and over again. Al Gore would be pleased. Hug a tree."

page break

Pronunciation: *paej braek.*

Meaning: In word processing, the point at which one page leaves off and another begins. There are two ways to accomplish this: *soft* page breaks and *hard* page breaks. A soft page break happens automatically as soon as you get to the last character of the last line on a page. If you add or delete text (or graphics, for that matter) from the page, the page break will change accordingly, adding room for the new text. A hard page break is one you put in yourself at a precise location. A new page will always start at that point even if you add or delete material before the hard page break. (See also *page* and *printer.*)

Sentence: "Because I wanted my term paper to come out to 20 pages and I only had 7 pages to start with, I made the type bigger and put in a lot of extra hard *page breaks.*"

Page Down key

Pronunciation: *Paej Down kee.*

Meaning: A glorified cursor key that moves you forward (down) in the document the exact length of a page every time you press it. Depending on the program, a "page" can either be the amount of information that fits on a screen or the size of a real page. Often abbreviated PgDn. (See also *Page Up key.*)

Sentence: "Page, off my knee. Off! Now! Down Page! *Page Down*!"

page frame

Pronunciation: *paej fraem.*

Meaning: The page frame is a place in memory where a bunch of memory pages are kept, like storing blocks of ice in a freezer. This happens on a PC when you use expanded memory. To access the extra memory, a page frame is created. Through that frame, individual pages of memory are stored that can access expanded memory. Is this complex or what? DOS lacks a true memory-management solution, so the Geeks That Be introduce obscure concepts like pages and page frames. Here are some more vitals:

- A page is 16K of memory.
- The page frame contains four 16K chunks of memory. Or sometimes it contains lots more chunks of memory.
- The page frame is located in "upper memory."
- The page frame is driving everyone nuts.

You don't need a page frame if none of your programs use expanded memory. (See also *expanded memory.*)

Sentence: "That memory looks bleak and ugly sitting there. *Frame* it and tell me what you think."

page layout

Pronunciation: *paej lae-out.*

Meaning: The design of text and graphics on a printed page and the software that you create it with, typically called desktop publishing (DTP) software. Most software programs that you can print from, such as word processors, databases, and spreadsheets, include some page layout capabilities. In word processing, you can set margins and specify typefaces; in a database, you can select where fields will be positioned in relation to each other; and, in spreadsheets, you can adjust column widths and row heights. That's page layout.

For the ultimate in page layout, however, you would go to desktop publishing software, such as PageMaker, Ventura Publisher, or QuarkXpress. Applications like these give you precision control over the elements of your design in relation to each other, such as wrapping text around a graphic, or reducing or magnifying the size of an element in relation to elements around it. Most DTP programs let you "import" previously created word processing, graphics, database, or spreadsheet files to polish up your presentation. (See also *desktop publishing software.*)

Sentence: "I want to start my own newspaper called *The Computer Chronicle For Dummies*, but I will need some *page layout* software and about 40 years to learn how to use it."

Page Up key

Pronunciation: *Paej Up kee.*

Meaning: The opposite of the Page Down key. This key moves you, page by page, backward through your document to the top. Often labeled PgUp on the keyboard. (See also *Page Down key.*)

Sentence: "If you're already at the top of the document, pressing the *Page Up key* won't take you anywhere."

pagination

Pronunciation: *pa-jin-ae-shun.*

Meaning: The act of making pages where there were none. Because everything you print eventually appears on a piece of paper — a *page* — the art of pagination shows you where those pages will be, right on the screen, before printing. It also allows you to see where various sections and titles appear in your document and make minor layout adjustments to see if everything will look hunky-dory when printed.

Sentence: "Since Steve can't figure out how the *pagination* works in my word processing program, he'll have to print his novel as one long scroll."

paint

Pronunciation: *pain-ta.*

Meaning: Just like in real life, but on the computer the paint is not wet, which also means that it doesn't need to dry when you're done with the picture. Paint programs give you "tools" that let you draw electronically on the computer screen for different effects, like different sizes of brushes, a roller (for large areas), a spray can, and so on. Artists are sometimes dismayed at how little precision control they have with a graphical paint program and a mouse. It feels like painting with ski gloves on. If you're not already an artist though, you will be amazed at how easy it is to use a computer to paint — you can make endless mistakes and do endless fine-tuning without wearing holes in your paper or mucking it up with "colors" like *mud bath brown* or *murky gray*. Paint programs range from the simple Paintbrush program that comes bundled with Windows, all the way up to professional packages like Aldus Freehand and CorelDraw.

Sentence: "With that new black velvet mode in the Adobe Illustrator *paint* program, we're going to put the Tijuana Elvis Painting Society out of business."

palette

Pronunciation: *pal-et.*

Meaning: The selection of colors available in a paint or drawing program. The palette is somewhat limited by your hardware, specifically your monitor and graphics card. Some paint colors are given to you; others you can mix yourself. Palettes can also hold fill patterns, border styles, and other types of painting stuff.

Sentence: "There are so many colors in this *palette* that they take up the whole screen, and I have only 2 square inches to paint my picture in."

pane

Pronunciation: *paen.*

Meaning: A window that has been split into multiple parts. For example, in Excel you have a single window and can see your spreadsheet inside that window. Further, you can create up to four panes in the window by splitting it vertically and horizontally. Different parts of your spreadsheet or document can be displayed in the different panes. The end result is probably like what those independent-eyed iguanas see, but it helps you scope out big documents and spreadsheets easily. (See also *window.*)

Sentence: "I've traveled on the ocean, I've tramped upon the plain, but I've never seen a Window cry because it had a *pane.*"

paper-white B/W VGA monitor

Pronunciation: *pae-per wiht bee dub-l-yoo Vee Gee Ae mahn-i-ter.*

Meaning: A VGA monitor whose display approximates the whiteness of paper and provides black text and graphics to go with it. But wait! There's more! Because the paper-white screen also gives you shades of gray, from 4, 8, 16, or up to 32 shades, it's much more true-to-life than a monochrome monitor, which usually gives you amber on black or green on black. Yawn! Paper-white monitors are a good value and are often clearer and easier to read than bad color monitors, such as the one you have now! (See also *VGA monitor.*)

Sentence: "Now that I've upgraded to a *paper-white monitor,* I can get the same kind of writer's block that I get when staring at a blank piece of paper."

Paradox

Pronunciation: *Par-ah-doks.*

Meaning: (1) The name of a relational database program marketed by Borland International because they originally wanted a database program to compete against dBASE, which Borland now also owns and markets after buying dBASE from the now-defunct Ashton-Tate Corporation. (2) Something that happens the same time something else can't happen, which is usually bad. (3) Two dox.

Sentence: "The name *Paradox* originally meant that it was a paradox that a powerful database could also be so easy to use. Now the name Paradox means that it's a paradox that Borland can market both Paradox and dBASE and still claim that each database is the number one database of choice by Fortune 500 corporations all over the world."

parallel

Pronunciation: *pare-ell-ell.*

Meaning: Side by side, as in two lines that never touch, unless you're not looking or your name is Albert Einstein. What's parallel? Two lines that travel in the same direction, about "yea" width apart, but never the twain do meet. With your PC, the term comes into play in the *parallel port,* which is covered just a few parallel inches below this term.

Sentence: "Actually, the universe isn't *parallel.* If a train travels along parallel rails that encompass the universe, and you're waiting to catch the 4:15 to Philly, eventually you'll see yourself get off the same train with a strange woman, ask yourself for $40, and then you'll never see yourself again."

parallel port

Pronunciation: *pare-ell-ell port.*

Meaning: A jack on the back of your computer that you can plug something into, especially a printer. The other kind of port is "serial." When a device is hooked up to the parallel port, it means that data is traveling at high speeds along parallel circuits in the innards of your computer. Parallel ports are known for their high-speed data transfer, but they poop out over long distances. (See also *printer* and *serial port.*)

Sentence: "The manual said to plug the printers into the *parallel ports,* so I arranged them neatly so that they each faced the door."

parallel processing

Pronunciation: *pare-ell-ell prah-sess-ing.*

Meaning: Having the computer be able to think about more than one thing at a time, which can cause neurotic behavior, as it does in humans. Technically, parallel process-ING comes from having parallel process-ORS, which is essentially only the case in computers far mightier than the average desktop PC or Mac. The top performers of any kind of computer can use several thousand processors in parallel, whereas the lowly desktop computer typically has only one. Parallel processing is the basis of artificial intelligence, or those computers that really can say "duh!"

Sentence: "Supercomputers, which are incredibly fast and powerful, use something called massively *parallel processing.* I never thought that one thing could be more parallel than another."

parameter

Pronunciation: *puh-ram-e-ter.*

Meaning: A value — which could be numbers, letters, or other characters — that you enter into an equation or statement, like an option. For example, the DOS FORMAT command is followed by a "drive" parameter. That's a drive letter telling the FORMAT command where the disk is that you want formatted. Parameter is just a fancy way of saying "option-thing that goes on the end of a command." You can also use parameters when searching for information. For example, Cornelia could enter the parameters "tall," "ugly," and "hairy" into the computer dating database to look for her dreamboat. (See also *option.*)

Sentence: "How about this error message: `optional required parameter missing`. How can something that's required be optional?"

paren(s)

Pronunciation: *pare-enz.*

Meaning: Slang for parenthesis (-theses). Sometimes you have to use a lot of them, so you don't want to waste your breath on extra syllables. They're used in mathematical calculations in programming, among other things. Paren is *not* the singular version of parentheses.

Sentence: "I don't know why the equation didn't work. Stick some *parens* in there and maybe it will."

parent/child

Pronunciation: *pare-ent-chil-da.*

Meaning: This describes the relationship (how cute!) between categories of information, which could be files, directories, levels of an outline, or families. The *child* is a subcategory of the parent. (See also *child process.*)

Sentence: "In my outline, 'Things to Eat' is the *parent* topic of the 'Candy' topic. 'Candy' is a *child* of 'Things to Eat.' This more than justifies what I put into my mouth for nourishment."

parity

Pronunciation: *pare-i-tee.*

Meaning: A way of testing whether data is OK or not by counting the number of bits (such as during data transmission). The number can be either odd or even, and that information is saved and compared with subsequent calculations that also see if the number is odd or even. If it isn't, then there is no parity and the computer will pout. (See also *parity bit.*)

Sentence: "Okay, Ivan, if you have enough nukes to blow up the world 530 times and we have enough to blow up the world 488 times — not counting subs, of course — then we've reached *parity.* Nyet?"

parity bit

Pronunciation: *pare-i-tee bit.*

Meaning: An extra bit included to check the parity in data bytes. The arrangement is specified, say, that a parity bit set to 1 means that the parity is odd (there is an odd number of 1s in the eight bits that it's monitoring), 0 if it's even. (See also *parity.*)

Sentence: "I made fun of the word *parity* by writing a parody, but then my modem bit me."

park

Pronunciation: *park* or *pahk.*

Meaning: To immobilize the heads of your hard drive so that they don't rattle around and do damage if the computer is moved. Not to be confused with parallel parking — an easy mistake to make because so many things are parallel in computers. Nowadays, most hard drives park themselves automatically when you turn off the computer. (See also *head* and *head crash.*)

Sentence: "In most of the country, when you want to make sure your computer is secure, you would *park* the hard drive. In Hahvuhd Squai-uh, however, you would pahk your hahd drive."

parse

Pronunciation: *pars.*

Meaning: (1) To split something up into separate pieces parts, as in programming, when a compiler specifies what "part of speech" each instruction component is. (2) In spreadsheets, the function used to distribute data imported from other applications into separate fields in your new spreadsheet. (3) Generically, the act of splitting up a group of items (such as a sentence of words) into individual components. (See also *compiler.*)

Sentence: "I tried to *parse* the spreadsheet I imported from Lotus, but the program couldn't figure out where to separate all the numbers — so now I have number soup."

partition

Pronunciation: *par-ti-shun.*

Meaning: A section of a hard disk set aside for use with a specific operating system, or the act of separating the hard drive into such sections (one of those devious nouns-turned-verbs). (See also *hard disk* and *logical drive.*)

Sentence: "It took so much disk space to set up the *partitions* on my hard drive that I now have no room left to install the operating system."

Pascal

Pronunciation: *Pass-kal.*

Meaning: A programming language used mainly for teaching programming concepts, with commands that look like regular English words — although they aren't strung together that way. Named after the 17th-century philosopher-mathematician Blaise Pascal, the language was created by Niklaus Wirth in the early '70s.

Sentence: "*Pascal* was a rascal."

passive matrix

Pronunciation: *pass-iv may-triks.*

Meaning: A type of laptop display that's cheaper and not as good as the active matrix type. Unlike active matrix, which uses transistors to control the screen, a passive matrix display uses some type of lame, logic board circutry or somesuch.

Sentence: "My new KneeCap 150 laptop uses the *passive matrix* display, so I can see color graphics of a parrot at 39,000 feet, but not as well as the guy with the active matrix display sitting next to me."

password

Pronunciation: *pass-werd.*

Meaning: Exactly like saying "Open sesame" to the computer. Usually encountered on a computer network, where a password is required to access certain parts of the network or on BBSs, where it is required to gain access to a forum. However, you can also use passwords to protect individual files.

Sentence: "Peggy wanted to make sure she would be able to remember her *password*, so she wrote it on a sign in big letters and stuck it on the wall next to the computer." (Tip for power users: This defeats the purpose of having a password.)

paste

Pronunciation: *paest.*

Meaning: To insert an item previously cut or copied from elsewhere. The item can be text, graphics, records from a database, a column of numbers from a spreadsheet, and so on. The item has been cut or copied into a mystical no-man's-land called the *Clipboard* until the next cut or copy event. Later, you can paste information from the clipboard into a document. (See also *clipboard, copy, cut,* and *cut and paste.*)

Sentence: "If you want to *paste* some of my term paper into your term paper, make sure that the fonts match so the teacher doesn't suspect."

path

Pronunciation: *path.*

Meaning: Otherwise known as *path statement*, the *path* is inserted into DOS's AUTOEXEC.BAT file, followed by names of whatever directories the user specifies. You can then start those applications from within any subdirectory in DOS without having to type the entire path name. Here's a typical PATH statement:

```
PATH=C:\DOS;C:\WINDOWS;C:\WINWORD;C:\EXCEL
```

(See also *path name.*)

Sentence: "When I said I could access my accounting program only from within the C:\PROGRAMS\ACCT directory, I was told to update my *path.* Now my front yard looks great, but I still can't access the accounting program from any directory."

path name

Pronunciation: *path naem.*

Meaning: The route the computer takes to get to a specified file, spelled out in excruciating detail. Sometimes programs require that you spell out the path name in this same kind of excruciating detail. You include the letter designating the drive, followed by a colon, followed by a backslash, followed by the directory, followed by any and all subdirectories, followed by the actual name of the file. Like this:

```
C:\PROGRAMS\GRAPHICS\PAINT.EXE
```

When you open or save files, you are usually required to specify the directory path (or path name) for the file to identify where the file is coming from or going. In Windows, you can specify a path name by typing it as shown or by working your way through folders that represent directories in a path statement. On a Macintosh, paths are not an issue, although an intricate maze of folders takes its place. (See also *path.*)

Sentence: "The *path name* that gets you to the file containing the manuscript for this book could be `C:\WINWORD\DUMMIES\P.DOC`. But it's not; it's something else, so don't go looking for it there."

Pause key

Pronunciation: *Paws kee.*

Meaning: A key that is often used to pause screen output, such as directory listings. Used within DOS and DOS applications, pressing Pause once usually freezes the display; pressing it again returns normal behavior.

Sentence: "The *Pause key* is on my keyboard, but what does it do? It seems to pause Windows when it's in the midst of opening but doesn't seem to have any effect elsewhere. Why would I want to wait any longer for Windows to open, anyway?"

PC

Pronunciation: *Pee See.*

Meaning: (1) Acronym for *Personal Computer.* Technically, refers to any stand-alone computer that fits on a desktop and is configured to address the computing needs of one user at a time. This format includes Macintoshes, IBM-compatibles, Commodores, and others. In ordinary usage, though, refers to only an IBM-compatible computer, as opposed to a Macintosh. (2) Acronym for politically correct.

Sentence: "Some would say it's more PC to buy a *PC* rather than a Mac, because Apple is so proprietary in its business practices."

PC-DOS

Pronunciation: *Pee See Doss.*

Meaning: Acronym for *Personal Computer-Disk Operating System.* The version of MS-DOS that is bundled with IBM-PCs. Either way, it's the most commonly used operating system on PCs. (See also *DOS* and *MS-DOS.*)

Sentence: "Do the upgrades for *PC-DOS* correspond to the upgrades for MS-DOS? I think not."

PC-XT

Pronunciation: *Pee See Ecks Tee.*

Meaning: Abbreviation for *Personal Computer - eXtended Technology.* A very early (relatively speaking — 1983) personal computer manufactured by IBM that used the Intel 8088 microprocessor. The XT, as it was called, was superior to previous PC computers. Now, you can't give one away. (See also *boat anchor.*)

Sentence: "You don't have to go to a computer museum to find a *PC-XT;* the technology changes so fast that most users can't afford to keep up with it."

PCI

Pronunciation: *Pee See I.*

Meaning: Acronym that stands for *Peripheral Component Interconnect,* which is a new bus standard developed by Intel. The dream of the PCI bus is to wipe out the VESA local bus standard and provide a faster bus for future computers that will require higher data processing speeds. Today's bus standards (ISA, EISA, and VLB) are like two-lane country roads. In comparison, PCI plans to be a five-lane interstate highway.

Sentence: "If you want a computer that won't become obsolete as fast, get one with the PCI bus. Then again, by the time you actually need to expand the capabilities of a PCI computer, it will probably be cheaper to buy a whole new computer instead."

PCL

Pronunciation: *Pee See Ell.*

Meaning: Acronym for *Printer Control Language.* A set of instructions used to control a specific brand of printer — not to be confused with *page description language*, nor with a *printer driver*. The printer driver might contain instructions written in a printer control language, but the PCL is germane to the printer itself. Also used commonly to refer to HP LaserJet compatibility.

Sentence: "I have a *PCL* printer that acts just like a LaserJet III, but it's a lot less expensive. It's called a LaserJet II."

PCMCIA

Pronunciation: *Pee See Em See I A.*

Meaning: Long-winded acronym that stands for *Personal Computer Memory Card International Association,* which is an organization dedicating its life to defining a standard for making and marketing credit card-size expansion cards for laptop and some desktop computers. PCMCIA expansion cards resemble metal credit cards that cost a lot and look like they could break just as easily.

Sentence: "Since laptop computers don't have room in them for ordinary-size expansion boards, you have to expand their capabilities using *PCMCIA* cards instead. In the future, more desktop computers will use PCMCIA because they're easier to use and can get lost easily, so you'll have to buy more."

PCX

Pronunciation: *Pee See Ecks.*

Meaning: A graphics file format (and therefore a file extension) for the PC. Originally developed for the PC Paintbrush program, PCX is supported by almost every program on the PC, both Windows and DOS. PCX files are bitmapped graphics files. (See also *bitmapped.*)

Sentence: "Bob thought *PCX* was a rating for the naughty graphics files he collected."

PDA

Pronunciation: *Pee Dee Ay.*

Meaning: Acronym that stands for *Personal Digital Assistant,* which describes hand-held computers that let you store notes, make phone calls, and cost a lot more than a pencil and a pad of paper.

Sentence: "The most popular *PDA* is Apple's Newton, which can recognize your handwriting. If you think using a PDA might come in handy, ask yourself how many times you misplace pens, and then ask yourself if you'd be willing to misplace a $1,000 computer by mistake."

PDF

Pronunciation: *Pee Dee Ef.*

Meaning: Acronym that stands for *Portable Document Format,* which is a type of file created by the Adobe Acrobat program. A PDF file contains text and graphics that can be viewed by anyone who uses an IBM or Macintosh computer, whether or not they actually have the Adobe Acrobat program on their hard disk. Unlike most files that can only be used on one specific type of computer (IBM or Macintosh), PDF files are meant to be shared among different types of computers.

Sentence: "I tried giving Bob my WordPerfect document, but, like a jerk, Bob didn't have WordPerfect on his computer so he couldn't read my document. Now that I converted my document into a *PDF* file, Bob can read the file on his computer, even though he's partially illiterate."

PDL

Pronunciation: *Pee Dee Ell.*

Meaning: Abbreviation for *Page Description Language.* A programming language, such as PostScript, that is processed by a CPU in the printer itself. The PDL, through its particular statements and commands, "describes" the information on a page of printed output, generally through vector graphics calculations. Although it may take thousands of lines of PDL code to describe a page, the result — bitmapped graphics — prints much faster than the previous method of sending information to the printer. The PDL is independent of the particular kind of printer you're using as long as the printer has the capability of understanding the language. (See also *PostScript* and *Vector Graphics.*)

Sentence: "PostScript is a *PDL* commonly used with Macintosh computers. TrueType is now the primary PDL for PCs. TrueType is PostScript-compatible, but PostScript is not TrueType-compatible."

peek

Pronunciation: *peek.*

Meaning: A BASIC command that lets the user "peek" at the contents of a precise address in memory. The user can then *poke* a new value into the address if desired. (See also *poke.*)

Sentence: "I took a *peek* into Santa's sack and saw that he was going to bring me a super duper fax/modem for Christmas!"

peer-to-peer

Pronunciation: *peer-too-peer.*

Meaning: A democratic arrangement in networking technology where all nodes are created equal. The other kind of network is a *client-server* arrangement, where one machine is specially designated as a file server that can allocate resources not available to the "client" nodes. A peer-to-peer relationship has no shared resources on a server. You can have a peer-to-peer relationship between computers in a network that contains servers. A *peer-to-peer file transfer* is the technology for accessing the available files of other members along the network. (See also *client-server, network, nodes,* and *server.*)

Sentence: "*Peer-to-peer* means that our computers communicate on a network without a file server. 'Pier to peer' means that we go to the end of the dock and peer over the edge."

pen

Pronunciation: *pen.*

Meaning: (1) Long, thin device used for writing, ranging from a quill to a felt-tip. (2) A computer that receives input from a stylus similar in shape to traditional, pencilesque writing implements, but which registers signals electronically so that users can write in their own handwriting rather than enter information on a keyboard or with a mouse. Pen-based input must be neatly printed. Hence, an ironic turnaround: when we lost touch with paper and became dependent on keyboards, our handwriting became a casualty of technological development. Now that the technology has advanced even further, tidy handwriting is once again becoming a necessity — to be able to take advantage of the technology! Industry analysts predicted that pen-based computing would be the hottest new technology in years. In reality, the pen has had little impact on the industry thus far. (See also *light pen.*)

Sentence: "The *pen* is mightier than the keyboard."

Pentium

Pronunciation: *Pent-ee-um.*

Meaning: A brand new chip (microprocessor) for personal computers, manufactured by Intel. It is the successor to the 486 chip, and even people who don't write ad copy for Intel consider it revolutionary because of its speed and efficiency. Intel was going to call this the 586 chip, but they couldn't copyright the term, so they called it the Pentium. (See also *coprocessor, Intel, microprocessor,* and *processor.*)

Sentence: "The *Pentium* is a hot new gift idea when you don't know what else to get the friend who has everything. This Christmas, get her a Pentium."

peripheral

Pronunciation: *per-if-er-ul.*

Meaning: Any machinery connected to the computer, including monitors, printers, scanners, mice, external hard or floppy drives, CD-ROM drives, speakers, and keyboards.

Sentence: "We are going to get so overwhelmed with *peripherals* that we won't be able to find the center anymore."

peripheralitis

Pronunciation: *per-if-er-ul-ih-tis.*

Meaning: A disorder characterized by having too many peripherals and nowhere to plug them in. Another problem is that you'll have a hard time getting them to talk to each other.

Sentence: "A very effective cure for *peripheralitis* is poverty."

permanent storage

Pronunciation: *perm-e-nent stor-ej.*

Meaning: Any data or means of storing it that is bolted down and won't go ka-blooie when you turn the computer off. Hard drives, floppy drives, and ROM are examples of permanent storage. RAM is the opposite — anything in RAM will go ka-blooie when you turn off the computer. (See also *nonvolatile memory.*)

Sentence: "I put all the names in my little black book into *permanent storage* on my computer."

Personal Information Manager (PIM)

Pronunciation: *Per-son-al In-for-may-shin Mah-nah-jer.*

Meaning: A program that tries to organize your appointments, meetings, or schedules so you can easily see how you're spending (wasting) your time at work. Sometimes abbreviated as PIM.

Sentence: "Because I never seemed to have any time, I bought a new *Personal Information Manager* for my computer. Now I still don't have any time because I'm spending it all trying to learn how to use my computer, MS-DOS, Windows, and my PIM all at the same time."

PERT

Pronunciation: *Pert.*

Meaning: Acronym for *Program Evaluation and Review Technique* (or Peripheral Envy Regression Training, for all you closet New Agers out there). An approach to project management that doesn't necessarily need the computer to implement it. You can perform PERT equally well on paper. PERT involves charting out the time and other resources needed to complete various components of a project. Project management software programs usually contain PERT charting features. (Isn't PERT a shampoo, too?)

Sentence: "I used a *PERT* diagram to show the vice president the schedule we intend to follow. He liked it so much that I'm now the official PERT manager at the company."

phosphor

Pronunciation: *fahs-fer.*

Meaning: The material used inside the CRT (cathode ray tube) to create the display. It works by being stimulated by an electron beam and emits the energy it absorbs in the form of light patterns that the user sees.

Sentence: "The *phosphor* in my monitor must be stimulated by now because I've been typing love poems all day."

phosphor burn-in

Pronunciation: *fahs-fer bern-in.*

Meaning: A ghost image that appears on the screen — and stays there — as a result of having the same particles activated for too long a time. Akin to sunburn of the monitor, phosphor burn-in occurs when you leave the same image on the screen for several hours. When you turn the screen off, you can still see an outline of the image. Screen savers help prevent this burn-in. (See also *screen saver.*)

Sentence: "When you get screen savers to prevent *phosphor burn-in,* they should have protection factor numbers like sunscreen."

Photo CD

Pronunciation: *Fo-to See Dee.*

Meaning: A format, developed by Kodak, for storing digital photographs on a compact disc. A Photo CD lets you store multiple photographs on a compact disc until the compact disc can't hold any more pictures. The Kodak dream is that you can own a Photo CD, take it into a film processing center with a roll of film, and the film processing center will store your photographs on your Photo CD for you.

Sentence: "After taking pictures of our vacation, we had the processing center store them all on a *Photo CD.* Now we can make multiple Photo CDs, distribute them, and bore people with our vacation pictures all over the world."

physical device

Pronunciation: *fiz-i-kul dee-vis.*

Meaning: An actual, physical, touch-and-feel device associated with your computer. *Physical device* would not require defining if it weren't for virtual devices, which are imaginary, make believe, can't-touch-'em devices. (See also *virtual device.*)

Sentence: "I put my virtual file, which contains my virtual income projection, onto a *physical device* for storage. I'm hoping it will become real."

physical drive

Pronunciation: *fiz-i-kul drih-va.*

Meaning: The actual floppy disk a user is writing to or reading from, with all its uniqueness, brand identity, and idiosyncrasies, as opposed to the *logical drive*, which is strictly an electronic concept, or the *virtual drive*, which is really just a file on a physical drive that acts like a separate drive. (See also *logical drive.*)

Sentence: "If you dissect the *physical drive* while saving data, you will have a virtual disaster."

pica

Pronunciation: *pih-ka.*

Meaning: An old-fashioned typographical measurement that rivals the English system (inches, pounds, and so on) for obsolescence. One pica equals 12 points, which is the measurement used to define typefaces. A pica equals *approximately* 1/6 of an inch, and each page layout program might have a different version of what this amounts to. Pages and parts of pages are measured in picas.

Sentence: "Since this is an emotional book, we'll make the gutters between those columns three *picas* wide. That should handle the run-off."

pico-

Pronunciation: *pee-koh* or *pih-koh.*

Meaning: A prefix meaning one-trillionth.

Sentence: "Give me a couple of *pico*seconds to back up my hard drive, and I'll be right with you."

PIF

Pronunciation: *Piff.*

Meaning: Acronym for *Program Information File*. PIF files are used by Windows to define parameters for DOS programs. A PC-type file that contains information about the logistics of running the application to which it corresponds.

Sentence: "*PIF*! Puff! Oy, oy, oy!"

PIM

Pronunciation: *Pimm.*

Meaning: See *Personal Information Manager.*

pin

Pronunciation: *pin.*

Meaning: The doohickeys in a dot-matrix printer that make an impression on the ribbon, which in turn makes an impression on the paper. The more pins, the sharper the image. Also, the doohickeys within a parallel or serial port that help configure the flow of information.

Sentence: "It was so quiet you could hear a 24-*pin* printer drop."

pin feed

Pronunciation: *pin feed.*

Meaning: Not the same kind of pins as above. This kind of pin is located on the sprocket wheel, and it's not as sharp as the other kind. It's the mechanism found on dot-matrix printers that use tractor-feed computer paper, the kind with the tear-off margins that have holes in them. The pins grab onto the holes and propel the paper through the machine. (See also *dot-matrix printer.*)

Sentence: "Sometimes the *pin feed* mechanism jams, and my document comes out looking like a Chinese paper fan."

Pink Floyd

Pronunciation: *Pink Flow-yd.*

Meaning: The name of one of the most successful rock bands in history, recording such notable albums as *The Dark Side of the Moon* and *The Wall,* which have sold over 23 million copies worldwide and have been banned by various dictatorships over the years for their anti-social messages. Pink Floyd is often the rock music of choice for hard-core programmers, hackers, and people who ingest illegal substances into their system.

Sentence: "When I program in an ancient language like COBOL or FORTRAN, I like listening to classical music. But when I really want to crank out good C++ code, I listen to *Pink Floyd.*"

pipe

Pronunciation: *pihp.*

Meaning: In UNIX and DOS, the technology for naming and connecting two or more programs so that the results of the first one named in the statement are fed as input to the second one named, and so on, ad infinitum. It's like sending water through a series of pipes. (See also *filter* and *pipe character.*)

Sentence: "This first program logs into my bank's computer database and locates my checking account to see how much money I need. This second program funnels the required money into my account. I use a *pipe* to connect these two programs."

pipe character

Pronunciation: *pihp kar-ek-ter.*

Meaning: A character found on the keyboard that you never see in real life, that looks like this: |. Sometimes it's one long line, and sometimes it's split in the middle. This character is usually found above the backslash, another character found only on computers. (See also *pipe.*)

Sentence: "My plumber's favorite key on the keyboard is the one with the *pipe character.*"

piracy

Pronunciation: *pih-re-see.*

Meaning: The copying of software without the permission of the writer or publisher, and, if you're really bad, distributing it as well. It is estimated that for every copy of a program that is purchased legitimately, two copies are pirated. Most pirates justify this practice by explaining that the software companies are making too much money on the products they sell and that pirated copies do not really take away revenue from the publishers because pirates would not have purchased the product anyway. Efforts to squelch this plague have included copy protection, registration of legal owners, and Just Saying No — besides the fact that you could also go to jail for it.

Sentence: "Software *piracy* allows people who become easily sea-sick to become buccaneers."

pitch

Pronunciation: *pit-cha.*

Meaning: Number of characters per inch, as on old-fashioned typewriters. Some old word processing software still uses this type of measurement, and will, for instance, give you a choice of printing in 10-pitch or 12-pitch.

Sentence: "Printing in 12-*pitch* saves space and looks classier. Printing in 10-pitch takes up more paper, so this is probably the way you want to go when writing term papers — or when writing for money, when you're getting paid by the page."

pixel

Pronunciation: *piks-ell.*

Meaning: Acronym for *PICture ELement.* As atoms are to molecules, pixels are to pictures. They are the smallest un-break-down-able units of a picture on the monitor's screen. When the image quality is poor, you are painfully conscious of looking at a bunch of square dots.

Sentence: "That thin coat of dirt on the front of your monitor is called *pixel* dust."

PL/1

Pronunciation: *Pee Ell Won.*

Meaning: Abbreviation for *Programming Language One,* an early programming language mostly used on IBM mainframes.

Sentence: "Not too many people use *PL/1* anymore, but it's still cool to have on your résumé."

plasma

Pronunciation: *plaz-ma.*

Meaning: The type of display or monitor used in laptop and notebook computers — adapted from LCD technology. Plasma monitors are flat, do not require tubes, and are therefore smaller and lighter than CRT monitors. The image is produced by stimulating a gas trapped between two panels. Also known as *flat panel display.* (See also *gas plasma display* and *monitor.*)

Sentence: "If I look at the *plasma* display on my laptop computer at just the right angle, I can see the ocean."

platen

Pronunciation: *play-ten.*

Meaning: In dot-matrix and daisy wheel printers, the roller that guides the paper through the printer. The character keys strike against the paper while it's rolling over this surface.

Sentence: "Do not let your *platen* get scratched or notched because that could make the letters come out looking funny."

platform

Pronunciation: *plat-form.*

Meaning: The hardware foundation on which an operating system sits, or the operating system on which a software application sits. For example, the Intel X86 processors constitute a platform on which operating systems are built. DOS/Windows is a platform on which application programs are built.

Sentence: "My friend told me he really likes the Macintosh *platform.* I told him to stop putting it on a pedestal."

plotter

Pronunciation: *plah-ter.*

Meaning: A type of printer that draws pictures with one or more pens, based on instructions fed to it from the computer. Especially useful with graphics or CAD applications.

Sentence: "When the ink jams up in a *plotter*-type printer, do you say, 'The plotter thickens?'"

plug

Pronunciation: *plug.*

Meaning: The thing at the end of a wire or cable that you stick into a jack to make information or electricity flow. Synonymous with *male connector.* (See also *male connector.*)

Sentence: "Sometimes when you can't get your computer to work, it's because you need to *plug* it in."

plug and play

Pronunciation: *plugg and play.*

Meaning: A wistful fantasy of engineers where all computer equipment works perfectly with equipment from other manufacturers, just by plugging the pieces together.

Sentence: "There will be no *plug and play* computers in this office! No! Give me plug and work computers!"

PMMU

Pronunciation: *Pee Em Em You.*

Meaning: Abbreviation for *Paged Memory Management Unit.* A chip or circuit in some later-model computers that enables them to invoke virtual memory. (See also *virtual memory.*)

Sentence: "I just love thinking about all the things in my Mac that are virtual rather than real, like *PMMU.*"

point

Pronunciation: *poynt.*

Meaning: (1) A move that the user makes with the mouse or "pointing device" that simply involves moving the mouse so that the mouse pointer moves to the desired location on the screen. (2) A measurement for typefaces. It's easy to specify or to change the point size in a typical word processing program, but if you want to measure text on a page, you need a special ruler. A point is equal to one-sixth of a pica, which makes it equal to *approximately* 1/72 of an inch. The exact measurement varies with each word processing or page layout program. Typical point size for books is around 11- to 12-point type. Display type, used for advertising, can get up to 72-point or larger. (See also *pica.*)

Sentence: "If you want your résumé to fit on one page, you can make the *point* size highly doinky."

point-of-sale system

Pronunciation: *poynt-uv-say-ell sis-tem.*

Meaning: Computer hardware and software for retail sales operations. The type of hardware can range from a personal computer to a mainframe, but its function is the same: it registers prices for individual items, gathers data from sales, tracks inventory, and maintains a customer database. It can include peripherals like a receipt printer, a bar code scanner, and a credit card verification capability.

Sentence: "Before we can install an expensive, new *point-of-sale system* in our store, we need to cut down on shoplifting."

pointer

Pronunciation: *poynt-er.*

Meaning: A symbol that appears on the screen and corresponds to the movement of the mouse or other pointing device. The pointer doesn't always look the same. It can take on different guises in different applications or even in different functions within the same application. A pointer is also a programming term relating to a variable that keeps track of an object (such as the next item in a linked list). (See also *I-beam pointer, linked list,* and *mouse.*)

Sentence: "On the Mac, the *pointer* changes from an arrow to a watch when the computer is busy doing something. That happens a lot."

pointing device

Pronunciation: *poynt-ing dee-vihs.*

Meaning: An input device like a mouse, trackball, joystick, or stylus that lets you move the cursor around the screen.

Sentence: "When Jerry uses a touch-sensitive monitor, his finger is no longer a picking device but becomes a *pointing device.*"

poke

Pronunciation: *pohk.*

Meaning: A BASIC command that allows you to place a specific value into a precise memory address. (See also *peek.*)

Sentence: "The object is to know where to *poke* the computer so it doesn't poke you back."

polymorphic virus

Pronunciation: *pah-lee-mor-fik vi-rus.*

Meaning: A special virus that modifies itself each time it infects a file on your computer. By modifying itself, a polymorphic virus makes it harder for anti-virus programs to find and kill all possible strains of the virus. Polymorphic viruses are usually created with the help of a mutation engine. (See also *mutation engine.*)

Sentence: "My anti-virus programs found and removed a *polymorphic virus* from my computer. But I'm afraid that the anti-virus program hasn't found all the different strains of the polymorphic virus, so I played it safe and switched my hard disk with Lyle's."

polymorphism

Pronunciation: *pahl-ee-morf-iz-um.*

Meaning: In the context of object-oriented programming, this means using the same name to specify different procedures within different contexts. A good analogy is the word *cook.* This term can involve a different method for bread, for pasta, for vegetables, and for meat. You can define *display,* for instance, to apply to text, graphs, pictures, spreadsheets, movies, sound effects, and anything else you choose to associate with the term. (See also *object-oriented programming.*)

Sentence: "I tried to describe the concept of *polymorphism* to my family, but then my mother-in-law blurted out that her sister is not a man and just has a tiny mustache problem."

pong

Pronunciation: *pawng.*

Meaning: (1) Say you're working on a computer that's part of a network. You want to tap into another computer on the network. There's a way to send out a signal (other than e-mail) to find out if that computer is available to connect with or not. Your status check is the "ping"; the other computer's response is the "pong." (2) The original computer game developed by Atari in the mid-'70s, now found in museums.

Sentence: "*Pong* was named after Ping Pong, the table tennis game invented by the Chinese. Do you know it's called Ping Pong in Chinese as well? Do you know what it means? Actually, 'ping pong' is the sound the ball makes. Same in Chinese and English. What a world!"

pop

Pronunciation: *pahp.*

Meaning: When data is arranged in a stack (like a stack of dishes), to retrieve the next record (or piece of data that is sitting on top of the stack) is to *pop* it. This doesn't happen much in an end-user situation but is more likely to happen within a programming context.

Sentence: "Pat's afraid that if his computer didn't have a lid, all those values he *popped* off the stack would fly up and hit him in the eye."

pop-up menu

Pronunciation: *pahp-up men-yoo.*

Meaning: Essentially the same idea as a pull-down menu, only it appears someplace other than the menu bar itself and is often the result of a keyboard command. In a Mac environment, a pop-up menu can appear when you highlight one of the choices on a pull-down menu. (See also *pull-down menu.*)

Sentence: "A *pop-up menu* is a little different from a pop-up book. You do not get a picture of the item in question sticking up from the surface of the screen."

port

Pronunciation: *port.*

Meaning as a noun: A jack in back of the computer where you can plug in a peripheral device. Ports are usually either serial or parallel. (See also *printer.*)

Meaning as a verb: To convert a software application to an operating system other than the one it was originally written for — that is, to *port* the application to another platform.

Sentence: "Many software companies just *port* their applications from the PC to the Macintosh rather than rewrite the application from scratch on the Macintosh. Then they often discover that the problems associated with porting applications often take longer to resolve than just rewriting the program from scratch."

portable computer

Pronunciation: *port-e-bull cum-pyoo-ter.*

Meaning: A computer that you can carry around with you without making yourself a candidate for the trauma ward. Classifications include laptops, notebooks, and hand-held computers. A portable computer that is really too heavy to lug around regularly may be called "transportable" or "a brick on a leash."

Sentence: "I have a new *portable computer* that can store pages of information and print them out instantanly. It even recognizes my handwriting. It's called a pad and pencil."

portrait orientation

Pronunciation: *por-tret aw-ree-en-tae-shun.*

Meaning: An amazingly convoluted way of saying "the usual direction" when discussing which way to turn the paper or which way the paper gets printed on. It means more vertical than horizontal, or "the long way," as opposed to "landscape orientation," or "the wide way." Usually you find this terminology in graphics applications. Like many other professionals, graphic artists seem to have an irresistible need to mystify even the simplest things. (See also *landscape orientation.*)

Sentence: "If you didn't print that picture of President Clinton with *portrait orientation,* you would be making the expensive mistake of cutting off the top of his hair."

POS

Pronunciation: *Pee Oh Ess.*

Meaning: Abbreviation for *Point of Sale.* (See also *point-of-sale system.*)

Sentence: "Our *POS* system was just installed. It consists of a receipt book, a pen, and a cash drawer."

POSIX

Pronunciation: *Pos-icks.*

Meaning: Acronym for *Portable Operating System Interface for UNIX.* A version of UNIX developed by the Institute of Electrical and Electronics Engineers. (See also *UNIX.*)

Sentence: "IEEE tries again, with POSIX, to impose some standardization on the many implementations of UNIX."

POST

Pronunciation: *Po-sta.*

Meaning: Acronym for *Power-On Self-Test,* a rigorous battery of tests the PC subjects itself to when first started. Rumor has it that if the computer fails any of the tests, it displays a cryptic error message and pouts in the corner until you call someone to tell you what to do.

Sentence: "Before I leave the house, I perform a personal *POST.* I check to see if I have my wallet, my keys, my glasses, that my hair is combed, and that I have my important stuff with me. Oh, and I check to ensure that I'm wearing pants."

post

Pronunciation: *po-sta.*

Meaning: To send an electronic message, usually to add a message to a news group or on-line bulletin board.

Sentence: "You never can feel involved with a BBS until you *post.*"

PostScript

Pronunciation: *Pohst-Skript.*

Meaning: A page description language developed by Adobe Systems used with laser printers and other high-resolution machines. To make PostScript work, you need to have a PostScript printer driver included with either the software application or the operating system. One of the great benefits of this technology is that you can create a document with an ordinary desktop computer, but the file can be read by very professional typesetting machines, such as a Linotronic. Thus, if you wanted to make a brochure or poster or print advertisement, you could do *all* of the design on your end and just take the disk to a print shop that would generate the output required by the printer. (See also *Linotronic.*)

Sentence: "If you need typeset-quality printouts, take your *PostScript* files to a laser bureau for output."

power down

Pronunciation: *pow-er down.*

Meaning: (1) To turn off the electric supply to the computer and/or peripherals. (2) To eat quickly and with vigor.

Sentence: "We have 30,000 more lines of code to write by 5:00; *power down* that Twinkie and get back to work!"

power up

Pronunciation: *pow-er up.*

Meaning: To turn something on.

Sentence: "Poor Ralph tried to *power up* his PC by plugging it into a 220-volt socket."

power supply

Pronunciation: *pow-er sup-plih.*

Meaning: The gizmo within the computer that changes the AC (alternating current) that comes out of your wall to the DC current that the computer actually uses. It's not a one-to-one correspondence. You need to make sure that your computer's power supply is adequate to cover the needs of all the machinery it's serving. (See also *AC* and *alternating current.*)

Sentence: "My computer's *power supply* gets so hot that I now use it to cook my breakfast in the morning."

power surge

Pronunciation: *pow-er serj.*

Meaning: You might think that because the shape of your plugs doesn't change and the size of your wires doesn't change, if you keep the same thing plugged into the same outlet you get the same amount of electricity. If only that were true. The amount of power flowing through your wires can vary considerably, and having it increase drastically and suddenly can cause damage to your computer's innards. Most of this surge (or *spike*) is beyond your control, but, regardless of the cause, every computer user needs to install a device called a *surge protector* between the computer and the wall. This offers full protection against power surges but offers no protection against other communicable diseases. (See also *spike* and *surge protector.*)

Sentence: "I read a science fiction story about a *power surge* that caused a computer to come alive. In reality, *power surges* are more likely to kill your computer."

power user

Pronunciation: *pow-er yoo-zer.*

Meaning: Somebody who's totally hip, adept, and cool in every way when it comes to doing things with computers. Power users not only know what to do to get something to happen, but they know *why* the thing works, as well. They can figure out shortcuts. They can hold down more than one key at a time with one hand. While munching on cocktail wieners, they can dazzle a roomful of people at a party with discussions of leveraged software, object-oriented programming, and cross-platform porting technologies.

Sentence: "When I was having problems with my computer, I asked our company's hottest *power user* what to do. He told me to turn the computer off and then turn it back on again. Can a person get paid to be a *power user?*"

PowerPC

Pronunciation: *Pow-er Pee See.*

Meaning: The name of a microprocessor from Motorola that uses reduced instruction set technology (also known as RISC), which uses simple instructions to carry out complicated programming commands. Apple Computers has replaced the older Motorola 68000 microprocessors in their Macintosh computers with the new PowerPC microprocessors.

Sentence: "According to the latest Apple ads, the new *PowerPC* Macintosh computers can run DOS, Windows, and Macintosh programs. Of course, many people are wondering that if you want to run Windows programs, why would you want to buy a Macintosh in the first place?"

PPM

Pronunciation: *Pee Pee Em.*

Meaning: Abbreviation for *Pages Per Minute.* The number of pages that come out of a printer in each minute. "In each," in this case, is the same as "per," so it's OK to say "Pages PER Minute" or PPM. Don't get stuck on the numbers, though. Eight pages per minute to one manufacturer might mean something different to another manufacturer (even if they both know how to count). You need to know whether that's eight pages of text only, eight pages of the printer's favorite font, eight pages with four-color graphics, eight pages only when the sun is shining, there's a gentle breeze, and the federal budget deficit is under control. . . .

Sentence: "When you are talking about buying a printer, ask about the *PPMs* as well as PCLs and PDLs. And while you're at it, ask about printers you can use with PIMs or PDAs. Whatever you end up getting, make sure to treat it with TLC."

PPP

Pronunciation: *Pee Pee Pee.*

Meaning: Acronym for *Point-to-Point Protocol.* This is a new standard for computers that want to join the Internet. It allows them to use TCP/IP (whatever that is), a high-speed modem, and regular phone lines to connect. This standard is replacing SLIP, just in case you were thinking of hooking up Mr. PC to the net.

Sentence: "Bob said we could use *PPP* to get on the net, but I've been pressing the P key for half an hour and nothing's happened."

precedence

Pronunciation: *pre-se-dens.*

Meaning: The order in which things are done in a mathematical operation. If operation A gets done (on purpose, mind you) before operation B, then operation A has *precedence* over operation B. An operation in the innermost parentheses in a statement has precedence over those in the outer parentheses. If there are no parentheses, the order of operations is determined by the natural order of operation.

Sentence: "Calculating the subtotal must take *precedence* over calculating the total."

precision

Pronunciation: *pree-si-zhun.*

Meaning: Exactness of a number, in terms of how many decimal places you take it out to. For instance, 3.17259324867 has a greater precision than 3.17. Precision is an area that triggers people's obsessive/compulsive tendencies, but, fortunately, computers have more of a sense of self-restraint than that.

Sentence: "You only need 2-digit *precision* to balance your checkbook, but plan on using more for sending a rocket into space."

presentation graphics

Pronunciation: *prez-en-tae-shun graf-icks.*

Meaning: A branch of software geared to creating impressive visual components that are used for speeches and other presentations. Essentially, such software translates data from a database or spreadsheet into a chart or graph, as well as being able to integrate text, titles, art, sound, and even multimedia activities. The end result is a high-tech slide show that can be viewed on a monitor or projected onto a screen from slides. (See also *graphics*.)

Sentence: "My speech is dreadful, but I have some *presentation graphics* that should keep them awake."

Presentation Manager

Pronunciation: *Prez-en-tae-shun Man-a-jer.*

Meaning: The old GUI and API for earlier versions of OS/2. (See also *OS/2.*)

Sentence: "*Presentation Manager* should have been renamed the Here It Is Whether You Like It Or Not Manager."

print

Pronunciation: *print.*

Meaning: To generate output from the computer onto pages of paper or mylar via any number of fascinating technologies. Also, a very standard command for any program or programming language, one of the few that are universally understood and not called by weird names in different programs in a forced effort to create brand identity. There are some choices involved in each print job. You can specify, for instance, how many copies, which pages of the file you want printed (if you don't want the whole file printed), whether the machine should collate the pages, and so on.

Sentence: "I used the *Print* command to print my document to the Print Manager, which holds it in a print queue while the printer completes its current print job."

print buffer

Pronunciation: *print buf-er.*

Meaning: A portion of memory that temporarily holds the print queue. The printer needs an area like this because its processing is much slower than the computer's, and this "holding cell" prevents a traffic jam. The computer sends information to the printer only as fast as the print buffer accepts it. (See also *buffer* and *screen buffer.*)

Sentence: "Joyce thought she didn't need a *print buffer* since the maid kept her printer clean for her."

print head

Pronunciation: *print hed.*

Meaning: The part of a dot-matrix printer's mechanism that contains the pins. The print head scans the paper while the pins strike the ribbon, creating images. (See also *dot-matrix.*)

Sentence: "The guarantee on my dot-matrix printer said that the *print head* will last for 300 million impressions. I'm sure I wasn't past one million impressions by the time I upgraded to the laser printer."

print job

Pronunciation: *print jahb.*

Meaning: An order to print certain material in a certain way at a certain time. Every time you hit the final OK key (or the equivalent) after making all your print specifications, that constitutes a print job — no matter how many times you might create an exact duplicate of that same order. A print job is also the unit you can cancel, delay, or perform other operations on. (See also *queue.*)

Sentence: "Don, your *print job* should have been fired."

Print Screen

Pronunciation: *Print Skreen.*

Meaning: An instruction to the computer to print the screen exactly the way it is, weird formatting commands and all. Also a key on your keyboard which, in some applications, prints the screen.

Sentence: "*Print Screen* is a key on most keyboards that never does what you'd expect."

print spooler

Pronunciation: *print spool-er.*

Meaning: Software that manages a print queue and lets print jobs line up one after the other — as if they were wrapped around a spool — patiently feeding them to the printer in the background while the user is busy writing novels, crunching numbers, playing Tetris, or doing other productive things in the foreground. (See also *background, foreground, queue,* and *printer buffer.)*

Sentence: "The Windows *print spooler* is called the Print Manager, which manages your print jobs and sends them to the printer in a queue."

printer

Pronunciation: *print-er.*

Meaning: An output device that translates signals from the computer into text and graphics on paper (or mylar, or any of a number of other materials, for that matter). Types of printers range from the old-fashioned dot-matrix printers that are so noisy their owners sometimes put boxes over them in a futile attempt to muffle the racket, to the wondrously, whisperingly quiet professional laser printers. Printers, like xerox machines, are subject to the most ultimate extrapolations of

Murphy's Law. Not only will anything that can go wrong actually do so, but it will go wrong more persistently and with less feedback than almost any other machine you've grown to love. The principal types of printers include *dot-matrix, daisy wheel, inkjet,* and *laser.* (See also *Murphy's Law.*)

Sentence: "My laser *printer* cranks out eight pages a minute. That's a little bit faster than I can type, so I guess the cost is worth it."

printer driver

Pronunciation: *print-er drih-ver.*

Meaning: The software that acts as an interpreter between the operating system or application software and the particular make and model of printer you're trying to talk to. In most cases, the set of printer drivers is written into the operating system, but in some cases, like DOS, each application has to have its own printer driver.

Sentence: "I can't seem to get the right *printer driver* for my printer. Maybe because it's from Korea, the instructions need to be in Korean."

printer font

Pronunciation: *print-er fahnt.*

Meaning: In the old days, fonts that the printer was capable of printing out but that the computer was *not* capable of displaying on the screen. This is rarely the case in these enlightened times. In fact, sometimes it's the other way around, where you can get fonts to show up on the screen that the printer can't necessarily produce. The term *printer font* also applies to a font that is created for the printer's PDL and that, hopefully, matches a screen font so that you can see something close to what the printer will print. (See also *font.*)

Sentence: "My printer has three *printer fonts*: Ugly, Uglier, and Too Ugly For The Human Mind To Comprehend."

printer port

Pronunciation: *print-er port.*

Meaning: The jack on the back of your computer that you plug your printer into — usually a parallel port. (See also *parallel port.*)

Sentence: "I'm waiting for the ultimate portable computer that will let me plug my electric razor into the *printer port.*"

processor

Pronunciation: *prah-sess-er.*

Meaning: The brains of the computer, the sine qua non of the computer experience. Generally, the processor of note is the CPU, but there are other kinds, second most notably the math coprocessor. Also, there are processors in probably every single type of consumer electronics. The hallmark of a processor is that it acts on instructions: sorting them, filtering them, or performing mathematical operations on them. (See also *microprocessor* and *coprocessor.*)

Sentence: "It's kind of foolish to call a *processor* like the Pentium a 'microprocessor' when it's more powerful than the old mainframes of 15 years ago."

Prodigy

Pronunciation: *Prah-di-jee.*

Meaning: An on-line service for computer users that offers electronic shopping, securities trading, games, downloadable files, and electronic mail, to name a few. Anybody can join; all it takes is a relatively new computer, a modem, and an indifference to the high cost of communications.

Sentence: "I went to Sears to buy the software for *Prodigy,* but the salesman didn't know what I was talking about. He asked me if it was some kind of Mozart thing."

program

Pronunciation: *proh-gram.*

Meaning: A set of instructions written in a programming language. Software is the same thing as a program. Also called an *application.* Either way you express it, a program is composed on a keyboard and assembled by machines or underpaid technicians. The most familiar types of programs on the consumer or end-user market are application programs, like word processing, databases, spreadsheets, graphics programs, games, and educational programs. However, there are other types of programs less visible to the naked eye, which can be thought of as the computer talking to itself (in a roundabout way). These include operating systems, communications software, and utilities — the ultimate computer navel-gazing program being the Norton Utilities, where the computer gazes inward to detect and repair problems on the hard and floppy drives. In a way, a computer can also imagine itself: you can get programs that can simulate the performance of a chip or other piece of hardware. (See also *application program.*)

Sentence: "I'm sorry, sir, but *Seinfeld* only comes on ABC. I don't believe it's a type of program for the Macintosh."

programmer

Pronunciation: *proh-gram-er.*

Meaning: Someone who writes programs. This involves designing the program — what it should accomplish and how — writing the code in a programming language, putting the source code through a compiler (which translates it into a form the machine can understand), and debugging it, or fixing any errors. Programmers come in three types: geeks, wizards, and hackers. (See also *programming language.*)

Sentence: "Scott went to school for eight years to become a *programmer,* and now he works for the local dairy, delivering milk."

programming language

Pronunciation: *proh-gram-ing lang-wij.*

Meaning: A way of talking to the computer, analogous to the ways humans have evolved for talking to each other. Like natural languages, programming languages include grammar, syntax, and vocabulary, as well as style and organization. Some programming languages are not too far removed from English (called *high-level languages*), while others are more like hieroglyphics (called *low-level languages*). Some languages are more suited to specific vertical markets, like Ada to the defense industry, FORTRAN to business, and C++ to applications building.

The lower the level of language, the closer it is to the guts of the machine. And when languages get close to the guts, they get really efficient, which is the case with assembly language. But when you're talking to a machine in a low-level language, you're talking to a specific machine, and your work can't be reused on a different platform. Higher-level languages, which include just about everything from BASIC to C++, approximate human languages more closely. (See also *Ada, BASIC, C, C++, Fortran, LISP,* and *Pascal.*)

Sentence: "Bill, our computer guru, prefers *programming languages* to human languages."

progress indicator

Pronunciation: *prah-gres in-di-kae-ter.*

Meaning: A graphic element that displays the progress of an event, such as opening a file or sorting a database. Progress indicators are often called *thermometer bars.* As an event progresses, the "level" of the thermometer rises until the entire bar is full, indicating that the event is 100-percent complete. Progress indicators can also be simple `percent complete` counts.

Sentence: "All the *progress indicator* does is keep you from falling asleep while your computer takes an incredibly long time to do something."

PROLOG

Pronunciation: *Proh-log,* short for PROgramming in LOGic.

Meaning: A programming language of special interest to mathematicians and computer science researchers. In real life, it's useful in diagnostic-type applications and expert systems, where the procedure involves proving or disproving that x is the case.

Sentence: "I use *PROLOG* to figure out whether my x will get off my case."

PROM

Pronunciation: *Pee Rom* or *Prom.*

Meaning: Acronym for *Programmable Read-Only Memory.* A semiconductor chip that allows a program to be written onto it once — and only once — by the computer manufacturer. This type of chip sits in the middle of the spectrum between the two extremes: chips that come with the programming etched in by the semiconductor manufacturer, and EPROM chips, which can be erased (that's what the "E" stands for) and reprogrammed. (See also *EPROM, EEPROM,* and *ROM.*)

Sentence: "Instead of letting me go to the Junior Prom with Luke Perry, my dad made me finish assembling the *PROM* chips I had started."

prompt

Pronunciation: *prahmpt.*

Meaning: A little character that appears on the screen to let you know the ball is in your court. In DOS, it often looks like the symbol for "greater than." In CompuServe, it is an exclamation point. In other programs, it may appear as a flashing underline or flashing pipe character. Sometimes it's just a question mark. Whatever the form, a prompt tells you that the program is waiting for you to enter something. Usually, you must type something and then press Enter. You can change the appearance of the DOS prompt by typing the PROMPT command, like this:

```
PROMPT = $p "What do you want now?"
```

Sentence: "The DOS *prompt* has nothing to do with being on time."

proportional pitch

Pronunciation: *pre-por-shun-ul pich.*

Meaning: The practice of letting a letter take up as much room as it needs to. If this sounds obvious, consider that older printers and typewriters did not use proportional pitch. On such typewriters, an *i* would be allotted the same amount of space as a *w*, even though it had no need for it. You can pretty well expect the newer, more advanced printers to offer proportional pitch, as our sensibilities have gotten used to this aesthetic.

Sentence: "Next time I think I'll pay the extra money and have our driveway done in *proportional pitch.*"

proprietary

Pronunciation: *pro-prih-e-tare-ee.*

Meaning: "Mine, all mine, and no one else's," to quote my favorite seven-year-old. Proprietary means the company that developed the design owns the design, and no one may duplicate it or distribute it without that company's permission. (See also *open architecture.*)

Sentence: "The Macintosh System 7 is a *proprietary* operating system developed by Apple Computer, Inc. But then, Apple considers everything it does to be proprietary. Apparently, it doesn't know how to share."

protected mode

Pronunciation: *pro-tektd mohd.*

Meaning: Used most notably in reference to 386 PCs or better. It means that each program is allotted its own niche in memory (RAM) so that, if you run more than one program at a time, the processing of one program is easy to keep separate from the processing of the other program. Without this capability, programs being multitasked could enjoy all the simple elegance and delicate choreography of rush hour in Boston. Protected mode is not accessed by DOS or any DOS programs, including Windows. However, new operating systems are available that take advantage of the protected mode of X86 processors. Such operating systems include Windows NT and OS/2. (See also *multitasking.*)

Sentence: "Your computer cannot contract any diseases while it runs in the *protected mode.*"

protocol

Pronunciation: *proh-te-kahl.*

Meaning: A set of standards that enables communication or file transfers between two computers. In a communications context, for instance, parameters need to be set for baud rate, parity, the number of data bits, the presence or absence of a stop bit, and type of duplex. Without such agreement, the two computers might as well be speaking different languages.

Sentence: "It's important that the computers in a network use the same network *protocol.* Otherwise, no one nodes what's going on."

prototype

Pronunciation: *proh-toh-tihp.*

Meaning: A model for later/more advanced versions of a piece of hardware of software. A prototype typically embodies the intentions of the designer but hasn't worked out all of the details.

Sentence: "My communications hardware is so difficult to use that I wonder if the manufacturer just shipped me the *prototype.*"

PrScr

(See *Print Screen.*)

ps

Pronunciation: *pee ess.*

Meaning: A UNIX command that shows you the *processor status,* or exactly what's going on in your UNIX computer at that time. Since a UNIX computer can be doing a number of things at once, as well as having several people using it at the same time, ps lets you know what's going on.

Sentence: "I just did a *ps* and discovered that Morgan is trying to break into the password file. Let's fry his modem."

PS/1

Pronunciation: *Pee Ess Won.*

Meaning: Abbreviation for *Personal System 1.* A PC actually made and marketed by IBM itself. The PS/1 computer was designed for personal/ home use and is IBM's second attempt at entering the home computer market. (See also *Bozo.*)

Sentence: "I got a *PS/1* computer to use at home. It's great for playing computer games and it keeps the door open when it's windy out."

PS/2

Pronunciation: *Pee Ess Too.*

Meaning: Abbreviation for *Personal System 2,* an IBM PC featuring a proprietary 32-bit expansion bus called the Microchannel bus. PS/2 computers are often shipped with the OS/2 operating system. The PS/2 continues to be a major player in computer wars. (See also *expansion bus, MCA,* and *OS/2.*)

Sentence: "The prices of computers like the *PS/2* are so low that I'm tempted to purchase a better clone."

pseudocode

Pronunciation: *soo-doh kohd.*

Meaning: The flow of a program expressed in fractured English — that is, part ordinary English, part programming language — so that the programmer can map it out without getting stuck in the details. (See also *p-code.*)

Sentence: "I wrote this program in *pseudocode* so that my mother could understand it. She's now a high-paid programmer in the Silicon Valley."

public domain

Pronunciation: *pub-lik doh-maen.*

Meaning: Software that has no copyright and can be copied and distributed without guilt or gelt. There are hundreds of public domain programs available through catalogs and PD distributors. Public domain is also called *freeware*. However, *shareware* is not public domain. Generally, public domain software is "at your own risk" stuff. If it makes your disk drive smoke and gives your computer a wet, hacking cough, that's your tough luck. (See also *freeware* and *shareware.*)

Sentence: "I got a great *public domain* program that lets me arrange my furniture on the computer. Now if only I could take out the trash on the computer, I would never have to get out of my chair."

public key encryption

Pronunciation: *pu-blik Kee en-Krip-shin.*

Meaning: A unique form of scrambling data that requires two separate passwords: a private key and a public key. The private key password can scramble and unscramble data that was scrambled with the public key. The public key password can only scramble data. If someone wants to send you a message, they must use your public key password, but only you can unscramble and read the message using your private key. This form of encryption is more secure than other forms of encryption that only scramble data with a single password.

Sentence: "To protect your privacy when using electronic mail, use *public key encryption.* The only hard part is scrambling and unscrambling your data all the time, and remembering your private key password."

pull-down menu

Pronunciation: *puhl-down men-yoo.*

Meaning: In a software application, a pull-down menu is a list of intriguing possibilities that appears when you select an option on the menu bar. To choose an item from the list, you drag the mouse down to it and let go, or use the appropriate keyboard strokes. The Macintosh popularized pull-down menus in its original operating system back in 1983. Now, pull-down, pop-up, and tear-off menus are commonplace.

Sentence: "I wish *pull-down menus* worked more like window blinds; when you pull them down far enough and let go, they should flap around the menu bar a few times."

punched card

Pronunciation: *punchd kard.*

Meaning: Old-fashioned, unwieldy style of data processing which used a separate heavy-stock card to transmit information. The computer would translate a hole pattern punched in the card — or the light coming through them — into electronic signals. I prefer to think they're obsolete.

Sentence: "Many eons ago when I went to college, we registered for our courses by using *punched cards.*"

purge

Pronunciation: *purj.*

Meaning: To get rid of unwanted/unneeded stuff, preferably in an automated fashion, as with a global search-and-delete operation or a PURGE command.

Sentence: "After pizza, I feel the urge to *purge.*"

push

Pronunciation: *push.*

Meaning: Related to the stacking of data, which usually happens far from the watchful eye of the end-user somewhere in the bowels of a program. Stacked data may be envisioned as a stack of dishes, and stacked data refers to the way data is stored in a part of computer memory. To push a record onto the stack means to install it at the top of the stack, where it will be the first one *popped* when the stack is addressed. (See also *stack* and *pop.*)

Sentence: "When I *pushed* that data onto the stack, I got a `Stack Overflow` error, and the computer told me not to be so pushy."

QBasic

Pronunciation: *Q-Bay-sik.*

Meaning: A version of the BASIC language that Microsoft includes with MS-DOS version 5.0 and up. The Q supposedly stands for Quick, though Quirky also comes to mind.

Sentence: "For people who want to learn to program their computer without spending a lot of money, learn *QBasic* because it's already on your computer for free. Then again, if you like blowing wads of cash on stuff you'll never figure out how to use, buy a C++ compiler instead."

Quadra

Pronunciation: *kwa-druh.*

Meaning: A fast, high-end (expensive) Macintosh with a 68040 processor. Ideal for use as a file server, for desktop publishing, for image processing, or for complex number-crunching.

Sentence: "I bought a new *Quadra* because I wanted to outdo Joe, the manager in the next department. He only has a Classic. Besides, Quadras have such a cool name, and the company was paying for it anyway."

query

Pronunciation: *kwr-ee, kweer-ee,* or *kway-ree.*

Meaning: To inquire of. To ask a database for specific information. For example, to find all records containing *Padlevski* in the Last Name field, you use a query such as this:

```
Last Name = Padlevski
```

The database then searches every record until it finds a match. Database queries can become rather complex and intricate, such as the following:

```
Last Name = or (ZIP > 80000 and < 99999)
```

This makes no sense, but queries the database to locate all records containing a Padlevski in the Last Name field or a ZIP code between 80000 and 99999. (See also *database.*)

Sentence: "That last customer started yelling when I couldn't find his record in our database; so I *queried* the database for all records containing 'Jerk' and found him!"

queue

Pronunciation: *kyoo* (as in the dreaded Q on *Star Trek:TNG*).

Meaning: A collection of documents or files waiting as patiently as they can in turn for printing or some other form of processing. For example, a *print queue* is a collection of documents waiting to be printed. In England, the word queue means *a line,* such as a line of people waiting to buy tickets. They say, "Queue up and buy your tickets. Jolly good. Tut-tut."

Sentence: "My document is waiting in the network *queue* to be printed. It's number four. And I'm still waiting. Yessir. I'm waiting. Here I sit. Waiting for that document. It's number four. Wait! Wait a sec. Look! Everything is moving up. Now it's document three in the queue. Okay. Pretty soon now. Just keep standing here patiently. Waiting for my document to print. Just waiting here. Looking at the queue on the screen. There's my document. It's number three now. Used to be number four. Waiting in the queue. . . ."

QuickTime

Pronunciation: *Kwik-Thyme*.

Meaning: A standard used on Macintosh computers for storing and displaying digital video on your computer, consuming lots of memory and hard disk space just so you can see a brief five seconds of a movie on your computer screen.

Sentence: "As a joke, I stored a film clip from an X-rated movie on my boss's Macintosh using *QuickTime*. How was I supposed to know that his wife moonlights as a porn star?"

Quit

Pronunciation: *Kwit.*

Meaning: (1) What to do if your company makes you work on a Macintosh Plus computer or on a 286 PC with 2MB of RAM. (2) A command that exits a program. Quit. Done. Kapeesh. All finished. All gone. Going bye-bye. (See also *exit.*)

Sentence: "The *Quit* command is one of the first commands you should know. There's nothing worse than getting into a program and not knowing how to get out again (total 'Hotel California')."

QWERTY

Pronunciation: *Kwer-Tee.*

Meaning: The name commonly given to a standard keyboard layout. The name comes from the combination of the first six keys on the keyboard in the third row. (See also *Dvorak keyboard* and *keyboard.*)

Sentence: "Several attempts have been made to replace the old *QWERTY* keyboard with something more sensible. It's like trying to switch the entire United States to the metric system. Can't be done."

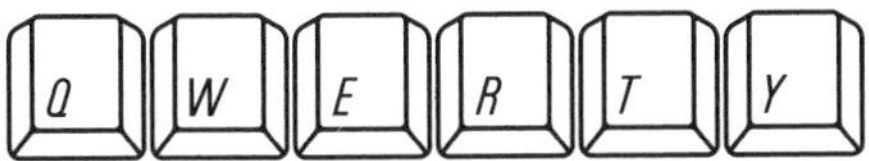

radiation

Pronunciation: *ray-dee-ay-shin.*

Meaning: An invisible form of energy that kills nuclear power plant workers, blows up hot dogs in microwave ovens, and smacks you in the face every time you look at a computer screen. Completely harmless.

Sentence: "Treating eye surgery with acupuncture is like treating hair loss with *radiation.*"

radio button

Pronunciation: *ray-dee-oh butt-in.*

Meaning: A type of mouse-clickable button in a graphical user interface. Radio buttons are grouped together and only one of the group can be "on" at a time. The name comes from the type of buttons that used to be on car radios; when you press a button to select a station, the other buttons all pop out. The same logic is applied to radio buttons, which are used to select only one of a group of options at a time. (See also *button* and *graphical user interface.*)

Sentence: "When I use the Format Tabs command in Microsoft Word, a set of *radio buttons* assaults me with several alignment options."

ragged justification

Pronunciation: *rag-ed jus-ti-fi-kay-shun.*

Meaning: An oxymoron that really means you have no justification at all. Ragged justification means that both the left and right margins in a document aren't lined up against anything. Specifically, it's usually applied to either the left or right margins individually. Ragged right justification, for example, refers to a paragraph of text that has an uneven right edge. (See also *justify.*)

Sentence: "When I asked John why he took a two-hour lunch, he gave me a *ragged justification* for his behavior."

RAID

Pronunciation: Ray-da.

Meaning: Acronym that stands for *Redundant Array of Inexpensive* Disks, though they could also be Independent Disks. Instead of storing all your valuable data on a single hard disk that may fail at any time, RAID takes the opposite approach by spreading your data among two or more cheap hard disks on the notion that multiple hard disks are less likely to fail than a single hard disk.

Sentence: "We couldn't think of a foolproof way to keep the records for our illegal gambling cartel when Garth piped up about a *RAID.* Rumor has it Garth is now doing intensive internal research on the alligators of certain Floridian swamps."

RAM

Pronunciation: *Ram.*

Meaning: Acronym for *Random-Access Memory,* a type of computer memory that can be written to and read from. The "random" means that any one location can be read at any time; it's not necessary to read through every bank of memory to find one location. RAM commonly refers to the internal memory of your computer, supplied by microchips and measured in kilobytes or megabytes. However, RAM can refer to any random-access memory medium, including magnetic disks and the human brain. RAM is usually a fast, temporary memory area where your data and programs live until you save them or the power is turned off on your computer. (See also *ROM* and *WORM.*)

Sentence: "The best way to improve the performance of Windows is to increase the *RAM* in your computer. Follow this formula: Figure out how much RAM you can buy without going over your credit card limit. Then buy that much RAM and install it in your PC."

RAM disk

Pronunciation: *Ram disk.*

Meaning: A portion of the computer's internal memory (RAM) that is configured to behave like a disk drive. You can use a RAM disk as you would use any normal disk drive — for storing and retrieving files — but a RAM disk is significantly faster than a standard disk drive because it's all electronic and has no moving parts. The drawback is that everything stored on the RAM disk disappears when you turn the computer off or reset. RAM disks are useful for storing some disk-intensive programs because RAM drives are so much faster than regular disks. The drawback here is that you usually need a large RAM disk to store the program, which means there's less RAM available for programs that need it.

Sentence: "The astrologer down the street says it's best to create a *RAM disk* under the sign of Aries."

RAM drive

(See *RAM disk.*)

random access

Pronunciation: *ran-dum ak-ses.*

Meaning: The ability to access any piece of information from a storage medium, such as a disk or RAM. The idea here is that random access gives you the ability to access any ol' information without having to read everything that comes before it. The opposite of random access is *sequential access.* Sequential access works like a videotape. If you want to watch the second half of a movie, you must fast forward to that spot in the tape. Random access works more like a laser disk (or a record player, if you're an old fogey). On the laser disk, you just tell the laser beam to "point to the second half of the movie" and it instantly goes there, no fast-forwarding involved. With RAM, random access means you can access any byte in memory any time you want. On a disk, random access means you can access any files without having to churn through all those written to disk before it. (See also *sequential access.*)

Sentence: "My uncle Marty tells jokes with *random access.* You give him a topic, and he'll have a joke."

random numbers

Pronunciation: *ran-dum nuhm-bers.*

Meaning: Numbers that are generated randomly (that is, without any particular aim, order, direction, or sequence), such as when you throw dice.

Sentence: "In light of new theories on the nature of chaos and randomness, many people argue that there is no such thing as a *random number.* These people have not seen my checking account."

range

Pronunciation: *rayn-ja.*

Meaning: A term used to describe a series of things, from a low-numbered thing to a high-numbered thing. For example, a range could be a block of cells in a spreadsheet. A range could also mean a span of values, such as the range between 1 and 10. Also a place where the deer and antelope play. (See also *block* and *cell.*)

Sentence: "A *range* can range from one cell in a spreadsheet to another, hither and thither, or to Amana Radar."

raster

Pronunciation: *rast-er.*

Meaning: A frame or pattern that an electron beam sends to the screen on your monitor. Scan patterns are sent to the screen continuously, a line at a time, to create the images and motion you see. The patterns displayed on the screen are sent using an electron "gun" that wipes the inside of your monitor like a firefighter's hose. The patterns are sent from top to bottom and each new pattern is sent before the last one is finished. This creates "bands" of images called raster images. If you look out of the corner of your eye at the computer screen, you can see a pulsating effect that the raster images cause. (See also *graphics.*)

Sentence: "It's the *raster* scan line you see when you look at a computer monitor on TV. Ugly, aren't they?"

RCA connector

Pronunciation: *Ar See Ay kon-nek-ter.*

Meaning: A standard type of connector used for stereo headphones and speakers. It has a long metal tip or prong surrounded by a quarter-inch diameter plastic jacket. This type of connector is used for some video systems but mostly for computer audio equipment.

Sentence: "Nothing will brighten your guru's heart like referring to the 'connector doohickey' properly as an *RCA jack*."

read

Pronunciation: *reed.*

Meaning: The act of transferring data from a storage medium to the internal RAM of a computer. For example, a computer "reads" information from a disk and then stores it into memory. If your disk drive were a video or cassette tape, "read" would be equivalent to "play."

Sentence: "My computer is not reading the file from this floppy disk; it says, 'Cannot *read* from Drive A.' Maybe the computer needs glasses."

read-only

Pronunciation: *reed ohn-lee.*

Meaning: A type of medium from which you can read data but to which you cannot write data. CD-ROM disks are read-only media, as are LP phonograph records; you can read from them (play), but you cannot write stuff to them (record). Also a file attribute in DOS. (See also *file attribute* and *write-protect.*)

Sentence: "*Read-only* media are used for information that you would not want to change, such as your weight when you were 18."

read/write head

Pronunciation: *reed/riht hed.*

Meaning: The mechanism in a disk drive that accesses and stores information on the disk. The "head" is usually a ceramic material that floats, or hovers, above the disk surface, creating a magnetic field that is charged by the magnetic impulses on the disk. When it writes information to the disk, the head changes the magnetic particles instead of being affected by them. This is how information is read from and written to a disk. (See also *head* and *head crash.*)

Sentence: "A *read/write head* is a delicate thing; small particles of dust between the read/write head and the disk surface can cause errors. This is why you don't go slamming melted cheese sandwiches into your disk drives."

README

Pronunciation: *Reed-mee.*

Meaning: (1) A name typically given to a text file that contains up-to-date information about a program, such as changes to the documentation, information about last-minute additions, and explanations of errors that were not fixed before the product shipped. When a program differs from the documentation, software developers turn to the README file to explain what happened. README files are usually text-only files, which is nice because they can be read with any text editor or word processor. (2) A file that nobody reads.

Sentence: "I was having some trouble with a new software package. When I looked at the *README* file, it said that a last-minute change prohibited the software from working on my system. When the company sent me the bill, I sent them a copy of my SUEME file."

real mode

Pronunciation: *reel mohd.*

Meaning: An operating mode of the 80286 and later microprocessors that operates just like the 8088 microprocessor in the first PC. DOS and all DOS applications use the real mode no matter which microprocessor lives inside your PC. (See also *protect mode.*)

Sentence: "Abigail wasn't sure if her virtual reality program would run in the *real mode.*"

real number

Pronunciation: *reel num-ber.*

Meaning: Basically, a real number is any value, usually a value that has some sort of fractional part. Contrast this with an integer, which is just a whole number, no fractions and no decimals allowed.

Sentence: "I gave my accountant a copy of my income projection, and he told me I should stop using imaginary numbers and try some *real numbers.*"

Real Soon Now

Pronunciation: *Reel Soon Now.*

Meaning: A phrase commonly heard by software companies in reference to the exact date they'll release a new version of their program that everyone's waiting for. This phrase is often leaked out to the press to con people who haven't yet learned that every new version is usually full of bugs and not worth getting in the first place.

Sentence: "Many companies promise to release a new version of their program *Real Soon Now* in a subtle attempt to keep you from defecting to a competing program."

real time

Pronunciation: *reel tihm.*

Meaning: A measurement of time based on actual time elapsed, rather than computer-time units. Real-time computer events can be measured with normal time-telling equipment. Many computer operations measure elapsed time based on computer processing time or other non-real systems, or they can simulate faster-than-normal or slower-than-normal time for experiments.

Sentence: "I'm sorry, Jenkins, but you can only clock in on *real time* here."

real-time clock

Pronunciation: *reel-tihm klok.*

Meaning: A computerized clock or timing device that tracks accurate time. For example, when DOS used to start, it would assume that "today" was January 1, 1980, at midnight. In those olden days, people would have to set the time and date manually whenever DOS started — unless they bought a device called a real-time clock, which would automatically keep track of the time and set DOS's clock every time the PC started.

Sentence: "I wish my VCR had a *real-time clock*. Maybe that way it wouldn't keep flashing 12:00 all day."

reboot

Pronunciation: *ree-boot.*

Meaning: To restart the computer. Starting the computer is called "booting" or "booting up." There are two ways to reboot the computer: you perform a cold boot by switching the computer off, waiting, and then turning it back on again. You perform a warm boot by pressing Ctrl-Alt-Del on a PC or by punching a reset button. Usually a warm boot is all that's required, but occasionally a cold boot is necessary to clear memory completely.

Sentence: "When you *reboot* by pressing Ctrl-Alt-Del, be sure to make the ka-chinka noise out loud because modern computers no longer ka-chinka by themselves when you reboot."

record

Pronunciation: *reh-kord* or *ree-kord.*

Meaning as a noun: An individual unit of data stored in a database. A record consists of one or more related fields, which are the actual pieces of data being stored. Fields combine to create a record the way blanks are filled in on a sheet of paper. The blanks are the fields and the sheet of paper is the record.

Meaning as a verb: To write information, usually applied when recording audio information and storing it in a computer file on disk. Normally, the word "write" is used when you record information to a disk or to memory (RAM).

Sentence: "Mr. Smith collects old LPs and stores information about them in his database. You could say that he's *recorded* a world record record record. "

recover

Pronunciation: *ree-kuhv-er.*

Meaning as a verb: (1) To restore a deleted file. You can often recover deleted files using an UNDELETE utility or command. (See also *undelete.*) (2) To put new cloth on an old piece of furniture.

Meaning as a noun: A program's ability to continue operating after any errors that would normally send it crashing into outer space. (See also *reboot.*)

Sentence: "Our database program is pretty sophisticated. It can *recover* from serious errors, such as when I shot the computer with a bazooka."

recursion

Pronunciation: *ree-ker-zhun.*

Meaning: An advanced programming concept not required by mere mortals. But, if you care to know, recursion is the process that occurs when a software routine (or procedure) calls itself while running. It would just blow your mind if I discussed this any further. Suffice it to say, the process keeps calling itself until it finds itself, and then it stops and the computer — miraculously — doesn't blow up.

Sentence: "I tried to write a program that used *recursion*, but every time the program called itself, it got a busy signal."

redirection

Pronunciation: *ree-dur-ek-shun.*

Meaning: The act of sending a program's output to a location other than the screen. Normally, output goes to the screen: you type it; you see it. Input normally comes from the keyboard. Using redirection, you can tell the computer where to send its output and from where to receive its input. For example, the following DOS command uses output redirection to send its output to the printer:

```
DIR > PRN
```

The > symbol is the output redirection symbol for both DOS and UNIX. The < is the input redirection symbol. Use these things with caution; consult a good DOS text for the lowdown. (See also *output.*)

Sentence: "I used output *redirection* to have the computer send all my network memos to the trash can."

redundant

See *redundant.*

reformat

Pronunciation: *ree-fohr-mat.*

Meaning: The act of formatting something again. You format it once; then the second (and any additional) time, it's a reformat. (See also *format* and *FORMAT.*)

Sentence: "You should never try to *reformat* a disk to a higher capacity. You'll get one of those 'Track 0 unusable' errors."

refresh rate

Pronunciation: *ree-fresh raet.*

Meaning: The rate at which a screen refreshes, or redraws, its image based on new information. The faster the rate, the less likely the screen is to flicker, which saves the wear and tear on your eyeballs and brain. It also means you pay a lot more for your monitor.

Sentence: "Allan didn't pay much for his monitor. The *refresh rate* is so slow that it works more like a strobe light."

register

Pronunciation: *rej-iss-ter.*

Meaning: (1) Tiny storage places inside your computer's microprocessor. A register is a row or bank of what are called flip flops (binary storage units) that store bits of information for processing by the computer. This is something you'll never need to know unless you program a computer at a very low level. (See also *assembly language, bit, flip flop,* and *word.*) (2) What software publishers want you to do with your software products so they can sell you upgrades through the mail.

Sentence: "Isn't it ironic that you have to *register* a software product before you can get customer service, yet you'll never have to register a gun?"

relational database

Pronunciation: *ree-lae-shun-ul dae-tah-baes.*

Meaning: A database that consists of several separate files that "relate" to one another through key words or values. Information stored in one file can be accessed through one or more of the other files because of the relations established in the database. For example, you might store customer address information in your Customer database and product order information in an Orders database. These two databases can relate to each other through the customer name. When you examine a customer record in the Customer database, you might be able to view all orders associated with that customer. Similarly, when entering an order into the Orders database, you can type a customer name and the entire customer record automatically appears at the top of the order form. Another advantage of relational database design is that each field (each type of information) in the database can be accessed individually (that is, you can search for an entry based on any field). (See also *data, database, field,* and *record.*)

Sentence: "It's *relational database* management that explains why you constantly have to tell the support people your name and address every time you call."

relational operator

Pronunciation: *ree-lae-shun-ul ah-per-rae-ter.*

Meaning: A symbol such as > or < that defines a relational operation between two variables or operands. Relational operators are used by programming languages, spreadsheet products, and database management systems for testing the relationships between two values. (See also *operator.*)

Sentence: "I used a *relational operator* to calculate whether meatloaf was better than sushi for dinner tonight."

relative reference

Pronunciation: *rel-uh-tiv ref-rens.*

Meaning: A cell address (or reference) entered into a spreadsheet formula using relative row and/or column designations. When you copy a formula containing relative references to other cells in a spreadsheet, the references are automatically updated to reflect cells that are relative to the new location of the formula. Relative references are applied only during copy procedures. (See also *absolute reference.*)

Sentence: "When it comes time to tell old, spooky Halloween stories, we all use Aunt Shirley as a *relative reference.*"

REM

Pronunciation: *Rem.*

Meaning: Abbreviation for *REMARK.* REM is a statement, or command, used in many programming languages (including the DOS batch file programming language) that lets you add a line to the program without affecting the program itself. In other words, it lets you enter remarks or comments to help explain what the program is doing. Here's an example:

```
REM This is a typical batch file
PATH C:\DOS;C:\WINDOWS;C:\WINWORD
PROMPT $p$g
C:\MOUSE\MOUSE.COM
```

Here, the REM command is just a comment and is ignored when the program runs.

Sentence: "Steve's really getting into programming. Last night I hear he even tried to *REM* his dog."

remote

Pronunciation: *ree-moht.*

Meaning: Something that is not near you. A remote computer is one that is connected to your network from a far off, really distant location — like across the hall. Remote access means you're using a computer that's not within arm's reach.

Sentence: "When I log onto our network from another location, my chances of making a connection are *remote.*"

removable disk

Pronunciation: *ree-moov-ah-bul disk.*

Meaning: Any disk that can be removed from its drive or from the computer. However, the term is generally used to describe a type of high-capacity disk (such as a hard disk) that can be inserted and removed from its drive, as in a Bernoulli disk drive. Another term for the unremovable disk is *fixed disk*, which means the disk is solidly attached to the computer — not that it was once broken.

Sentence: "Uh-oh, there goes Fred down the hall with the Jaws of Life. I guess we better tell him that his hard drive isn't a *removable disk.*"

repetitive

Same as *redundant.*

ResEdit

Pronunciation: *Rez-Edit.*

Meaning: Abbreviation for Resource Editor, a Macintosh utility that lets you access and edit system resources. ResEdit lets you mess with the various components of a Mac file. You can actually use it to rename menus and buttons, rewrite text in dialog boxes, copy or paste graphics and sounds, and so on. It's a fun tool, which implies that it's also quite technical and using it is a sure key to goofing up your system.

Sentence: "You can use Johnson's office while he's off in sensitivity training. He used *ResEdit* to change all the Mac's error messages to dirty limericks."

reserved word

Pronunciation: *ree-zervd werd.*

Meaning: Any word or code used for a special purpose that cannot be used for any other purpose. Reserved words happen in programming languages, operating systems, and some applications. For example, in DOS the words COPY, DEL, and REN are all names of DOS commands and therefore reserved words. Other programs cannot use these names or DOS will, well, get mad.

Sentence: "Around our house, blockhead is a *reserved word.*"

reset

Pronunciation: *ree-set.*

Meaning: To restart the computer or restore previous settings. Reset is also a key on some Macintosh keyboards that performs a warm boot when you press it. (See also *warm boot.*)

Sentence: "There. I just finished the final page of my speech, and I must admit it's brilliant. Now I have a few idle moments to sit back and brain-relax and . . . hey? I wonder what this button labeled *Reset* does. . . ."

resolution

Pronunciation: *rez-oh-loo-shun.*

Meaning: A way of measuring the clarity of an image. Resolution involves the number of elements per inch — the number of pixels on your screen or dots your laser printer can produce — which indicates

how clear and sharp an image is. For example, some laser printers produce 300 dots-per-inch (dpi) resolution. High-resolution printers display from 600 to 2400 dots per inch. Video graphics resolutions are measured horizontally and vertically. A resolution of 320 x 200 indicates large dots to create an image; a resolution of 1240 x 800 means smaller dots and a finer image, and therefore a higher resolution. When examining the resolution of an image, your naked eye can discern the dots in resolutions below 600 dpi. However, 300 dpi laser printers are considered adequate resolution for most printing needs.

With color displays, the resolution is also tied to the number of colors that can be displayed at once. For example, a relatively low-resolution picture may be able to display several hundred colors at once. This gives an illusion that the image has a higher resolution, but that's only because the eye is tricked by the multiple colors. Higher resolution images generally use fewer colors. (Most computer games use a medium resolution as a trade-off.) Resolution may be abbreviated as res (pronounced rez) — as in, for example, "high res" or "low res" to indicate high or low resolution. (See also *pixel*.)

Sentence: "I made a New Year's resolution that I'd get myself a high-*resolution* printer this year."

resource

Pronunciation: *ree-sohrs.*

Meaning: Just as humans have natural resources, a computer has its own resources. A resource may be memory, disk drive storage, the printer, a monitor, and so on. In Windows and on networks, you always want to watch that your resources aren't running out.

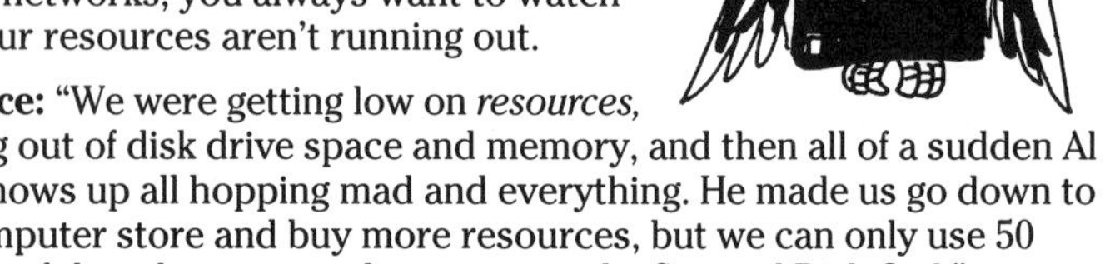

Sentence: "We were getting low on *resources,* running out of disk drive space and memory, and then all of a sudden Al Gore shows up all hopping mad and everything. He made us go down to the computer store and buy more resources, but we can only use 50 percent of them because we have to save the Spotted Disk Owl."

restore

Pronunciation: *ree-stohr.*

Meaning as a verb: (1) To return to normal, as in "Yes, Mary is fully restored after her conniption fit." (2) The act of copying files from an archive or set of backup disks or tape drive to their original locations on the hard drive. This is the opposite of backing up, usually done after something bad has happened. For example, after losing all your data you would restore your files from a recent backup disk. Or, if you deleted a file, you could restore it from a backup disk. Needless to say, this only works if you back up frequently.

Meaning as a noun: In DOS, the RESTORE command returns backed-up data to the hard disk.

Sentence: "Don't panic, Dave. You can *restore* the missing files from your backup diskettes. You do back up, don't you?"

retrieve

Pronunciation: *ree-treev.*

Meaning: (1) Fancy talk for accessing or opening a file, as in Lotus 1-2-3's Worksheet Retrieve command. (See also *open.*) (2) May refer to opening a file that's inside another file, as in WordPerfect.

Sentence: "Most people use the word 'open' when they refer to getting a file from disk into a program. Some use *retrieve.* Old Microsoft Word fans may remember 'Transfer Load.' Doesn't that bring back memories?"

Return key

Pronunciation: *Ree-tern kee.*

Meaning: Same as the Enter key, but it gets its name from the carriage return key on a typewriter. Currently found on some Mac keyboards.

Sentence: "Both Enter and *Return* generally perform the same function, but don't quote me on that."

reverse engineer

Pronunciation: *ree-vers in-jin-eer.*

Meaning: The process of decoding a program based not on the program's code but on what the program does and how it affects things. Also applies to the act of analyzing hardware to determine how it works. Reverse engineering is primarily performed when engineers want to figure out how a black box gizmo works, and they're either unable to take it apart or forbidden from taking it apart for legal reasons. For example, the reason we all have "IBM-compatible" computers today is that someone somewhere reverse engineered the chips in the first IBM PC (the BIOS) and created a working counterpart without infringing upon IBM's copyrights.

Sentence: "I bet IBM really regrets not sicking their legions of lawyers on the first company to successfully *reverse engineer* the guts of the IBM PC."

revision history

Pronunciation: *ree-vee-zjun his-toh-ree.*

Meaning: A revision history tracks the various revisions of a program and what improvements or adjustments occurred in each. For example:

> Version 1.0 Product introduced. They'll love this.
> Version 1.1 Annoying "all files accidentally deleted" bug removed.
> Version 1.2 Annoying "erased hard drive" thing fixed.
> Version 2.0 Networking features added, flock sheared for $50 upgrade fee.
> Version 2.1 Annoying "network not found" bug fixed.
> Version 2.2 Support for tall people added.
> Version 2.3 Support for left-handed people added.
> Version 3.0 DOS 5 update, sheared flock for another $50.
> Version 3.1 DOS bug fix.

Sentence: "Obviously, most major applications don't include a *revision history* because it would prove to be a source of embarrassment."

RF

Pronunciation: *Ar Ef.*

Meaning: Acronym for *Radio Frequency*, which includes a certain chunk of the electromagnetic spectrum that you would find terribly uninteresting. Mostly used with *RFI,* discussed below.

Sentence: "Tune to KRUD, 1240 AM on your *RF* dial."

RFI

Pronunciation: *Ar Ef Eye.*

Meaning: Acronym for *Radio Frequency Interference.* This is the type of interference that occurs when two devices emitting electromagnetic waves interfere with each other. Computers, radios, TVs, and many other radio transmission devices emit waves that can interfere with other devices' waves, causing fuzzy noise, snow on the monitor, an annoyed cat, and other anomalies. RFI is why you can't use your mobile phone on an airplane, and it's why notebook computers undergo monstrous testing for FCC approval. Proper grounding and quality cables help to minimize RFI in computers.

Sentence: "This *RFI* is causing some strange effects on my computer. I could swear I just saw a fuzzy image of Bill Gates giggling on my monitor."

RGB

Pronunciation: *Ar Jee Bee.*

Meaning: Acronym for *Red Green Blue*. A type of color process that involves mixing intensities of red, green, and blue reflective (or additive) colors. Based on the mixture and intensity of these colors, you can produce many of the colors in the normal spectrum. TVs and computer monitors use RGB to produce color on the screen. You light individual red, green, and blue pixels to mix colors.

Sentence: "I have an *RGB* monitor, but in this case RGB stands for Randomly Goes Blank."

ribbon cable

Pronunciation: *ree-bun kay-bul.*

Meaning: A type of computer cable in which the wires are flat like a ribbon. Ribbon cables are often used for the printer and, inside the PC, for disk drives. In the old Apple II days, the ribbon cables were multicolor — like rainbows. Today, they're usually all a pasty hospital-blue. (See also *cable.*)

Sentence: "Doris is so nice. She thought the office looked rather dreary, so she went around and tied bows in all our *ribbon cables.*"

Rich Text Format

Pronunciation: *Rich Teks-ta For-mat.*

Meaning: A type of document file format, usually readable by most major word processors. The Rich Text Format (RTF) file is basically a text file. However, included in the text are various instructions that describe the document's formatting. This looks utterly gross when you see it in the raw, text-only format. But word processors that understand RTF can read in the files and translate the ugly text into formatting codes, making the document look really nice.

Sentence: "The *Rich Text Format* was an attempt to create a common document file format compatible with all word processors and people living in Scarsboro."

RIP

Pronunciation: *Rip* (rhymes with *trip, dip,* and *slip*).

Meaning: Acronym that stands for *Remote Imaging Protocol*, which is a graphics language that lets modem users use their mouse to give commands to another computer through the phone lines. Many of the newest electronic bulletin board systems offer RIP so users can use their mouse instead of typing arcane commands.

Sentence: "Before bulletin boards started using *RIP,* you had to type commands to get anything done. With RIP, you can use your mouse instead of typing to choose most commands. (Then again, have you ever tried typing your password using a mouse?)

RISC

Pronunciation: *Risk.*

Meaning: Acronym for *Reduced Instruction Set Computer.* A RISC system is a computer that runs very fast because the microprocessor can only do a limited number of things. The idea here is that those little things make the building blocks for larger things, so the RISC processor isn't hindered by its limited number of instructions.

Sentence: "I don't care how fast it is. Putting something called *RISC* into my computer doesn't sit well with me."

RLL

Pronunciation: *Ar El El.*

Meaning: Abbreviation for *Run-Length-Limited.* A type of hard disk controller (now deceased) that increases the capacity of the hard drive by using disk-compression technology directly from the hard disk controller. An RLL controller can increase disk storage capacity by as much as 50 percent. (See also *IDE.*)

Sentence: "Wow! Where did you get the antique *RLL* drive?"

robot

Pronunciation: *roh-baht.*

Meaning: An automated mechanism that simulates or reproduces (or replaces) human activities, such as assembly-line work and deep space work. R2D2 from *Star Wars* is an example of a robot. Robots are used in many applications, including computer assembly and testing.

Sentence: "Perhaps the most famous *robot* of all time is Robby the Robot from the film *Forbidden Planet.* He was charming, polite, a good friend, and could crush your head like a grapefruit."

robotics

Pronunciation: *roh-baht-iks.*

Meaning: (1) The study and application of robots. (2) Mechanical bugs that suck your blood (pronounced *robo-ticks*).

Sentence: "My nephew studied *robotics* in school. Now he's working at Burger King. I suppose he's experiencing what it's like to be a robot."

ROM

Pronunciation: *Rahm.*

Meaning: Acronym for *Read-Only Memory.* ROM is any type of memory that can be read but not written to. For example, compact discs (CDs) are ROM media. ROM is also used to describe the chip inside your computer that permanently contains basic information for the computer. (See also *RAM, PROM,* and *ROM BIOS.*)

Sentence: "I think 'crash randomly' is a special instruction in my computer's *ROM.*"

ROM BIOS

Pronunciation: *Rahm Bye-ahss.*

Meaning: Acronym for *Read-Only Memory Basic Input/Output System*. It's a BIOS that is stored in ROM. (See also *ROM* and *BIOS.*)

Sentence: "No, Mr. Pinkston, *BIOS* is not ROM's 'last name.'"

Roman

Pronunciation: *Roh-mun.*

Meaning: A classification of type styles (fonts), including Times and many others. Also refers to the normal, non-slanted version of type, as opposed to italic type. (See also *font.*)

Sentence: "A *Roman* man once said, 'Hello, my name is Gaius Julius Caesar, and I'm looking for a specific type of font. What do you suggest?'"

root

Pronunciation: *root.*

Meaning: The main user of the UNIX computer. Also called the "root user," it's a special account that allows full access to all the commands, directories, and places secret on the computer. This is truly holy stuff. To be a root on a UNIX computer is akin to being a true computer god.

Sentence: "Bill keeps trying to log in as the *root,* hoping that someday the computer will be his. I don't like the grin on his face when he says that."

root directory

Pronunciation: *root duh-rek-toh-ree.*

Meaning: The first and often only directory on a disk. The root directory doesn't become important until you have subdirectories and a disk tree structure. Then the other directories — the subdirectories — branch from the root like a tree. In DOS, the symbol for the root directory is the single backslash. Under UNIX, the symbol is a single forward slash. (See also *tree structure, directory, subdirectory, path,* and *pathname.*)

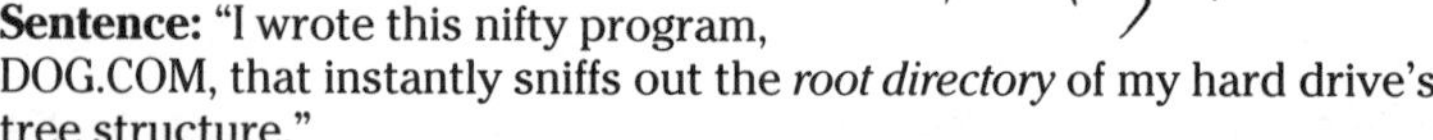

Sentence: "I wrote this nifty program, DOG.COM, that instantly sniffs out the *root directory* of my hard drive's tree structure."

rounding error

Pronunciation: *rown-ding eh-rohr.*

Meaning: A one-cent error that occurs when the computer converts decimal numbers into binary code (for internal processing) and back again. This always happens, but it's nothing to be overly concerned about — unless you're doing nuclear physics or thousands of lives are at stake, in which case you can use the "blame Microsoft" defense at your U.N. Crimes of Humanity trial. The reason for the rounding error is that certain numbers can only be approximated in the computer's memory as binary digits. As a result, there's a little bit of a fudge factor since the computer's approximations are mathematically manipulated.

Sentence: "I tried to explain that all the wrong answers on my math final came from *rounding errors,* but the professor declines to believe that I'm a computer."

row

Pronunciation: *roh.*

Meaning: A horizontal array of data, as in a spreadsheet or table. Spreadsheets organize data into rows and columns to make totals and other calculations faster and easier. Row may also refer to a line of text in a word processing document or just a line of text across the screen.

Sentence: "The typical PC screen has 25 *rows* of text, only four of which may make sense at any one time."

RPM

Pronunciation: *Ar Pee Em.*

Meaning: Acronym for *Revolutions Per Minute*. A measurement of the number of times something turns around. Disk drives and phonograph records (remember those?) spin at specific RPMs. Phonograph records spin at 33$^{1}/_{3}$ or 44 RPMs.

Sentence: "I like CD players because I don't have to worry about the *RPM."*

RS-232

Pronunciation: *Ar Ess-too-thur-tee-too.*

Meaning: Abbreviation for *Recommended Standard-232*, also known as RS-232C. This is not a Radio Shack part number. Instead, it's a standard method of transmitting data across serial cables and is used by modems, printers, and other serial devices. There's lots of technical stuff surrounding the standard and it can be boring, so that's all I'm going to say here. (See also *serial* and *serial port.*)

Sentence: "If *RS-232* is the 232nd standard they came up with that year, then I'd hate to have sat through the first 231 meetings."

RTF

Pronunciation: *Ar Tee Ef.*

(See *Rich Text Format.*)

run

Pronunciation: *ruhn.*

Meaning: (1) What to do when the computer starts to smoke. (2) To execute or use a program. Other terms for run are *start, launch, execute,* and *initiate*.

Sentence: "The customer service operator told me to *run* my program, but I couldn't find a leash to fit it."

run time

Pronunciation: *ruhn tihm.*

Meaning: (1) The time spent while a program is running. (2) A special version of a program, such as a database or spreadsheet, that performs a specific task. For example, a run-time version of Excel lets you use your Excel worksheets but does not let you use any Excel commands or options.

Sentence: "*Run time* is a misnomer when you work with Windows. Then, it's more like walk or crawl time."

S-100

Pronunciation: *Ess-won-hun-dred.*

Meaning: A type of expansion card and also the name of a CP/M computer from the late 1970s that used that type of expansion card. These systems are called dinosaurs today. (See also *expansion card* and *CP/M.*)

Sentence: "During their heyday, the *S-100* systems were the Cadillacs of PCs."

SAA

Pronunciation: *Ess Ay Ay.*

Meaning: Acronym for *Systems Application Architecture*, a set of guidelines that IBM developed for standardizing the way computers work. Most people follow these guidelines and then add just enough "improvements" to destroy the whole purpose of a standard in the first place. (See also *IBM.*)

Sentence: "My computer follows IBM's *SAA* standard. That seems odd because my computer is a Macintosh."

sans serif

Pronunciation: *san ser-if.*

serif

san serif

Meaning: A typeface that lacks *serifs*, which are tiny ornamental curves and such that appear at the edges of letters. Believe it or not, serifs actually make letters easier to read. Sans serif typefaces (*sans* is the French word for *without*) are harder to read. (See also *serif.*)

Sentence: "A simple desktop publishing rule is to use *sans serif* fonts for headlines or titles and serif fonts for the text. I once followed that advice painstakingly in Microsoft Word for Windows, only to save and then reload my document and have WinWord switch everything around."

save

Pronunciation: *save* (rhymes with *shave, knave,* and *wave*).

Meaning: To store data (from RAM) onto a floppy or hard disk in hopes that you'll be able to find it again. Nearly every program has a Save command to store your work. (See also *RAM.*)

Sentence: "Use the *Save* command periodically to store your work in case the power goes out or the computer short-circuits itself."

save as

Pronunciation: *save as.*

Meaning: To store an existing file under a different name. The Save As command saves a file, but it allows you to change the file name and maybe also to change the format under which the file is saved.

Sentence: "All top-secret documents have file names like SECRET1 and SECRET2. So I just loaded each file into my word processor, used the *Save As* command, and saved each file under a different name. Now I can sneak out these secret files without the guard getting suspicious."

scalable font

Pronunciation: *skay-lah-bull faunt.*

Meaning: A type of font that can appear in different sizes and still look good. Non-scalable fonts can also appear in different sizes, but at certain sizes they look as horrible as seeing your skin pores through a magnifying glass.

Sentence: "I use *scalable fonts* only in my desktop publishing work, just in case some customer wants to change the type sizes at the last minute."

scan

Pronunciation: *skan.*

Meaning: To read text, images, or bar codes into the computer. Accomplished by a device called a *scanner.* (See also *scanner.*)

Sentence: "I brought a zebra to the supermarket, forced it to lie flat on the checkout conveyor belt, and *scanned* in its skin to see how much it was worth."

ScanDisk

Pronunciation: *Skan Disk.*

Meaning: A utility program that comes with MS-DOS 6.2 and identifies and repairs problems on floppy or hard disks, which were usually caused by using MS-DOS 6.0. ScanDisk is a more advanced and easier program to use than the ancient MS-DOS CHKDSK command.

Sentence: "After MS-DOS 6.0 screwed up my hard disk beyond repair, I had to dish out another ten bucks for the MS-DOS 6.2 upgrade so I could run *ScanDisk* and fix everything that shouldn't have gotten wrecked in the first place."

scan rate

Pronunciation: *skan ray-ta.*

Meaning: The speed at which a monitor constantly draws an image on-screen. Sometimes called the *refresh rate*, the scan rate is measured in hertz (Hz), which sounds like the name of a popular rental car agency found in airports near the baggage claim. The higher the scan rate, the more expensive your monitor. And, as anyone familiar with computers knows, the more you pay for it, the better it is. (See also *refresh rate.*)

Sentence: "My monitor has a *scan rate* of 72 Hz. Most clerks in the grocery store have a scan rate of about 18 items a minute."

scanner

Pronunciation: *skan-ner.*

Meaning: (1) A device that can electronically "read" printed text or images into a computer. Scanners come in two sizes: flat-bed and hand-held. Flat-bed scanners can scan an entire page at one time while hand-

held scanners can scan in widths of approximately four inches. (2) In 1981, Hollywood released a bad horror movie called *Scanners,* where people could use mental powers to make other people's heads explode. (See also *scan.*)

Sentence: "While watching *Scanners* on TV and trying to concentrate hard enough to make my dog's head explode, I decided to buy a *scanner* so I wouldn't have to retype newspaper articles into my word processor."

scope

Pronunciation: *sko-pa.*

Meaning: (1) A mouthwash typically not used by halitosis-happy computer programmers. (2) A term used by programmers to describe the area within a program in which a variable can be used.

Sentence: "While rinsing my mouth out with Scope, I noticed that the *scope* of my subprogram's variables actually included my own subprogram and those subprograms written by Bob as well. But that subject is really beyond the scope of this book."

Scrapbook

Pronunciation: *Skrap-book.*

Meaning: A desk accessory found on the Macintosh that stores frequently used graphic images or text for pasting into documents.

Sentence: "Whenever I use MacPaint to draw a picture of my sister shoving pencils into her ear, I store the images in the *Scrapbook* so that I can paste them into a PageMaker document and blackmail her later."

screen blanker

Pronunciation: *skreen blayn-ker.*

Meaning: A special program that periodically blanks out the screen and replaces it with utter darkness — on purpose. Screen blankers prevent the same image from appearing on your screen and being "burned-in" permanently. For example, a lot of older PCs have images of 1-2-3 or WordPerfect permanently etched into their monitors. Some screen blankers can be quite creative. Instead of just blanking the screen, they show images of some sort such as flying toasters, lightning flashes, or raindrops; these are called *screen savers.* (See also *phosphor burn-in* and *screen savers.*)

Sentence: "If I don't touch my keyboard or mouse for five minutes, my *screen blanker* shuts off my screen and displays fish in an aquarium to protect my monitor from burn-in. Then my stupid brother thought it was a real aquarium and poured water in the top, ruining my monitor anyway."

screen buffer

Pronunciation: *skreen buf-fer.*

Meaning: An area of memory used to store the graphic or text image displayed on-screen. Also called *screen memory* or *video RAM.*

Sentence: "And all this time I thought a *screen buffer* was this thing from Ronco for only $19.95 that you used to clean your monitor."

screen dump

Pronunciation: *skreen dump.*

Meaning: A printout of the image that appears on-screen. The unflattering term *dump* is often used in computer lingo to mean a wholesale copying of information from one place to another. We could dwell on this for a long time and get very descriptive. But one of the editorial matrons at IDG Books, Diane Steele, would doubtless frown upon such verbosity.

Sentence: "Whenever my computer crashes for no apparent reason, I try to get a *screen dump* so I can show the technician what happened and why his last solution didn't really work after all."

screen font

Pronunciation: *skreen fawnt.*

Meaning: A bit-mapped font that mimics the appearance of printer fonts. Because printers often print with a resolution of 300 dots per inch or more, the fonts tend to look better printed than they do on-screen. As a result, the fonts that appear on-screen may look plain and simple compared to the fonts that appear on the printer, resulting in confusion when you try to figure out what you're doing.

Sentence: "I hate *screen fonts* because you can never tell what they'll look like until you print them out and waste paper in the process."

screen saver

(See *screen blanker.*)

scroll

Pronunciation: *sk-roll.*

Meaning: To move text or graphics vertically or horizontally on-screen as if your monitor were a porthole, looking at a much larger image a little bit at a time.

Sentence: "With a 250-page document, your monitor can show only half a page at any given time. To see the rest of your document, you have to *scroll* up or down. Then again, you can just pretend that you only saw part of the document so you can't be held responsible for the rest of it."

scroll bar

Pronunciation: *sk-roll bar.*

Meaning: A horizontal or vertical rectangular strip that often appears at the right and bottom sides of a window. The scroll bar lets you use a mouse to scroll the image up/down or left/right. The scroll bar also shows you the approximate position of the current screen in relation to the beginning or end of the file.

Sentence: "After a hard day of philosophizing, the typical ancient Greek would venture off to the *scroll bar* for drinks and lewd entertainment."

scroll box

Pronunciation: *sk-roll boks.*

Meaning: Sometimes called an *elevator box*, the scroll box appears in the middle of a scroll bar. By using the mouse, you can scroll through a file just by moving the scroll box within the scroll bar. By looking at the position of the scroll box within the scroll bar, you can see how close the current screen is to the beginning or end of the file. (See also *elevator.*)

Sentence: "Don't waste time pressing the Page Up/Down keys. Move the *scroll box* wildly up and down in the scroll bar and pretend there are people in there alternatively being slammed into the floor and ceiling."

Scroll Lock key

Pronunciation: *Sk-roll Lok kee.*

Meaning: (1) A key on keyboards that appears to do absolutely nothing when you press it. (2) In some (but not all) programs, pressing the up/down cursor keys causes the cursor to scroll up or down. But if you press the Scroll Lock key and then press the up/down cursor keys, the cursor remains fixed on-screen, but the text or graphics seems to slide up or down underneath. If you try this with your program and nothing happens, then you know that your program ignores the Scroll Lock key.

Sentence: "Sometimes I like to press the *Scroll Lock key* while using different programs just to see which programs actually use the Scroll Lock key. I guess this key is the computer equivalent to wisdom teeth in people today."

SCSI

Pronunciation: *Scuz-zee.*

Meaning: Acronym for *Small Computer System Interface*, which is yet another standard for connecting tape drives, hard disks, and scanners to computers. This is a truly whimsical and easily pronounceable acronym, like WYSIWYG, but not like GUI.

Sentence: "I bought a *SCSI* hard drive and then found I couldn't hook it to my computer without a SCSI port. Now I have a SCSI port, a SCSI hard drive, and a $1,000 credit card bill I can't pay."

SEA

Pronuncation: *See.*

Meaning: Acronym that stands for *Self-Extracting Archive*, usually a Macintosh archive that was compressed using the StuffIt program. Files with the SEA extension can automatically uncompress themselves on a Macintosh floppy or hard disk.

Sentence: "Sometimes when I copy files from CompuServe, they have the SIT or *SEA* file extension. If they have the SIT extension, I have to use StuffIt to uncompress them, but if they have the SEA extension, they'll uncompress themselves if I double-click on them."

search

Pronunciation: *ser-cha.*

Meaning: To examine a file for specific data such as words, characters, or symbols. Word processors let you search for words, and databases let you search for specific records. (See also *sort*.)

Sentence: "Because the board can't decide who we should lay off, we're going to conduct a *search* of everyone's hard drive and fire all of those who have the words `I hate this company` in one or more of their files."

search and destroy

Pronunciation: *ser-cha and dee-stroy.*

Meaning: A military term made popular during the Vietnam war, which is a nice way of saying to look for someone so you can kill him. In computers, search and destroy is a form of search and replace when you replace what you found with nothing. The proper term is really *search and delete*, but no one would turn to that entry. (See also *search and replace.*)

Sentence: "Someone told me my computer program had bugs in it, so I spent the last few days on a *search and destroy* mission using pesticides long since outlawed by the government."

search and replace

Pronunciation: *ser-cha and ree-play-sa.*

Meaning: To look for specific characters in a file and substitute them for another character or group of characters. Every word processor offers a search and replace command so that you can quickly change multiple words or phrases at the touch of a button.

Sentence: "When Margaret Mitchell wrote *Gone With The Wind,* she originally named her heroine Pansy O'Hara. At the last moment she changed it to Scarlett O'Hara. If she had used a word processor, she could have just used the *search and replace* feature to make the changes instantly. Instead, some poor editor had to go through each page and change it all by hand."

search string

Pronunciation: *ser-cha string.*

Meaning: The group of characters that the computer looks for when given the Search or Search and Replace command. A string is a group of characters. (See also *string.*)

Sentence: "If you want to replace all occurrences of *Pansy* with *Scarlett* in your word processor document, tell the computer to use *Pansy* as the *search string.*"

sector

Pronunciation: *sek-ter.*

Meaning: To store data, disks are formatted into concentric rings called *tracks*, and each track is further divided into sectors. When a disk gets screwed up to the point where the computer can't read information off it anymore, it's usually because one or two sectors are damaged. A damaged sector on a disk is like a book with one or more pages ripped out of it. (See also *track.*)

Sentence: "The technician said that I couldn't use my floppy disk because the boot *sector* was destroyed by a virus. He said this was like someone ripping out the battery and starter from my car to keep it from working. I thanked him for this analogy and took my computer to another technician who didn't aspire to lofty literary pretensions."

seek

Pronunciation: *seek* (rhymes with *geek, Greek,* and *reek*).

Meaning: To move the read/write heads of a disk drive so data and program instructions can be loaded, much the same way as you might move a needle over a record on your grandmother's old turntable. This is actually quite a religious term for a computer, don't you think? You'd expect a term like Go To or Find or Search. Seek, of course, always implies that there may be some chance at failure, which is probably why the computer gods selected it instead. (See also *read/write head.*)

Sentence: "I bought a Bible program and wanted to find the passage where `Seek and ye shall find` occurs. When I started looking, I could hear the disk drive heads sliding back and forth, *seeking* the information I wanted off the floppy disk."

segment

Pronunciation: *seg-ment.*

Meaning: A portion or part of something. With worms, a segment is like a new piece of the worm that makes it longer — a worm-slice, should the worm chance to crawl over an upended razor blade. In the PC, a *segment* refers to a 64K chunk of memory.

Sentence: "Programs generally run slow under DOS because they must fit their parts into puny little 64K memory *segments.*"

select

Pronunciation: *seh-lekt.*

Meaning: To highlight and choose text or graphics that appear on-screen, usually by dragging the mouse, using the cursor keys, or randomly punching keys while cursing intensely. Selecting is the same thing as "marking it as a block" or "highlighting it."

Sentence: "Before you can delete, copy, or cut anything off the screen, you have to *select* it first so the computer knows what you want to delete, copy, or cut."

select all

Pronunciation: *seh-lekt all.*

Meaning: To highlight and choose all text and graphic images on-screen or in your document at one time. This is a good command to use to erase everything at once, adjust everything on-screen, or copy everything at the same time. If used carelessly, this is also a good way to delete four years' worth of work at the touch of a button.

Sentence: "I chose the *Select All* command and everything in my room became highlighted."

selected

Pronunciation: *sel-ekt-ed.*

Meaning: Highlighted text or graphic images that show you what objects will be affected by the next command you give (cut, copy, delete, and so on).

Sentence: "I told my grandfather I had to click on the mouse to make objects *selected*. He thought I joined a new cult or something."

self-modifying

Pronunciation: *self-mod-if-fi-ing.*

Meaning: When a program makes changes to itself while running. Many virus programs are self-modifying (also called *mutating*) to prevent detection by anti-virus software. Many artificial intelligence programs are also self-modifying, to give the illusion of correcting themselves or adapting to outside stimuli like a living organism.

Sentence: "I wrote a chess program that's *self-modifying*. It started out playing chess very well, but eventually rewrote itself into an accounting program."

semiconductor

Pronunciation: *sem-i-kon-duk-ter.*

Meaning: A material that is neither a good insulator nor a good conductor of electricity. Semiconductors are used to make transistors, diodes, integrated circuits, and all the other neat stuff that make up the parts of a computer. Silicon and germanium are two popular materials used for semiconductors. (See also *silicon* and *germanium.*)

Sentence: "Before he got a job designing *semiconductors* in the electronics industry, George used to work part-time as a conductor on Amtrak."

separator bar

Pronunciation: *sep-er-ray-ter bar.*

Meaning: On pull-down menus, the separator bar appears between groups of commands, making it easier to see each command without your eyes going buggy. (See also *pull-down menu.*)

Sentence: "The File menu of my word processor has a *separator bar* between the Church and State commands."

sequential access

Pronunciation: *see-quen-chal ax-sess.*

Meaning: To scan information starting from the beginning, such as a tape backup or a cassette tape on your stereo. In comparison, random access lets you scan for information anywhere, such as on a CD-ROM disk. Sequential access is usually much slower than random access, although if you want to kill some time so that you can goof off for a while, it's a fine method for searching on your computer. (See also *random access.*)

Sentence: "Every time I want to play my favorite song stored on a tape cassette, I have to use *sequential access* by fast-forwarding or rewinding. If I had the song stored on a CD-ROM disk, I could use random access and start playing the song immediately."

serial

Pronunciation: *cereal.*

Meaning: To transmit data, one bit after another, through a single cable. This is akin to marching single file. Serial contrasts with *parallel,* which is where data is sent eight (or more) bits abreast — like marching in a parade. The advantage of serial is that the information can be sent over longer distances. (See also *parallel.*)

Sentence: "Talking is a *serial* activity because you have to speak the words one after another. Arguing is more parallel in nature because nobody bothers listening to what the other person has to say before shouting right back."

serial communications

Pronunciation: *cereal kom-mew-ni-kay-shins.*

Meaning: To transfer data one bit at a time through a single cable, usually through a modem. (See also *modem.*)

Sentence: "Ted's our *serial communications* expert. He knows all about modems, transmission protocols such as ZModem and Kermit, and who manufactured cereals such as Quisp and Quake."

serial mouse

Pronunciation: *cereal mow-sa.*

Meaning: A mouse that plugs into the serial port of a computer. The other type of mouse, called a *bus* mouse, plugs into a special expansion card which is plugged into the computer. (See also *bus mouse.*)

Sentence: "My *serial mouse* is doing 15 to life for cheese theft."

serial port

Pronunciation: *cereal port.*

Meaning: A port (connector on the back of a PC) that allows data transfer, one bit at a time. Serial ports are sometimes called *RS-232* ports or "that hole in the back of the computer." They come in 9-pin and 25-pin sizes. (See also *RS-232* and *parallel port.*)

Sentence: "Lois bought a serial port for her PC, but was crushed to find out there wasn't a milk or sugar port available."

serial printer

Pronunciation: *cereal print-her.*

Meaning: A printer that plugs into the serial port of a computer. Most printers plug into the parallel ports for faster data transfer and easier setup. Some printers only plug into a serial or parallel port, some printers can plug into either a serial or parallel port, and some printers don't work at all. (See also *serial port* and *parallel port.*)

Sentence: "I decided to buy my boss the slowest printer possible, so I got him a *serial printer.* Now he has to buy another serial port so he can use his external modem, mouse, and serial printer simultaneously."

serif

Pronunciation: *ser-if.*

Meaning: Tiny ornamental curves on letters to make them easier to read. Most typefaces have serifs. (See also *sans serif.*)

Sentence: "This book uses a typeface with *serifs* so the printing won't strain your eyes and give you headaches while reading it. Too bad the same can't be said for legal documents, tax forms, or textbooks."

server

Pronunciation: *ser-ver.*

Meaning: Usually the most expensive computer that nobody can use because it's busy controlling the entire network. You would think that the server would be the "slave" on the network, but this isn't so. The server is really the "master computer," the one all the other computers hook into and beg for the use of disk drives and printers. This is the same evil concept that dominated mainframe computing during the last three decades. (See also *client/server network.*)

Sentence: "If you want to sabotage a network, don't bother wrecking each computer. Just unplug the *server* and then the whole network will sink like the Titanic."

session

Pronunciation: *se-shin.*

Meaning: (1) A fifty-minute hour spent with a psychiatrist to help repair the mental trauma of having to use a computer. (2) An individual activity being carried out by a multitasking computer. (See also *multitasking.*)

Sentence: "Psychiatrists love multitasking computers. Since they charge $120 for an hour *session*, a computer running three sessions gets billed $360."

setting

Pronunciation: *set-ting.*

Meaning: The configuration of a program that defines its appearance on-screen (color, window size, memory usage, and so on).

Sentence: "By the time the sun got done setting in the west, I had finished modifying the program's *settings* so it wouldn't keep appearing as hot pink on purple every time you loaded it up."

setup

Pronunciation: *set-up.*

Meaning: The modification of a program or computer so it works in a particular way each time you use it. The first time you set up a program or computer is when you install it. Later, you can adjust the settings. (See also *configure* and *install.*)

Sentence: "Here's the *setup*: You build the hardware and I'll build the software; no one will understand how it works; then we'll write books that are even more confusing. We'll be rich in a picosecond."

sh

Pronunciation: *shell* or *ess-aech.*

Meaning: The Korn shell in UNIX. An interface that lets you use UNIX, which was actually what Microsoft modeled DOS on (in case you didn't know). sh is also the command you use to start the shell. Another UNIX shell is csh (See *csh.*)

Sentence: "Dale uses UNIX all the time, and he thinks that the *sh* command is two letters too short."

shareware

Pronunciation: *shar-wear.*

Meaning: Software that you can legally copy and give away but must pay for if you use it regularly. Many shareware programs often rival the features of commercial programs but cost far less. Once you pay for shareware, you will get a printed manual, telephone support, and notice of future upgrades. (See also *freeware* and *public domain.*)

Sentence: "*Shareware* programs let you try before you buy, which is like asking your local Ford dealer if you could drive around the latest Mustang for a few weeks before deciding if you want to buy it."

sheet feeder

Pronunciation: *sheet feed-er.*

Meaning: A tray that holds paper and feeds it one page or sheet at a time to a printer. Sheet feeders let you use special stationery or letterhead that you may have lying around instead of using computer paper every time.

Sentence: "Every time my boss hands me a memo, I just flip it over, store it in my *sheet feeder,* and print on the other side, thereby saving valuable computer paper."

shell

Pronunciation: *shell* (rhymes with *bell, sell,* and *well*).

Meaning: (1) A program that makes another program easier to use. DOS shells are the most common shell programs and often provide menus for choosing common DOS commands. (2) The name given to any program that someone uses to control a computer. In DOS, the shell is really a program called COMMAND.COM. That program displays the DOS prompt, interprets your commands, and runs other programs. (3) The name given to the command that runs another program from a first program. For example, the Shell command in WordPerfect allows you to run a second program without having to first quit WordPerfect. When you quit the second program, you're back in WordPerfect.

Sentence: "Sue sells sea shells by the sea shore and uses a DOS *shell* for making her IBM computer easier to use. Sue likes using pull-down menus instead of memorizing cryptic DOS commands."

Shift key

Pronunciation: *Shift kee.*

Meaning: The key labeled Shift (really?) that you have to hold down to produce uppercase letters LIKE THIS. The Shift key can also be used with function keys for commands like Shift-F4.

Sentence: "Hold down the *Shift key* while tapping the F4 key once and then let both of them go. That's what Shift-F4 means when you see it printed in the manual. Shift-Tab means hold down the Shift key and press the Tab key."

Shift-arrow

Pronunciation: *Shift-air-row.*

Meaning: To hold down the Shift key, tap one of the arrow keys (up, down, left, right), and then let both of them go. This command is often used for moving the cursor to highlight text in a word processor.

Sentence: "Press *Shift-left arrow*, and the cursor highlights all the text you just wrote. Now if you press Del, you'll just wipe out all your valuable work in an instant."

shift-click

Pronunciation: *shift-klik.*

Meaning: To hold down the Shift key while clicking on the mouse button at the same time. Shift-clicking is used to select two or more objects on-screen. (See also *click*.)

Sentence: "In your drawing program, you can select two objects by clicking on the first object and then *shift-clicking* on the second one. If you just clicked on the second object, the first object would no longer be selected. If you turn off your computer at this point, you won't have to worry about anything at all."

shoulder surfing

Pronunciation: *shoal-der ser-fing.*

Meaning: To look over another person's shoulder without being seen. Shoulder surfing is often used to see which keys someone types for their password, or to read someone's phone calling card numbers at a public phone.

Sentence: "Be careful for people *shoulder surfing* you whenever you use your calling card at a public phone. They might be trying to inhale your cologne or perfume, or they might be trying to read your calling card numbers."

Show Clipboard

Pronunciation: *Show Klip-bored.*

Meaning: A command that lets you see the last item that was cut or copied from the screen. By choosing the Show Clipboard command first, you can see what will appear on-screen if you choose the Paste command next.

Sentence: "I chose the *Show Clipboard* command and found out the Clipboard only keeps one item at a time. I think it needs a bigger clip."

shrink wrap

Pronunciation: *shrink rap.*

Meaning: To cover a box completely with clear plastic, giving it the illusion that it hasn't been touched by the grubby little hands of other people before reaching your computer desk intact and pristine. Most software is sold in shrink-wrapped boxes for that sanitized look, much like finding a 'Sanitized For Your Protection' paper loop covering the toilet seat at a motel.

Sentence: "No, madam, *shrink wrap* will not make you thinner."

sidelit

Pronunciation: *siyd-lit.*

Meaning: Additional illumination from the side of a liquid crystal display (LCD) to make it easier to read. (See also *backlit.*)

Sentence: "If it weren't for my *sidelit* LCD, I wouldn't be able to use my laptop computer in a dark plane ride. I'd really miss all those 36,000-ft. games of Solitaire."

SIG

Pronunciation: *Sig* (rhymes with *big wig*).

Meaning: Acronym for *Special Interest Group*, which is a collection of people who share the same interest in computers, such as a specific computer like an Amiga, a type of program like dBASE IV, or a field such as artificial intelligence or desktop publishing.

Sentence: "Cool people say that they belong to a *SIG*. Uncool people say they belong to a Special Interest Group, because everyone knows that only cool computer people use acronyms whenever possible."

sign on

Pronunciation: *sine on.*

Meaning: To call another computer, such as a local BBS, CompuServe, or Prodigy, and type your name and password so that you can start using the services. (See also *logon.*)

Sentence: "Before breaking into the Pentagon's computers, we put the 'Do not disturb' sign on the motel door and then plugged our portable computers into the phone jack so we could dial out and *sign on* without anybody watching us."

signature

Pronunciation: *sig-na-choor.*

Meaning: A special file containing information to be put at the end of a mail message or USENET posting. These files typically contain your name, contact information, and, if you're a sophomore in college, about 4K of useless ASCII graphics and *Star Trek* quotes.

Sentence: "Howie was able to create a delightful *signature* using only three lines of text. Obviously he's net-sensitive."

silicon

Pronunciation: *sil-i-kon.*

Meaning: An element — sand — that's used in making glass and the ceramic wafers out of which computer chips are punched. Do not pronounce this "silly con."

Sentence: "The hors d'oeuvres wouldn't be complete at any computer party without a tray of *silicon* wafers."

Silicon Valley

Pronunciation: *Sil-i-kon Val-lee.*

Meaning: The place in Northern California that is world-famous for making semiconductors, microprocessors, and other computer electronic circuitry. They also have a few good pizza parlors and take-out Chinese restaurants, too.

Sentence: "We drove through *Silicon Valley* up El Camino Real to look for a job in the computer industry. But with computers so prevalent in that area, we wound up getting a job with a computer company in Fresno instead."

silicone

Pronunciation: *sill-ee-kone.*

Meaning: An element (Si) with atomic number 14 and an atomic weight of 28.0855. It has very little to do with computers.

Sentence: "I thought *silicone* was the same stuff they made Silly Putty from."

SIMM

Pronunciation: *Sim* (rhymes with *rim* and *brim*).

Meaning: Acronym for *Single In-line Memory Module*, which is a tiny circuit board that holds several memory chips. Several SIMMs plugged into a computer look like headless cockroaches stuck face first in the surface of a Roach Motel. (See also *SIP.*)

Sentence: "*SIMMs* make it easier to install large amounts of memory. Instead of plugging individual memory chips in your computer, you can just plug in a couple of SIMMs."

simulation

Pronunciation: *sim-yoo-lay-shin.*

Meaning: A program or device that mimics the operation of something else. A flight simulation program mimics flying an airplane (although how many airplane cockpits do you know that use a keyboard to control the plane?), while a stock market simulation mimics the actual rise and fall of stocks on Wall Street. (See also *emulation.*)

Sentence: "To give my kids an idea of what driving a real car is like, my computer has a driving *simulation* they can play with."

single-density

Pronunciation: *sin-gull-den-si-tee.*

Meaning: The earliest form of storage on magnetic media that has been replaced with double-density and quad- or high-density. A single-density $5^{1}/_{4}$-inch floppy disk might contain 180K of data, a double-density $5^{1}/_{4}$-inch floppy disk might contain 360K, and a high-density 5 $/_{4}$-inch floppy disk might hold 1.2MB. (See also *high-density* and *double-density.*)

Sentence: "Don't buy *single-density* floppy disks because they're obsolete. Then again, so will be everything else in another month or two."

single-sided disk

Pronunciation: *sin-gul-si-ded disk.*

Meaning: A floppy disk that stores data only on one side. Sometimes you can cut a notch in the side of these disks, flip them over, and store data on the other side, although disk manufacturers recommend against this (because if you follow their instructions,

you have to buy twice as many floppy disks).

Sentence: "Give me all your *single-sided disks* and I'll punch holes in them so you can use the other side. Better yet, why don't we just toss these disks and buy high-density ones instead?"

single-user

Pronunciation: *sin-gull yoo-zer.*

Meaning: Equipment that only one person can try to use at any given time. A laptop computer is a single-user computer, because if two or more people tried to type on the keyboard simultaneously, it might look obscene. Some database programs are single-user, meaning that only one person can use them at a time. Multiuser database programs let two or more people use the program. (See also *multiuser.*)

Sentence: "Lots of companies want to eliminate *single-user* computers and connect everything in a network. That way, they can watch what everyone's doing and keep people from playing games on their computers at work. Too bad that destroys morale and reduces productivity in the long run. And then people wonder why the Japanese are more productive than Americans."

SIP

Pronunciation: *Sip* (as in "I want a small drink of what you have but will gulp it anyway").

Meaning: Acronym for *Single In-line Processor*, a type of memory expansion card similar to a SIMM. The difference between a SIP and a SIMM is that the SIP uses a row of tiny pins as a connector — like a cheap comb. SIPs generally aren't user-upgradable and are usually installed at the factory only. (See also *SIMM.*)

Sentence: "I need more *SIPs* because my PC gulps down memory."

SIT

Pronunciation: *Sit*, as in the command given to a dog, "Sit!"

Meaning: File extension given to a file that has been compressed using the StuffIT program.

Sentence: "If you have a *SIT* file, uncompress it using StuffIt. If you have a ZIP file, uncompress it using PKUNZIP. If you have a CPT file, uncompress it using Compact Pro. If you have any other types of files, leave me alone and figure out which program you need to use by yourself."

site license

Pronunciation: *siyt liy-senz.*

Meaning: A software agreement that lets you legally use multiple copies of the same program on several computers at the same time. Site licenses are cheaper than buying multiple copies of the same program, and they're legal, whereas software piracy is not.

Sentence: "We have a *site license* for WordPerfect and DOS, but the folks who make the Space Zombies game want us to have a site license for 500 copies of it as well."

Skipjack algorithm

Pronunciation: *Skip-jak al-gore-rhythm.*

Meaning: The specific instructions for encrypting and decrypting files, used in the Clipper encryption chip that the government wants everyone to use so they can read our mail.

Sentence: "The *Skipjack algorithm* is classified as a government secret because if we know how it works, then we can figure out how to crack its code. So if you want to learn how the Skipjack algorithm works, get a job with the government and then defect back to the people."

SLED

Pronunciation: *Sled* (as in Rosebud).

Meaning: Acronym that stands for *Single Large Expensive Disk*, which is another way of putting all your eggs in one basket. Computers that use a SLED often have a multimegabyte hard disk that costs a fortune.

Sentence: "After we lost all our data because we bought lots of cheap hard disks, we decided to buy a *SLED* and get our money's worth. Then it failed anyway."

slimline case

Pronunciation: *slim-line case.*

Meaning: A computer case that's short and narrow, perfectly suited for squeezing into tight spaces on desks that have no room. Slimline cases usually offer fewer expansion slots and disk drives than do normal computer cases (referred to as *desktop cases*). If you have absolutely no plans to upgrade a computer in the future, get a slimline case. Otherwise get a bigger computer case that offers more room for expansion.

Sentence: "I bought a *slimline case* because I didn't have much room on my desk to put a computer. Now I can't add a hard disk or another disk drive because the slimline case has no room. Wow, do I feel like I just got ripped off."

SLIP

Pronunciation: *Ess El Eye Pee* or *slip.*

Meaning: Acronym for *Serial Line IP* (Internet Protocol), a method of hooking your computer up to the Internet using a high-speed modem and standard phone line.

Sentence: "This is how we *SLIP* on the net, SLIP on the net, SLIP on the net. This is how we SLIP on the net, so early in the morning."

slot

Pronunciation: *slaught.*

Meaning: A long, thin hole into which an expansion card is plugged. These are usually called *expansion* slots, though in advertising you may see that a PC comes with "8 slots," meaning you can plug in up to eight expansion cards. The term *slot* is actually the easy term. Nerds call all the slots *the bus* and refer to it by terms such as MCA, ISA, EISA, and NuBus. (See also *expansion card* and *expansion slot.*)

Sentence: "Plugging things into your PC's expansion *slot* makes upgrading your hardware Tinkertoy-simple. Just remember to turn your computer off before you do this or your PC's guts will look like burnt toast."

small caps

Pronunciation: *small kaps.*

Meaning: A text attribute or style where lowercase letters are replaced by capital letters of a smaller size. For example, the following title is in small caps:

BOSCO SLUGWORTH LANCES A BOIL

The first letter of each word is capitalized. That's called *initial caps.* The subsequent letters are still uppercase, but in a smaller size than the other letters. That's *small caps.* If all the letters were capitalized, it would be called *all caps.*

Sentence: "These three charming old ladies came into the computer store looking for *small caps,* so I told them to go to the milliner instead."

Smalltalk

Pronunciation: *Small-tawk.*

Meaning: One of the first object-oriented programming languages in the world. Originally developed at the Xerox Palo Alto Research Center, the Smalltalk interface has been responsible for the graphical user interface ideas of the Macintosh and Microsoft Windows. So now you know who to blame.

Sentence: "Blake thinks he's cool because he programs in a pure object-oriented programming language like *Smalltalk* instead of C++. I'd believe him if any of his programs ever worked the way they're supposed to."

smart terminal

Pronunciation: *smart ter-min-al.*

Meaning: A computer, connected to a network, that can function independent of the network. Smart terminals are usually just personal computers with their own hard disk, disk drive, and memory. In comparison, *dumb terminals* are usually nothing more than a monitor and a keyboard. (See also *dumb terminal.*)

Sentence: "*Smart terminals* scare most managers because they can't control them as easily. Who knows if that employee is working on a report or his résumé? Managers who distrust smart terminals are called 'dumb managers,' and managers who trust smart terminals are called 'smart managers'."

smiley

Pronunciation: *smi-lee.*

Meaning: An emoticon or ASCII "picture" that conveys a happy mood or something fun. It consists of a colon, a hyphen, and the right parenthesis, which looks like a face turned sideways:

:-)

E-mail fanatics use this symbol to denote a light mood since their writing skills are often limited and jokes that would be taken as such in verbal communications often lose their meaning once written down.

Sentence: "I would have busted you in the chops for that message, had you not appended a *smiley*."

SMM

Pronunciation: *Ess Em Em.*

Meaning: Acronym that stands for *System Management Mode*, which is a standard developed by Intel for automatically reducing energy consumption in their chips when the computer isn't being used. The idea behind SMM chips is that they will conserve energy and prolong the batteries of laptop computers.

Sentence: "The latest Intel processors offer *SMM* to cut off power consumption by your computer if you're not using it. SMM is great for people too lazy to hit the on/off switch on their computers."

smoke and mirrors

Pronunciation: *smoke and mir-ors.*

Meaning: Slang term describing verbal special effects to make a product sound more enticing and powerful than it really is. Smoke-and-mirrors techniques are commonly used in advertising and sales. A great smoke-and-mirrors story has to do with the ancestor of the Macintosh, the ill-fated Lisa computer. (In many ways, the Lisa was the "father," or is it "mother," of the Macintosh and Windows, but in a way it isn't because they stole the idea from elsewhere.) When the original Lisa was demonstrated for the computer industry, it wasn't a computer at all! Instead, under the table, the designers had rigged several Apple II computers, which actually controlled the Lisa. This is classic smoke and mirrors.

Sentence: "The product demo had us floored. But then a little dog pulled back the curtain on the left and the computer said, 'Pay no attention to that nerd behind the curtain!' I suppose the whole thing was just *smoke and mirrors*."

SNOBOL

Pronunciation: *Sno-ball.*

Meaning: Specialized language for processing character strings (text). Developed at Bell Laboratories in 1962, SNOBOL is rarely used today, except as an answer for computer trivia questions.

Sentence: "*SNOBOL* isn't the Latin of ancient computer languages. No, it's more like Aramaic."

snow

Pronunciation: *sno.*

Meaning: Small flickering dots that sometimes appear on certain monitors, caused when the screen image changes too fast for a lame monitor to handle. Usually found only on CGA monitors or really bad VGA monitors. (See also *VGA*.)

Sentence: "Edna, this isn't *snow* on your monitor. I think we need to go to the pharmacy and get you some Head & Shoulders."

soft hyphen

Pronunciation: *sof-ta hi-fen.*

Meaning: A hyphen in a word processing document that appears only when a word hangs precariously close to the right margin, in which case the hyphen hyphenates the word. At times, the term may also apply to any hyphen character that is used to split a word. This contrasts with hard hyphens that are not supposed to split a word when that word is too close to the right margin.

Sentence: "No, if you poke a *soft hyphen*, you won't get gunk all over your fingers."

software

Pronunciation: *sof-ta wear.*

Meaning: Computer programs. Software generally refers to any type of computer program, from an operating system such as DOS, to a utility, to an application, to a program stored on a ROM chip. This contrasts with *hardware*, which is the physical side of computing. It's the software

that makes the hardware go. Without it, the hardware would be nothing but potential — like an uneducated kid but minus the hyperactivity. (See also *hardware.*)

Sentence: "Og know difference between *software* and hardware. Hardware hard. Software soft."

SOHO

Pronunciation: *So-ho* (rhymes with "Ho, ho").

Meaning: Acronym that stands for *Small Office/Home Office*, which hardly anyone uses but computer magazines that are trying to create another acronym for everyone to remember. SOHO is often used to describe products that people think would be just perfect for a small office or home office, such as a computer desk that folds up into an aquarium or flower pot, or a portable lamp that doubles up as a food warmer or plant light.

Sentence: "If a big company buys a product, then it's not considered a *SOHO* product. If a big company wouldn't be interested in a product, then it's considered a SOHO product or something absolutely useless that nobody in their right mind would consider buying in the first place."

sort

Pronunciation: *sort.*

Meaning: To organize according to some pattern or rule. The typical sort is alphabetical, though you can also have numeric sorts. Sorts can also be ascending or descending. An ascending sort is from first to last, smallest to biggest, or A to Z. Descending goes the other way.

Sentence: "Kinkaid should be busy for a while. I just told him to *sort* our list of Japanese clients — in Japanese."

source

Pronunciation: *sores.*

Meaning: The original or the location of the original, normally used when copying files. The source file is the original file; the *source* directory or disk drive is the place from which the files are being copied. The *target* is the final destination, the place to which files are being copied or moved. (See also *target.*)

Sentence: "The first *source* for anything has to be your brain. Or it could be the devil, if you're possessed."

source code

Pronunciation: *sores kohd.*

Meaning: The original file or instructions from which a program is created. A programmer, call him Melvin, starts by writing a computer program using a text editor. The text editor creates a file that contains source code. That's swallowed and manipulated in several mystical manners until another file is created, the final program itself.

Sentence: "Melvin is such a deft programmer that his *source code* reads like poetry. Okay, you have to be pretty weird to appreciate it."

space character

Pronunciation: *spa-sa kear-ik-tor.*

Meaning: The character, or blank, produced by pressing the spacebar. With computers, the space is actually a character on-screen, just like A or $ or the ~ thing.

Sentence: "I keep having to tell Tom that 'alot' is really two words. I told him to insert a *space character*, so he drew a picture of Captain Kirk."

spacebar

Pronunciation: *spa-sa-bar.*

Meaning: The longest key on your keyboard, the one that produces the space character.

Sentence: "Is it called the *spacebar* or the spacebar key? Is it a bar or a key? And, no, there will be no tired and obvious outer space cocktail lounge jokes here."

spaghetti code

Pronunciation: *spa-geh-tee kohd.*

Meaning: A program written so sloppily that it has no flow or logic to it. It's said of such a program that reading it is like following a noodle around a plate of spaghetti. Such programs are typically written by those new to programming or by a programming committee.

Sentence: "Well, I guess if Sergio Leone wrote a program, it could be called *spaghetti code.*"

spam

Pronunciation: *spam*

Meaning: A worthless electronic message, even lower than paper junk mail, it's usually sent out in batches, unsolicited, and met with great anger on the Net. Sending spam is taboo. Being spammed is justification for electronic retaliation.

Sentence: Typically some lawyer gets on the Net and decides to "advertise" to everyone. Unwittingly, he sends out a *spam* and gets flamed for it.

SPARC

Pronunciation: *Spark.*

Meaning: Acronym for *Scalable Performance ARCitechture*. A RISC processor developed by Sun Microsystems for their line of workstations. It must be cool; I've never seen one. (See also *RISC.*)

Sentence: "This Sun workstation is running kind of slowly. Maybe it needs another *SPARC* plug."

special characters

Pronunciation: *spesh-el kar-ek-ters.*

Meaning: Any oddball or unusual characters or those characters that perform special functions. For example, the trademark character (™) is considered a special character because it's not found on the keyboard. Most characters that aren't alphanumeric or a handful of symbols are special characters. Other special characters may look like normal characters but carry out special functions. For example, a wildcard character, such as the ?, may be a special character.

Sentence: "Will you look at that J *character*? What's so *special* about him?"

speed

Pronunciation: *speed.*

Meaning: A measure of how fast something is. With microprocessors, the speed is measured in MHz (megahertz). Disk drive speed is measured in access time by the millisecond. Generally speaking, the larger the number, the faster the thing operates (and the faster the money comes out of your wallet). (See also *MHz.*)

Sentence: "I wouldn't say this new printer is fast. Its *speed* is probably one notch above stop."

spell checker

Pronunciation: *spell che-ker.*

Meaning: A program, usually built in to a word processor, that examines every word you've typed for correct spelling and offers possible corrections when it finds a word it doesn't recognize. This is really necessary only in English, where spelling still remains a mystery some 150 years after Webster made up the whole idea."

Sentence: "Now I never have to learn to spell because my computer *spell checker* does it for me."

spike

Pronunciation: *spi-ka.*

Meaning: A power surge that can potentially fry electronic equipment but most likely does nothing other than cause the screen to flicker momentarily. Look out your window. Find a tall tree. If a bolt of lightning hits that tree, it will send a power spike through all the circuits in the room you're sitting in, making your PC's guts go pop. Also, the name of Joan Rivers's dog. (See also *surge suppressor.*)

Sentence: "I bought a surge suppressor to protect against power *spikes,* but I still unplug the computer during an electrical storm."

Spock

Pronunciation: *Spahk.*

Meaning: The character played by Leonard Nimoy on the original *Star Trek* television show. Spock is admired by the computer-loving crowd because he, too, enjoyed using computers. Some great Spock-computer *Star Trek* moments:

> "This computer here is the key. Destroy this one and the whole planet goes."
> "Computer? Compute to the last digit the value of pi." (The computer starts screaming here.)
> "Landru is a computer."
> "The computer lied."

Spock is also the name of a real doctor, well-known for his expert advice for caring for babies and for blocking trains carrying nuclear waste.

Sentence: "Okay, *Spock.* It's your turn to wear a red shirt and beam down to the planet."

spool

Pronunciation: *spool* (rhymes with *school, pool,* and *cruel*).

Meaning: To store data temporarily before printing it. The main reason for spooling files is to free up your computer so you can use it without waiting for the printer to finish printing it out. This feature is less important with multitasking operating systems such as OS/2 or Windows. (See also *buffer* and *print buffer.*)

Sentence: "Be sure to *spool* your document to a print buffer or else you'll have to wait until the printer is done before you can use your computer again."

spooler

Pronunciation: *spoo-ler.*

Meaning: A chunk of memory that's either built in to a printer, carved out from the computer's main memory, or stored in a separate box connected between a printer and a computer. Sometimes called a *print spooler* or a *print buffer.*

Sentence: "If it wasn't for my *spooler,* I would have to wait until my printer got done printing before I could use my computer again. I know some fast food restaurants that could use a drive-through spooler."

spreadsheet

Pronunciation: *spred-sheet.*

Meaning: A program that organizes numbers, labels, and formulas in rows and columns for calculating results. Spreadsheets rapidly and accurately calculate results using mathematical formulas. Accountants love spreadsheets, as do scientists, mathematicians, and people with nothing better to do on a Saturday night. Many spreadsheets have built-in statistical, mathematical, or financial equations (called *functions*) so users can focus more on entering in their numbers and less on creating the necessary equations. Some of the more popular spreadsheets are Lotus 1-2-3, Excel, Quattro Pro, and the backs of envelopes and cocktail napkins.

Sentence: "I told my mother I'm learning *spreadsheets* at the office and she thought I was demoted to a maid."

sprite

Pronunciation: *sprite* (rhymes with *right, kite,* and *bite*).

Meaning: (1) A moving element in a graphic display, such as those found in video games. (2) A sugar-flavored, carbonated beverage with exaggerated claims of refreshment that two out of three hard-core programmers and computer users prefer over Coke, Pepsi, or Kool-Aid.

Sentence: "Whenever I get tired of watching *sprites* on my computer, I drink a Sprite."

SRAM

Pronunciation: *Es-Ram*

Meaning: Acronym for *Static Random-Access Memory.* Another type of memory, but one specifically designed for high-speed purposes, such as assisting the microprocessor with a cache (see *cache*).

Unlike DRAM, static RAM or SRAM memory is expensive, doesn't store as much information in the same amount of space, and doesn't require a lot of electricity to keep it refreshed. (Gatorade helps.) This is why this type of memory is only used in specific parts of the computer, not as main memory.

Sentence: "I think Bill misunderstands what static RAM is. He thought it would be nice to add some *SRAM* to his computer, so he opened up the case, rubbed his socks on a shag pile carpet, and then touched the RAM chips."

SS/DD

Pronunciation: *Ess Ess/Dee Dee.*

Meaning: Acronym for *Single-Sided/Double-Density.* This type of disk is obsolete, although older computers still use these disks. An SS/DD $5^1/_4$-inch floppy disk can typically store 180K of data.

Sentence: "We found an old *SS/DD* disk in the storage room the other day. Stood around for about an hour marveling at such an antique."

SS/SD

Pronunciation: *Ess Ess/Ess Dee.*

Meaning: Acronym for *Single-Sided/Single-Density.* These types of disks are obsolete, although some older computers still use them. An SS/SD $5^1/_4$-inch floppy disk can typically store 90K of data.

Sentence: "I found this old box of *SS/SD* floppy disks in my closet. I could use them, but I'd rather cut them open and toss them around the house as frisbees instead."

stack

Pronunciation: *stahk.*

Meaning: A data structure that programmers use to store and remove data in a last-in, first-out (LIFO) order (especially used in assembly language). (See also *LIFO* and *POP.*)

Sentence: "Programmers who like pancakes prefer using *stacks.*"

standard

Pronunciation: *stan-dard.*

Meaning: A stubborn, mythical belief held by scientists that they can define specific methods, appearances, or equipment that everyone else in the world will voluntarily follow.

Sentence: "The American National Standards Institute (ANSI) keeps trying to define the C language. The International Standards Organization (ISO) keeps trying to define the Pascal language. Too bad no one ever bothers to define the English language."

Star Trek

Pronunciation: *Star Trek* (not *Star Trick*).

Meaning: A science fiction TV show, with a rabid following, that tells the story of a spaceship sent from Earth to explore the galaxy, confront alien life forms that look surprisingly like actors wearing lots of makeup and speaking perfect English, and earn residuals from the sales of *Star Trek* T-shirts, action figures, and annual conventions.

Sentence: "I'm very thankful for *Star Trek.* Without it, we'd have to put up with lame *Voyage to the Bottom of the Sea* computer humor."

Star Trek: The Next Generation

Pronunciation: *Star Trek The Nekst Jen-er-a-shin.*

Meaning: The very popular first sequel to *Star Trek* (see preceding). *ST:TNG* has several beloved characters, including an android named Commander Data, a Klingon named Worf, and the very poised, sophisticated Captain Picard. Some two-year-olds know who these guys are before they even recognize Ernie or Bert (we're not even going to discuss Barney).

Sentence: "If you don't watch *Star Trek: The Next Generation,* you may have trouble conversing with nerds, geeks, and gurus."

star-dot-star

Pronunciation: *star-dot-star* (just like it looks).

Meaning: The *.* wildcard in MS-DOS that tells the computer to look for all files no matter what the filename or file extensions may be. Some less computer-literate people call it "asterisk-period-asterisk," but the cool people always say "star-dot-star." (See also *wildcard.*)

Sentence: "*.* means everything. The whole ball o' wax. The big enchilada. The whole shootin' match. You get the idea."

start bit

Pronunciation: *start bit.*

Meaning: The tiny chunk of information that signals the beginning of data transfer.

Sentence: "Before my wife starts yelling at me for spending too much time at my computer, she starts wringing her hands. To me, that's a *start bit* signalling she's about to start nagging again."

start-up disk

Pronunciation: *start-up disk.*

Meaning: The floppy or hard disk that the computer uses when you turn it on for the first time. The start-up disk differs from other disks because the start-up disk has special commands and programs that tell the computer what to do to wake itself up.

Sentence: "My hard disk is my *start-up disk.* But when the hard disk starts acting flaky, I have a special floppy disk that I use for my start-up disk. If that floppy disk doesn't work, then I cry."

static

Pronunciation: *stah-tik.*

Meaning: Random electrical noise that garbles voice and modem communication through the phone lines.

Sentence: "Every time I try to dial into NASA's computers, *static* interferes and I have to hang up. Every time my mother-in-law calls, I make crackling noises with my mouth and pretend that static is preventing me from hearing what she has to say."

stealth virus

Pronunciation: *stelth vi-rus.*

Meaning: A sneaky type of virus that tries to make itself invisible to anti-virus programs that might kill it.

Sentence: "I'm sorry, Jay, but pointing that expensive Air Force radar detector at your PC just won't work. It might be infected by a *stealth virus* that our technology cannot detect."

stop bit

Pronunciation: *stop bit* (just like it looks).

Meaning: The tiny chunk of information that signals the end of successful data transfer. Hanging up the phone in the middle of a call is NOT an example of a stop bit.

Sentence: "Some communications programs let you choose between one or two *stop bits.* Most of the time, one stop bit is fine, unless the other computer doesn't stop, in which case you'll need two stop bits."

storage

Pronunciation: *stow-r-age.*

Meaning: A place to put valuable information in the hopes you'll be able to find it again. Common storage devices are tape drives, floppy disks, hard disks, and CD-ROM discs.

Sentence: "We use a special optical disk for *storage.* That way our data will survive a nuclear attack, even though we might not."

string

Pronunciation: *string* (rhymes with *sting, sing,* and *ring*).

Meaning: A group of letters. Humans call groups of letters *words*, but computers call them *strings*.

Sentence: "I consider my name to be a representation of ancient history, but when I type it into my database, the computer just thinks of it as a *string* of meaningless characters."

string variable

Pronunciation: *string var-ee-ah-bull.*

Meaning: A symbol that a program uses to represent a group of characters. Most databases use the string variable NAME to represent a person's name.

Sentence: "Yes, you should store the word 'yarn' in a *string variable.*"

structured programming

Pronunciation: *struk-sured pro-gram-ming.*

Meaning: A method for writing programs in small subprograms or modules so they are easy to read and understand. A myth pursued by computer scientists with the same vigor that early Spanish explorers had when they searched the New World for the Fountain of Youth and the Seven Cities of Gold. Structured programming emphasizes that programs can be written using three types of statements: sequential, conditional, and loops. Sequential program statements occur one after another. Conditional statements are IF-THEN or CASE statements. Loop statements are WHILE-DO, DO-WHILE, FOR-DO, and REPEAT-UNTIL statements. If you have no idea what these last few sentences mean, you probably don't need to know anything about structured programming, except for the fact that it rarely works and that's why programs today have so many bugs in them.

Sentence: "The closest I've come to *structured programming* is building a little house out of old issues of *TV Guide*."

StuffIt

Pronunciation: *Stuf-it.*

Meaning: A compression program for the Macintosh that can smash multiple files into a single file to take up less space. StuffIt is a shareware program that you can copy and try for free. If you use it, then you're supposed to pay for it.

Sentence: "My Boss asked me how to decompress the files he downloaded from CompuServe and I told him to *StuffIt.* Now I'm out of a job, but he still can't get to his files."

style

Pronunciation: *stiy-el.*

Meaning: Text formatting and character attributes all combined into one. Style refers to the way text looks. In some programs, you can format your text using a Style command. Other times, Style may refer to a collection of formatting and character attributes that can be slapped onto text all at once.

Sentence: "I have two *styles* I use for my memos: Fancy Sycophant, for writing letters to my boss, and Ugly Automaton, for writing letters to those who work for me."

stylus

Pronunciation: *stiy-less.*

Meaning: A long pointy thing, like a pencil. The stylus is a type of input device like a mouse. You use the stylus to draw on an electronic pad embedded with sensors. What you draw shows up on-screen. These things are more expensive than your typical computer mouse but offer a higher degree of control. (See also *digitizer.*)

Sentence: "If Baron Lytton had known computers, he might have said, 'The *stylus* is mightier than the mouse,' but he'd have run the risk of being locked up for that."

subdirectory

Pronunciation: *sub-dir-ek-toh-ree.*

Meaning: A directory within or "under" the current directory. All disks have directories in which they store files. The directories can also store other directories, which are then called subdirectories. Technically, the term applies only to directories "beneath" another directory. Generally, any directory on disk — save for the main or root directory — is called a subdirectory. The Macintosh operating system also uses the subdirectory concept, but they call subdirectories "folders" instead. (See also *tree structure* for more confusion.)

Sentence: "I'm sorry, Private, if you want to find a *subdirectory*, you'll have to look on the Navy's computers."

submenu

Pronunciation: *sub-men-yoo.*

Meaning: A menu below another menu. For example, if you're presented with a menu of choices and selecting one of them displays another menu, you have a submenu. In a GUI, a submenu is often a secondary or tertiary menu that hangs on to the main menu like an ugly piece of gum.

Sentence: "Today's *submenu* offers several items: Ham, Pastrami, Turkey, Provolone, Swiss, Cheddar, and a variety o' fixins."

subroutine

Pronunciation: *sub-roo-teen.*

Meaning: A miniprogram within a larger program. For example, a program may have a subroutine that displays text on-screen. The main program would "call" that subroutine any time it wanted to display text on-screen.

Sentence: "My son just can't seem to finish his homework. I think his brain is missing some *subroutine*."

subscript

Pronunciation: *sub-skr-ipt.*

Meaning: Text that appears smaller than and below the surrounding text. Subscript is a text formatting attribute available in word processors and other programs that let you manipulate text. The number 2 in H_2O is a subscript. (See also *superscript.*)

Sentence: "Jacob was trying to explain to me that the printer was broken, but it turned out he accidentally turned on *subscript* mode and didn't know it. Ah, the joys of WordPerfect. . . ."

suite

Pronunciation: *sweet.*

Meaning: A collection of separate programs, usually a word processor, database, and spreadsheet, sold together at an attractive price. Theoretically, all programs in a suite are supposed to work together and use similar commands. Realistically, all programs in a suite are together simply because some company packaged them together in an effort to sell more programs (especially when it comes time to upgrade). Ideally, once you learn how to use one program in a suite, you can quickly learn the others. Also, once you create data in one program, you can effortlessly (supposedly) share that data within other programs of the same suite.

Sentence: "An integrated program is a single program that offers a word processor, spreadsheet, and database. A *suite* is a collection of three or more separate programs that some marketing genius thought would look nice packaged together, regardless of whether they work alike or share data."

Super VGA

Pronunciation: *Soo-per Vee Gee Ay.*

Meaning: Faster than regular VGA. More powerful than EGA. Able to leap puny old CGAs in a single bound. Look, up on-screen, it's high-resolution, it's colorful — yes! — it's SuperVGA. IBM introduced its best PC graphics standard in 1987, the VGA. Other manufacturers liked it but offered an improvement called SuperVGA, also known as SVGA. If you're buying a graphics card for your PC, Super VGA is the way to go. (See also *VGA.*)

Sentence: "*Super VGA* gives Phil the graphics horsepower he needs to see his naked lady GIF collection at full resolution."

supercomputer

Pronunciation: *soo-per-kom-pyoo-ter.*

Meaning: Faster than a regular computer, a supercomputer is a very large, powerful, and fast computer. Supercomputers are used for important things like drawing dinosaurs in *Jurassic Park.* Unlike a mainframe, the super computer has an interesting design that makes it very, very fast. That's about all you need to know because you can't have a supercomputer in your house; turning it on would dim all the lights in the neighborhood.

Sentence: "I hear the boys in the lab just love the new *supercomputer.* They bow to it each time they enter the room."

superscript

Pronunciation: *soo-per-scr-ipt.*

Meaning: Text that appears smaller than and above the surrounding text. Superscript is a text formatting attribute available in word processors and similar programs that manipulate text. The number 10 in 2^{10} is superscripted. (See also *subscript,* unless you've already come here from there.)

Sentence: "Simon Nathaniel the Fourth thinks it's really nifty if he prints his name with a *superscripted* four: Simon Nathaniel^{4}."

superstore

Pronunciation: *soo-per-stor.*

Meaning: A large store that sells lots of different computer equipment, software, books, and furniture, except for the ones you really need. Most superstores give the illusion of offering the lowest prices for name brand equipment, but they're often priced higher than competing stores that aren't part of a nationwide franchise.

Sentence: "Superman, Batman, Spiderman, and Wonder Woman all bought their computers at a *superstore.*"

support

Pronunciation: *suh-port.*

Meaning: (1) What you pay extra for when you pay extra. (2) What you don't get when you pay extra. (3) What you're supposed to get with each computer you buy, whether you pay extra or not. (4) Training or someone available to help with your new PC, or a place to get it repaired. Support is the most important factor in buying a computer, one many people often neglect as a trade-off for a low price. Support includes service after the sale, as well as phone help, classroom help, and other assistance. Software vendors offer support in the form of phone lines, toll free or not, over which you can ask questions. Sometimes this actually works.

Sentence: "The only *support* that comes out of waiting on hold is support for the long-distance phone company."

surfer

Pronunciation: *ser-fer.*

Meaning: A slang term that describes someone who spends an inordinate amount of time exploring an electronic network, such as the Internet, CompuServe, or local electronic bulletin board systems. Often used with the slang term "net," such as in "net surfer."

Sentence: "If you have questions about using the Internet, ask Ted because he's the local net *surfer* around here. "

surge

Pronunciation: *serge.*

Meaning: An increase in the power level coming through the wall socket. Surges are gradual and build to a point where they may do some damage to your PC's components. Usually this is prevented by a circuit breaker or sometimes — in an utterly unbelievable twist of altruism — the power supply may actually give up its life to save the rest of the PC's components. A surge is the opposite of a *brownout*, when the power drops to low levels, and your PC may not even start at all. (See also *spike* and *surge suppressor.*)

Sentence: "Serge was expecting the power *surge* to make his computer run faster. However, the circuit breaker popped and, though he lost my data, his computer is once again saved from the perils of the electric company."

surge protector

Pronunciation: *serge pro-tek-tor.*

Meaning: (1) A device that guards against power surges (I think it kind of eats them) so that your computer doesn't blow up. (2) A device the protects you against Serge.

Sentence: "Although a *surge protector* is a good thing to have for your PC, it won't protect your computer against other power line nasties, such as spikes, line noise, and people who trip over cords."

suspend

Pronunciation: *sus-pend.*

Meaning: To temporarily halt — not completely stop, more like freeze.

Sentence: "When I answer the phone, I must *suspend* my dot-matrix printer. Otherwise, I can't hear a darn thing."

SVGA

Pronunciation: *Ess Vee Gee Ay.*

Meaning: An acronym for *Super VGA*, a PC graphics adapter standard. (See also *Super VGA*.)

switch

Pronunciation: *swi-cha.*

Meaning: (1) A knob or lever that has two positions, usually ON and OFF. It can also be a graphical representation of a knob or button in a GUI. (2) A command option or parameter. For example, the /F switch on DOS's FORMAT command is used to tell FORMAT how big of a disk to format. (3) To move from one program to another in a multitasking environment. In Windows and OS/2, you accomplish this by pressing the Ctrl-Esc key combination.

Sentence: "In IBM lingo, the Big Red Switch used to mean the on-off *switch* on the computer. Back in the early PC days, the switch was really big and red. Today, on-off switches are no longer red, nor are they necessarily big."

SX

Pronunciation: *Ess Ecks.*

Meaning: A suffix added to Intel microprocessor numbers, one that usually indicates that the chip is something less than a DX model. The 386SX was crippled by running at half its bit-width internally. The 486SX was crippled by lacking a built-in math coprocessor.

Sentence: "Steer clear of any *SX* microprocessor, unless you're completely destitute."

synchronous

Pronunciation: *sing-kro-nuss.*

Meaning: Happening at the same time, in synch. Usually this term applies to synchronous communications. In that mode, two computers communicate at a specific pace with each other, sending bits back and forth "on the beat." Microcomputer modems are asynchronous devices and do not send information at a specific pace. (See also *asynchronous.*)

Sentence: "No, Bob, *synchronous* communications doesn't mean we have to sing to each other."

syntax

Pronunciation: *sin-taks.*

Meaning: (1) A tax on beer, alcohol, or cigarettes. (2) The rules regarding the way a language is put together. This applies to programming languages as well as human languages.

Sentence: "Computers are persnickety. Disobeying their laws of *syntax* is akin to telling your neighbor, 'Day nice outside hot not it is.'"

syntax error

Pronunciation: *sin-taks air-or.*

Meaning: You have violated the rules of syntax. This usually happens when writing a computer program. If you flip-flop words or misspell something, the program compiler spits out a syntax error and then you're left scratching your head to figure out what you did wrong.

Sentence: "Computers say `Syntax Error` because the people who programmed them are too lazy to make the message any more precise."

sysop

Pronunciation: *siss-op* (not *sy-sop*).

Meaning: Abbreviation for *system operator*, the head honcho in charge of the system. This term revolves primarily around computer bulletin boards (BBSs). The person who owns the computer and the BBS and in whose house it sits is the sysop. This is an exalted position among the modeming crowd. Everyone wants to be a sysop or be in the sysop's favor. (See also *BBS.*)

Sentence: "I begged the *sysop* for advanced access to his system; finally he gave me level six access. But the funny thing is, there's no one on level six."

system

Pronunciation: *siss-tim.*

Meaning: (1) A way of doing things. (2) The program that controls the entire computer. (3) The whole computer. (4) The network. (5) The Powers That Be. (6) What you can't fight.

Sentence: "Something has to be in charge, and that's the *system.* It rules the computer. In real life, there's a system too, but it doesn't rule anything. Instead, it's The Conspiracy who's in charge. And they watch everyone through cable TV and listen to our phone calls. And there's a helicopter over my head right now, and they're watching me type this. And that gnat is a spy for a terrorist group."

System 7

Pronunciation: *Sys-tem seh-vin.*

Meaning: The operating system used on most Macintosh computers. System 7 is not the same thing as DOS on a PC. Most of the Macintosh's operating system is encoded in its ROM. System 7 provides the Finder interface, plus other extensions to the Mac's internal operating system.

Sentence: "I upgraded to *System 7* because I thought it would bring sanity to my Mac. Alas, the computer may be sane, but it's still as slow as ever."

System 7.5

Pronunciation: *Sys-tem seh-vin point fyv*

Meaning: The operating system Apple wants most Macintosh owners to install on their computers in an admission that System 7 probably wasn't the best they could do.

Sentence: "Morgan won't upgrade to the new *System 7.5.* He says he only upgrades his Mac's system to whole-numbered versions."

system clock

Pronunciation: *sis-tim klaughck.*

Meaning: An internal time clock maintained by the operating system. This clock is primarily used to record the time when files were saved to disk.

Sentence: "I once reset my PC's *system clock* wrong on purpose to prove to the boss that I was getting work done way ahead of the deadline."

system disk

Pronunciation: *sis-tim dis-ka.*

Meaning: A disk that contains the system, or all the programs required to start your computer. For most of us, the system disk is our hard drive, which starts the computer each time we turn it on. You can also start your computer from a floppy drive, which some people do just to kill time.

Sentence: "You can't start your PC without a *system disk.* Because of this, we recommend that everyone create an 'Emergency Boot Floppy' with which you can start your PC in times of woe."

System Folder

Pronunciation: *Sis-tem Fold-her.*

Meaning: A special subdirectory on a Macintosh computer that contains all the system files. This is roughly equivalent to the DOS subdirectory on a PC. Into the System Folder you put (or have already installed) all the files necessary to make Mr. Mac boot up properly, special files and programs such as fonts, desk accessories, control panel thingys, and other stuff I can't think of.

Sentence: "The term *System Folder* makes it sound so neat and tidy. But the truth is that the System Folder is perhaps the junkiest folder on my disk."

system font

Pronunciation: *sis-tem fahnt.*

Meaning: A font built into the operating system or GUI. System fonts are those fonts that *must* be there. Text on menus and in dialog boxes is usually composed using the system font. Yes, there can be more than one system font.

Sentence: "Truly, the *system font* is the most boring font you have. I recommend buying other, more exciting fonts and doing your documents with those instead."

system unit

Pronunciation: *sys-tim yoo-nut.*

Meaning: The main computer box, also called the *console*. The system unit typically houses the computer's microprocessor, memory, and disk drives and usually contains expansion slots. All other items outside the system unit are peripherals.

Sentence: "Earl is such a card. He cleverly disguised his *system unit* in an old Philco TV box."

tab

Pronunciation: *tab.*

Meaning: A chunk of blank spaces created by pressing the Tab key. This chunk of spaces is treated as a unit so that if you wanted to delete the tab space, it would delete the whole thing, not one blank character at a time. In most database and spreadsheet programs, you move from one field or cell to another by pressing the Tab key. You can move backwards through the fields or cells by pressing the Shift key with the Tab key. This is known as a "back tab."

Sentence: "This is absolutely amazing. I pressed the *Tab* key, and this diet beverage rolled out of my disk drive slot."

Tab key

Pronunciation: *Tab kee.*

Meaning: The key on the keyboard that produces the tab "character." In most programs, when you write something, pressing the Tab key moves you forward one tab stop, whether that's a chunk of spaces in word processing, a field in a database, or a cell in a spreadsheet.

Sentence: "On most PCs, the *Tab key* has two arrows pointing in opposite directions printed on it that leads me to believe the key doesn't know which direction is which."

table

Pronunciation: *tay-bull.*

Meaning: A way of organizing data or text into rows and columns, especially in a database context. You don't need a tablecloth for this kind of table, nor do you need good table manners. A data table is simply a way to store information or, in word processors, to present text in a neat and tidy manner.

Sentence: "Tax *tables* list income on the left side and tax categories along the top. In the middle you can find out what outrageous amount the government would like you to pay."

Taligent

Pronunciation: *Tah-li-jent.*

Meaning: An object-oriented operating system developed by Apple, IBM, and Hewlett-Packard in a desperate attempt to wrest the operating system market away from Microsoft. Although most people will use Microsoft Windows for the future, Apple and IBM hope that Taligent will be so wonderful that people will abandon Windows and use Taligent instead.

Sentence: "As a programmer, I have to write programs for the most popular operating system so I can make lots of money. So far I've written programs for CP/M-86, GEM, OS/2, and *Taligent.* Am I doing something wrong?"

tape

Pronunciation: *tay-pa.*

Meaning: A magnetic data storage medium (long, thin brown stuff), essentially the same material as audio and video cassettes. The advantages of this medium are its low cost and high density (ability to store lots of information). The disadvantage is that it offers only linear or sequential access, which means you have to rewind or fast forward through the whole tape in order to find what you're looking for. In contrast, disk drives offer random access so that you can get to any given point within a fraction of a second, no rewinding or fast forwarding involved. You generally use tapes only to store backup copies of data. (See also *sequential access.*)

Sentence: "Okay. Who's the joker who put the Scotch tape into the *tape* backup unit?"

tape drive

Pronunciation: *tay-pa dry-va.*

Meaning: A machine into which you insert a tape cassette that records data and stuff. The machine is like a tape recorder and player, reading and writing information to the tape. This is how sophisticated PC users back up their data. They buy these backup tape cartridges, slam them into the tape drive, and then run special tape backup software. There's no swapping involved (providing the tapes can hold enough data), and the backup takes only a few minutes. Tape drives are about as expensive as new hard drives. Many formats are available: 1/4-inch cartridge, 8-mm VCR cartridge, 4-mm audio, and nine-track.

Sentence: "I'm sorry about the demotion, Jason, but what you thought was a toaster oven was really our new $2,000 DAT *tape backup system.*"

tar

Pronunciation: *tahr* (as in "tar and feather").

Meaning: A contraction of *tape-archiver*, a backup and archiving program used on UNIX computers. In addition to copying files to a tape backup, tar can also be used to clump a bunch of files together, slapping the TAR extension on them. Getting the files out again will lead most people to madness (and, yes, if there were a simple solution, I'd offer it here).

Sentence: "Darryl was overjoyed to get FTP to work on the Internet, but getting his files out of the *tar* proved to be very messy."

task

Pronunciation: *tas-ka.*

Meaning: A task is something you do with a computer. For example, if you're word processing, the computer's task is word processing. This would be an utterly redundant thing if it weren't for multitasking, which is the capability of a computer to do several things — several tasks — at the same time.

Sentence: "Most of the time, my computer's main *task* is to ignore me."

task switching

Pronunciation: *tas-ka swi-ching.*

Meaning: When computers can multitask (run more than one program at a time), the art of switching between the running programs is called task switching. In Windows, you can do this by pressing Ctrl-Esc, Alt-Esc, Alt-Tab, or by clicking on a specific window that represents a program. When you move from one open application (task) to another, you are task switching.

Sentence: "The boss told me I was *task switching* too often between Word and Solitaire."

TCP/IP

Pronunciation: *Tee Cee Pee Ih Pee.*

Meaning: Take Caffeine Periodically/Intravenously, Preferably. Har, har. Actually, it stands for *Transfer Control Protocol/Internet Protocol*, and it means information can be shared between two strange networks. Only severe networking dweebs will use — and understand — what it's all about.

Sentence: "I went for a job interview that asked for *TCP/IP* knowledge. When I asked what it meant, they said, 'We were hoping you knew!'"

TeachText

Pronunciation: *Teech-Tekst.*

Meaning: A simple text-editing program that the Mac uses to read and display README files.

Sentence: "I don't think the *TeachText* program is teaching me anything."

tear-off menus

Pronunciation: *taer-off men-yoos.*

Meaning: Menus that you can actually tear off the menu bar (symbolically, of course) and place at any convenient location on the screen. For example, you might press Ctrl while clicking on the File menu to tear it off. You can then drag it to any location on the screen. Tear-off menus are not widely used.

Sentence: "Baby Jonah accidentally got ahold of the computer. He found the *tear-off menus,* and now they're all over the floor."

techno weenie

Pronunciation: *tek-noh weenee.*

Meaning: Person who aspires to be a full-fledged geek, nerd, or dweeb, but either isn't smart enough about computers, isn't overly obsessed about computers, or has too many social skills. The guru at the office is a geek. Bill, your "computer literate" neighbor, is a techno weenie.

Sentence: "In college, you can tell who the *techno weenies* are because they take classes like Physics for Poets . . . and fail."

technology

Pronunciation: *tek-nal-uh-jee.*

Meaning: A stone used to shape another stone (as in the Stone Age) could be considered technology. You could say, in the broad sense, that technology means the use of tools. Power tools. Big anti-torque drills. Large dirt-moving vehicles. Ah, technology. More often, the word is used to refer to "high" technology, which is characterized by being abstract and not accessible to the naked eye. If you opened the hood of a vintage American car, you could tell exactly what was going on by seeing how the parts fit together and how they move. This is not-so-high tech. When you're talking about electronics, though, the relationships are not apparent. There could be millions of transistors on one silicon chip, and you would have no idea what the relationship of each was to its neighbors, nor where to fit the crescent wrench.

Sentence: "*Technology* actually comes from the ancient Greek term that roughly translates as 'If your VCR is blinking 12:00 all the time, you probably won't get any of this stuff.'"

telecommunications

Pronunciation: *tel-e-kom-yoo-ni-kae-shuns.*

Meaning: The field of technology dealing with communicating at a distance. It includes, but is not necessarily limited to, telephony, telegraphy, consumer radio, broadcast television, cable television, satellite television, radar, ham radio, CB radio, two tin cans connected by a string, and data transfer.

Sentence: "*Telecommunications* allows you to get confused at greater and greater distances."

telephony

Pronunciation: *tel-ih-fa-nee.*

Meaning: The art and science of making telephones happen. (Could just as well have been called "telephonology," but there was an editor on the loose that day, and the word got cut short.) Essentially what happens in the telephone process is that the voice — and all embarrassing or annoying background noises — get converted into electrical signals that travel through the wires and then get reconverted to sound at the other end. All this, even though Alexander Graham Bell used only two ordinary cups and a length of wire to make the World's First Telephone happen.

Sentence: "Using our new voice discriminator technology, it's easier to *telephony* call from a real one."

teletype

Pronunciation: *tel-e-tihp.*

Meaning: The old clunky typewriter-like things that typed "by magic" thanks to remote wires that controlled the keyboard. In the early days of computing, teletype machines were used to communicate with the behemoth computers of the time. You would type, Klunka-wunka, and then the computer would type back at you, Klunka-wunka-faster. All this would be transcribed on a long sheet of paper that fed into and out of the teletype machine. In these exciting, carefree computer days, teletype is used to describe the dumbest and least sophisticated way to connect one computer to another. The teletype is nothing more than a keyboard and monitor (also called a Dumb Terminal) that allows you to send and receive information from another computer. It's abbreviated TTY because most computer nerds can't remember if teletype has one or two L's in it.

Sentence: "In the early '80s, I used to communicate with my friends on home computers using then-speedy 2400 bps modems. At the same time, the 'hot line' connecting the White House with the Kremlin was run on a sluggish old *teletype* machine running at only 300 bps. That meant that in the time Ronald Reagan could send 'Ivan, kiss your *@# goodbye,' I could have downloaded Tetris."

telnet

Pronunciation: *tell-net.*

Meaning: The closest thing UNIX has to a DOS modem program. Telnet is a command you can use to dial up another UNIX computer, and you can also use it like a dumb old modem program to call up any old computer with a modem attached.

Sentence: "Al uses *telnet* to dial up the local university, which then dials up Berkeley, which then dials up his own computer again. He spends a lot of money just to talk to himself."

template

Pronunciation: *tem-plate.*

Meaning: A "master" document for a word processor, spreadsheet, or other application that is used as the starting point or rough draft for other documents. Generally, the template contains all the formatting, so all you have to do is fill in the blanks. Some software packages come with numerous templates so that you really don't even need to learn to use the software. Word for Windows, for instance, comes with 17 different templates that let you easily generate form letters, reports, memos, proposals, and fax cover sheets. You can create your own templates by performing the formatting and composing the text that will appear in every document of that type. Then, each time you need, say, an invoice, you open up the template file, fill in the blanks, and print out the document. Then you can either save the additions to the file (as a new file, now, so you don't mess up the template) or not.

Sentence: "I'm going to use a *template* to write a letter to Santa Claus this year."

tera-

Pronunciation: *ter-a.*

Meaning: A prefix meaning trillion (the same prefix from which we get the words *terrible* and *deficit*, by the way). Usually seen in computer use when talking about terabytes, which are pretty close to a trillion bytes (which is the same as 1,000 gigabytes, or a million megabytes). The actual measurement of a terabyte is 1,099,511,627,776 bytes.

Sentence: " If you had one dollar for each byte in a *tera*byte, it would take Bill Gates 134 years to catch up with you if he made 8 billion dollars a year (not including interest or subtracting taxes)."

teraFLOP

Pronunciation: ter-a-flop.

Meaning: A very powerful computer, one capable of calculating one trillion (a tera) floating point operations (FLOPs) per second. That would be the equivalent of equipping all 1 billion Chinese with abacuses and expecting all of them to do 1,000 mathematical problems in one second. Boggling, no? Presently no computer is capable of such a feat.

Sentence: That new Steven Segal film is a total *teraFLOP*.

terminal

Pronunciation: *term-un-nel.*

Meaning: A monitor hooked up to a mainframe computer, from the root of the Latin word for *death*. Like people, terminals can either be smart or dumb, and the only way to find out how smart or dumb they are is to check how they relate to the computer. If a terminal has a mind of its own, then it's a smart terminal. This means it has some processors, maybe even a CPU, and maybe even a disk drive so it can store its own data. With such capabilities, the terminal doesn't need to rely on the mainframe for all its operations. If all it's got is a monitor and keyboard (and/or similar peripherals), then it's pretty dumb.

Sentence: "People can get terminally ill from sitting at *terminals* their whole lives."

terminal emulation

Pronunciation: *term-in-el em-yoo-lae-shun.*

Meaning: The ability of an average, run-of-the-mill desktop computer to cleverly disguise itself as a certain type of terminal hooked up to a mainframe computer. This can only be done with the right software, called terminal emulation software. You only need to worry about this when you actually *want* to be hooked up to a mainframe computer — a rare circumstance for most of us mortals.

Sentence: "They've finally perfected Macintosh *terminal emulation* for the PC. Everything works really slow, and the system crashes just before you save your file to disk. (You think we're kidding.)"

terminate-and-stay-resident program

Pronunciation: *ter-min-aet-and-stae-rez-i-dent proh-gram.*

Meaning: A special type of program that always stays in RAM and can be easily activated by a keystroke or "hot key." Also known as a TSR or memory resident program. These programs became popular when Borland's SideKick was introduced in the mid-'80s. SideKick gave you instant access to a slew of interesting little programs, all by pressing the Ctrl-Alt keys at the same time. SideKick would "pop-up" right on top of whatever other program you were running. At the time, this proved immensely handy. Other programmers learned SideKick's secret, and soon dozens of TSRs and pop-up programs appeared. The problem was that Borland cheated to get the pop-up effect, and because of this method of cheating, none of the TSRs would cooperate with each other. A TSR-laden PC would often crash, and the programs would conflict. Today, the pop-up type of TSR program isn't popular any more, thanks to multitasking programs such as Windows and advanced operating systems such as OS/2. TSRs still exist, primarily as programs that enhance DOS's features, but without conflicting with other programs. Popular TSRs include the mouse driver, CD-ROM driver, the DOSKEY keyboard enhancer, and certain file undeleting utilities. (See also *memory resident programs.*)

Sentence: "Please, Mr. Cooper, don't get all upset just because the old folks' home has adopted *terminate-and-stay-resident* software."

text

Pronunciation: *tek-sta.*

Meaning: Letters, numbers, and other characters or symbols found on your keyboard. Just plain writing; no formatting or other fancy stuff. (See also *ASCII.*)

Sentence: "*Text* is boring."

text box

Pronunciation: *tek-sta bahk-sa.*

Meaning: A box on the screen, outlining an area in which you can type text. This may also be called an input box. Oh, and you can edit text in the text box. What else? Nothing that we can think of right now. It's late, and *Star Trek* is on in three minutes.

Sentence: "Here's a good one: When you're searching for text, type 'my brain' into the *text box.* Then click the OK button. The computer won't find the text, and it will display a message that says 'Error: Can't find my brain.' Ha, ha."

text editor

Pronunciation: *tek-sta ed-i-ter.*

Meaning: A program, actually a crude form of a word processor, that lets you modify ("edit") text files. Text editors are used by programmers to edit program source code files. This is handy because text editors don't use formatting or graphics or anything fancy. All programmers want is something to easily type in their programming instructions without being bothered by the formatting. We mere mortal users can take advantage of text editors as well, even using them as a word processor if we like. They come in handy for working with small files. Indeed, this book was initially created using a text editor so that Dan, Wally, and Chris had a common file format (plain text or ASCII files) in which to work. (Eventually we all moved up to Microsoft Word for Windows because IDG Books told us we were working too fast.) (See also *editor.*)

Sentence: "My award for the worst *text editor* ever goes to DOS's old crummy EDLIN."

text file

Pronunciation: *tek-sta fi-el.*

Meaning: A file that contains only text or ASCII characters. Many word processing, database, and spreadsheet programs give you the option of saving your stuff as "text only," or a text file. This means that you lose all the formatting and special characters not associated with text files, but it also means the information can be easily digested by just about any other program on any other computer. (See also *ASCII.*)

Sentence: "*Text files* are the most common type of file format."

thermal wax printer

Pronunciation: *ther-mel waks print-er.*

Meaning: An old-fashioned type of printing technology that uses a special kind of paper onto which the letters are transferred using heat. For example, Sheryl is lying out at the beach. She's rubbed her bod with this new special wax that gets you tanned quickly. Between Sheryl's back and the sun, Karl, her boyfriend, holds up this piece of cardboard that has his name punched out and, lo, over the course of time the sun tans this image — KARL — onto Sheryl's back. That's how thermal printing works, but the printer supplies the heat, and the image is burned onto the paper.

Sentence: "My *thermal wax printer* has a reputation for having a smell as bad as a dot-matrix printer's noise."

thesaurus

Pronunciation: *the-saw-rus.*

Meaning: Seriously, this is a collection of words and other words with the same meaning. In computers, it refers to the capability of a word processing program to come up with synonyms to match a word you've chosen. You can highlight a word, ask the thesaurus for some synonyms, and the software generates a list of alternatives or suggestions. There is a Murphy's Law of Thesauruses: the more certain you are that a synonym with exactly the right flavor exists, the more certain your thesaurus is not to even list the word you're referencing, let alone its synonyms.

Sentence: "What would the *thesaurus* offer if you looked up synonyms for 'molecular beam epitaxy'?"

three-dimensional spreadsheet

Pronunciation: *three-dim-en-shun-el spred-sheet.*

Meaning: In spreadsheet technology, a group of spreadsheets organized like the pages of a book; in addition to the usual rows and columns, three-dimensional spreadsheets also have depth.

Sentence: "I started to learn how to work on a *three-dimensional spreadsheet,* but I got lost because I only had a two-dimensional brain."

tick

Pronunciation: *tik.*

Meaning: (1) Another name for the apostrophe character. (2) In a chart-drawing utility such as the one found in Excel, a tick mark is a notch on the axis of a chart that denotes an increment. For example, if the Y axis represents Dollars, every tick mark might represent 100 dollars. (3) A beat in your computer's internal clock-ticking, timekeeping thingamabob. PC computers generate 18.5 ticks per second. So if you hear some nerd say, "How many clock ticks was that interrupt?" you know that a clock tick is just about one-eighteenth of a second and can nod your head knowingly.

Sentence: "There was this German POW camp in World War II. And one summer day, the Kommandant assembled all the prisoners out under the hot sun. He said, 'Today we will do special exercises. I want you to tilt your heads left to right, left to right. When you tilt your head to the left, you will say *tick!* When you tilt your head to the right, you will say toc! Everyone!' So all the prisoners started tilting their heads, tick-toc, tick-toc, out under the hot sun — sweat just pouring from their faces. Everyone did this but one prisoner. He just tilted his head to the left over and over, going 'tick, tick, tick.' The Kommandant walked up to the man, looked him over, and said, 'Ve have vays to make you toc.'"

TIFF

Pronunciation: *Tif.*

Meaning: Acronym for *Tagged Image File Format.* A bitmapped graphics file format used frequently for images read in using a scanner. TIFF files are high-resolution dot images.

Sentence: "No, we don't support that graphics standard here. We support PCX, GIF, *TIFF,* and anything painted by Lichtenstein or Klee."

tiling

Pronunciation: *tih-ling.*

Meaning: A technique for arranging various windows in a graphical user interface, such that they're all nicely sized and laid out like a mosaic, without overlapping each other. The key here is "without overlapping." Another arrangement possibility is "cascading." (See also *cascade.*)

Sentence: "*Tiling* is a good choice when it doesn't matter if the images in each window are chopped off and difficult to read."

time sharing

Pronunciation: *tihm shaer-ing.*

Meaning: A strategic use of resources (microprocessor, printer, disk drives) with mainframe or networked computers. The time that is being shared is the computer's processing time. Typically, it's being shared among several users and also may be shared among several programs as well. In a time-sharing situation, the computer is programmed to know how to use its processing resources to attend to a hierarchy of priorities.

Sentence: "Because our computer knows how to manage *time sharing* so well, I think I should have my own time-sharing program so my time will get divided properly among my kids, my spouse, and my job."

time slice

Pronunciation: *tihm slihs.*

Meaning: Amount of processor time allocated to an application, usually measured in milliseconds. For example, if you're running several programs at once in Windows, each program gets a "slice" of the computer's time. The size of the slice can be adjusted, allowing some important programs to use up more time than other not-so-important ones. (See also *multitasking.*)

Sentence: "Roy found this old film from the '40s. It shows Albert Einstein creating *time slices* with a Ginsu knife."

title bar

Pronunciation: *tiht-el bar.*

Meaning: In a GUI like Windows or the Mac system, this is the, well, title that is prominently displayed in a long bar that stretches across the whole window. It is an especially effective invention because you always know where you are and don't need to call customer service to get you unlost. It typically includes the name of both the application you're using and the document you're working in. Even when you haven't named the new file yet, the program will provisionally call the document something like "Untitled" or "Document," until you come up with your own name for it.

Sentence: "I was hopelessly lost until I looked up at the *title bar,* which said that I was working in Microsoft Word on the T.DOC document."

TLA

Pronunciation: *Tee El Ay.*

Meaning: Acronym for *Three Letter Acronym.* The computer industry (and the government) is fond of these.

Sentence: "Nope, our manual just makes too much sense. Why not fill it with more *TLAs* and have Mr. Fujimori stick some raw Japanese in there, too."

toaster

Pronunciation: *toh-ster.*

Meaning: A computer device that's so homegrown, so user-friendly, and so intuitive, it's almost like the toaster you use to toast bread. The original Macintosh design was fondly called the "toaster" by its fans. A device called the Video Toaster is used in the Amiga computer to allow you to create studio-quality videos in your own home.

Sentence: "The original Macintosh was fondly called 'the *toaster*' at the height of its popularity. Now it's often called 'the footstool.'"

toggle

Pronunciation: *tog-el.*

Meaning: A type of switch that typically alternates between two modes, on or off. An example would be the button on your TV that both turns it on and off. When the TV is off, the button turns it on, and vice versa. In a computer program, a toggle may be a graphical button or some other option that can be either on or off. Selecting the button once turns it on, again turns it off.

Sentence: "I keep *toggling* between slow and slower mode on my PC. I don't think I paid enough money for this thing."

token ring network

Pronunciation: *toh-ken ring net-werk.*

Meaning: A networking format in which PCs are connected in some way. They use this token thing, passed between the computers on the network hose, to decide who's on first. That's the most I can make out of this definition. This is heady, IBM stuff. Most people use Ethernet networks because they are easier to understand. I always think of bus tokens when I see token ring network in print.

Sentence: "No, sir, I don't think you'll find a book on the *token ring network* in the Fantasy section."

toner

Pronunciation: *toh-ner.*

Meaning: The black, icky stuff laser printers print with. Technically, toner consists of highly carcinogenic, electronically charged ink particles. It's used to form the image on paper. Actually, the laser printer "welds" the toner to the paper using heat and tiny laser beams manned by elves.

Sentence: "Marcia was changing the *toner* when it broke open. Now she looks like she works in a coal mine."

toner cartridge

Pronunciation: *toh-ner kar-trij.*

Meaning: A cartridge, or container, for a laser printer (or other type of machine, like a copier or fax machine) that holds the toner. This technology makes an unbearable job simply horrible. In older machines, you had to fill the toner container with powdered toner, which had the advantage of allowing you to approximate the effects of six years' worth of cigarette smoking in a mere 10 minutes. Today, toners equate themselves to just about a pack of cigarettes.

Sentence: "I told Phil about having his old *toner cartridges* re-charged, but he misunderstood and tried to plug one into the wall."

toolbox

Pronunciation: *tool-bahks.*

Meaning: For software developers, a set of programs that can be used as building blocks for creating applications, so the programmers can avoid re-inventing the wheel every time they write a program. For software users, a collection of tools that serve a common purpose. (See *tools.*)

Sentence: "Using a *toolbox,* anyone can create a cool-looking program with only several weeks of intensive training."

tools

Pronunciation: *toolz.*

Meaning: A set of electronic "tools" that you can use within a given software application, each of which has effects like the real-life tools they're named after. (Bear with me on this one.) As an example, in a paint program you might have "brushes" of different diameters, a roller, and a spray can. These are tools you can use in the program to get a specific job done.

Sentence: "I'm having such a good time playing with all these *tools* that I don't know when I'll get around to actually painting a picture."

top-down programming

Pronunciation: *tahp-down proh-gram-ing.*

Meaning: Starting a program, and each of its modules, with a statement (in English) about what it's supposed to do and how it's supposed to do it — kind of like a mission statement.

Sentence: "*Top-down programming* doesn't mean you build the program's roof and then the foundation later. It's more along the lines of you write the overall feeling for the program first and then fill in the holes later."

topology

Pronunciation: *tahp-ah-le-jee.*

Meaning: Topology refers to the configuration of a local area network — how the network is physically laid out. The basic types are centralized and decentralized; the basic formats are the star topology (centralized) and the bus and ring topologies (decentralized). Understand this and you, too, can make massive sums working as a network coordinator.

Sentence: "*Topology* refers to the way your network is laid out, as well as the study of the actor, Topol."

touch pad

Pronunciation: *tuhch pad.*

Meaning: An input device for which all you need to do is touch a spot and it will register as a signal to the computer. The "spots" are actually cleverly disguised keys or buttons, and the whole front of the touch pad display is a layer of soft plastic.

Sentence: "I was walking down the input aisle in the computer store and came upon the *touch pad* section. They all whispered at me, 'Touch me!' 'No, touch me!' 'Touch me, here!'"

tower PC

Pronunciation: *tow-ur Pee See.*

Meaning: A desktop computer on its side, but really a computer that was made to stand vertical (up and down). These computers usually have more room and tend to be more powerful than mere mortal desktop models.

Sentence: "Since Kevin lives by an airport, the FAA told him to put little red lights on top of his *tower PC*."

TPI

Pronunciation: *Tee Pee Eye.*

Meaning: Abbreviation for *Tracks Per Inch*. It measures the amount of information that can be stored on a disk. The more tracks per inch on the disk, the higher the disk's "density" and the more data it can store. It's also a good way to tell some high-density disks from low-density. The lower density disks use 40 or 80 TPI. High-density disks use 135 TPI.

Sentence: "I've been using computers for over 12 years now, and no one I know uses the term *TPI* when they talk about a floppy disk."

track

Pronunciation: *trak.*

Meaning: A "ring" of information on a disk. Most disks record information on disks by storing that information on several concentric rings or "tracks" prerecorded on the disk's surface. This is complex, disk-formatting stuff. The track contains sectors which each contain 512 bytes of information — the stuff you save on the disk. Knowing about tracks and sectors isn't important in using a disk. The information may only come up when you use special disk utilities (disk repair and diagnosis programs) or when formatting the disk. The term cylinder may also be used to refer to a track of information on a disk.

Sentence: "This disk is no good. I guess my AMTRAK file keeps jumping the *tracks.*"

trackball

Pronunciation: *trak-bahl.*

Meaning: An input device that operates very similarly to a mouse. Where a mouse has a ball you roll on your table top, in the case of the track ball, the ball part is on top and you rotate it using your fingers. Trackballs are very popular with artists, who find the large ball easier to manipulate than the clumsy soap-on-a-rope-like mouse. They're also common on notebook computers because then you don't have to have this device hanging outside the case, nor do you have to roll it around on a flat surface, such as your thigh.

Sentence: "Not only is this *trackball* easier to use than a mouse, but it also doesn't have a tendency to roll itself off the desk as much."

TrackPoint II

Pronunciation: *Trak-Point Too.*

Meaning: A tiny knob, embedded between the G and H keys on the keyboard, developed by IBM as an alternative pointing device that substitutes for a mouse. The TrackPoint II looks and feels like the red tip of a rubber eraser and is actually easy to use once you get the hang of it and realize it won't rub pink stuff off all over your fingertips.

Sentence: "Tim tried to yank out the *TrackPoint II* in his laptop with a pair of pliers. That was until I told him it was supposed to be there, and that he could use it like a mouse."

tractor feed

Pronunciation: *trak-ter feed.*

Meaning: A mechanism for feeding paper through dot-matrix printers. This kind of paper is what is commonly known as "computer paper," the stuff with the holes on either side. This would be a good time to tell you that there is actually a name — chosen in a contest — for the edges of such paper, which form the row of holes that the mechanism grabs to push the paper through. It's called "snaf."

Sentence: "I always have trouble lining up the little holes so that the paper will go through the *tractor feed* without getting overly perfed."

tractor food

Pronunciation: *trak-ter food.*

Meaning: Your most valued documents, caught in the jaws of a tractor feed mechanism.

Sentence: "I watched as my precious annual report became *tractor food* in a matter of seconds."

transparent

Pronunciation: *tranz-par-ent.*

Meaning: Not there. Didn't see it. Automatic. Silent. Sneaky. Beyond the realm of perception. In computers, *transparent* refers to anything that happens without your being directly involved or requiring your input or attention. For instance, a fax being sent while you continue to work on another document would be a transparent operation. (Unfortunately, trying to print your document and getting a blank page is not.)

Sentence: "My communications software sends documents to other users *transparently*. They don't even see the document on the other end."

Trash

Pronunciation: *Trash.*

Meaning: In the Mac system, a special place to put unwanted documents and files. The Trash icon on the Mac desktop looks just like a trash can, and all you have to do to dispose of your unwanted stuff is to click on the item in question with the mouse and drag it to the trash can. A handy feature of the Mac

Trash can is that its sides bulge out when it has discarded files in it, and it doesn't ultimately dump the stuff until you give it the command to Empty Trash — just like in real life!

Sentence: "The nicest thing about the Mac *Trash* can is that the dogs don't knock it over every Thursday night."

tree structure

Pronunciation: *tree struk-cher.*

Meaning: One of the more visual concepts in organizing files on a hard drive. Files are stored in "directories," each of which is connected to other directories like branches in a tree. The main directory on every disk is called the root directory. Other directories branch from the root, and still other directories branch from them, making the thing look like an electronic family tree. (See also *path* and *pathname.*)

Sentence: "I almost had a heart attack when Earl walked by with the pruning shears, claiming he was going to fix his hard drive's *tree structure.*"

trigonometry

Pronunciation: *trig-en-ah-me-tree.*

Meaning: A branch of mathematics having to do with relationships of parts of a triangle. If you hear terms like sine, cosine, and tangent, you can nod wisely and say, "Ah, trigonometry!" Trigonometry helps you figure out unknown measurements of a triangle (such as an angle or a side) based on known elements.

Sentence: "You could use *trigonometry* to figure out the height of a distant mountain, if you know how far it is to the mountain and what the angle of view to the peak is, and also if someone whispers its height in your ear."

triple-clicking

Pronunciation: *tri-pel-clik-ing.*

Meaning: Clicking the mouse button three times in rapid succession to access very weird and arcane functions. Triple-clicking is uncommon and is used only in programs whose designers could not figure out more effective means of accessing features.

Sentence: "When I *triple-click* on this icon, I get a message telling me to stop drinking so much coffee."

troglodyte

Pronunciation: *trahg-le-diht.*

Meaning: From the Greek word meaning "cave dweller." A special class of nerd who prefers to dwell in the dark recesses of computer rooms. Troglodytes have developed nocturnal feeding habits like bats and moles.

Sentence: "The university cafeteria is keeping special hours — not to mention a special diet — for the *troglodytes* on campus."

Trojan horse

Pronunciation: *Troh-jen hors.*

Meaning: A nasty computer program cleverly hidden inside a legitimate program. It comes from a strategy used in the Trojan War, where the Greeks pretended to give a gift of a huge wooden horse as a peace offering to the city of Troy. As Troy slept, the many soldiers hidden inside the horse clambered out and attacked the city, which most historians agree was a sneaky thing to do. Sneaky computer programs that pretend to do one thing while disguising a more nefarious deed are called Trojan horses. You are more likely to find a Trojan horse packaged inside shareware or freeware than in off-the-shelf commercial software.

Sentence: "There is argument behind the notion that Microsoft Windows is a *Trojan horse.*"

true

Pronunciation: *troo.*

Meaning: The opposite of "false." Or it could also mean "yes" or "on." In binary math (also called Boolean math), true means a 1 or positive, and false means a zero or negative.

Sentence: "Believing that a computer would save me time and effort proved too good to be *true.*"

TrueType font

Pronunciation: *Troo-Tihp fawnt.*

Meaning: A category of fonts created jointly by Apple Computer and Microsoft that bypass the need for a page description language (see *PDL*) or a utility that enables fonts to be displayed on-screen. Instead, the smarts that translate the font to the screen or to the printer are kept inside the font itself. In the olden days, you had to pay dearly for computer programs and printers that understood a multitude of fonts and displayed and printed them well. TrueType fonts take care of the details, making everything look and print swell. TrueType fonts are also called scalable fonts, which means you can select any type size and make it larger or smaller without having to worry about distortions.

Sentence: "Using these widely available and inexpensive *TrueType fonts,* I've been able to design a document that looks just as bad as my handwriting."

TSR

Pronunciation: *Tee Ess Arr.*

Meaning: See *terminate-and-stay-resident program.*

TTFN

Pronunciation: *Tee Tee Eff En.*

Meaning: On-line acronym for *Ta Ta For Now*. Another way to say goodbye in an e-mail or news group posting.

Sentence: "I was worried when Ryan always signed his electronic epistles *TTFN*, until I found out it wasn't anything dirty."

TTL

Pronunciation: *Tee Tee Ell.*

Meaning: Here's a doozey: *Transistor-to-Transistor Logic* is what this acronym is all about. What is it? Who knows, who cares, why bother? You'll often see TTL listed as a type of computer monitor, typically the old style monochrome monitors. Everyone always asked, "What's TTL stand for?" Now you know.

Sentence: "I feel so culturally enriched now that I finally know what *TTL* stands for."

tty

Pronunciation: *tee tee y.*

Meaning: A UNIX command that tells you which terminal you're using. (See *TTY* next.)

Sentence: "I typed in *tty* on my laptop, and the computer told me I was about to land at O'Hare."

TTY

Pronunciation: *Tee Tee Why.*

Meaning: An abbreviation for *teletype*. It's also the name of a type of terminal emulation, usually (and this is a secret) meaning "absolutely no emulation whatsoever." TTY rears its ugly head a lot in UNIX and is incorporated into many UNIX commands. Those commands are used to control the various terminals, monitors, and keyboards — even modems — connected to the UNIX machine. You need to be a real UNIX dork to understand it all. (See also *terminal emulation*.)

Sentence: "Oh, so you're the jerk who keeps logging in on *TTY*P3 and crashing the system!"

Turing machine

Pronunciation: *Ter-ing ma-sheen.*

Meaning: A simple computer developed by A.M. Turing in the 1930s. It was supposed to be able to diagnose which problems were solvable by machines. It did this by reading a piece of paper tape. Turing's machine could only move the tape forward, put a mark on it, erase the mark, or stop it in its tracks. Turing claimed that the machine could solve any problem that could be expressed as an algorithm (a step-by-step procedure for solving a problem).

Sentence: "I don't think I'd have a use for a *Turing machine.* I just want to solve the problems; I don't care whether they *can* be solved or not."

turnkey system

Pronunciation: *turn-kee sis-tem.*

Meaning: A computer system all packaged and ready to go for a specific task. The system will be complete with computer, monitor, keyboard, disk drives, software, and other peripherals. The term comes from the automotive industry — where you can put a key into your car, turn it, and operate the vehicle without anything else to buy, install, set up, or learn.

Sentence: "I always thought that *turnkey* had something to do with sardines."

tutorial

Pronunciation: *too-tor-ee-ell.*

Meaning: A training session that guides the student step-by-step through a procedure. Of particular interest are the tutorials that are packaged with many contemporary software programs. Generally, they are interactive, so that you can play along and push keys to get the program to continue.

Sentence: "The *tutorial* for my accounting package comes with instructions for loading a gun."

Twain

Pronunciation: *Twayn* (rhymes with *pain, drain* and *inflame*).

Meaning: A standard for acquiring graphics, such as input from a scanner, computer video, or something else that brings graphics into the computer. The term comes from the saying "never the twain shall meet," a phrase that seems especially true if you've ever wrestled with incompatible graphics file formats.

Sentence: "Since Adobe Photoshop can gobble up a *Twain* image, we should buy a Twain scanner."

tweak

Pronunciation: *tweek.*

Meaning: To customize, tailor, adjust, rearrange, cajole, or otherwise mess with. More specifically, it means changing settings on a piece of hardware or software so that your needs are more closely attended to.

Sentence: "I want to *tweak* my word processing program so that it stops beeping when I misspell a word."

Twinkie

Pronunciation: *Twink-ee.*

Meaning: A staple in the diet of computer programmers and other nerds. Fits into most of the four basic food groups. Also, consumption of Twinkies has been used as a defense in the most egregious crimes. Thus, if you need a scapegoat, invoke the Twinkie defense. (See also *M&Ms.*)

Sentence: "Because I had some heavy-duty programming to do, I had some *Twinkies* for a power breakfast."

twisted pair

Pronunciation: *twist-ed paer.*

Meaning: A wire that's secretly a pair of wires wrapped around each other. It is the kind of wire typically used in commercial telephone systems. The wire is "twisted" because you talk into the mouthpiece and it's heard in the earpiece. If the wire weren't twisted, you would talk into the mouthpiece and the sound would come out the mouthpiece. The term is also used in local area networks, especially those that use common phone wiring to connect the computers (common phone wiring is the same thing as "twisted pair"). The good thing about twisted pair is that it's cheap and ubiquitous; the drawback is that it doesn't carry nearly as much information as the thicker coaxial cable (the stuff cable TV comes over).

Sentence: "Here come our network guru and his female companion. Geez. Aren't they a *twisted pair?*"

TXT

Pronunciation: *Tee Ecks Tee.*

Meaning: Abbreviation for *Text.* A suffix used for text files, generally in DOS-based computing. Examples include LETTER.TXT and GOFISH.TXT.

Sentence: "When I tell my word processor to save my files as 'text only,' it automatically slaps the *.TXT* extension to the filename."

type-ahead

Pronunciation: *tihp-ah-hed.*

Meaning: A term for a buffer (a part of memory) that allows you to type ahead of what you see on the screen. For example, you can start typing the next DOS command even though DOS is currently copying files to the floppy drive. Of course, DOS's type-ahead buffer is only 15 characters big, so after you type the 15th character, DOS starts beeping at you: Beep! I'm full! Stop typing! Beep! The stuff you type appears as soon as DOS is un-busy.

Sentence: "Because of the *type-ahead* buffer in Windows, I can enter several commands and wait for the computer to catch up. I seem to do that a lot."

typeface

Pronunciation: *tihp-faes.*

Meaning: The design of characters in a font. Typeface refers to the physical characteristics of a family of letters and numbers. Typesetting has grown into a major art form, and the number of available typefaces — even to personal computer users — is almost endless. The main division between the categories of typefaces lies in their use of serifs — the little hooky things at the ends of the letters. Thus, they are called either serif typefaces or sans serif (without serif) typefaces. Other categories include display faces and decorative faces.

Sentence: "One of my favorite *typefaces* is Omar Serif."

UART

Pronunciation: *Yoo Ahrt.*

Meaning: Acronym for *Universal Asynchronous Receiver/Transmitter.* The UART is the gizmo — actually the integrated circuit — in a computer that changes the parallel data stream inside the computer into the serial data stream. So it takes the bits marching eight abreast inside your computer and lines them up single file for the serial port. This is required for devices that use the serial port, such as a modem. (See also *bit, modem,* and *serial port.*)

Sentence: "There seems to be a traffic jam in my *UART.*"

UMB

Pronunciation: *Yoo Em Bee.*

Meaning: Abbreviation for *Upper Memory Block*. It's an area of upper memory that can be "filled in" with real memory using some sort of memory-management magic that only the eggheads can comprehend. A memory device driver, such as DOS's EMM386.EXE, is required to create UMBs. Then, using other memory-management magic too mental to mention here, programs can be *loaded high* into those UMBs, which makes more memory available to your programs. It's magic! (See also *conventional memory, low memory, high memory, memory,* and *terminate-and-stay-resident program.*)

Sentence: "Hi. My name is Jim. On my PC, I once had a paltry 384K of available memory. Not enough to run WordPerfect. I was devastated. Then I bought a memory manager for my 386 clone. And, now, I can stuff all my device drivers and TSRs into *UMBs.* Not only do I have more memory available, but I also learned some really cryptic terms and acronyms that have bolstered my Tech-IQ rating at cocktail parties."

undelete

Pronunciation: *un-duh-leet.*

Meaning: To put something back the way it was before you deleted it. That is, to restore a file after you have deleted it, to resuscitate it, to resurrect it. DOS includes an undelete command that attempts to restore files you may have accidentally blasted to smithereens. Other operating systems have similar commands because it's apparent to those who write computer software that people who use computers (that is, you and me) are apt to accidentally delete things we didn't intend to delete. (See also *Del key* and *unerase.*)

Sentence: "Just because DOS has an *undelete* command doesn't mean you should be careless with the delete command."

underline

Pronunciation: *un-der-lihn.*

Meaning: (1) In word processing or desktop publishing, the attribute applied to text that makes it look underlined. Underlined text was once used in typed manuscripts to indicate that the typesetter should use italics. That's because typewriters could underline but not italicize text. Computers can italicize, so underlining is left as a text attribute for the narrow-minded and bureaucratic out there who are still amazed by underlined text. (2) The underline character on your keyboard, which is a very important character by itself in some programming languages. (See also *underscore.*)

Sentence: "I knew a guy who tried to underline things by typing a word, backspacing (which erased the word), and then typing the *underline* character. While that would work on a typewriter, with a computer you must use a special command that underlines the text for you."

underscore

Pronunciation: *un-der-skor.*

Meaning: Another term for underline, probably introduced by the more musical-minded among computer users. (See also *underline.*)

Sentence: "Now that you're a power user, Michael, you'll need to stop saying underline. It's *underscore.*"

undo

Pronunciation: *un-doo.*

Meaning: To put the situation back to the way it was before you messed it up. It's the command in most applications that enables you to cancel the effects of whatever you just did. You can undo typing and formatting commands, but don't get careless about your work, because you can't undo everything.

Sentence: "I just hope that when I die and get to Heaven, God offers me an *undo* command."

undocumented

Pronunciation: *un-dok-yoo-men-ted.*

Meaning: A way of describing a feature of your hardware or software that is not explained in the user manual. This happens either because the manufacturer forgot, didn't think it was important, hasn't figured out itself how the feature works, or wants to keep it a secret from you or its competition. Computer book authors love to find undocumented features in software products; it's their life!

Sentence: "I stumbled upon an *undocumented* feature that makes Windows run 100 times faster."

unerase

Pronunciation: *un-ee-raes.*

Meaning: Just like undelete, this term was coined by DOS utility guru Peter Norton when he first came upon the idea of undeleting files in the early 1980s. Norton created a program called UnErase — the first of its kind — that recovered deleted files. He made tons of money and founded a complete category of computer software called *utility programs.* (See also *guru, undelete,* and *utility.*)

Sentence: "All praise be to Peter Norton on high! Thank you, O Peter, for thy grace and thine *UnErase.*"

Unicode

Pronunciation: *Yoo-neh-kowd.*

Meaning: A new "universal" standard for sharing information between different programs and computers. Unicode is meant to replace the ancient ASCII standard and includes all the characters represented by the ASCII standard as well as additional characters for displaying languages such as Greek, Hebrew, Arabic, Russian (which uses Cyrillic), Chinese, Japanese, and Korean.

Sentence: "Now that computers are being used all over the world, computer companies want to adopt the *Unicode* standard for sharing documents, because that means more market share for them in countries like Taiwan, Pakistan, and Greece."

unicorn

Pronunciation: *yoo-ni-korn.*

Meaning: A mythical creature that looks like a horse with a spiral horn jutting out from its forehead. According to legend, a unicorn could only be tamed by a pure virgin maiden, who could tempt the unicorn to lay its head and horn in her lap. Obviously, the origin of this legend has sexual overtones that aren't polite to discuss in public.

Sentence: "Many girls love *unicorns* when they're growing up. Then, when they get older and start dating men, they realize that mythical creatures really have a lot more to offer than real-life human beings."

UNIX

Pronunciation: *Yoo-niks.*

Meaning: An operating system used especially in multiuser computing contexts, such as with minicomputers and workstations. You also can install UNIX on personal computers and mainframes. UNIX was written in C and developed in the late 1960s at AT&T's Bell Labs. It first became popular on minicomputers on college campuses and in scientific communities.

The advantages of UNIX lie in its portability from one system to another and in its support of a wealth of applications programs, many programmer's utilities, and programming languages, making it popular among the techno-nerd and geek-whiz faction. Primarily, UNIX is a command-line operating system, very similar to DOS but much more crude and cryptic. Several GUIs are available for UNIX, including X Windows, Open Look, NeXTStep, and others. Incidentally, the name

UNIX is a pun of sorts; it's a take-off on an operating system called Multics. Multi, Uni — get it? (See also *C, DOS, K&R, operating system, OS/2, platform,* and *Windows.*)

Sentence: "When a programmer must protect his harem of PCs, he gets some *UNIX.*"

up

Pronunciation: *up.*

Meaning: In the general direction of the sky or ceiling, unless you're in Australia (just checking to see whether you were paying attention). "Up" is used to refer to the direction of the top of the document, even if the top is nowhere on the screen and is in fact just another happy electronic memory to your computer. (See also *down* and *up arrow.*)

Sentence: "To scroll *up,* keep jabbing at the up arrow key."

up arrow

Pronunciation: *up ar-oh.*

Meaning: An arrow pointing upward, as found on one of your cursor keys. Pushing the up arrow key moves the cursor up in the document by one line of text. There is also an up arrow at the top of the vertical scroll bar in most graphical applications. Clicking the up arrow in graphical applications with the mouse usually moves the contents of the window down a line or so. Yes, the up arrow moves the contents down, but that's so you can see "up" to the preceding line on the screen. Weird, backward, hard-to-understand — yes, this is how a computer makes life easier for everyone. If only the steering wheel on your car worked that way. . . . (See also *down* and *up.*)

Sentence: "You won't believe this: I pressed the *up arrow,* and my computer levitated."

upload

Pronunciation: *up-lohd.*

Meaning: To transmit a file from your computer to another computer. If you're sending a file to another computer, you're uploading. That computer, on the other hand, is downloading the file from you. It doesn't matter who started the file transmission or which computer you're using. If you're sending a file, you're uploading it. (See also *BBS, download,* and *network.*)

Sentence: "I often *upload* my word processing files onto CompuServe to send to publishers in remote parts of the world, such as Indiana."

uppercase

Pronunciation: *up-er kaes.*

Meaning: Capital letters. The terminology comes from the earliest days of typesetting, when the individual metal letters mounted on blocks were stored in trays. The typesetter would pick out the letters that he needed for the job and arrange them on a plate. He would then store the capital letters in the top (or upper) case and the small letters in the bottom (or lower) case. (See also *case-sensitive* and *lowercase.*)

Sentence: "Text typed in all *uppercase* letters is hard to read. In fact, it almost seems as if the writer is SHOUTING AT YOU."

upper memory

Pronunciation: *up-er mem-o-ree.*

Meaning: On a PC, this term refers to the portion of memory not used by DOS for running programs. It was originally called Reserved Memory, set aside by IBM in the first PC for "future expansion." DOS was given the rest of memory, a total of 640K, to play with itself and run programs. The rest of the first PC's memory, 384K of memory, was set aside. In memory-management terminology, that area is called upper memory. And, in a break with all logic, the memory DOS uses isn't called "lower memory"; it's called conventional memory. (See also *conventional memory, high memory, lower memory, memory,* and *UMB.*)

Sentence: "Every time Phil gets a haircut, he loses some *upper memory.*"

UPS

Pronunciation: *Yoo Pee Ess.*

Meaning: Abbreviation for *Uninterruptible Power Supply.* A fancy term for battery backup — an emergency supply of power in case the power coming out of the wall suddenly stops or when Jim, the dork from Marketing, trips over the PC's cord. Having a UPS often means that you have just enough time to save your stuff and turn off the computer while you're in the dark. You can't really work from the backup battery in the UPS.

Sentence: "This blackout is horrible, but there's Jim, sitting in his office with the only working PC hooked to a *UPS.* Let's unplug him and run something useful instead, like the Nintendo."

uptime

Pronunciation: *up-tyme.*

Meaning: The time that the computer is actually working and you can get stuff done, as opposed to downtime, when the computer isn't feeling well and nothing works. (See also *downtime.*)

Sentence: "The dog is pretty lethargic, Doctor. How can we increase his *uptime?*"

upward compatible

Pronunciation: *up-werd kum-pat-i-bel.*

Meaning: Upward compatible means that something is designed with the future in mind. The item in question, usually a document or file created by some application or piece of hardware, will work with the next version of the product or with components that are not on the market yet. Generally, software is downward compatible only, meaning the newest versions of the application will work with files generated from previous versions, but the previous versions will not work with files created with the new version. (See also *compatibility* and *downward compatible.*)

Sentence: "Wow! This new computer is really designed for *upward compatibility.* There's a plug in the back marked R2-D2 Connection."

Uruguay

Pronunciation: *Yoor-eh-g-way.*

Meaning: The second smallest country in South America. Mostly agricultural, Uruguay exports meat and textile products. Its capital is Montevideo, which has some lovely museums. (See *Montevideo.*)

Sentence: "Our sojourn to South America just wouldn't be complete without a trip to lovely *Uruguay.*"

USENET

Pronunciation: *Yooz-Net.*

Meaning: Acronym for *USEr NETwork.* A facility of the Internet that offers a wide variety of newsgroups, bulletin boards, and public forums. It runs on the UUCP (UNIX-to-UNIX copy) network, an international wide area network of all sorts of UNIX computers, all interconnected a la the Tholian Web. (See also *BBS, Internet, network, UNIX,* and *wide area network.*)

Sentence: "From your cozy office chair in Silicon Valley, you can get up-to-the-minute news from, say, Helsinki, Finland, just by accessing *USENET.*"

user

Pronunciation: *yoo-zer.*

Meaning: The person using the computer and software as a tool, as opposed to the programmer or hardware engineers. The term has nothing to do with the skill level of the person at the keyboard. Even nerds of the high programming priesthood are mere users when they sit at a computer. (See also *user-friendly, user group,* and *user-hostile.*)

Sentence: "The computer industry is the only legitimate industry that calls its customers *users.*"

user group

Pronunciation: *yoo-zer groop.*

Meaning: A club or gathering of computer users devoted to the study of a particular piece of software or hardware. There are user groups for the Macintosh, for dBASE, for Adobe Photoshop, and many, many more. User groups often include Special Interest Groups (SIGs) for users that share common interests or products. (See also *America Online, CompuServe, GEnie, Internet, network, Prodigy,* and *SIG.*)

Sentence: "*User groups* are a great source of information and a good place to ask questions about your computer or a software package. But if you show up late, stick around and listen to the conversation. You might have accidentally stumbled upon a meeting of the Older Guys with Pen Packs and Pot Bellies Society."

user ID

Pronunciation: *yoo-zer Eye Dee.*

Meaning: Yes, you can get "carded" by your computer. The user ID is a number or code word assigned to you by the system administrator or one you make up yourself. It's used to tell the computer who you are, often in place of your name. For example, Bill Gates's ID on the Microsoft internal mail system is "billg."

Don't confuse the user ID with the password. The ID is something that identifies who you are to other people using the computer. In contrast, the password is secret and proves to the computer that the guy who logs in as billg is really Bill Gates and not some joker from the competition who's trying to learn all Microsoft's secrets. (See also *password* and *user.*)

Sentence: Recently overheard in the system administrator's office at a major software vendor: "No, I'm sorry, the *user ID* 'god' is already taken. You'll have to think of something else."

user interface

Pronunciation: *yoo-zer in-ter-fays.*

Meaning: What you see when you turn on the computer. This is the set of prompts, cursors, and software devices with which you interact to get something done in a program. The interface is what you see — in your face — and how you communicate with the computer and (hopefully) get things done. (See also *DOS, GUI, interface,* and *Windows.*)

Sentence: "The best *user interface* is on Star Trek, where they actually tell the computer what to do. Did you ever hear the Enterprise's computer say `Bad command or file name`?"

user name

(See *user ID.*)

user profile

Pronunciation: *yoo-zer proh-fyle.*

Meaning: In a network or bulletin board situation, a little blurb about a member or user that others on the system can access so they'll have a better sense of whom they're talking to. Users write their own blurbs that might include their name, age, geographic location, the kind of computer they're using, and their interests as they relate to that specific bulletin board. (See also *BBS, network,* and *user.*)

Sentence: "Fortunately, my *user profile* didn't include the fact that I have twelve designer pocket protectors."

user-friendly

Pronunciation: *yoo-zer frend-lee.*

Meaning: Trendy marketing term supposedly implying that the software or hardware is easy enough for even you or me to understand. Also called intuitive or idiotproof. It means you can easily figure out what to do without having to look it up in the manual or the on-line help. Yeah, right! (See *user* and *user-hostile.*)

Sentence: "You know, the computer industry must figure that *user-friendly* means slow and plodding."

user-hostile

Pronunciation: *yoo-zer hoss-till.*

Meaning: The opposite of user-friendly. This means that no matter how well you treat your computer and the software installed in it, they never lift a finger to make your life any easier. The epitome of user hostility is a cursor blinking on an otherwise totally blank screen — the DOS prompt. (See also *user* and *user-friendly.*)

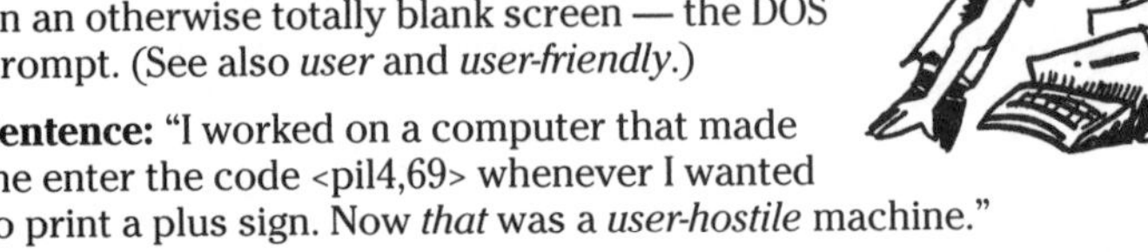

Sentence: "I worked on a computer that made me enter the code <pil4,69> whenever I wanted to print a plus sign. Now *that* was a *user-hostile* machine."

utility

Pronunciation: *yoo-til-i-tee.*

Meaning: Software intended to help you fix, tweak, or enhance your system. Unlike a true application, a utility doesn't produce any concrete output or documents. Instead, utilities are designed to make working with the computer or your operating system easier. Utilities were once called software tools, and they were intended for use primarily by programmers to help ease programming drudgery. Today, utilities are a legitimate software category. Popular utilities include the Norton Utilities, PC Tools, Stacker, and FastBack. (See also *backup, debugger, file compression, undelete, unerase,* and *virus.*)

Sentence: "At the time of the Michelangelo virus scare, sales of computer anti-virus *utilities* went way up. It makes you wonder who thought up that Michelangelo thing."

UUCP

Pronunciation: *Yoo Yoo See Pee.*

Meaning: Acronym for the *UNIX-to-UNIX Copy Program,* a program used to copy information from one Unix computer to another, which is sort of the backbone of the whole Internet system.

Sentence: "We've hooked up our top security project on a computer with *UUCP.* This allows us to exchange mail with other Unix sites and to read USENET user groups, and it allows hackers to try to crack into the computer."

V.Fast

Pronunciation: *Vee-Fast.*

Meaning: A fast (for now) modem standard, set up according to the CCITT V standards (and there are a lot of them). These standards all start with V followed by a dot and a number. The number indicates how fast the modem can go (though there is no relationship between the number and the modem's speed), and other modems that share that standard can communicate with each other. Supposedly, a V.Fast modem toots along at 14,000+ bps, maybe even 28,000 bps.

Sentence: "After the *V.Fast* standard proves too slow, will there be a V.Faster and V.Fastest standard?"

vaccine

Pronunciation: *vaks-seen.*

Meaning: A disinfectant or anti-virus utility that helps your computer fight computer viruses. It works by looking for the symptoms of virus activity, such as suspicious attempts to infiltrate relatively secluded areas of the hard drive, drowsiness, and high fever. The vaccine then removes the virus, making your PC infection-free. (See also *virus.*)

Sentence: "So let me get this straight. You tried to cure your PC of any possible virus by sticking a moldy orange into your disk drive? Why not just try a *vaccine* next time."

vacuum tube

Pronunciation: *vak-yoom tewb.*

Meaning: An old-fashioned technology used in early computers. It is a device that transmits information by controlling the flow of electrons, as semiconductor diodes and transistors do in modern computers.

Sentence: "A *vacuum tube* is something you can look for in a computer museum, such as the marvelous Boston Computer Museum, which, incidentally, is in Boston."

vaporware

Pronunciation: *vae-per-way-er.*

Meaning: Products, whether hardware or software, that have yet to materialize on the market but are promoted as if they were about to revolutionize the computer industry. In many cases, there is plenty of good reason to believe that the product will never even make it to the market, at least not in the lifetime of its purveyors.

Sentence: "Anything that you've read about or heard about in the computer industry but have yet to see in a store is *vaporware.*"

VAR

Pronunciation: *Vahr.*

Meaning: Acronym for *Value-Added Reseller.* An individual or business that integrates components provided by Original Equipment Manufacturers (OEMs) and gets them properly packaged and documented for end users who usually need all the bells and whistles. VARs often package hardware, software, training, documentation, and even custom software services for specialized industries. (See also *OEM, end user,* and *bells and whistles.*)

Sentence: "We purchased a large medical system from a *VAR.* The advantage is that we can complain to one source for all our problems."

variable

Pronunciation: *vaer-ee-a-bowl.*

Meaning: In programming, a symbol that represents a numerical value or string of text used in the program. Using variables gives the programmer the flexibility of changing the value at any point in the program, even if there seems to be no need for that kind of flexibility at the outset. (See also *wildcard.*)

Sentence: "The content of a *variable* can change at any time. This leads me to believe that Bill Clinton's brain contains way too many variables."

VAX

Pronunciation: *Vaks.*

Meaning: A line of computers produced by Digital Equipment Corp. (DEC). In the olden days, the term VAX was often used to mean a large, cumbersome, yet highly capable and powerful computer. The notion of "a VAX on your desktop" used to be thought of in science-fiction terms. In 1988 or thereabouts, it became a reality as the microcomputers of the time reached the processing capabilities of the early VAX computers.

Sentence: "No, it's not true that the first Apple computer was the result of the engineers leaving a Mommy *VAX* and Daddy *VAX* alone overnight."

VBX

Pronunciation: *Vee Bee Ex.*

Meaning: Acronym that stands for *Visual Basic eXtension*, but often just called a Visual Basic custom control. VBXes are reusable programs, written by other people, that you can add to your own Visual Basic or C++ programs so you don't waste time writing part of a program that somebody has already written. VBXes first appeared in Visual Basic, and, just as their popularity has peaked, Microsoft plans to make them obsolete and make everyone use a new standard called OCX instead. (See *OCX.*)

Sentence: "Visual Basic is so popular because you can buy loads of *VBXes*, paste them together, and make powerful programs quickly with almost no effort besides shelling out lots of money to buy VBXes from different companies."

VDISK

Pronunciation: *Vee-Disk.*

Meaning: See *virtual disk.*

VDT

Pronunciation: *Vee Dee Tee.*

Meaning: Acronym for *Video Display Terminal*, otherwise known as a monitor (with a keyboard). The term VDT, however, is more apt to be used when talking about the negative health effects of these machines, which have been implicated in everything from eye strain to birth defects. They produce a substantial amount of electromagnetic radiation, which may or may not be enough to cause the various maladies that monitors have been accused of causing. For protection, it is possible to get screens that filter out these electromagnetic fields. Screens that polarize the visual output so as to avoid glare are even more widely available. (See also *radiation.*)

Sentence: "I like my *VDT*, but I'm worried about the EMFs it produces. I'm worried that I might get RSI or CTS from all that typing, too. It's that dangerous side of computing that gives me so many of life's thrills."

vector graphics

Pronunciation: *vek-tor graf-icks.*

Meaning: Graphics that are drawn using lines or vectors. A vector is a line that starts at a certain point and goes off in a certain direction for a certain distance. (Certainly, you knew that.) Vector graphics are fine for CAD programs, though don't expect to see many flower vases done that way. (See *graphics.*)

Sentence: "Victor loves *vector* graphics over bitmaps."

verify

Pronunciation: *ver-i-fy.*

Meaning: To confirm the existence of something. In computing, this often refers to the double-checking that takes place after a file is copied. You verify that the duplicate is identical to the original. This makes the copy process take a bit longer because the computer has to double-check, but it ensures that no errors were produced during the duplication process.

Sentence: "Because disk media is much more reliable than in the old days, most DOS users don't bother to *verify* file copies."

Veronica

Pronunciation: *Ver-on-eh-ka.*

Meaning: Acronym that stands for *Very Easy Rodent-Oriented Net-wide Index to Computerized Archives*, which is a program developed at the University of Nevada to help you search through various Internet Gopher servers to find the information you need. If you have no idea what the Internet or Gopher Servers are, you don't need to know about Veronica. (See also — and we're not kidding — *Archie.*)

Sentence: "The real *Veronica* would probably have nothing to do with any Gopher."

version

Pronunciation: *ver-zhun.*

Meaning: An edition of a product. Versions are usually designated with a number, such as "Word 2.0 for Windows," in which 2.0 is the version number, second version, first release. You can't count on the numbers being in numerical order (we don't know why this is so), but typically 1 comes before 2, 2 comes before 3, and so on. The decimal portion of a version number generally represents a small enhancement or bug fix to the initial version release so that version 2.1 is always more reliable than 2.0. Intermediary releases have more digits following the decimal, such as Windows 3.1.1, which is really just Microsoft's way of avoiding the fiasco caused by releasing a whole new version.

Sentence: "*Version* 1.0 of any product — the first one out the shoot — is generally the worst. Of course, the computer industry knows we know that, so we can't recommend version 1.1, either."

vertical

Pronunciation: *ver-ti-kel.*

Meaning: Relating to the up-and-down direction. In computers, we can talk about vertical markets, vertical centering, vertical columns, vertical justification, and vertical scrolling. All of which apply in some way to up-and-down-ness.

Sentence: "Charlie told me he was feeling *vertical* today."

vertical market

Pronunciation: *ver-ti-kel mar-kit.*

Meaning: A relatively small group of consumers who want or demand a specific piece of software. Most programmers who don't work for major software vendors create programs for the vertical market. For example, real estate agencies are a vertical market that needs specific software written for it — stuff you can't find on the shelf in the Software-o-Rama.

Sentence: "Elevator software is a *vertical* market."

vertical scroll bar

Pronunciation: *ver-ti-kel skrohl bahr.*

Meaning: The bar on the right side of a window in a graphical application. By clicking the scroll bar with your mouse or using the arrow keys, you can move the contents of the window up or down in various increments. The little marker that travels along the bar is called the *elevator box.* It shows you how far along you are in the document. (See also *horizontal scroll bar.*)

Sentence: "To get to the end of my document, I put these little people in the *vertical scroll bar's* elevator box. Then I say, 'Free fall!' and drag the elevator box quickly to the bottom of the scroll bar. It may scare the little people, but I get to the bottom of my document quickly."

VESA

Pronunciation: *Vee-za.*

Meaning: Acronym that stands for *Video Electronics Standards Association,* which is an organization devoting its existence to setting video standards for computers. The most prominent standard set by VESA has been the development of the VESA local bus, which was designed to make IBM computers run graphics faster. (See *PCI, VL-Bus.*)

Sentence: "Actually, *VESA* is dead. Everything is PCI today."

VGA

Pronunciation: *Vee Gee Ay.*

Meaning: Acronym for *Video Graphics Array* or Video Gate Array. It is a color graphics display standard that was an improvement over its predecessors in color selection, resolution, and accuracy of image. A VGA monitor can display up to 256 colors at one time. The resolution measures image sharpness, and with VGA that's 640 pixels horizontally by 480 lines vertically. Super VGA monitors are even more impressive, with resolutions reaching 1,024 x 768. (See also *monitor, CGA, EGA, graphics, resolution,* and *SVGA.*)

Sentence: "The current standard in PC graphics is *VGA.* If you have anything else, we encourage you to upgrade — especially because we just bought a wad of VGA stock."

video

Pronunciation: *vi-dee-oh.*

Meaning: This word is used loosely to describe all activities in which moving pictures (movies) are involved. More specifically, it can refer to the display function of your computer (that is, video display) or the act of incorporating video devices (VCRs and video recording equipment) with computer technology. Video standards established by the Video Electronics Standards Association help to assure that our computer components work together in such a way that you can actually see something on the screen (which is nice). That's the kind of video that's common to all computers.

Sentence: "I got my father *video* software for his birthday. Now he sits around all day in dark glasses in front of his computer yelling, 'Cut!' into a megaphone."

video adapter

Pronunciation: *vid-ee-oh a-dap-ter.*

Meaning: An expansion card that plugs into one of your PC's expansion slots, allowing your software and your PC's monitor to talk with each other. Standard video adapters include VGA, SVGA, EGA, CGA, and Hercules. Also called a *video card.* (See also *expansion slot, VGA, EGA, CGA,* and *SVGA.*)

Sentence: "The graphics on your PC consist of two elements: the monitor and the *video adapter.* The monitor you see. The video adapter lurks inside your PC's guts."

video card

(See *video adapter.*)

video memory

Pronunciation: *vid-ee-oh mem-ree.*

Meaning: A special part of RAM in which the computer stores images displayed on the screen. (See also *memory* and *RAM.*)

Sentence: "Fran must have a lot of *video memory.* He remembers seeing the old *Gary Moore Show* live on TV."

video mode

Pronunciation: *vid-ee-oh mohd.*

Meaning: The various resolutions and number of colors available for the different types of graphics adapters used by IBM-compatible computers. Presently, there are 20 video modes, ranging from 0 to 19. Characteristics of a video mode include graphics or text only, color or monochrome, the number of colors, the resolution (height and width in pixels), and, in a text-only mode, the number of columns (the number of characters you can fit on a line). (See also *mode.*)

Sentence: "Jane pasted some flowers on her monitor to help cheer up its *video mode.*"

video RAM

Pronunciation: *vid-ee-oh Ram.*

Meaning: The RAM chips used to make up video memory. These are built into high-end video adapter boards. (See also *RAM* and *video memory.*)

Sentence: "The Megalons used a *video RAM* to break into Captain Video's secret fortress."

videotext

Pronunciation: *vid-ee-oh-text.*

Meaning: Words and numbers that come to your computer (or your TV, for that matter) over the wires. Types of videotext that are commonly transmitted include news, weather information, and stock quotes. In Europe, a videotext system was designed for use with their cable television. Using a special type of computer, Europeans can hook into the system and access information right at home on TV. Americans must have thought this was too dumb because we never bothered with it.

Sentence: "*Videotext* is an appropriate format for up-to-the-minute news that must be transmitted quickly to be valuable. Stuff such as, 'Hey! Some guy just broke into your house. Go check the bedroom window.'"

virtual disk

Pronunciation: *ver-choo-ul disk.*

Meaning: A make-believe disk that doesn't exist in reality, like most flying saucers. Actually, a virtual disk is a fancy term for a RAM disk, a disk created from the computer's memory. (See also *RAM disk.*)

Sentence: "Father Matthew wants to put all her sermons on a *virtual disk.*"

virtual machine

Pronunciation: *ver-choo-ul ma-sheen.*

Meaning: A software simulation of another computer. A virtual machine is useful for testing software on large computers such as mainframes. For example, a group of engineers typically create a new computer on a larger mainframe and then run tests to see how the computer performs. All of this is done before the first real machine is created, primarily to work out the bugs. New microprocessors are created in a similar manner. On 386 and later PCs, a virtual machine refers to a special operating mode, the V86 mode, in which the microprocessor can pretend it's actually several 8088 computers all running at the same time. This is how programs such as Windows and DESQview can *multitask* (run more than one program at a time).

Sentence: "Programmers amaze their friends by creating *virtual machines* that contain virtual machines. They can get a job done . . . with virtue."

virtual memory

Pronunciation: *ver-choo-ul mem-er-ee.*

Meaning: A use of disk drive storage that simulates RAM. Some operating systems (not DOS) borrow parts of the disk drive and swap out massive chunks of memory to a file on disk — a *swap file.* That way, true memory (RAM) is made available for programs that need it. The memory saved on disk can be put back into real memory when it's needed later. (See also *RAM, memory,* and *hard disk.*)

Sentence: "You can tell when your computer uses *virtual memory*; your system slows w-a-y d-o-w-n."

virtual reality

Pronunciation: *ver-choo-ul ree-al-i-tee.*

Meaning: An oxymoron that describes a brave new world of computer technology that creates a simulated multidimensional environment for the user. The user is actually encased in the environment, or can be, with paraphernalia that can include a helmet, goggles, gloves, and a belt, all used as input devices. Getting "inside the space" makes you feel as if you're trapped in a dream world. Within a virtual reality environment, you can see, hear, and feel your way around a software application. Currently, the main uses of virtual reality are games and design/engineering.

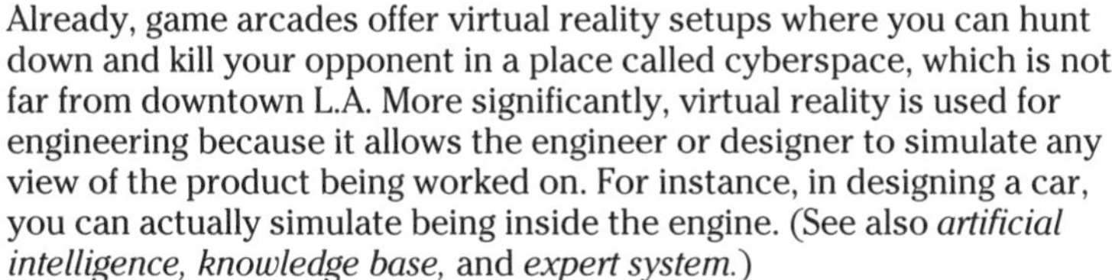

Already, game arcades offer virtual reality setups where you can hunt down and kill your opponent in a place called cyberspace, which is not far from downtown L.A. More significantly, virtual reality is used for engineering because it allows the engineer or designer to simulate any view of the product being worked on. For instance, in designing a car, you can actually simulate being inside the engine. (See also *artificial intelligence, knowledge base,* and *expert system.*)

Sentence: "Sometimes I think my whole life is one big *virtual reality* machine — especially when the cat talks to me."

virus

Pronunciation: *vih-ress.*

Meaning: A nasty type of program created by nasty people that is capable of replicating itself and doing severe damage to the contents of other users' systems. To protect your system against viruses, you should (1) get your software only from reputable places, (2) run an anti-virus utility, and (3) religiously back up your hard drive so that lost data can be quickly and reliably replaced. (See also *vaccine.*)

Sentence: "If you can't cure your computer of a *virus* it's caught, you should at least let it rest and feed it plenty of chicken soup."

Visual Basic

Pronunciation: *Vi-shoo-ell Bay-sik.*

Meaning: A Microsoft dialect of the BASIC language that lets you create programs by drawing your user interface on the screen and then writing BASIC commands to make the program actually do something worthwhile. Besides marketing Visual Basic to write DOS and Windows programs, Microsoft also uses Visual Basic as a common language for all of its business applications, such as Excel, Word, and Access. Theoretically, in the future, you will be able to write Visual Basic commands to make Excel or Access easier to use. Realistically, most people will probably never attempt this unless they want to drive themselves crazy.

Sentence: "*Visual Basic* is so popular because it makes programming a whole lot easier than using an arcane language like C++ or Pascal. The only thing Visual Basic doesn't make easier is figuring out why you want to write a program in the first place."

visual programming

Pronunciation: *vizh-oo-ul proh-gram-ing.*

Meaning: A way of creating software by making menu choices with the mouse and cutting and pasting items so that actual typing and linear thought are minimized. Examples are Visual BASIC by Microsoft and ObjectVision by Borland. The plus side is that you don't have to know much about programming to be able to work with this technology and produce results. The minus side is that many of your choices are made for you and there is often no way to customize certain options. (See also *programming.*)

Sentence: "*Visual programming* makes it possible for someone such as Uncle Ralph to create custom applications. Remember his spice rack? Doesn't the thought of Ralph programming make you cringe?"

VLB

Pronunciation: *Vee Ell Bee.*

Meaning: Acronym that stands for *VESA Local Bus*, which is a special type of bus to make computers run graphics faster. (See *VESA.*)

Sentence: "Because Windows is so slow, get a fast computer that uses *VLB*. Otherwise your computer will run Windows so slowly that you'll go out of your mind waiting for something to happen."

VL-Bus

Pronunciation: *Vee-Ell Bus.*

Meaniong: Yet another term for a VESA Local Bus. (See *VESA.*)

Sentence: "Boy, my computer has VESA, VLB and *VL-Bus* and it only has one slot!"

VLSI

Pronunciation: *Vee El Ess Ih.*

Meaning: Acronym for *Very Large Scale Integration*, a technology that refers to semiconductor chips. This means engineering the chip so that it can accommodate a large number of transistors and do more. (See also *CMOS, MOS,* and *semiconductor.*)

Sentence: "*VLSI* circuits are not larger than other chips; they just contain more information."

voice recognition

Pronunciation: *voys re-kug-ni-shun.*

Meaning: Technology that can recognize and work with the spoken word. It translates sound signals into digital signals that can be processed and analyzed by a computer. The prospect offers a whole new world of opportunity for computers: being able to talk to your computer as you talk to your friends (or, more appropriately, to your children) and being able to repot your plants or remodel your kitchen while you're doing your computer work. Voice recognition technology is in a fairly primitive state at present. (See also *voice synthesis.*)

Sentence: "The first thing I'd do with *voice recognition* technology is tell DOS exactly what it can do with the `Bad command or filename` error message."

voice synthesis

Pronunciation: *voys sin-the-sis.*

Meaning: The opposite of voice recognition. Here, the computer is able to create something that sounds like speech from text that it reads from a hard or floppy disk. Voice synthesis is a lot easier to create than voice recognition, which is why computers talk like computers. (See also *voice recognition.*)

Sentence: "I had always imagined my computer was female. But when I plugged in that *voice synthesis* expansion unit, it sounded like Arnold Schwarzenegger on a slow day."

volatile memory

Pronunciation: *vol-uh-till mem-o-ree.*

Meaning: Another term for RAM. Computer memory is often called volitile because it requires a constant flow of electrons to maintain its contents. Turn the power off and — poof! — there goes memory. (See *RAM.*)

Sentence: "Walk gingerly around the computer. You don't want its *volatile memory* to go off."

volume

Pronunciation: *vahl-yoom.*

Meaning: Another name for a disk, whether hard or floppy. Comes from the old computer days when instead of having a disk inside your computer, the lab technicians mounted a volume on a high-speed tape machine. The term works for computer storage the same way that a volume is a single book in a larger collection of works. (See also *floppy disk, disk,* and *hard disk.*)

Sentence: "I got an error message that said, `No volume in drive A`, so I turned up my stereo."

volume label

(See *label.*)

von Neumann

Pronunciation: *vahn Noy-man.*

Meaning: The guy who invented an architecture that created a data bottleneck named for him. Basically, this type of computer uses a very fast CPU and fast storage, but the processing is slowed down to the rate of the transmission of the data from one place to another. Yes, his name is von Neumann, but you pronounce it von Noyman.

Sentence: "Yes, Dr. *von Neumann* and not two guys named Steve really started this computer revolution."

voodoo

Pronunciation: *voo-doo.*

Meaning: Tried-and-true technology to apply when all else fails. Instead of pressing keys and clicking a mouse, you can chant invocations, do ritual dances, or feed weird concoctions of exotic herbs to your computer in an effort to get it to cooperate. Similar to voodoo economics; see the *Republican Dictionary For Dummies.*

Sentence: "If your PC worked fine yesterday and for some reason it won't today — even though you didn't change a thing — it's *voodoo.*"

wait state

Pronunciation: *wayt stayt.*

Meaning: A short delay that occurs when a microprocessor accesses data from memory. Because the microprocessor is generally faster than the memory chips, it waits for the memory chips to "catch up" by sitting around and having a cup of coffee for the duration of one wait state each time it accesses the memory. A *zero wait state processor* is much faster and takes advantage of faster memory chips. How long is a wait state? It depends on how fast the processor is. In any case, it's a slice of time way too fast for a human to experience. (See also *microprocessor* and *zero wait state.)*

Sentence: "I had to call tech support yesterday about my laptop. They said it had only one *wait state,* but when I took it to the post office it suddenly gained about 40 wait states!"

WAIS

Pronunciation: *Ways.*

Meaning: Acronym that stands for *Wide Area Information Server,* which is a valiant attempt by the Internet to make it easy to search for specific types of information.

Sentence: "Most people have no idea how to search for information on the Internet. Rather than waste time, you can learn how to use *WAIS* to find and retrieve the information you want quickly and easily. Now the hard part is trying to figure out how to use WAIS."

wallpaper

Pronunciation: *wahl-pay-per.*

Meaning: A graphic image placed on the desktop, or background, of your GUI. If you close all windows in your GUI, you'll see the wallpaper underneath. Wallpaper serves no particular purpose, but it can be interesting and amusing to your friends.

Sentence: "My favorite *wallpaper* is the Nagel painting called 'Sushi.'"

wapro

Pronunciation: *wah-pro.*

Meaning: The Japanese term for word processor. We just thought we'd throw it in here because it's one of those terms you usually don't see in computer dictionaries.

Sentence: "The proper response to the question *'Wapro?'* is 'Wa-kari-mas-en,' or 'I don't understand.'"

warm boot

Pronunciation: *wohrm boot.*

Meaning: The process of restarting your computer by pressing Ctrl-Alt-Delete or an equivalent reset button. A warm boot occurs when you restart the computer without turning it off. Warm booting is much faster than cold booting, which occurs when you turn the computer off and then back on. (See also *cold boot, reboot,* and *Ctrl-Alt-Del.*)

Sentence: "After installing certain software on my hard disk, the programs tell me to restart the computer by pressing Ctrl-Alt-Delete, which *warm boots* the computer. That seems so much cozier than the cold boot approach."

warp coils

Pronunciation: *wohr-pa koy-els.*

Meaning: (1) The massive hoops of metal that allow a starship to glide through space at high speeds without any chiropractic injuries to the crew. (2) Any sufficiently advanced or mysterious thing inside a computer that you don't understand.

Sentence: "The PC won't boot! Why doesn't someone check the innertubular couplers, quantum phase adjustment wing nuts, or the *warp coils?*"

watch icon

Pronunciation: *wahch eye-kahn.*

Meaning: An icon shaped like a tiny little watch. The watch icon, indigenous to the Macintosh computer, tells you that the computer is thinking and that you'll have to wait. In the early days of the Macintosh, the watch's little hands did not move. Today's watch icons are much more sophisticated. (See also *hourglass icon* and *beachball pointer.*)

Sentence: "Spacelab, this is Houston. You'll have to wait on that emergency meteor collision avoidance program. We're still getting the *watch icon* here."

watt

Pronunciation: *waht.*

Meaning: A unit of measure for power consumption. Watts equal volts times amperes. Hence, a 10 volt, 10 amp power source puts out 100 watts of power. It helps if you think of watts in terms of a lightbulb. A 100W lightbulb is much brighter than a 60W bulb. TV studios use 1000K bulbs to light their sets, which are terribly bright. The typical PC uses 250W of power, just like a 250W light bulb. (See also *amp* and *troglodyte.*)

Sentence: "I use 50 *watt* lightbulbs in my computer room, so I don't get too much glare on the screen. Also, I'm a troglodyte, so it reminds me of my cave-dwelling forefathers."

WFWG

Pronunciation: *Win-doze For Werk-groops*

Meaning: An acronym for *Windows for Workgroups,* one that's very hard to say as an acronym so no one does anyway. (See *Windows for Workgroups.*)

Sentence: "I told my Mom I was working on *WFWG* and she thought I'd become a professional wrestler."

what-if

Pronunciation: *wut ef.*

Meaning: A term used for testing a spreadsheet with various values, generating different results for analysis. Like, "If I made a gazillion dollars, what percentage would my house payment be?" And then you can enter another value, "Now what if I worked at McDonald's? Hey, can this thing deal with negative numbers?" What-if testing is commonly used in spreadsheets, in which you can enter different values into cells of the spreadsheet and the formulas recalculate their results based on the different scenarios.

Sentence: "Jimmy used a spreadsheet to calculate various *what-ifs* for the money he embezzled. Now he's doing 5 to 10 but is trying to get the judge to work out a what-if for good behavior."

Whetstone

Pronunciation: *Wet-stohn.*

Meaning: The name of a program used for testing the speed of a microprocessor. The Whetstone was used as a standard test for microprocessor speed until they invented the more accurate Dhrystone test. (See also *Dhrystone, MIPS,* and *microprocessor.*)

Sentence: "Hey, my computer can do 1,500 *Whetstones* — and that's with one cable tied behind its back!"

wide area network (WAN)

Pronunciation: *wihd ae-ree-ah net-werk.*

Meaning: A network of computers that spans a large distance, as opposed to a local area network, which involves computers in the same building. (See also *LAN, network, network operating system,* and *node.*)

Sentence: "Realtors can access a *wide area network* that provides multiple listings and other services for your computer. That way they can send messages such as 'Hey! Mr. and Mrs. Turkey looking for duplex — completely real-estate ignorant. Be on the lookout!'"

widow

Pronunciation: *wih-doe.*

Meaning: The first line of a paragraph of text that is separated from the rest of the paragraph. A widow line appears at the bottom of the page, whereas the rest of the paragraph appears at the top of the next page. Many word processors provide widow suppression to avoid this embarrassing problem. (See also *orphan.*)

Sentence: "Sometimes, if your document is full of *widows,* simply writing about a bunch of elderly bachelors makes the widows disappear."

wildcards

Pronunciation: *wihld-kahrds.*

Meaning: Characters or symbols used in place of a number of possible combinations. Wildcards represent one or more characters that "could be anything" in a search or command. For example, if the * symbol is a wildcard, the search text *s*ing* matches any word or item that starts with an *s* and ends in *ing.* (See also **.* (star-dot-star)* and *?.*)

Sentence: "*Wildcards* come in handy when you search for text and don't know how to spell, when you search for files and don't know their whole names, or when you play Shanghai with the in-laws and have a lousy hand."

WIMP

Pronunciation: *Whimp.*

Meaning: A disparaging acronym for *Windows, Icons, Menus, Pointing device.* It's the wimpy GUI way of using a computer as opposed to using the command line. (See also *window, menu, mouse, icon,* and *command line.*)

Sentence: "Don't show me that *WIMP* interface! I'm a real man! Give me the DOS prompt any day!"

WIN.INI

Pronunciation: *Win I-En-I* or *Win-innie* (or just the "Windows initialization file").

Meaning: The most important file in the world if you're running Windows (yes, even in Windows 95). This file contains commands that determine how Microsoft Windows looks and behaves on your computer. The WIN.INI file is an ASCII file, so you can edit it using a text editor. If you ever lose or modify your WIN.INI file, Windows may not work properly on your computer.

Sentence: "Every time you install a new program, it automatically updates your *WIN.INI* file. For the fun of it, I copied my WIN.INI file to my boss's computer so now his computer refuses to work properly."

Winchester disk

Pronunciation: *Whin-ches-ter disk.*

Meaning: A type of hard disk. For years, hard drives were called Winchester disks. This had nothing to do with any company named Winchester that made hard drives. Instead, it referred to the first IBM hard drive that stored 30 megabytes of information on each side. Because the drive was a 30-30, people dubbed it a Winchester disk after the famous Winchester rifle. Until the mid-'80s, hard drives were often called Winchester disks. This drove everyone nuts because they assumed some person or some company named Winchester made the disks. It just wasn't so. Today they're called hard disks, plain and simple. (See also *hard disk* and *disk.*)

Sentence: "Yes, ma'am, our hard disks come in three sizes: *Winchester,* Colt, and Daisy."

window

Pronunciation: *win-doe.*

Meaning: A window is a *viewport* (outline through which you see stuff) on the screen that displays data, programs, or information. A window can be moved, resized, opened, and closed, allowing you to organize the data on your computer screen. In most GUIs, you can open numerous windows at the same time and juggle information on the screen. You can switch between windows by simply clicking the window you want. However, you can work in only one window — called the *active window* — at a time. (See also *active window.*)

Sentence: "Sometimes I get carried away and open 20 or 30 *windows* at the same time. This usually results in the building inspector coming in with a worried look on his face and muttering something about earth-quakes."

Windows

Pronunciation: *Win-dohs.*

Meaning: Short for Microsoft Windows, a graphical user interface for DOS computers. Microsoft Windows provides a common way of using programs, making them easier to learn. Plus, Windows manages the way your PC works and takes care of common chores, such as working with the printer and disk drive. For example, when you set up a printer in Windows, that printer is automatically available in all your Windows programs. This lets us poor users concentrate on our work rather than on fussing with the computer and printer drivers or some such. Microsoft Windows provides access also to your computer's *extended memory* (memory above the first megabyte in your computer) and allows multitasking on 386 and higher computers. (See also *GUI* and *Microsoft.*)

Sentence: "Sometimes *Windows* can be a fun place in which to work. And then there's now."

Windows for Workgroups

Pronunciation: *Win-doze For Werk-groops.*

Meaning: A special version of Microsoft Windows designed for a local area network. With the right cables and hardware, you can use Windows for Workgroups to connect several computers together for exchanging electronic mail, sharing printers and modems, or writing nasty messages to one another in an attempt to sabotage the morale of a corporation. Often abbreviated as WFWG.

Sentence: "We bought all the networking cables and expansion cards we needed, but we didn't buy any network software to run the whole thing. Then we bought *Windows for Workgroups* and installed it on every computer. Now networking is as easy as using Windows. Of course, that explains our problems since not everyone knows how to use Windows."

WinMarks

Pronunciation: *Win-Marks.*

Meaning: A measurement unit used to determine the speed of a computer when running Windows-based programs. The two most common WinMark measurements are Graphics WinMarks (which measure the speed of displaying graphics) and the Disk WinMarks (which measure the speed of accessing a hard disk). The higher the WinMark value, the faster the computer.

Sentence: "My computer is better than your computer because *PC Magazine* rated mine as scoring 21.8 on their Graphics *WinMark* test while your computer only scored 17.4. Nya, nya, nya."

wiz

Pronunciation: *wiz.*

Meaning: A computer user who is sharp fast and looks good at the computer. A wiz is not quite as adept as a wizard. (See also *wizard, guru,* and *hacker.*)

Sentence: "Thank you for writing and calling me a computer *wiz*. Please note that wiz does not contain an *h*. That means something else entirely."

wizard

Pronunciation: *wiz-erd.*

Meaning: A computer user of high caliber. Not quite a guru, a computer wizard can solve most problems in most cases without assistance of any kind. (See also *guru, wiz,* and *hacker.*)

Sentence: "No, Amy isn't quite a guru. She's a *wizard,* one who knows how to solve a problem but just can't quite explain how she does it."

WMF

Pronunciation: *Double-yoo Em Eff.*

Meaning: Acronym that stands for *Windows MetaFile,* which is a special graphic file that was once used in earlier versions of Microsoft Windows. It was yet another attempt at a common file format.

Sentence: "Any time you see a graphic file with the *.WMF* file extension, it's either really old or was created by someone who doesn't know that the .WMF file format is obsolete."

word

Pronunciation: *werd.*

Meaning: (1) A collection of data bits that are processed as a unit. On the PC and with most microcomputers, a word is 2 bytes of data, 16 bits "wide." Sometimes a word is as little as a byte (8 bits). The size varies, which is why we're being vague here. (2) A word processing program created by Microsoft (Word). (3) A unit of the English language, such as *duh.*

Sentence: "Yes, Microsoft *Word* can write whole documents, which makes us wonder why they didn't call it Microsoft Document."

word processor

Pronunciation: *werd prah-ses-ser.*

Meaning: An application that lets you write and edit documents. Word processors generally include the capability to copy and move text (by individual words, phrases, or paragraphs), search for specific words or phrases, insert and delete text, format the document (including margin settings, fonts, and character styles), and, of course, print the document. Popular word processors include Microsoft Word, WordPerfect, and AmiPro. (See also *application* and *text editor.*)

Sentence: "My *word processor* has features that let me create tables and columns. Hey, you'd almost think this was a construction project instead of a memo."

WordStar

Pronunciation: *Werd-Star.*

Meaning: One of the first word processors ever sold and also one of the first to lose its dominance in the market through mismanagement and the failure to upgrade the program for three years.

Because WordStar existed in the days when computer keyboards lacked function and cursor (arrow) keys, WordStar defined certain keystrokes that are still used by many programs today. These keystrokes are usually referred to as "WordStar commands."

WordStar Keystroke	*What It Does*
Ctrl-S	Moves cursor one character to the left
Ctrl-D	Moves cursor one character to the right
Ctrl-E	Moves cursor one line up
Ctrl-X	Moves cursor one line down
Ctrl-A	Moves cursor one word to the left
Ctrl-F	Moves cursor one word to the right
Ctrl-Y	Deletes a line

Sentence: "Although hardly anyone uses *WordStar* anymore, lots of programs still use WordStar commands because they're based on ancient computer history. With Windows becoming more popular, WordStar commands may finally fade from memory like a bad dream."

word wrap

Pronunciation: *werd rap.*

Meaning: Word wrap refers to the way a word processor automatically determines whether the word you are typing will fit within the right margin, or, if it won't fit, whether the word processor needs to put that word on the next line. With word wrap, you don't have to press the

Enter key at the end of each line, as you once had to do with a typewriter. You just keep typing. Text editors do not have word wrap; you have to press Enter at the end of each line. (See also *hyphenation.*)

Sentence: "*Word wrap* used to be considered a bonus feature for early word processors. Today, a bonus feature is the built-in space shuttle simulator and advanced physics calculation module."

worksheet

Pronunciation: *werk-sheet.*

Meaning: A data file created by a spreadsheet program. Not all spreadsheet programs refer to their data files as worksheets; some call them spreadsheets, others call them pages or sheets, and some even call them documents. In any event, you can save a worksheet as a file on disk. (See also *document* and *spreadsheet.*)

Sentence: "I saved my Budget *worksheet* on disk as BUDGET-A and then saved the Budget I show to the IRS as BUDGET-B."

workstation

Pronunciation: *werk-stay-shun.*

Meaning: A nebulous term used to describe a powerful computer generally used for scientific or engineering applications, such as CAD. A workstation usually has tons of RAM, gobs of disk storage space, a high-resolution graphics adapter and monitor, and a powerful microprocessor. Workstations often use the UNIX operating system, but some high-end Macintosh, DOS, and OS/2 machines qualify as workstations. (See also *network, PC,* and *mainframe.*)

Sentence: "At work I have a 486 computer *workstation*, and at home I have a 386 computer playstation."

WORM

Pronunciation: *Werm* (as in a naked, snake-like, soft-bodied animal).

Meaning: (1) Acronym for *Write Once Read Many.* WORM refers to a disk medium to which you can write data only once but you can read the data as often as you like. First-generation optical disks are WORM media. CD-ROM disks, however, are not WORM media because only the manufacturer can supply the information on the disk. There is no "writing to" a CD-ROM; they are read-only memory (ROM). (2) A type of virus. (See also *RAM, ROM,* and *SCSI.*)

Sentence: "The best two acronyms in all computing are SCSI and *WORM.* It's entirely possible to have a SCSI WORM drive and, if you do, to constantly refer to it as that. It's bound to upset someone somewhere."

WPG

Pronunciation: *Double-yoo Pee Jee.*

Meaning: Acronym that stands for *WordPerfect Graphic,* which is a special graphic format that gives WordPerfect the ability to display pictures in your documents. WordPerfect comes with several .WPG files for you to play with, although none of them are very useful when you want to get some real work done.

Sentence: "If you're going to draw a picture of me with a clueless look on my face, at least store the graphic as a *.WPG* file so I can display it in my WordPerfect document."

wristwatch pointer

(See *watch icon.*)

write error

Pronunciation: *rite ehr-er.*

Meaning: An error that occurs when you try to save data to a disk. Write errors can occur because of glitches on the disk surface, not enough space on the disk, or attempts to save to a write-protected disk. A good user interface "traps" the write error, gives you some clue as to the exact problem that occurred, and maybe, if the computer's in a good mood, tells you how to fix it. Otherwise, the system might crash.

Sentence: "Nothing induces computer panic like having a beautiful document created in memory but not being able to save it to disk, thanks to a *write error.* Try another disk."

write protect

Pronunciation: *rite pro-tekt.*

Meaning: To modify a disk or file so that it's unwilling and unable to edit or erase its data. You can write-protect a disk by activating the write-protect tab, a doohickey that makes the disk un-writeable. On 3½-inch disks, this is done by flipping the write-protect tab such that it exposes (or opens) the hole in the disk. On 5¼-inch disks, this is done by placing a piece of opaque tape over the write-protect notch on the side of the disk. Write protection is useful when you are copying disks and want to protect the originals.

Sentence: "When I gave my files to a coworker to examine, I *write protected* the disk so that she couldn't change the files. But, just in case, I also made a backup copy. And I'm holding her husband and children hostage."

WW II

Pronunciation: *Double-yoo Double-yoo Too* (or World War Two).

Meaning: Acronym that stands for *World War Two,* a major war that most young people today are oblivious to. This lack of concern for history explains why many American high school students think the Nazis were involved in the Vietnam War and why British teenagers dress up like Nazis, inadvertently glorifying a government that once bombed their own nation.

Sentence: "The movie *Schindler's List* was set in *WW II.* Even today, many people claim that the Holocaust never took place. These same people also claim that *Schindler's List* was never made into a movie, either."

WWW

Pronunciation: *Double-yoo Double-yoo Double-yoo* (or World Wide Web).

Meaning: Acronym that stands for *World Wide Web,* which is a program that organizes related information together on the Internet. Sometimes called "The Web," this program uses hypertext to link separate documents for fast and easy retrieval. (See *hypertext.*)

Sentence: "The *WWW* program is just another valiant attempt to make the Internet easier to use and navigate. If you don't want to learn yet another set of arcane commands, it's even easier to pay a starving college student to find what you want on the Internet instead."

WYSIWYG

Pronunciation: *Whiz-Zee-Wig.*

Meaning: Acronym for *What You See Is What You Get.* WYSIWYG describes the phenomenon of seeing on the computer screen exactly what you will see on the page when you print your document. There are degrees of WYSIWYG in computerdom, but most people agree that the Macintosh and Windows environments offer true WYSIWYG. In fact, WYSIWYG is so common now that the term is quickly falling out of common usage.

Sentence: "If this page layout program offers a *WYSIWYG* display, why does it need a Print Preview command?"

X-ray

Pronunciation: *Eks-ray.*

Meaning: An electromagnetic radiation of a short wavelength (less than 100 angstroms) that can pass through walls, bodies, and other solid objects. Computers don't produce X-rays (but don't quote us on that one). Airport X-ray machines may or may not damage your computer or laptop PC. The best advice is to hand your computer to the guard and not X-ray it.

Sentence: "Superman had *X-ray* vision."

X.25

Pronunciation: *Eks Dot twen-tee-fihv.*

Meaning: A protocol for arranging data in packets that includes identification of the recipient and sender of the data. This is mostly advanced network stuff, not required knowledge unless you plan someday to bring in the big bucks by being a network guru. (See also *network.*)

Sentence: "Our network no longer functions because someone rewrote all our *X.25* protocols without telling the network manager." (I know, vague sentence, but it makes you sound important when you repeat it.)

Xanadu

Pronunciation: *Zan-uh-doo.*

Meaning: A mythical city in Kubla Khan, known for its incredible beauty and romance. It's also rumored to be an advanced network and information system available to all PCs all over the world. Someday. Soon. (See also *network.*)

Sentence: "I thought I had somehow stumbled into *Xanadu,* but it was only the local computer superstore."

xBase

Pronunciation: *ex-Bay-sa.*

Meaning: A generic term for any program that can read, write, edit, modify, and otherwise totally destroy database files that are compatible with the dBASE program. Some popular xBase programs are Microsoft FoxPro, CA-Clipper, and Alpha Four.

Sentence: "Back in the '80s, everyone used to advertise that their database was dBASE-compatible. Then Ashton-Tate, the makers of dBASE, threatened to sue everyone because they claimed that dBASE was a trademark, like Kleenex or Xerox. So everyone started calling their databases *xBase*-compatible, which meant they were really dBASE-compatible. Fortunately, Ashton-Tate is no longer around, but, to avoid lawsuits, everyone still calls their dBASE-compatible programs xBase-compatible."

XCMDs

Pronunciation: *Eks See Em Dees.*

Meaning: External commands available for the Macintosh HyperCard programming language. Accessing the XCMDs means a HyperCard programmer has more functions and pizzazz available than when using HyperCard alone. (See also *HyperCard.*)

Sentence: "Josh used a bunch of cool *XCMDs* to spice up his fungi HyperCard database."

XENIX

Pronunciation: *Zee-Niks.*

Meaning: A version of the UNIX operating system that was adapted by Microsoft to run on personal computers. In the old days, you couldn't "buy" a copy of UNIX like you could buy DOS or System 7 or OS/2. So Microsoft packaged its own version of UNIX, which it called XENIX. Now people use SCO XENIX or SCO UNIX from Santa Cruz Operation, Inc. (See also *UNIX.*)

Sentence: "Lauren had the computer science club rolling with her repertoire of archaic *XENIX* puns."

XGA

Pronunciation: *Eks Gee Ay.*

Meaning: Abbreviation for *Extended Graphics Array.* A type of video adapter that provided a higher resolution than previous adapters. (See also *VGA* and *SVGA.*)

Sentence: "No one really needs *XGA* graphics. I'd stick with SuperVGA."

XMODEM

Pronunciation: *Eks-Moh-Dum.*

Meaning: A protocol for transferring files between computers (often across phone lines) and catching errors that occur during transfer. This ensures that the file sent is identical to the file received. XMODEM was actually the name of a program that included the XMODEM file transfer protocol. Today, it refers to the way the file is sent. Other transfer protocols, such as YMODEM and ZMODEM, improve on the XMODEM idea by allowing faster data transmission through larger packets (chunks) of data and the capability to continue transmitting data when the checksum values don't match. (See also *CRC, YMODEM, Kermit, checksum,* and *protocol.*)

Sentence: "Oh, Charles, darling, get with the times! No one uses plain old boring *XMODEM* anymore."

XMS

Pronunciation: *Eks Em Ess.*

Meaning: Abbreviation for *Extended Memory Specification.* A memory-management standard for allowing DOS applications to access extended memory. XMS memory-management software provides access to the extended memory through the XMS standard, a set of rules developed by Microsoft and other industry bigwigs. DOS comes with an XMS memory manager called HIMEM.SYS. (See also *expanded memory, extended memory,* and *extended memory specification.*)

Sentence: "I'm going to need a new *XMS* manager on my PC. All my extended memory is threatening to go on strike."

XON/XOFF

Pronunciation: *Eks-Ahn/Eks-Ahf.*

Meaning: Signals for stopping and starting the flow of data during transmission between computers. XON/XOFF lets the receiving computer stop the flow of information so that it may process the information as it comes in. The XON character is actually Control-S, produced by pressing the Ctrl-S key combination. That stops data from being sent and also allows you to catch up and read the screen. For example, if DOS is TYPEing out a file, you can press Ctrl-S so that DOS is on hold for a while until you press any other key. The XOFF character is Ctrl-Q. It isn't used by DOS for anything interesting, but on other systems, only the Ctrl-Q character gets things moving after being frozen by a Ctrl-S.

Sentence: "We used *XON/XOFF* signals with our walkie-talkies."

XOR

Pronunciation: *Zor* or *Ek-skloo-siv Or.*

Meaning: A logical operation, otherwise known as Exclusive OR or sometimes an EOR. (See *Exclusive OR.*)

Sentence: "The wee little bit said, '*XOR* me once and I'll look strange, XOR me twice and I'll be back again.' Then I just deleted him."

XT

Pronunciation: *Eks Tee.*

Meaning: Abbreviation for *Extended Technology.* XT applied to a model of PC computer that extended the architecture of the original 8080 PC computers by adding extra expansion slots and a larger disk drive. Today, XT computers make good boat anchors. (See also *AT, PC,* and *boat anchor.*)

Sentence: "An *XT* computer might have been something back in 1983, but remember that was before most TV sets were sold with remotes."

yacc

Pronunciation: *yack.*

Meaning: Acronym for *Yet Another Compiler Compiler,* a UNIX tool used to create other languages and compilers. (See also *UNIX.*)

Sentence: "The *yacc* tool usually hangs out with lex and sed at the UNIX Cryptic Acronym Bar & Grill."

YMODEM

Pronunciation: *Wie-Moh-Dum.*

Meaning: A transfer protocol based on the XMODEM standard. YMODEM allows faster data transmission. (See also *XMODEM* and *protocol.*)

Sentence: "My communications package offers XMODEM, *YMODEM,* and ZMODEM protocols. What comes next, AAMODEM?"

Z80

Pronunciation: *Zee ay-tee.*

Meaning: The name of an old, 8-bit microprocessor used in the days of CP/M. The Z80 microprocessor was overshadowed by the faster 8080, the brain for the first IBM PC. (See also *CP/M.*)

Sentence: "Nary ten years ago, the *Z80* was considered the cutting edge of technology. Today, that and $2.25 will buy you a tall double latté."

Zamboni

Pronunciation: *Zam-bo-nee.*

Meaning as a noun: The machine used to clean the ice in an ice skating rink.

Meaning as a verb: The act of cleaning the ice using a Zamboni machine.

Sentence: "Our hockey team is so bad that the best part of the game is watching the *Zamboni.*"

zap

Pronunciation: *zap.*

Meaning: To zap a file is to remove it permanently from the disk. Unlike deleting a file, zapping a file removes it without possibility of being undeleted. (See also *undelete.*)

Sentence: "I *zapped* my tax files from the disk, just in case the IRS auditor knows how to undelete files."

Zephram Cochrane

Pronunciation: *Zef-ram Kak-ran*

Meaning: The man who invented warp drive or the space warp (though the term "space warp" was copyrighted by IBM and he had to call it something else). He was lost in deep space and ended up on a remote planet where a feminine energy force was keeping him alive, young, and virile for centuries — like an outer space *Sunset Boulevard.* Of course, Captain Kirk stumbled upon him and rescued him by letting the energy force inhabit the body of Betty from *Father Knows Best.* Zephram and Betty lived happily ever after on that planet.

Sentence: "In the future, *Zephram Cochrane* will have colleges, universities, cities, and spelling bees named after him."

zero wait state

(See *wait state.*)

ZIF

Pronunciation: *Ziff* (rhymes with *Biff* and *Jiff*).

Meaning: Acronym that stands for *Zero Insertion Force,* which describes a socket for plugging in chips, usually the CPU such as the Pentium or 80486. Unlike other types of chip sockets that force you to push a chip into place, a ZIF socket lets you drop the chip into the socket and then close a lever to hold the chip securely in place.

Sentence: "In the old days, you had to shove a chip into a socket and pray that you didn't break off any pins in the process. Nowadays, you just drop the chip in the *ZIF* socket and you're done. Isn't it amazing how the obvious can be dubbed 'advanced technology' by the computer industry?"

ZIP

Pronunciation: *Zip.*

Meaning as a noun: A suffix applied to files that have been compressed with the PKZIP utility. A ZIP file may be anywhere from five percent to 95 percent smaller than the original file — or the original group of files, if more than one was compressed at a time. Compressing files like this is useful for transferring them over a modem or for saving disk space.

Meaning as a verb: The act of creating a ZIP file. I zip. You zip. He zips. We all zip now.

Sentence: "Deloris always *ZIPped* her files twice. She was afraid they might accidentally become unZIPped on the hard drive and embarrass themselves."

ZMODEM

(See *XMODEM* and *YMODEM*.)

zoom

Pronunciation: *zoom.*

Meaning: The ability to change the way your data appears on the screen. You can zoom in to magnify the data, making it appear quite large on the screen, or you can zoom out to see how the data looks in relation to the page it's on. Zooming is usually accomplished (and this will shock you) by using a Zoom command.

Sentence: "I tried using the *Zoom* command to make my computer go faster, but it made my text bigger instead."

zoom box

Pronunciation: *zoom boks.*

Meaning: An area or button on a graphical window that increases the window size to full-screen proportions. (See also *button.*)

Sentence: "I was just poking around the window when, all of the sudden, Yikes!, it got as big as a house! I must have stumbled upon the *zoom box.*"